HARRY AUSTRYN WOLFSON

JUBILEE VOLUME

HARRY AUSTRYN WOLFSON

JUBILEE VOLUME

ON THE OCCASION OF HIS SEVENTY-FIFTH BIRTHDAY

ENGLISH SECTION

VOLUME II

JERUSALEM 1965

AMERICAN ACADEMY FOR JEWISH RESEARCH

Published with a Subvention of the Alexander Kohut
Memorial Foundation
and the Lucius N. Littauer Foundation

Copyright 1965 by
THE AMERICAN ACADEMY FOR JEWISH RESEARCH

PRINTED IN ISRAEL
AT CENTRAL PRESS, JERUSALEM

TABLE OF CONTENTS

SCHWARZ, LEO W.: A Bibliographical Essay 1
ALTMANN, ALEXANDER: Ibn Bājja on Man's Ultimate Felicity 47
ANASTOS, MILTON V.: The Ancient Greek Sources of Byzantine Absolutism 89
ATLAS, SAMUEL: Solomon Maimon's Conception of the Copernican Revolution in Philosophy 111
BARON, SALO W.: John Calvin and the Jews 141
BLUMBERG, HARRY: The Problem of Immortality in Avicenna, Maimonides and St. Thomas Aquinas 165
BONIS, CONSTANTINE G.: Basil the Great and the Philosophical Thoughts Developed in His Homily "Give Heed to Thyself" 187
COHEN, BOAZ: Conditions in Jewish and Roman Law 203
FINKEL, JOSHUA: The Guises and Vicissitudes of a Universal Folk-Belief in Jewish and Greek Tradition 233
FISCHEL, WALTER J.: From Cochin (India) to New York 255
FLOROVSKY, GEORGES: Theophilus of Alexandria and Apa Aphou of Pemdje 275
GEIGER, L. B.: Le Traité de la Vie de la *Summa Fratris Alexandri* 311
GOLDSTEIN, HELEN TUNIK: Averroes on the Structure and Function of *Physics* VII, 1 335
GRANT, ROBERT M.: Early Christianity and Pre-Socratic Philosophy 357
HYMAN, ARTHUR: Aristotle's "First Matter" and Avicenna's and Averroes' "Corporeal Form" 385
JAEGER, WERNER: "We Say in the *Phaedo*" 407
JOFFE, JUDAH A.: Mutual Borrowings Between Yiddish and Slavic Languages 423
KALLEN, HORACE M.: Secularism, God and Freedom 447
KRISTELLER, PAUL OSKAR: A Thomist Critique of Marsilio Ficino's Theory of Will and Intellect 463

LIEBERMAN, SAUL: Some Aspects of After Life in Early Rabbinic Literature 495
MCKEON, RICHARD: Spinoza on the Rainbow and on Probability 533
MILLÁS–VALLICROSA, J. M.: Aspectos Filosoficos de la Polemica Judaica en Tiempos de Ḥasday Crescas 561
MOODY, ERNEST A.: Buridan and a Dilemma of Nominalism 577
NEUMAN, ABRAHAM A.: Abraham Zacuto Historiographer .. 597
NOCK, ARTHUR DARBY: The Synagogue Murals of Dura-Europos 631
PERLMANN, MOSHE: Ibn Al-Maḥruma a Christian Opponent of Ibn Kammuna 641
RAHMAN, F.: Avicenna and Orthodox Islam: An Interpretative Note on the Composition of his System 667
ROTENSTREICH, NATHAN: The Problem of the *Critique of Judgment* snd Solomon Maimon's Scepticism 677
SHEPHERD, MASSEY, H. JR.: The Occasion of the Initial Break Between Judaism and Christianity................... 703
SILVERSTEIN, THEODORE: Guillaume de Conches and Nemesius of Emessa: On the Sources of the "New Science" of the Twelfth Century 719
SMITH, MORTON: The Account of Simon Magus in Acts 8 .. 735
SPERBER, ALEXANDER: How to Edit the Septuagint 751
STRAUSS, LEO: On the Plan of The *Guide of the Perplexed* 775
WERNER, ERIC: Post-Biblical Hebraisms in the Prima Clementis 793
WHITE, MORTON: Moral Judgment and Voluntary Action .. 819
WILLIAMS, GEORGE HUNTSTON: Camillus Renatus Called Also Lysias Philaenus and Paulo Ricci (c. 1500–c. 1575): Forerunner of Socinianism on Individual Immortality .. 833
ZEITLIN, SOLOMON: Proselytes and Proselytism during the Second Commonwealth and the Early Tannaitic Period 871

לוח העניינים של הכרך העברי

אברמסון, שרגא: מפתחות לתשובות גאונים . . . . א

אפרת, ישראל: תורת הנפש האימננטית במשנתו הפילוסופית של רב סעדיה
גאון . . . . כה

בלקין, שמואל: המדרש הסמלי אצל פילון בהשואה למדרשי חז״ל . . . לג

גולדין, יהודה: משהו על בית מדרשו של רבן יוחנן בן זכאי . . . . . סט

הלקין, א.ש.: לדמותו של ר' יוסף בן־יהודה אבן עקנין . . . . צג

השל, אברהם יהושע: ר' נחמן מקוסוב, חבירו של הבעש״ט . . . . . קיג

וכסמן, מאיר: המחשבה הפילוסופית והדתית של אברהם ב״ר חייא הנשיא . קמג

טברסקי, יצחק: על השגות הראב״ד למשנה תורה . . . . קסט

פינס, שלמה: הצורות האישיות במשנתו של ידעיה בדרשי . . . . . . קפז

פינקלשטיין, אליעזר ארי' הלוי: שוב על המו״מ בין הלל ובני בתירא . . רג

שלום, גרשם: תעודות שבתאיות על ר' נתן העזתי מגנזי ר' מהללאל הלויה
באנקונה . . . . רכה

שפיגל, שלום: לפרשת הפולמוס של פירקוי בן באבוי . . . . רמג

SECULARISM, GOD AND FREEDOM

by HORACE M. KALLEN

NOT LONG AGO, a bishop of the Protestant Episcopal Church and a one-time chaplain of Columbia University declared secularism "a dirty word," "the enemy, the front."[1] By implication, this would confirm the well-known sentiments of the Roman Catholic hierarchy. To them "secularism" was long "a dirty word." They expounded their detestation of it in their communication "On Secularism," in 1947. In 1948 they warned against "the impending danger of a judicial establishment of secularism that would ban God from public life" and directed "the Christian in Action" to combat secularism. In 1952 they charged that "secularists distort and blot out our religious traditions." Repeatedly they attack "secularism" as an assault on religion and on the freedom of religion. Their more recent[2] aggression was published six days after the newly crowned pope, in his coronation homily, repeated the traditional papal claim to be Christ's vicar on earth, to be the sole vehicle of Christian salvation, and to continue to seek the submission of all mankind to this papal role. The bishops asserted: "If a man is truly free, he is free to accept the revelation of our Lord and to embrace the society he established. It is this freedom, essentially, which is attacked and denied by modern secularism."

On the other hand, not all Protestants go as far as Episcopalian Bayne and the Roman establishment in the United States. No less radically concerned over the freedom of religion than the former, many have long recognized a threat to this freedom in the very

[1] Bishop Stephen F. Bayne, at a dinner of the Division of College Work of the National Council of Churches, Miami, October, 1957.
[2] See the New York *Times*, November 26, 1958.

claims which the Roman establishment makes in freedom's name. Thus Methodist Bishop Bromley Oxnam declared: "Protestants must be alert lest in a blind march on 'secularism' they become allied with forces that would destroy public education, deny the right of private judgment and shackle the free mind."[3]

On the face of it, these diverse deliverances present a conflict of interests, one being signalized by the word "secularism" the other by the word "God," with the spokesmen for each charging against the other enmity to the freedom which both require. Each supports the interest it advances on "freedom" — either for itself alone, or for its opponent as well. "Freedom" seems to signify the common matrix of their warring interests.

What on the record, does freedom stand for?

However different, and perhaps, irreduceable, be the experiences which the word is used to designate, they are somehow brought together in the idea that freedom is a right, equally inherent and inalienable to each human being. Certainly this has been the case since the Democratic Revolution, whose ideal has been to change the ancient subordination of many men's freedoms to the service and support of a few men's freedoms into a reciprocal insurance by all men of equal freedom for each man. This is the intent of our American Declaration of Independence, of the French Declaration of the Rights of Man and Citizen, of the Universal Declaration of Human Rights of the United Nations Organization and of the many similar affirmations which come between. They all postulate that the experience of freedom is not an illusion but a reality. The belief that it is such is older than philosophy and the doubt of it is as old as philosophy itself. The belief is shared no less by necessitarians who prove with arguments that it is a disguised error than by libertarians who affirm, like the signers of the American Declaration of Independence, that it is a self-evident truth.

Both start from an experience of freedom, the first moving to deny, the second to confirm, the reality of that which they start

[3] *The Churchman*, March 1, 1952.

from. And the deniers could not deny if they lacked the continuing freedom to search out and to devise the means whereby they strip away the disguise and expose the error. Many, indeed, such as the Stoics or Augustinians or Jesuits, conserve human freedom in their configurations of metaphysical necessity, whether as natural law or supernatural omnipotence. Be they scientific determinists or theological predestinarians, their ratiocination assumes something other than inevitable effects following ineluctable causes or infallible obedience to Allah's omnipotent providence; something that resists and struggles and will not yield, that must be forced to yield, and be subdued to the laws of nature or the will of God.

Experience realizes this something in man as his freedom. Freedom is that which we become aware of as we respond to the changing manifold of persons and places and thoughts and things, amid which we live and move and struggle for our being, and choose one to fix upon and have and hold against competing alternatives. Freedom is that which we become aware of in our acts of decision, our literally cutting off and stopping something from passing on, and adopting it, holding fast to it, and thus shutting out its rivals from our interest. Champions of the rivals, if they be theologians, will signalize such decisions as *pride, sin, evil*; those who approve will call them *conscience*. Their surrogates among men of science might be *chance, contingency, indeterminance*.

Pervading every event of living our lives and earning our livings, this freedom comes most vividly to consciousness in patterns of push and pull against obstruction, constrainment or compulsion. When we say freedom *from*, freedom *of*, freedom *to*, the prepositions signify some such barrier we strive to break out of. Men of science conceptualize these barriers in terms of necessary connexion, causal necessity, determinism, natural law. Supernaturalists hypostatize them as fate, fortune, providence, the will of God, revelation, truth, divine authority, and employ them for sanctions of harnessing other men's freedoms to the service and support of their own. The authoritarian imperialist, Bluntschli declared:[4]

---

[4] *Allgemeine Staatswelt*, V. 1, 39.

"When error prevails, it is right to invoke liberty of conscience; but when, on the contrary, truth predominates, it is proper to use coercion." The ultra-montanist, Louis Veuillot, told his opponents in 1870: "You believe in freedom, therefore you owe it to us who don't. But since we don't, we shall refuse it to you." Decision as to what is truth and what is error is here the exclusive right of the authoritarians, who also claim the right to impose their choice whenever they are able to. Not to agree with them is to choose error instead of truth; and how could disagreement have the same rights as agreement? The truly "free" man is free only "to accept the revelation of our Lord and to embrace the Society he established;" but he is not equally free not to accept the dogmas of the Roman church. Modern secularism, however, does assert this freedom. Hence the assertion is equated to attacking and denying freedom to accept and embrace. To "modern secularism" the creed is error, and the authoritarian church is anti-democratic. But it holds that disagreement has the same right as agreement, and it defends this right for the mistaken and the authoritarian as it does for the correct and democratic. But since it disagrees with the former, they charge it with attacking and denying their freedom. In fact, the charge applies to all who are committed to equal liberty whether or not secularists. Holding that disagreement does have the same rights as agreement, they are admonished that this requires them to acquiesce in the freedom of such as deny this to suppress and destroy the freedom of those who affirm it. In a word, they are advised that it is the nature of equal liberty to intend and invite its own destruction. Not only is such freedom suicidal; it does not deserve to survive.

The dialectic points up the predicament of the *bona fide* libertarian. Must the logic of equal liberty be the logic of suicide? Does the libertarian faith require its true believers to set its foes and killers in places where they can work their declared will against it? Or must they themselves become authoritarians in order to survive as libertarians? Or does their commitment to equal liberty entitle them to safeguard its survival and growth from foes endeavoring to use it as a weapon against itself? They must needs decide at what point the declared enemies of freedom have rendered themselves by means of it a clear and present danger to its upkeep and extension. As the guardians of a society of equal liberty they must needs be vigilant to find the limits of toleration for those who are themselves intolerant of toleration. Their commitment is to keep society as equally open to disagreements as to agreements. Near to a millenium ago dissident Monk Abelard disclosed the disingeniousness of the authoritarian pretensions: "If we have no right to say *no* to a proposition," he asked in *Sic et Non*, "how can there be a right to say *yes*? For then, 'Yes' would result from blind coercion, not deliberate choice."

The recognition that freedom is the mother of alternatives, the matrix of change, of the processes of suspending judgment, doubting, inquiring, examining, and of finally choosing and deciding, goes back to the skeptics who became Plato's heirs in his Academy. Among many others it had its later prophets in Pyrrho, Hume and Kant, as it has its modern spokesmen in such figures as William James and John Dewey.

The record of men's struggles over freedom makes clear why the Democratic Revolution should proclaim freedom as an inalienable right; why John Locke should define it as "the power of a man to do or forbear doing any particular action according as its doing or forbearing has an actual preference in the mind;"[5] why, when considering government he should identify it also as "the natural liberty," which "is to be free from any superior power on earth and not to be under the will or legislative authority of any man, but to have the law of nature for his rule."[6] The record makes clear why Kant, in his own way, should outdo Locke while confirming him. Thus: "Freedom is being independent from the coercion of another's will. Insofar as it can coexist with the freedom of all according to a universal law, it is the one, sole, original inborn right belonging to every man in virtue of his Humanity. There is indeed an inborn equality belonging to every man which consists

---

[5] *Essay on the Human Understanding* II, 341, 15.
[6] *Of Government* II, 422.

in his right to be independent of being bound by others to anything more than that to which he may reciprocally bind them. It is consequently the inborn quality of every man in virtue of which he ought to be his own master by right (sui juris)."[7]

The record makes clear why there should be a consensus on this between personalities so different as John Locke, Immanuel Kant and John Stuart Mill, and why the last should set forth as he does the role of the idea of equal liberty in the mores of public discussion. Mill makes this point in his great *Essay on Liberty*. Where freedom to choose is suppressed, opinion, he shows, is solely imposed opinion, and it is impossible to displace error by truth. Where opinion is free, the collision of truth with error clarifies truth. Where it isn't free, authority must pretend to infallibility. In freedom, the merits of alternatives can be checked and tested by means of free competition on equal terms. Under these conditions errors won't be foisted, truths have a better chance to become evident. Where persecution prevails, truth is rendered scarce and dangerous. To win out it needs a fair field and no favor. But it can't establish itself without them, since a true idea is as idea no more potent than a false one. For these reasons equal liberty is the *sine qua non* of public discussion. They are why such discussion requires intellectual fairplay, sportsmanship, in the presentation, exploration and weighing of alternatives. These behaviors constitute the morality of all discussion, not alone public discussion, a morality regularly violated by want of candor, by bigotry, by malignity, by intolerance of feeling. Not the ideas argued or the conclusions advocated violate this morality, the violation is the attitude which these words denote. What manifests the morality is calmness of vision, honest and just consideration of the competing alternatives, exaggerating nothing to its discredit, keeping back nothing to its credit.[8]

[7] *The Philosophy of Law.*

[8] The kind of morality of public discussion which Mill held the opposite of the morality of equal liberty was of course, and continues, an enduring trait of the folkways and mores of the western world. This trait is presently outstanding in the discourses of the Communists, especially the Russian and

Given the record, this is the enduring morality of scientific inquiry; it is the vital differentia of the method of science. Where it is followed men are able to appeal to truth for authority instead of having to submit to authority for truth.

In the nature of things, authority, with its pretensions to infallibility, must denounce and repudiate this morality. For once it agrees to equal liberty of the different, it renounces infallibility and gives up its claims to primacy and privilege. Everywhere in the world it is the case that authority, to make good its claims, seeks, by whatever means, preponderant power, and wages a perennial war, hot or cold or both, against whatever refuses to concede this power by accepting the creed and conforming to the code which are the authority's chosen vehicles. Everywhere in the world, Church States or State Churches, be they sacerdotal like the Roman Catholic, non-sacerdotal like the Communist, are engaged in a struggle for power over the minds and hearts of men. Everywhere they demand of them belief, obedience, loyalty unto death as soldiers and as workers. Everywhere they claim their creeds to be the revelation, and their codes the ordination, of an absolute omnipotent metaphysical energy to which they alone

---

the Chinese, whose officials have developed it into a high art of insult and denigration. But it used to be the method of parliamentary and academic as well as theological discussion. How far it has fallen into desuetude in free societies may be inferred not alone from the extensions of the religious theme to all the denominational diversities that Harvard professors can profess as well as study, but symbolically, from what has happened to the themes and utterance of the Dudleian Lectures set up at Harvard College by the will of the Honorable Judge Dudley, January 1, 1750. Four lectures are provided for, "the third lecture to be, for detecting and convicting and exposing the Idolatry of the Romish Church, their tyranny, usurpations, damnable heresies, fatal errors, abominable superstitions, and other crying wickednesses in their high places; and finally, that the Church of Rome is that mystical Babylon, that man of sin, that apostate Church, spoken of in the New Testament." So far as I know, nothing of the sort has been at Harvard in the 20th century, perhaps longer; perhaps the trend has even been toward something more favorable than intellectual fairplay and sportsmanship in the judgment of these ideas and institutions.

have access. The newer word for it is "Dialectical Materialism," the older one is "God."

The word "God" has a global acceptance, a circulation as wide as mankind. Philologists opine that it is native, with the natural vernacular variations, in all Teutonic tongues. It seems not to point to any such perceptions as its synonyms *deus* or *theos*, which intend the heavens above. It seems not to have had any connotation of gender, to have been originally a neuter term. Some have suggested that its meanings disclose certain resemblances to the meaning of mana, which is also neuter. But ongoing usage multiplied its significations, and their ongoing rivalries lead to doubt that any signified anything other than the uses and the condition which prompted the usings. As the late Monsignor Ronald Knox observed:

> O God, forasmuch as without Thee
> We are not able to doubt Thee,
> Help us by all Thy Grace
> To teach the whole race
> That we know nothing whatever about Thee.

He called the limerick "Prayer of a Skeptic," but he could also have called it "Prayer of a True Believer" such as Reinhold Niebuhr, or Paul Tillich or Martin Buber or Angelus Silesius or John the Apostle,[9] each with his own functional signification of his *deus absconditus*. For the "hidden God" is also an ineffable God, and the traits which the true believers assign to him turn out to be altogether as diverse and incommensurable as the individual believers themselves. "As to the word 'God,'" George Santanyana wrote in *Reason in Art* (p. 9), "all mutual understanding is impossible. It is a floating literary symbol, with a value which, if we define it scientifically, becomes quite algebraic. As no experienced object corresponds to it, it is without fixed indicative force and

---

[9] "No one has at any time seen God; the only-begotten son, who is in the bosom of the Father, he has beheld him." (1:18)

admits any sense which its context in any mind may happen to give it." Such meanings could be events or values created by the meaner's ineluctable struggle for survival. Voltaire suggested that "If there were no God it would be necessary to invent him," and that mankind do not cease from invention nor from warfare over whose invention reveals the one, sole, living God.

In an endeavor to reconcile this warfare, John Dewey, whose centenary has recently been celebrated, expounded "a common faith" rooted "in the distinctively religious values inherent in natural experience," developing through free enquiry and free communication of whatever "glimpses... we may obtain of the truth of which we are in search." Such glimpses were to Dewey experiences of union which feel so momentous that we call them supernatural. Actually, they are events in nature taking us actively beyond the present toward ideal ultimacies of human relationships. They are experiences of God, for "God" is the name Dewey would give "to this active relation between the ideal and the actual." This God could signify that which is dynamic in the gods of all peoples of all times and all places: the vital meaning common to the diverse and singular meanings of mankind's multitudinous pantheons. "We who now live are parts of a humanity that extends into the remote past, a humanity that has interacted with nature. The things in civilization we most prize are not of ourselves. They exist by grace of the doings and sufferings of the continuous human community in which we are a link. Ours is the responsibility of conserving, transmitting, rectifying and expanding the heritage of values we have received that those who come after us may receive it more solid and secure, more widely accessible and more generously shared that we have received it. Here are all the elements for a religious faith that shall not be confined to sect, class, or race. Such a faith has always been implicitly the common faith of mankind. It remains to make it explicit and militant."

But as a signer of the Humanist Manifesto (published in 1933), Dewey committed himself to a diversity of assertions whose configuration makes up one more "God," incompatible with the God that is this "active relation between the ideal and the actual," and is the One implicit in the countless many. These assertions are set to be barriers rather than framed to be bridges. They establish those who affirm them as aficionados of one more amid the rival claimants of exclusive rightness and thus of over-ruling authority among the establishments using "God" or an equivalent for their battle-cry.

Yet, for the hopes and fears of the plain people struggling for survival the rival definitions of "God" are indifferent. All, any, or none, will do, provided there is promise that the hopes will be realized, the fears allayed, and the future assured. It is the *how*, not the *what*, the workings, not "the nature," of divinity which relate to the passions and purposes of the peoples of the world.

Whatever else "God" means for them, it means some sort of cause invoked to account for all those undesired, unwilled accidents, contingencies, and compulsions in a person's daily life or "in the course of human events," to which no conventionally determined or determinable causes get assigned. Lawyers bespeak "the hand of God," plain folks talk about "God's will" and say "God knows" whatever they neither do nor can know. God also means a cause hoped and prayed for at times when other causes, tried and true, get doubted or have actually failed to bring on a much-desired effect. People want the feeling of security and certainty that the word awakens in them. They want to "go with God," to stand "under God," to "trust in God," at home, in public edifices, on coins and documents, in pledges to flag and country such as are used in American public schools. Who doubts that "God" stands for any efficacy, save that of the believer's belief, is "godless," "atheistic," an enemy of the right and the good, without faith or morals, a communist, a reproach to humanity. On the record, as Buber concedes, "belief in God" — my God, no other — figures as one of the major motivations of man's inhumanity to man.

Functionally, the symbol "God" seems to signify for each believer a definition and control of undefined, undefinable, uncontrolled and uncontrollable fate and fortune as they bear on whatever is happening to the believer's struggle to go on struggling which he calls his survival. So he will wage war over the word's use or disuse, regardless of any other role it may play. He is betting his life. He invokes "God" to reenforce the efficacies of the causes regularly at work in nature and society and to confirm those disclosed by the sciences and harnessed to men's service by the technologies. Daily usage indicates that "God" serves him as a term of completion, closure, reassurance or vindication. He wants it everywhere at hand. But his behavior indicates that he feels all the while that he cannot be betting on a sure thing. His inhumanity to the non-believer is his way of making the unsure thing a little surer. "God" is a stake as well as a weapon in the war of all against all. Every cult keeps asserting that its "God-concept" alone is the right concept and keeps striving to impose acceptance of its rightness by all who deny it or assert a different "concept."

Reasonable men recognized here that there could be but one way of assuring religious peace not imposed and maintained by force. This way was for each of the diverse companies of true believers to agree that its rivals were making their claims by the same right as they themselves asserted, and that it could live on safe and free only if the competitors joined together to assure to one another equal liberty of conscience and equal security in the exercise of this liberty to believe and to disbelieve, without fear and without favor. This would involve a certain consensus that beliefs about *what* God is and about what he requires of the believer, are functions of free choice to be made without privilege and without penalty and to be appraised not by what they are, but by their consequences to the life together of the doubters, the disbelievers and the believers in different creeds and codes. "No man," wrote John Locke, "is by nature bound unto a particular church or sect. But every one joins himself voluntarily to that society in which he believes he has found that profession and worship which is truly acceptable to God. A church is a society of members voluntarily uniting to that end."

This view postulates the complete naturalness of differences among human beings and the consequent equality of the different as *different*, in their rights to "life, liberty and the pursuit of happiness." It is from these postulates that James Madison concluded: "This freedom arises from that multiplicity of sects which pervades America and which is the best and only security for religious liberty in any society. For where there is such a variety of sects, there cannot be a majority of any one sect to oppose and persecute the rest." Many years later he wrote to Governor Livingston: "I observe with particular pleasure the view you have taken on the immunity of religion of a civil government in every case where it does not trespass on private rights or public peace."[10]

When our fourth President made these observations, only about ten percent of all Americans were enrolled in churches. Can it be reaffirmed today, when in the safety assured by the nation's commitment to equal liberty, churches have been able to count in their memberships more than half of all Americans, with a plurality of all members enrolled under the hierarchical establishment of authoritarian Rome? The answer is debated among Romanist theologians. But until the Papacy itself has made a change, infallibly a matter of faith and morals, binding upon the true believers, the late Father John A. Ryan's statement sets forth the authentic papal program. He wrote: "Constitutions can be changed, and the non-Catholic sects may decline to such a point that the political proscription of them may become feasible and expedient. What protection would they then have against a Catholic State?" The answer may be read in the penalties laid upon non-Catholic religious societies simply as non-Catholic by the Spanish State and in the privileges and monopolies provided for the Roman church.

What is imposed in Spain and threatened in freer countries like the United States or Great Britain is the tyranny of the religious majority that Madison and the other Founding Fathers hoped to keep from recurring in the new Republic. This inheres in every sect and denomination, Catholic or non-Catholic, sacerdotal or secular. The threat is endemic, its potential is greater locally than on the national scale. A while ago a television panel of distinguished lawyers, moderated by Edward A. Murrow, dis-

[10] July 10, 1782.

closed the case of the Hutterites of North Dakota, penalized by the law of that state, because like the early Christians of the New Testament, the Kibbutzim of the new Israel, and like contemporary monastic brotherhoods of other cults, they renounce personal possession of worldly goods, choose to hold all things in common, yet successfully practice modern farming for their commonwealth; and because, believing that true Christians must be men of peace, they refuse military service. The laws forbid their acquiring land or enlarging their activities.

The event illustrates what Jefferson and Madison had feared and had endeavored to ensure the liberties of Americans against when they insisted on integrity of religious liberty and its safeguarding by the separation of church and state and the liberation of all civil functions from churchly prescription and control. The Secularism which is under discussion here is the conception of the relationships to one another of different religions with their different "Gods," creeds and codes which shaped the Jefferson-Madison-Lee program for a free society of free men. The Declaration of Independence, to which believers of all denominations and none jointly and severally pledged their lives, their fortunes and their sacred honor, postulates this Secularism. The Constitution assumes it and patterns implementing this Secularism. It is something quite different from a particular creed and code which sets the true believer against the fact and idea of a priestly authority, holding by vocation and training a privileged relationship to "God" and to the rest of the supernaturalist establishment and imposing its creed and code on the laity. In Europe that Secularism is known as anti-clericalism and its program is to liberate the people from the domination of the sacerdotal hierarchy. Another usage of the word "Secularism" is to signify a non-supernaturalist faith first professed about 100 years ago by George Jacob Holyoake.[11] This religion was not atheistic but agnostic *vis a vis* the "God" of the churches and the immortality of the soul. It was skeptical of theology, because theology discourses of the Hidden, the Un-

[11] See his *The Principles of Secularism*, 1859.

known and the Unknowable. It chose to rely on the sciences and on the arts based on them because their role in improving the human condition can be observed and measured. It preferred "the piety of usefulness" to "the usefulness of piety," and while it made common ground with supernaturalism regarding the conduct of men, it held that they had contributed nothing to the knowledge of its nature or causes. In its view, theism and atheism were alike more overbeliefs than truly operative working hypotheses. It chose to rely in religion as in science on free inquiry, reason and the tests of experience. Persons so believing could form a congregation, define a creed, ordain a code. The urbanity, sobriety and good-will of this secularist communion received favorable consideration from such figures as Jeremy Bentham, John Mill, G. H. Lewes.

But it is still not the Secularism here under discussion.

This Secularism is not one more creed and code adding itself independently to the already existing aggregate. Dynamically, it is a creation of this aggregate as the Federal Union is a creation of the independent and sovereign states uniting to form and maintain it. Thus it denotes a relation; it signifies a rule of association. Failing the rule, each church, each cult struggles for its own existence in rivalry with all others, and where it is able, to dominate and displace, if not to destroy, the others. This Secularism is born when each of the competitors has recognized that a union of their diverse and irreduceable configurations of creed and code can take such a form that this union of all will assure equally to each its safety and freedom. The creed and code of the union cannot therefore be identical with those of any single member of the union. For them to be such would be tantamount to subordinating the others to the doctrine and discipline of that one cult. It would render them second-class citizens of the republic of religions. The creed and code of the republic, as a union of the diverse, must needs be other than those which the members of the union are separately committed to, and for the safeguarding of whose equal liberty they have formed their union, to serve them as the joint insurance of their several freedoms of religion. Being such, this common faith displaces none, but safeguards and supplements all, jointly and severally. Insofar as it is operative, it is the faith of an open society of religious societies, shutting none out, cutting none off save to stop aggression against the equal liberty and safety of any other.[12] It assures the morality of the public discussion; it assures that issues shall not be fought out, but talked out, on equal terms of free enquiry and decision. In virtue of this it cannot, in the nature of things, be anything but secular, and the Secularism it intends is *de facto*, the common faith of all believers, however diverse and "ultimate" their beliefs or ideologies. Thus, let the signification they give the word "God" be what it may, this Secularism is by the wills of their gods the revelation conjoined to their singular and separate revelations, establishing all the diversities as alike elect and alike equal in their rights to be free and safe.

[12] The Universal Declaration of Human Rights is the most comprehensive utterance to date of the spirit and program of this Secularism.

A THOMIST CRITIQUE OF MARSILIO FICINO'S THEORY OF WILL AND INTELLECT

FRA VINCENZO BANDELLO DA CASTELNUOVO O.P. AND HIS
UNPUBLISHED TREATISE ADDRESSED TO LORENZO DE' MEDICI*

by PAUL OSKAR KRISTELLER

WHEREAS THE CONTRIBUTIONS made by the Italian humanists to thought as well as to learning and literature have been studied and justly emphasized by students of the Renaissance, the history of scholastic philosophy and theology in the fifteenth century is still a largely unexplored area. The unpublished text which we shall discuss in this paper offers not only a contribution to this subject, but also throws new light on the place of Florentine Platonism within the context of fifteenth-century thought. As I have tried to show elsewhere, the Platonism of Marsilio Ficino and of his circle represents an independent philosophical movement, although it is related in a number of specific ways to both humanism and scholasticism.[1] Since the scholastic authority most frequently quoted by Ficino, aside from Averroes, is Thomas Aquinas, and since Ficino's views resemble those of St. Thomas in a number of instances, it is significant that we learn from our treatise that on a rather important issue, that is, on the superiority of the will and intellect, Ficino adopted, at least at one period of his career, the position held by Duns Scotus and his followers,

---

* This study was made possible by travel and microfilm grants made by the American Philosophical Society and by the Columbia University Council for Research in the Social Sciences.

[1] For the place of Florentine Platonism in Renaissance thought, I may be permitted to refer to my previous studies: "Florentine Platonism and Its Relations with Humanism and Scholasticism," *Church History*, VIII (1939), 201–211; *Studies in Renaissance Thought and Letters* (Rome, 1956), esp. pp. 35–50; *The Classics and Renaissance Thought* (Cambridge, Mass., 1955).

and thus evoked the criticism of an orthodox Thomist, who was a Dominican friar (as most orthodox Thomists were at that time), and a rather distinguished member and future general of his order. The fact that this prominent Thomist took the trouble to refute Ficino in a lengthy treatise, and in a rather polite and respectful fashion, tends to show that Ficino was taken seriously by his scholastic contemporaries, and that they felt he was dealing, at least in part, with the same problems which were treated by themselves and by their own masters. The problem under discussion, the relative importance of will and intellect, happens to be a central problem in the history of Western thought that can be traced from Augustine to Kant, and that has retained its importance, if we make allowance for a variety of changes in context and in terminology, up to the present day.

The author of our treatise, Vincentius Bandellus de Castronovo, was born in 1435 in Castelnuovo in the diocese of Tortona in Northern Italy and entered the Dominican Order at an early age, studying and later teaching in the monastery of S. Domenico in Bologna.[2] He first acquired some fame after having participated in a public disputation in Ferrara where he argued against the doctrine of the Immaculate Conception of the Virgin Mary.[3]

[2] For the life and works of Vincenzo Bandello, see Leander Albertus, *De viris illustribus Ordinis Praedicatorum* (Bologna, 1517), f. 7–8, 47–49v (copy in the Spencer Collection of the New York Public Library); J. Quétif and J. Echard, *Scriptores Ordinis Praedicatorum*, II, (Paris, 1723, reprinted New York, 1958), 1–3; G. Mazzuchelli, *Gli scrittori d'Italia* II, 1 (Brescia, 1758), 206–208; J.A. Fabricius, *Bibliotheca Latina mediae et infimae aetatis*, ed. J.D. Mansi, VI (Florence, 1859), 589; H. Hurter, *Nomenclator Literarius Theologiae Catholicae*, IV (Innsbruck, 1899), col. 932–934; R.P. Mortier, *Histoire des Maîtres généraux de l'Ordre des Frères Prêcheurs*, V (Paris, 1911), 66–127; *Dictionnaire de Théologie Catholique*, II (1910), col. 139–140 (by P. Mandonnet); *Dictionnaire d'Histoire et de Géographie Ecclésiastiques*, VI (1932), col. 483–484 (by L. Charlier). For further references, see U. Chevalier, *Répertoire des sources historiques du Moyen Age*, I (*Bio-Bibliographie*), I (1903–04), col. 420; *Archivum Fratrum Praedicatorum*, XV (1945), p. 95, note 53.

[3] F. Borsetti, *Historia almi Ferrariae Gymnasii*, I (Ferrara, 1735), 97–98. Most biographers give the date 1481 for this disputation, that is, the same year in which the treatise based on it was printed. C. Le Bachelet (*Dictionnaire*

In 1484, the degree of a master of theology was conferred upon Vincenzo by Pope Innocent VIII in Rome. Vincenzo lived for a number of years in S. Maria delle Grazie in Milan, served for some time as prior of that monastery, and was confessor of Lodovico Sforza who bestowed many favors on him and on his monastery.[4] During his stay in Milan, he is reported to have held another successful disputation against a group of Jewish rabbis. In 1500, Alexander VI appointed him Vicar General of his Order, and at a general chapter held in Rome on May 30, 1501, he was elected General. He devoted the remaining years of his life to the reform of his order, visiting many of its monasteries in Italy, France, the Low Countries, and Spain. On one of these journeys, he died in Altomonte, Calabria, on August 27, 1506, and was buried in Naples. Fra Vincenzo Bandello is known to students of Italian literature as the uncle of the famous novelist Matteo Bandello,[5] and to historians of art because he was prior of S. Maria delle Grazie when Leonardo da Vinci painted his Last Supper for its refectory.[6]

---

de *Théologie Catholique*, VII, 1922, col. 1120 1124) gives the date 1477. Since the edition is dated February 12, 1481, and since Fra Vincenzo in his preface to Ercole states that the disputation took place "preterita quadragesima," the date 1480 seems preferable. Easter fell on April 22 in 1481.

[4] V. Cian, "Isabella d'Este alle dispute domenicane," *Giornale storico della letteratura italiana*, LXVII (1916), 376–386. Apparently Fra Vincenzo was opposed to Savonarola. See A. Gherardi, *Nuovi documenti e studi intorno a Girolamo Savonarola*, Second ed., (Florence, 1887), pp. 56–57. Also, J. Schnitzer, *Savonarola im Streite mit seinem Orden und seinem Kloster* (Munich, 1914), esp. pp. 62–66, 98–99.

[5] Matteo Bandello, *Novelle*, pt. III, no. 12 (vol. IV, Bari, 1911, p. 195). E. Masi, "Vita italiana in un novelliere del Cinquecento," *Nuova Antologia*, CXXV (Ser. III, vol. XLI, 1892), 432–461, 672–694, esp. 442.

[6] G. d'Adda, "Lodovico Maria Sforza e il Convento di Santa Maria delle Grazie," *Archivio Storico Lombardo*, I (1874), 25–53; F. Malaguzzi Valeri, *La Corte di Lodovico il Moro*, II (Milan, 1915), 518; E. Müller, *Das Abendmahl des Lionardo da Vinci* (Baden–Baden, 1952), pp. 11–12; C. Pedretti, *Documenti e Memorie riguardanti Leonardo da Vinci a Bologna e in Emilia* (Bologna, 1953), pp. 213–215. The anecdote that Leonardo gave the features of Vincenzo Bandello to the Judas of his Last Supper, in order to punish the prior for his

Fra Vincenzo published two different treatises on the Immaculate Conception,[7] edited and annotated the Rule of St. Augustine and the Constitutions of his order,[8] and many of his letters dealing with church affairs have been preserved and partly published.[9] Among his unpublished writings, the bibliographical sources mention a treatise which is of some interest for the history of philosophy.[10] I found the text of this treatise in a manuscript in Florence in 1952,[11] and shall study it in this paper as a document

insistence on the completion of the work, is rejected by all modern historians, also on iconographical grounds.

[7] See Quétif-Echard, Mazzuchelli, Le Bachelet, *l.c.* The first treatise is entitled in the colophon: Libellus recollectorius de veritate conceptionis Beate Virginis Marie (Hain, 2352; *Gesamtkatalog der Wiegendrucke*, 3237). The second treatise has at the end of the text: Explicit tractatus de singulari puritate et prerogativa conceptionis salvatoris nostri ex auctoritatibus ducentorum sexaginta doctorum (Hain, 2353; *Gesamtkatalog*, 3238). I have seen both first editions at the Pierpont Morgan Library. The bibliographers list several later editions of the second work.

[8] Milan, 1505 (copies in the British Museum and Bibliothèque Nationale), and many later editions. R.-M. Louis, *Archivum Fatrum Predicatorum*, VI (1936), 334–350.

[9] *Registrum litterarum Joachimi Turriani 1487-1500, Vincentii Bandelli 1501-1506, Thomae de Vio Caietani 1507-1513*, ed. B.M. Reichert (*Quellen und Forschungen zur Geschichte des Dominikanerordens in Deutschland*, vol. X), (Leipzig, 1914). *Archivum Fratrum Praedicatorum, pass.* Mortier, *l.c.*

[10] Most detailed of all is Quétif, *l.c.*: "Extat hoc opus (sc. tractatus de singulari puritate) Ms Florentiae ad S. Marci Arm. III cod. 19, cui et aliud adiunctum eiusdem Vincentii opusculum ad magnificum et generosum virum Laurentium Medicem. Titulus: Quod beatitudo hominis in actu intellectus et non voluntatis essentialiter consistit. Occasio huius scripti fuit sententia Marsilii Ficini ea aetate florentis et aliter opinantis. Idem opusculum item habetur ibidem Arm. IV cod. 89." Arm. III cod. 19 is evidently identical with the manuscript cited below. Mazzuchelli also gives the title of the treatise, and mentions that it is found in ms. III, 19 of the library of S. Marco in Florence. He does not mention the other manuscript, nor indicate the connection of the treatise with Lorenzo and Ficino. The mere title of the work is repeated by Fabricius–Mansi, *l.c.*, and by L. Charlier (*Dictionnaire d'Histoire et de Géographie Ecclésiastiques*, VI, 1932, 483–484).

[11] See the appendix for a description of the manuscript and for the text of the preface and of the main arguments.

for the history of the Platonic Academy of Florence, leaving it to others to publish the entire text of the work, and to determine its place in the history of Thomism.

Fra Vincenzo's treatise begins with a preface addressed to Lorenzo de' Medici. The tone and content of this preface suggest that Vincenzo had recently visited Florence, and had met both Lorenzo and Ficino on that occasion. He states that he had read a few days before a letter or treatise by Ficino in which the latter related a disputation held by Ficino himself and Lorenzo on the ultimate happiness of rational creatures. Vincenzo assumes that in the debate Ficino maintained the superiority of the will, and Lorenzo that of the intellect, and states that he decided to present his own opinion in a short work, since Ficino's conclusion contradicts that of Aquinas and of other distinguished theologians.

The work of Ficino to which Fra Vincenzo alludes and which he attempts to refute is evidently Ficino's letter to Lorenzo de' Medici, which is included in the first book of his letters, and has the heading "Quid est felicitas, quot habet gradus, quod est aeterna."[12] This letter is cited by Ficino himself as "epistola de felicitate,"[13] and it may have circulated for a while as an independent work. In the beginning of this letter, which was probably composed in 1474,[14] Ficino reports that he had recently held a disputation with Lorenzo on the subject of happiness, and that they both finally agreed on the same opinion. In the next sentence Ficino credits Lorenzo with some new arguments proving that happiness consists in the act of the will rather than in that of the intellect. This sentence is missing in one of the oldest manuscripts, and appears as a marginal addition in several others, and hence it was probably added by Ficino as an afterthought in 1475 or 1476, in order to emphasize Lorenzo's active part in the discussion.[15] Fra Vincenzo must have read Ficino's text without this sentence,

[12] Ficino, *Opera*, (Basel, 1576, reprinted Turin, 1959) I, 662-665.
[13] *Ibid.*, 619; II, 1252; 1425.
[14] *Supplementum Ficinianum*, ed. P.O. Kristeller (Florence, 1937), I, XCI.
[15] *Suppl.* I, 28. Another manuscript copied on Feb. 21, 1477 (*Suppl.* I, X) contains the passage.

for otherwise he could not have assumed, as he does in his preface, that in the discussion with Ficino, Lorenzo had defended the superiority of the intellect. This dates Vincenzo's treatise between 1474 and 1475, and we may even wonder whether Ficino inserted the sentence in question, after having seen Vincenzo's preface, in order to show that Lorenzo concurred with his own position. Ficino then relates that he and Lorenzo had agreed to write down the content of their discussion. Lorenzo had done his share by composing an elegant poem (*L'Altercazione*), whereas Ficino is now carrying out his part of the agreement by composing a piece in Latin prose.[16] In the first part of his letter, Ficino presents a hierarchy of goods, and concludes that the ultimate happiness of man consists in God alone. To this part of Ficino's letter Fra Vincenzo makes no reference. The second and longer part of Ficino's letter actually discusses the question to which Fra Vincenzo devotes his entire treatise. Ficino maintains that in the ultimate happiness of the soul, which has God for its object, joy which is an act of the will is superior to vision which is an act of the intellect. This statement is then followed by a series of arguments. In the third part of his letter, which Fra Vincenzo again does not discuss, Ficino argues that different souls enjoy God in different ways, and that the soul that has once attained true happiness will never lose it again. He concludes with a reference to his commentary on Plato's *Symposium* and to his *Platonic Theology* where some of the problems are discussed more fully than is possible in the compass of a short letter.

The reasons why Fra Vincenzo decided to attack Ficino in his treatise are easy to see. The notion that the will is superior to the intellect was one of the main points on which Duns Scotus had disagreed with Thomas Aquinas who asserted the superiority of the intellect. In defending the superiority of the will in his letter, Ficino was in fact endorsing the Scotist position, and in arguing for the superiority of the intellect against Ficino, Fra Vincenzo

[16] Lorenzo de' Medici, *Opere*, ed. A. Simioni (Bari, 1939), II, 33–70, esp. 41–63. A. Buck, *Der Platonismus in den Dichtungen Lorenzo de' Medicis* (Berlin, 1936), pp. 70–94. P.O. Kristeller, *Studies*, pp. 214–216.

defended the Thomist view against the Scotists and Franciscans as well. That the point was of some importance to him, appears from the preface of one of his other works, which was written about the same time.[17]

Although Ficino states at the beginning of his letter that he had discussed the question of happiness with Lorenzo "ultro citroque," there is no reason to believe that this discussion had taken the rigid form a scholastic disputation where each of the disputants had argued for one side of the question. However, this is the kind of disputation to which Fra Vincenzo was accustomed through his training. In dealing with the central section of Ficino's letter, Fra Vincenzo thus takes it for granted that Lorenzo had acted as a respondent and had argued in favor of the intellect, and that Ficino, after having refuted all arguments of his respondent, had "determined" the question in favor of the will. In other words, Fra Vincenzo treats the central part of Ficino's letter as a truncated *Quaestio*, in which the counterarguments and their refutations are omitted, and only the arguments supporting the main thesis remain. Consequently, Fra Vincenzo first repeats the issue of the question, namely whether ultimate happiness consists essentially in an act of the intellect or of the will, and then gives a somewhat formalized version of the arguments advanced in Ficino's letter in favor of the will. These arguments come to eighteen, and on the whole, they are rendered rather faithfully by Fra Vincenzo who merely omits a few characteristic nuances.[18] In the second part of his treatise, Fra Vincenzo presents eighteen counterarguments in favor of the intellect. He then proceeds to the third part of his treatise which is entitled *Decisio et determinatio questionis*. This part is much more systematic than the others, and it presents sixteen conclusions with their respective proofs. In the fourth and last part of his treatise, Vincenzo refutes Ficino's arguments one by one, and concludes his work with a short epilogue addressed to Lorenzo.

Fra Vincenzo's *Opusculum* follows on the whole the familiar

[17] *Libellus recollectorius* (1475), f. 1.
[18] I noted such omissions in arguments 1 e, 6 and 17.

pattern and structure of a scholastic *Quaestio*. It has a main proposition or thesis which is formulated in the beginning and considered proven in the end. There are series of arguments for and against the thesis (parts two and one), and also a one by one refutation of the contrary arguments (part four). Due to the fact that this is the refutation of Ficino's letter (which Fra Vincenzo treats as a *Quaestio*), the normal order of the arguments is inverted, and the arguments against the thesis (that is, Ficino's arguments for the contrary thesis) precede the arguments for it. The third part consists of a series of independent conclusions with their respective proofs, and hence seems to fall outside the scheme of the *Quaestio*, but it may be said to lay the foundations on which the refutation of Ficino's arguments in the fourth part is based. In adding a prefatory epistle and a short epilogue, both addressed to Lorenzo de' Medici, Fra Vincenzo, in spite of his disclaimer, pays his tribute to humanist literary conventions. His Latin style is on the whole fluent and simple, and his use of technical terminology fairly moderate. His arguments are often repetitious and at times pedantic, but as a rule well reasoned and to the point. His presentation of Ficino's opposite views is fair and dispassionate, although he does not always seem to grasp his intentions. His frequent quotations and references show the range of his learning: the Bible, Aristotle and Thomas Aquinas are quoted most frequently, and occasionally at length; there are a few references to Augustine, fewer to Boethius, two to Dionysius the Areopagite, one each to Cicero, Gregory the Great, and Hugh of St. Victor. Origen and the Platonists are mentioned for their opinions, probably at second hand.

If we want to understand the significance of this controversy, we must realize first of all that the two contestants share a number of common terms and premises which they obviously inherited from the preceding philosophical and theological tradition. For both of them, the ultimate happiness of man consists in a conjunction of the soul with God that is permanently attained, on the part of the blessed, in the future life. Both of them also take it for granted that intellect and will are involved in the attainment of this ultimate happiness which includes the vision and fruition of God on the part of the soul and presupposes the love and desire of the soul for this ultimate end. For desire, love, pleasure in all their forms are considered acts of the will, and the will is taken as a distinct faculty of the soul, distinct from the intellect, and somehow on the same level with it: the will is the rational part of the appetitive power of the soul. It is within this broader common framework that the question arises which is the subject of Ficino's letter and of Fra Vincenzo's treatise: does the ultimate happiness of man essentially and primarily concern the intellect or the will, and what is implied in it: is the intellect or the will the more excellent among the two faculties? It is comparatively easy to see which side of the issue each of the contestants is taking, and how many arguments of quite unequal value each of them is trying to accumulate in support of his chosen thesis. It would be more important and more difficult to find out which of the many arguments really carry the burden of the respective conclusions, and which were the real philosophical reasons that prompted each of the two contestants to adopt his chosen position. In the case of Fra Vincenzo, a basic factor is, of course, his commitment to the doctrine of Thomas Aquinas who had taken a clear and explicit stand on the question. Fra Vincenzo quotes Aquinas at great length, and he follows him in the use he makes of specific Aristotelian and Christian theories and quotations. If we compare the arguments on both sides, the following differences seem to be especially important. Fra Vincenzo introduces a number of nice distinctions which are absent from Ficino's discussion, and which allow the former to restate the problem in different terms. Especially noteworthy is the distinction, taken over from Aquinas, between the internal and the external ultimate end of man, that is, between God and the possession of happiness. Another basic difference concerns the theory of pleasure. Fra Vincenzo stands firm on the Aristotelian theory presented in the last book of the *Nicomachean Ethics* that pleasure is the accompanying perfection of an activity, and hence should not be considered as a primary good or end of desire. Ficino, on the other hand, was at one time deeply influenced by the hedonism of Epicurus and Lucretius, and actually refers in his letter to his early treatise *De voluptate*, in which his views on this subject are developed. Moreover, he was influenced by the Neoplatonic view that the good, and the appetite directed towards it, have both a higher and broader metaphysical significance than the order of truth and intellect. Obviously, Fra Vincenzo did not know or appreciate these ideas or their sources. The most profound and pervasive difference between the two views concerns the analysis of the acts of knowledge and of love. The intellect grasps its object through images or species while resting in itself, and when this object is God, the intellect lowers and narrows it to conform with its own capacity. Love, on the other hand, moves the soul towards its object as it is in itself, and when this object is God, love will lift and enlarge the soul to the infinity of God. Ficino's eloquent words reflect Neoplatonic and medieval theories, but also his own spiritual experience, and as they were rendered into Italian verse by Lorenzo de' Medici, they made a deep impression on Jacob Burckhardt who considered them as a noble expression of Renaissance thought, and cited them with emphasis towards the end of his famous book.[19] Fra Vincenzo's reply to this important argument is characteristic: the distinction between the acts of the will and of the intellect as given by Ficino is true for the present life. In the future life, the knowledge of God will be aided by the *lumen gloriae*, the soul will know God immediately in His essence, and thus be enlarged to His infinity through the vision of God, rather than through fruition.[20] This reply discloses another fundamental

---

[19] J. Burckhardt, *Die Kultur der Renaissance in Italien*, 13th ed. (Stuttgart, 1921), p. 415.

[20] Part IV, no. 7 (f. 186v–187): In statu autem patrie ubi essentia divina non per aliquam creatam speciem sed ipsa immediate per se ipsam intellectui creato unietur ut forma intelligibilis.... non habebit divina essentia nobilius esse in se ipsa quam in intellectu beato et per hoc non nobiliori modo attingetur a voluntate quam capiatur ab intellectu.– no. 15 (f. 192): In illo inquam statu amplitudinem divinam non contrahemus ad capacitatem nostre mentis atque conceptus... sed potius anima per intellectum amplificabitur ad latitudinem

difference of outlook. For Fra Vincenzo, there is a radical difference between the present and the future life, and even between the knowledge of God in the one and in the other. The ultimate happiness as it is attainable in this life and as it is known to the philosophers including Aristotle has but a remote resemblance to the real happiness in the future life,[21] and he does not hesitate to postulate for the future knowledge of God certain characteristics that have no counterpart in the experience of our present life. Ficino, on the other hand, as an heir to the Neoplatonic tradition, does not know such a radical difference between the present and the future life. He is convinced that the highest experience of contemplation as it is accessible to the Platonic philosopher is a genuine foretaste of the future life, and that the latter can be legitimately described through analogies drawn from this experience. He would not deny the importance of the Christian faith, or of grace and of the *lumen gloriae*, but he would stress that the present and future experience are fundamentally alike; their basic difference is one of degree: the perfect knowledge of God in this life is attained but by a few people and for a short while, whereas in the future life it will be attained by a large number and for eternity.[22]

So far we have discussed Ficino's theory of will and intellect exclusively on the basis of his letter to Lorenzo since this letter alone was the target of Fra Vincenzo's critique. However, the problem was discussed by Ficino and his pupils in a number of other passages, and although the question was obviously of great importance to him, his views on it were not as simple or consistent,

divine bonitatis, quia per lumen glorie in tantum dilatabitur quod totam divinam perfectionem capiet intra se que ei ut forma intelligibilis unietur.

[21] Part IV, no. 16 (f. 192v–193): Huius autem perfecte et ultime felicitatis que omne desiderium complet nihil in hac vita est adeo simile sicut vita contemplantium veritatem. Et ideo philosophi qui de illa ultima felicitate plenam notitiam habere non potuerunt, in contemplatione veritatis que in hac vita possibilis est ultimam felicitatem hominis posuere... Incipit enim contemplatio veritatis in hac vita et in futura consummatur.

[22] P.O. Kristeller, *Il pensiero filosofico di Marsilio Ficino* (Florence, 1953), pp. 259–273.

as an isolated analysis of the letter to Lorenzo might suggest. Although Fra Vincenzo was probably not acquainted with these other texts, a very brief consideration of these texts will help us to see Ficino's letter and Fra Vincenzo's critique in a better historical perspective.

If we scan Ficino's writings from different periods of his life for relevant passages, it becomes apparent that he is quite consistent in making a distinction between intellect and will, between knowledge on the one hand, love and joy on the other, between an order of truth and an order of goodness; he also tends to establish a kind of parallelism between these two sets of concepts, and uses both of them when he defines the ultimate end of man as including both the knowledge and the enjoyment or love of God.[23] However, when it comes to facing the question whether intellect or will is superior, and which of them plays the more important part in the relationship between the soul and God, Ficino's answers differ in his various writings, and this difference seems to reflect a development of his views during different phases of his thought. I am inclined to distinguish roughly three phases of his thought on this particular issue. The earliest phase is represented by Ficino's commentary on Plato's *Philebus*, which originated in public lectures delivered around 1468 and was revised much later. In an important section of that commentary, Ficino starts from the passage where Plato recommends the mixture of wisdom and pleasure, and comments that in this mixture wisdom is greatly superior to pleasure.[24] Then he states explicitly that the intellect is superior to the will, and presents several arguments in support of this thesis. He asserts that happiness or the attaining of the ultimate end consists in an act of the intellect, and not in an act of the will, and adds a series of arguments. Ficino does not cite Thomas or any other sources, but he does not only endorse the Thomist position on this issue, but also uses some of the same arguments which we encounter in Fra Vincenzo's treatise. The intellect directs the

[23] *Ibid.*, pp. 274–291.
[24] *Opera*, II, 1250–1252, cf. *Il pensiero*, pp. 291–292; for the date, see *Suppl.* I, CXXII–CXXIII.

will. The intellect attracts objects to itself, whereas the will is attracted by them. Pleasure is not the ultimate end, but merely its companion. The first object of the will is not an act of the will. True and false happiness are distinguished by the intellect, not by the will. Pleasure is not the ultimate end of nature, but it is chosen for the sake of certain operations. Finally, the soul attains God primarily through the intellect.

Yet a few years later, Ficino changed his view on this matter rather radically. The letter to Lorenzo which we have examined in detail and which was composed around 1474 is an important testimony of this change, but it is by no means the only one. In this letter, Ficino cites his major philosophical work, the *Platonic Theology*, which was composed between 1469 and 1474. In the fourteenth book of this work, Ficino argues that in this life the love of God is superior to the knowledge of God, and repeats in part verbatim the same arguments which we know from his letter to Lorenzo, including the impressive sentence on the enlarging effect of love upon the human mind.[25] The same emphasis on the superiority of will, love and joy over the intellect and knowledge occurs in other passages of the *Platonic Theology* and of Ficino's letters,[26] as well as in an undated short text on the supreme good,[27] and this must have been Ficino's view during the middle period of his career.

However, during his last years he seems to have wavered again, and to have attempted a compromise, while being still inclined to favor the superiority of the will. We are unable to say whether Fra Vincenzo's critique made an impression on him, but we know that his inconsistency was known to himself as well as to others. When he revised his commentary on Plato's *Philebus* for the second time around 1492 and gave it the final form in which it was printed in 1496, Ficino added several sentences to the passage which we have discussed. He states explicitly that he had given

---

[25] *Opera*, pp. 324–325, *Il pensiero*, pp. 292–294. For the date, cf. *Suppl.* I, LXXIX–XXXI.
[26] *Opera*, p. 309, 409, 658, 704, 710, 862–863, cf. *Il pensiero*, p. 294.
[27] *Suppl.* II, 96–97.

probable arguments for the opposite view, that is, for the superiority of the will, in his letter to Lorenzo, and then suggests as a "safe attempt" the compromise of treating the will as included in the intellect, and not as separate from it.[28] This sounds very much like a concession made not only to his own earlier view, but also to the Thomist position. He returns to the question in a letter to Paolo Orlandini, written probably in 1496 and printed during the same year with his commentaries on Plato. Orlandini had asked him about the contradiction between his commentary on the *Philebus* and his letter to Lorenzo. Ficino replies that he could say that he proposed in the former text Plato's opinion, and in the latter his own, but he does not wish to use this way out. He rather replies that we must distinguish between the natural and the supernatural or "ecstatic" activity of our mind. In the former, the intellect guides the will, whereas in the latter it is the will which leads the intellect. In the commentary on the *Philebus* he was concerned with the former, in the letter to Lorenzo with the latter.[29] In this way, Ficino manages to achieve an apparent reconciliation between his own former and later views, and to give greater emphasis to the latter. In a sense, he reverses the stand taken by Fra Vincenzo. For him, the superiority of the intellect applies to the ordinary activity of the mind, whereas the superiority of the will and of love holds for the highest ascent of the mind towards God. The context shows that he is here thinking of Plato's theory of love, and of Plotinus' doctrine of "ecstasy."

As further evidence for the interest taken by Ficino and his circle in the problem of will and intellect, we may cite a short treatise written between 1481 and 1488 by Ficino's pupil Alamanno Donati that was published, without philosophical comments, by Lamberto Borghi some years ago.[30] The work is entitled "Disputationes de intellectus voluntatisque excellentia" and addressed

---

[28] *Opera*, p. 1252, cf. *Suppl.* I, 79. *Il pensiero*, pp. 295.

[29] *Opera*, p. 1425–1426. *Il pensiero*, pp. 295–296.

[30] *La Bibliofilia*, XLII (1940), 108–115. Guglielmo Capponi later became bishop of Cortona (F. Ughelli, *Italia Sacra*, I, Venice, 1717, col. 628).

to Guglielmo Capponi. In the introduction, the author refers to a recent disputation on the question held in the house of the addressee in the presence of his brother Bernardo Capponi and of Cristoforo Marsuppini. Donati wishes to supplement the discussion with relevant arguments from the "Christian theologians," that is, probably from Thomas Aquinas and Duns Scotus, or from some of their followers. He begins with ten arguments supporting the superiority of the intellect. Of special interest is the third argument that the intellect is peculiar to man whereas the will as an appetite is common to all animals, and peculiar to man only in so far as it is dependent on the intellect; hence man attains happiness with reference to his intellect. According to the fourth argument, the action of the intellect is desired for its own sake and completely self-sufficient. According to the eighth, the intellect moves the object to itself, whereas the will moves itself to the object. According to the ninth, ultimate happiness is attained in the act of the intellect, whereas the acts of the will, that is, desire, love and joy, precede or follow it.

Donati then presents ten other arguments in favor of the superiority of the will. The first argument states that the will has freedom. According to the second, we can misuse knowledge, but not love. According to the fifth, joy is desired for its own sake, vision for the sake of something else. Finally, according to the last argument, *charitas* is the highest of virtues, and it belongs to the will rather than to the intellect. Donati does not solve the dilemma, but concludes with a praise of the dignity of the human soul, that is demonstrated by the excellence both of his intellect and of his will. The treatise suggests that also for Donati's teacher, Ficino, the question of the superiority of will and intellect, on which he oscillated, was less important than their parallelism, and their common excellence which expresses the dignity of man understood as the dignity of his higher self.

The problem with which we have seen Ficino struggling was by no means new with him or with his century, and it was no coincidence that his views as expressed during his middle period should have been criticized by a theologian trained in the Thomist tradition, although there is some irony in the fact that his critic defended against him a thesis which Ficino himself had advanced in another work a few years before, and partly with the same arguments. The question whether the intellect or the will is superior, and which of these two faculties of the soul is more directly involved in man's ultimate happiness had been discussed in exactly the same terms and with a great number of arguments by Thomas Aquinas and Duns Scotus, as we have repeatedly indicated. Let us see as briefly as possible how the formulation of the problem and of the supporting arguments by Ficino and his opponent compare with the corresponding passages in Thomas and Duns. The matter is of some interest, for this is one of the rare instances where we can watch Ficino, a non-scholastic philosopher of the fifteenth century commonly labeled as a Platonist, discuss a typical problem of high scholasticism, in the terms laid down by his scholastic predecessors, and without any but indirect help from his favorite ancient sources.

Thomas Aquinas discusses the question in a number of passages some of which are cited at great length by Fra Vincenzo. In his Commentary on the *Sentences*, book IV, dist. 49, Thomas discusses the opinion that happiness concerns the will rather than the intellect, and gives five arguments.[31] In the third, he says that *caritas* is the highest of all virtues; in the fourth that the will commands the intellect, and in the fifth, that man is joined to God more perfectly through the will than through the intellect. Then he rejects this view with four arguments drawn from Scripture and Aristotle. Another passage in the Commentary on the *Sentences* deals with the superiority of knowledge and love.[32] After having given some arguments on both sides, Aquinas concludes that the intellect is more excellent with reference to its subject, and the will with reference to its objects. For through his will and law man is drawn towards his objects, whereas through his knowledge the objects are reproduced in him through their images. Hence we may say that with reference to higher things,

[31] Quaestiuncula 2 (*Opera omnia*, ed. Fretté, XI, Paris, 1874, 458).
[32] Book III, dist. 27, qu. 1, a. 4 (*Opera*, IX, 1873, 426–429).

love is superior, and with reference to lower things, knowledge. After having refused to identify will with the active life and intellect with the contemplative life, Aquinas here admits that in the present life, will surpasses intellect.

More detailed is the treatment in the *Summa Theologica*. In the *Pars Prima*,[33] Thomas discusses the question whether the will is superior to the intellect. In the third argument for the will, the superiority of *caritas* over the other virtues is again emphasized. Referring to Aristotle for the superiority of the intellect, Aquinas argues again that in an absolute sense, the intellect is superior to the will, whereas the will is superior in relation to the object, especially if this object is higher than man, since the will tends towards the object as it exists in itself. In the *Prima Secundae*,[34] Thomas asks specifically whether ultimate happines is an operation of the intellect or of the will. Among the arguments for the will, he mentions that the love of God is superior to the knowledge of God. Yet he concludes that the essence of happiness consists in an act of the intellect, and that the delight which belongs to the will is merely an accompanying factor of happiness. In the act of attaining God, knowledge is superior to love. In another passage, Thomas argues that in the ultimate happiness, vision is more essential than delight.[35] In the *Summa Contra Gentiles*, Thomas devotes a whole chapter to the same question.[36] Arguing first for the view that ultimate happiness consists in an act of the will, he states that delight is desired for its own sake, that desire is more widely shared than knowledge, and that the will directs the intellect. Yet then he rejects this view, and advances stronger arguments in favor of the intellect. Will in so far as it is appetite is not peculiar to man. The ultimate object of the will is not itself an act of the will. The distincton between the true and the false good is made by the intellect and not by the will. The acts of the

[33] *S. Th.* I, qu. 82, a. 3. Cf. E. Gilson, *Le Thomisme*, 5th ed. (Paris, 1945), pp. 341–342.
[34] *S. Th.* I–II, qu. 3, a. 4.
[35] *Ibid.*, qu. 4, a. 2.
[36] *S. c. gent.*, III, 26.

will, desiring, loving and enjoying, either precede or follow the ultimate end of man. Pleasure is not always to be desired for its own sake, but only that which accompanies good actions. Man attains God primarily through knowing. Hence we may say that ultimate happiness is the object of our will, but it is not its action.

Another important passage is found in the *Quaestiones disputatae*.[37] Thomas presents again several arguments for the superiority of the intellect and for the superiority of the will, and concludes that in an absolute sense the intellect is superior, but that in relation to a superior object, especially to God, the will is superior.

We cannot analyze all arguments of Aquinas in detail, but from the points we have mentioned it appears that Aquinas, although he does in the end favor the superiority of the intellect, seems to make greater concessions and qualifications in favor of the opposite view than does his fifteenth-century follower Fra Vincenzo, and that he gives a sufficient number of arguments in favor of will and love to supply at least in part the needs of those who were inclined to hold the opposite thesis, as Ficino was during his middle period.

The historical significance of the problem is heightened by the fact that Duns Scotus differed from Aquinas on this very issue and thus arrived at his distinctive "voluntaristic" position. In his larger commentary on the *Sentences*, the *Opus Oxoniense*, Scotus discusses the matter in book IV, distinction 49, question 4, which is entitled "Whether happiness consists absolutely in an act of the intellect or in an act of the will."[38] The discussion of the question is minute, but consists primarily in a formalized restatement and detailed refutation of some of Thomas' arguments. Duns Scotus then adds a *Quaestio ex latere* which discusses the broader problem whether the intellect or the will is superior.[39] Among other points, Scotus argues here that the will in this life has a greater capacity than the intellect, and hence also in the

---

[37] *De veritate*, qu. 22, a. 11.
[38] Duns Scotus, *Opera omnia*, XXI (Paris, 1894), 93–100.
[39] *Ibid.*, 123–164, esp. 93, 123, 141, 163.

future life. While Thomas had cited Aristotle in favor of the superiority of the intellect, Scotus remarks that Aristotle does not consistently distinguish between will and intellect.[40] The intellect is not the total cause of the will, otherwise the freedom of the will would be excluded. To hate God is worse than not to know him, hence love is superior to knowledge. The act of the will joins the soul to the object as it is in itself, the act of the intellect only to the object as it is in the knower; hence in the state of ultimate happiness, the act of the will joins the soul with God more perfectly.

The same question is discussed by Duns Scotus in the corresponding passage of his *Reportata Parisiensia*.[41] He refutes Thomas' arguments for the view that ultimate happiness consists absolutely in an act of the intellect. The conjunction between the soul and God in the state of happiness is more immediately accomplished by an act of the will. The most perfect habit, that is, *caritas*, and the greater capacity belongs to the will, not to the intellect, both in this and in the future life. The will is also nobler because its corruption is worse. The will is superior because it joins the soul with its external object, provided that it is a perfect object. Thus happiness consists essentially in an act of the will. Duns then rejects the intermediary position according to which happiness consists both in an act of the will and of the intellect, and finally argues at length that happiness consists in fruition which is an act of the will, whereas vision does not belong to the essence of happiness.

I cannot discuss the very complicated arguments through which Duns Scotus develops his views, yet I should like to sum up the impact which Thomas and Scotus seem to have had upon our two fifteenth-century authors. In the case of Fra Vincenzo, it is quite obvious that he is defending the position of Aquinas. At the same time, he seems to be aware of Scotus' critique and different

---

[40] *Ibid.*, 141: Posset aliter dici, quod Philosophus communiter non distinxit intellectum a voluntate in ratione principii operativi sive operatione ad extra.

[41] IV, dist. 49, qu. 2-4 (*Opera omnia*, XXIV, 1894, 620–640, esp. 625 and 629). Cf. E. Gilson, *Jean Duns Scot* (Paris, 1952), pp. 600-603.

position, and is thus prompted to restate Aquinas' view in some respects more explicitly and with fewer qualifications than the master had done himself, and to use a few Scotist distinctions and arguments in discussing it. Ficino, on the other hand, adopts the Scotist position during his middle period, and was probably aware of this fact in a general way. Yet there is no evidence that he actually read Scotus, as he surely had read Aquinas, and his rather simple arguments do not resemble the intricate discussion and terminology of Scotus at all. He drew some of his arguments from Thomas himself, by using the arguments advanced by Thomas for the view he rejected, and by inverting some of Thomas' positive arguments. Other arguments he added from his Neoplatonic sources, and a few he may have invented himself. The famous argument 15, according to which our soul is enlarged through love to the infinite vastness of God, may very well be Ficino's own contribution. The notion presupposed in it, that love tends towards its external object whereas knowledge assimilates the object to itself, is clearly taken from Aquinas.

We may add that the problem of intellect and will was also one of the few scholastic problems in which some of the early humanists were strongly interested. In his treatise on his own and other people's ignorance, where Petrarch speaks about the true task of the moral philosopher, he stresses in eloquent words the superiority of will and of love over intellect and knowledge.[42] And in his treatise on the nobility of law and medicine, Coluccio Salutati devotes a whole chapter to the task of proving that the will is nobler than the intellect.[43] The will rules the intellect, and it is free. Aristotle who seems to assert the contrary does not really separate will and intellect. I should not think that Petrarch or Salutati derived their views or arguments from Duns Scotus, but it is interesting to note that on this particular problem they

---

[42] Pétrarque, *Le traité De sui ipsius et multorum ignorantia*, ed. L.M. Capelli (Paris, 1906), p. 70.

[43] Coluccio Salutati, *De nobilitate legum et medicinae*, ed. E. Garin (Florence, 1947), ch. 23, pp. 182–196.

took essentially a Scotist position, as did Ficino in his middle period.

Whereas the specific terms in which the problem of will and intellect was discussed by Ficino and Fra Vincenzo, and before them by Petrarch and Salutati, received their classical formulation in the thirteenth century by Thomas Aquinas and Duns Scotus, this discussion is but a special phase within a much broader problem which has played a decisive role in the history of Western thought from the end of antiquity to fairly modern times, that is, at least from Augustine to Kant: the conception of the will and of its relation to the intellect. The history of this important problem has been treated by a few historians,[44] but seems to deserve a more complete and detailed investigation than it has received so far. I must limit myself to indicating a few major points, and to clearing up a few widespread misconceptions.[45] First of all, the conception of the will as a faculty distinct from the intellect should not be confused with the defense of the freedom of the will, as is often done. We have seen that Duns Scotus uses the freedom of the will as an argument to prove the superiority of the will over the intellect. Yet even the term freedom of the will (*liberum arbitrium* and its Greek equivalents) does not presuppose a distinct faculty of willing (*voluntas*), as the terminology in English and other modern languages might suggest, and vice versa, it is quite possible to assume a separate faculty of willing, but to believe that it is determined and not free. The doctrine of free will was assumed or defended by many Greek philosophers, but I am inclined to hold that the conception of the will as a distinct faculty, equal or even superior in status to the intellect, was alien

---

[44] W. Kahl, *Die Lehre vom Primat des Willens bei Augustinus, Duns Scotus und Descartes* (Strassburg, 1886); Archibald Alexander, *Theories of the Will in the History of Philosophy* (New York, 1898); E. Benz, *Marius Victorinus und die Entwicklung der abendlaendischen Willensmetaphysik* (Stuttgart, 1932). See also the discussion in Harry A. Wolfson, *Philo* (Cambridge, Mass., 1947), I, 430–438; 456–458.

[45] My ideas on this subject were much clarified by discussions with my colleague, Prof. James Walsh.

to classical Greek philosophy.[46] According to the view of Socrates, which dominated most later Greek ethics, the good is known by reason, and once it is known, it is also done. Plato assigns an important role to love in some of his dialogues, but he does not oppose it to reason or identify it with will, or even treat it as a faculty of the soul. Where he introduces a distinction between such faculties, desire and "wrath" are not only distinct from reason, but clearly inferior to it, and in no way "intellectual." In Aristotle we find a variety of concepts and theories that resemble various aspects of the medieval doctrine, and that hence were cited by his medieval commentators, but in his own work, they are disconnected and do not form a unified theory of the will. Where he distinguishes between various faculties of the soul, he treats the power of desiring as an inferior and irrational faculty, as Plato had done, and never uses a term reminiscent of willing. In an obscure chapter of the *De anima*,[47] Aristotle links the terms desire, willing and practical intellect, but it is not at all clear whether desire is here really treated as belonging to the practical intellect, and certainly willing is merely considered as an act of the intellect, as it is also elsewhere, but not as a separate faculty of the soul. The same is true of his concept of deliberate choice which plays such an important part in his *Ethics*. In the tenth book of the *Nicomachean Ethics*, he discusses pleasure in its relation to the intellect, as Plato had done in the *Philebus*, but neither of them even remotely suggests that pleasure is to be considered as an act of the will, as it is for the medieval philosophers. Hence Duns Scotus seems to have observed correctly that Aristotle when discussing these activities does not clearly distinguish the will and the intellect. The Stoics distinguish in their epistemology between representations passively received and the assent freely given to these representations, or withheld from them. Yet the power that grants or withholds the assent is still

[46] Cf. G. Gentile, *Sistema di logica*, 3rd ed. (Florence, 1940), I, 33–34.

[47] III, 10, 433a, 9–30. In the discussion of incontinence (*Nic. Eth.* VII, 2 ff.), Aristotle criticizes the Socratic position, but does not introduce the concept of will.

the faculty of reason. Finally, Plotinus expands Plato's theory of love, and in an important but isolated treatise,[48] he attributes to his first principle the faculty of willing that induces it to bring forth all other beings, and to the human soul the choice, not only between specific actions, but between the basic alternatives of the life of reason and the life of the senses. This is as close as we come to a doctrine of will in Greek philosophy.

The credit for having introduced the concept of will into Western philosophy seems to belong to St. Augustine. It has been rightly shown that he built upon the work of many predecessors, including Plotinus and other Greek thinkers. It has been suggested that the importance of the will in Augustine's thought was due to his Christian faith, and the praise bestowed upon *caritas* by St. Paul was cited by medieval (and modern) authors in support of the will. However, Paul does not yet treat *caritas* as an act of the will, or distinguish between will and intellect. We should also make allowance for the Latin language, and for the tradition of Roman jurisprudence embodied in that language, as well as for the originality of Augustine's thought. In any case, in his *De Trinitate*, Augustine places the will as a distinct and independent faculty besides the intellect, and treats them, along with memory, as the triad which represents the divine Trinity on the level of the human mind. The definitions Augustine gives of the will are somewhat elusive, but he suggests already a close link between love and will, and between joy and love, and there is no doubt that the concept of the will occupies a central place in his thought.[49] Yet neither St. Augustine, nor his early scholastic followers such as St. Bonaventura, seem to have asserted that the will is superior to the intellect, as Duns Scotus was to maintain.

Thus we may conclude that the distinction between will and intellect was explicitly formulated for the first time by St. Augustine, and was left by him as a heritage to subsequent Western thought. The question whether the intellect or the will is superior was

---

[48] *Enn.* VI, 8.
[49] E. Gilson, *Introduction à l'étude de Saint Augustin*, 3rd ed. (Paris, 1949), pp. 170–184.

answered largely in favor of the intellect by Thomas Aquinas, under the influence of Aristotle's emphasis on the intellect (although Aristotle did not know the distinction between will and intellect). Duns Scotus placed the will above the intellect, and thus did not merely restate the distinction made by Augustine, but also went beyond his explicit views. In these terms, the problem remained alive for many centuries, and it is still present, in a way, in Kant's distinction between pure and practical reason, and in the primacy he assigns to the latter. With Hegel, the primacy reverts to pure reason, we might say, and with Schopenhauer the will stands again for what the Greek used to call irrational desire. What modern thought has opposed to reason has not been the will in the sense formulated by Augustine, but irrational feeling or emotion. In contrasting the irrational with reason, recent thought after Romanticism has in a sense reverted to the position of the Greek philosophers. Yet when recent thought has at times defended the superiority of the irrational, this attitude has been made possible by the earlier tradition from Augustine to Kant that contrasted the will with the intellect and at times emphasized its superiority. The neglected episode which we have tried to study in this paper, receives its significance from the fact that it belongs as a modest phase to the history of a broad and important problem in Western thought. In a more specific way, it illustrates the way in which Renaissance Platonism was linked, not only with ancient thought, but also with the traditions of medieval philosophy and theology.

Appendix

The manuscript which contains our text is cod. S. Marco 482 of the Biblioteca Medicea Laurenziana in Florence. It consists of 196 fols., and was written on parchment by two different hands during the second half of the fifteenth century. The first part which goes to folio 156 and has decorated initials contains Fra Vincenzo's treatise on the Immaculate Conception addressed to Ercole d'Este. Since this treatise is followed by the laudatory verses of Antonius (Cittadinus) Faventinus and of M.L. iurisperitus, by a letter attributed to St. Bernard, and by an epilogue of the author (f. 153–156), as in the Bologna edition of 1481, this part of the manuscript may be a copy of that edition, and this is confirmed by an old note on the fly-leaf (f. I verso), which reads: compilatus per... Vincentium de Castro Novo... anno salutis MCCCCLXXXIII scriptus ex elemosinis.... (Another copy of the same treatise, with the preface and the two accompanying epigrams, appears in cod. 17-6 of the Biblioteca del Cabildo in Toledo, fols. 1–66; communication of Professor Eugenio Massa). The second part of the manuscript (f. 157–196) is written in a different hand and begins with the title of our treatise. The text is complete and neatly written, but hardly autograph since it shows a few errors attributable to a copyist rather than to the author. Since the text is in a different hand and seems to begin with a new gathering, we are not obliged to assign to this copy or to the composition of the treatise the same date as to the preceding treatise on the Immaculate Conception. A few months ago, Prof. Zofia Ameisenowa called my attention to another manuscript containing our text, which was offered for sale by Maggs Bros. in 1960 (Catalogue 871, no. 82). This manuscript was kindly shown to me in 1961 by its present owner, Mr. Laurence Witten (New Haven). See now his Catalogue Five (1962), pp. 16–17, n. 9. It is written on paper, consists of 41 fols., and has the Medici coat of arms. It contains no other text besides our treatise. A note on the fly-leaf, written in an Italian hand during the eighteenth century, suggests that the ms. comes from S. Marco in Florence. I am convinced that this is the second S. Marco ms. cited by Quetif with the shelf mark Arm. IV cod. 89. The ms. is not included in the S. Marco inventory of 1768, and hence must have disappeared from the library before that date. I am indebted to Dottoressa Irma Merolle Tondi, director of the Biblioteca Laurenziana, for the detailed information on which this statement is based. Additional information was supplied by Dott. Alberto Giraldi of the Biblioteca Nazionale Centrale in Florence, and by the Rev. T. Kaeppeli of the Istituto Storico Domenicano in Rome.

Florence, Biblioteca Medicea Laurenziana, cod. S. Marco 482.

(f. 157) Opusculum Fratris Vincentii de Castro Novo Ordinis Predicatorum ad Magnificum ac generosum virum Laurentium Medicem quod beatitudo hominis in actu intellectus et non voluntatis essentialiter consistit incipit.

Frater Vincentius de Castro Novo Ordinis Predicatorum Laurentio Medici viro magnifico s.p. dicit. Superioribus diebus nihil tale cogitanti querentive mihi casu oblata est epistola sive magis tractatus quidam ornatissimi viri Marsilii Ficini, in quo sicut sui semper moris est dilucide eleganterque determinat inter te et ipsum in agro Charegio de ultima rationalis creature felicitate habitam disputationem, cum ut reor is in voluntatis, tu contra intellectus actu beatitudinem hominis sitam esse confirmares, tandemque in eandem sententiam convenistis. Ex qua rationum diversitate admirabilis mihi reddita est tum tua religio probitasque, qui inter domesticas et publicas curas divinarum rerum scientiam contemplationemque non negligas, tum illius singularis viri peritia[1], utpote qui efficacibus argumentis et sustinere et quam[2] plurimis persuadere potuerit opinionem suam. Verum quoniam

[1] Ex. *periticia* corr. cod.   [2] suprascr cod.

ea Marsilii nostri determinatio non tantum celesti theologo Aquinati Thome, sed et potioris partis ceterorum illustrium doctorum sane sententie adversatur, inter multiplices occupationes meas lucubratiunculam aliquam tue magnificientie censui dedicandam, ac iam notissima apud omnes amicissimi mihi Marsilii benignitate fretus, presertim cum, ut dici solet, opinionum diversitas (157v) non frangat amicitiam, quid hac de re tenendum esse arbitrarer in hoc opusculo breviter exposui. Nec tamen est intentionis nostre, si de extrema perfectione rationalis nature quid nos quoque sentiamus sequenti tractatulo notissimum fiet, Marsilii talis ac tanti viri doctrine vel minima ex parte detrahere, neque vero derogari ei quicquam potest.[3] Protulit is quid sibi de hac questione videatur.[3] Edam et ego licet sine iniuria sententiam meam. Reliquum est magnifice Laurenti ut si in verborum compositione ornatuque sententiarum nos deficere tua eloquentia iudicarit, non propterea munusculum hoc minus gratum habeas. Siquidem theologorum consuetudinem imitamur qui longo suo exemplo docuerunt oratione simplici huiuscemodi gravissimas questiones clarius ab omnibus intelligi posse. Tue sinceritatis atque innocentie etiam erit iuxta iudicium Aristotelis utrumque nostrum ut facis amare, persuasionem autem certioris accipere. Nam quia in eligendis seu repudiandis opinionibus non debet homo duci amore vel odio ipsam opinionem inducentis, sed magis veritatis certitudine, in libro Metaphisice [cf. II, 1, 993b, 12–15] princeps philosophorum oportere ait utrosque amare, et eos scilicet quorum opinionem sequimur, et eos quorum opinionem repudiamus, quia utrique inquirende veritati operam dedere nobisque suo studio ambo profuere. Sed tamen oportet si sapientiam querimus nobis persuaderi a certioribus, id est eorum opinionem sequi qui certius ad veritatem pervenerunt. Vive diu foelix, et cum licuerit urgentes aliquantisper ponere curas, ex nostrorum rationibus ac deinde Marsilii primo loco positorum argumentorum responsione dissolutioneque tui ingenii perspi- (158)cacia quid verius de hac materia tenendum sit eligito. Vale. Explicit epistula.

[3] – – [3] In marg. add. cod.

Incipit tractatus et primo ponuntur decem et octo rationes in contrarium.

Cum ergo questio verteretur utrum beatitudo in actu intellectus vel voluntatis existat essentialiter, Marsilius actui voluntatis inherens his rationibus arguit.

1. Ille actus qui est potior in premio est ultimus finis.... Nam illa potentia que est potior in merito est etiam potior in premio.... a. Quia vere voluntas amat Deum quoquomodo cognitum... intellectus autem in hac vita non vere cognoscit Deum... b. Sed odisse Deum quod est dilectionis oppositum deterius est quam ignorasse quod est oppositum cognitionis. (158v) c. Sed cognitione Dei possumus male uti... dilectione autem eius male uti non possumus. d.[4] Sed amans Deum se et omnia que possidet Deo tribuit,[4] qui vero Deum prospicit nihil ob hoc tribuit Deo. e. Sed amando brevissimo tempore plurimum proficimus, perscrutando vero Deum paululum longo vix tandem tempore. f. Sed amando Deum meliores efficimur quam intelligendo.

2. Sed gaudium propter se ipsum desideratur... visio autem non propter se desideratur...

3. (159) Sed nullum gaudium natura ipsa respuit unquam, respuit tamen aliquam interdum cognitionem.

4. Sed gaudium presupponit et includit aliquo modo cognitionem, et non e converso.

5. Nam dolorem semper et ubique propter se fugit natura... non autem ignorantiam propter se respuit.

6. Per amatorium[5] autem gaudium... perfectius unimur et coniungimur Deo quam per cognitionem.

7. (159v) Sed actus voluntatis extra protenditur et in obiectum quod est extra transferre se nititur, intellectus autem modo quodam imaginario obiectum intra se capit.

8. Sed actus appetitus in pluribus invenitur quam cognitio.

9. Si Deus mentem a voluntate seiungeret... mens non esset beata... voluntas autem adhuc suo bono frui posset.

10. (160) Sed ad voluntatem pertinet initium motus in Deum....

---

[4]--[4] In marg. add. cod.   [5] Amotorium, cod.

Intellectus autem... res ad se ipsum quodammodo magis videtur attrahere quam animam ad res movere. Magis ergo ad voluntatem pertinet finis et consummatio talis motus...

11. Sed labor et cura stimulusque consequendi bonum malumve vitandi in affectu potius est quam in intellectu.
12. Quia quanto quis ardentius amat, tanto evadit beatior.
13. [6]Sed amatoria via est hominibus tutior et ad infinitum bonum consequendum pluribus accommodatior.[6]
14. (160v). Sed amando gaudendoque potius quam intelligendo angelos in beatitudine superare valemus.
15. [7]Sed amando mentem amplificamus ad latitudinem divine bonitatis, Deum vero cognoscendo eius amplitudinem contrahimus[7] ad mentis nostre capacitatem atque conceptum. Hic in nos Deum quasi deicimus, illic vero attollimus nos ad Deum. Noscimus enim quantum ipsi capimus, amamus autem et quantum intuemur et quantum ultra perspicuum intuitum nostrum vaticinamur bonitatis divine reliquum superesse. Hoc divine infinitatis abissum remisse quidem et obscure prospicimus, voluntate autem intense ardenterque amamus similiterque gaudemus.
16. Sed ipsa visione Dei non contentatur anima nec quietatur quia nulla res creata gradibusque perfectionis finita qualis est visio Dei potest animam contentare vel quietare.
17. (161) Sed per gaudium quod est actus voluntatis anima convertitur dilatatur atque diffunditur in Deum visum....
18. Sed voluntatis actus fertur in Deum ut in se ipso infinitus est... actus vero intelligendi est quedam notio Dei pro mentis capacitate....

Rationes probantes beatitudinem in actu intellectus et non voluntatis essentialiter consistere.

Iam secundo ponende sunt rationes quibus oppositum eius in quo tua magnificentia cum Marsilio convenerat efficacius iudicio meo probari videtur.

1. Sed in perfecta Dei cognitione consistit vita eterna.
2. (161v) Sed visio Dei est finis omnium actionum nostrarum.

[6 – – 6] In marg. add. cod.   [7 – – 7] In marg. add. cod.

3. Sed visio Dei est tota merces nostrorum operum.
4. Sed visio Dei complectitur omne bonum.
5. (162) Sed speculatio prime veritatis queritur propter se et non propter aliud.
6. Sed intellectus secundum se est proprium intellectualis nature.... Voluntas igitur ut est appetitus non est proprium nature intellectualis, sed ut ab intellectu dependet.
7. (162v) Sed beatitudo precedit omnem actum voluntatis, igitur beatitudo non consistit in actu voluntatis essentialiter.
8. (163) Sed intelligere est operatio per quam natura intellectualis primo attingit ad Deum.
9. Omnis actus voluntatis est aut desiderare aut amare aut delectari sive gaudere, sed beatitudo substantialiter in nullo eorum consistit.
10. (163v) Sed delectatio non est secundum se ipsam appetenda.
11. (164) Sed intelligere perfectissimum intelligibile quod est Deus est propria et perfectissima operatio substantie intellectualis...
12. Sed omnis delectatio est propter aliquid aliud.
13. (164v) Sed speculatio prime veritatis est propter sese diligibilis et ad eam omnes humane actiones ordinantur.
14. (165) Nam quies in bono et in fine iam adepto non est finis intellectualis nature.... Ergo quietatio inclinationis nature intellectualis quam ipsa delectatio importat non est finis eius, sed aliquid consequens finem iam assequutum.
15. (165v) Sed cognitio primi veri quod est Deus est ultimus finis omnium actionum humanarum... Sed inter omnes hominis partes intellectus superior motor invenitur. Intellectus quippe movet voluntatem....
16. Vera autem beatitudo non (166) differt a falsa secundum actum voluntatis sed intellectus.
17. Sed perfecta Dei cognitio est bonum perfectum omnem tollens indigentiam.
18. (166v) [8] Sed visio Dei per essentiam est perfectissima operatio nobilissimae potentiae respectu optimi obiecti[8].... (167) quod intellectus sit voluntate nobilior.

[8] — — [8] In marg. add. cod.

(168v) Decisio et determinatio questionis.

Tertio loco subiungenda est questionis huius decisio, pro cuius pleniori explanatione nonnullas conclusiones cum probationibus breviter subiciam.
1. Omnes actiones humane sunt propter finem.
2. Quecumque appetit homo propter finem ultimum appetit.
3. (169) Beatitudo est ultimus finis hominis.
4. (169v) Finis ultimus hominis primo modo sumptus non consistit in re aliqua creata.
5. Finis ultimus secundo modo sumptus est aliquid creatum.
6. (170) Beatitudo causaliter et obiective sumpta est bonum increatum.
7. Beatitudo formaliter et essentialiter sumpta est aliquid creatum quod est operatio.
8. (171v) Beatitudo formaliter et essentialiter sumpta est actus intellectus et non voluntatis.
9. (174) Delectatio que est actus voluntatis est quoddam accidens proprium beatitudini.
10. (175) Beatitudo formaliter et perfective sumpta est obiectum voluntatis et non intellectus.
11. (176) Fruitio proprie sumpta est actus voluntatis presupponens actum intellectus.
12. Fruitio proprie sumpta non est substantialiter beatitudo.
13. Fruitio proprie sumpta est quedam perfectio beatitudinem accidentaliter perficiens.
14. Deus clare visus est obiectum fruitionis.
15. (176v) Voluntas videntis clare divinam essentiam non potest velle non frui ea.
16. (177v) Illi qui ultimam felicitatem consequuntur ex clara Dei visione nunquam ab illa decident.

(179) Sequitur solutio rationum que obiecte fuerunt.
Quia cognitio veritatis ut ait Aristoteles in III. Metaphisice solutio est dubitatorum, in hac postrema parte rationes in oppositum primo loco adducte ut veritas iam declarata magis elucescat sunt clare aperteque solvende.

(196) Missa facio Laurenti clarissime quam plura alia argumenta que contra perspicuam hanc veritatem quam tenemus et in hoc opusculo probavimus ac defensavimus a nonnullis aliis fieri solent, tum propter urgentes atque cotidianas occupationes meas, tum ne nimia prolixitate tuas aures eruditas offenderem, tum quia efficaciora communioraque Marsilius acumine sui perspicacis ingenii in sua questione delegerit, tum etiam quia si responsiones ac solutiones horum lumine preclaro interioris oculi et acie tue mentis eximie perspexeris atque perlegeris, facillime poteris quecunque alia dissolvere. Vale in Cristo foelix et me, quod tua benignitate facis, semper ama. Finis.*

---

* I have just learned that the second manuscript of our text has been acquired by the Biblioteca Laurenziana.

SOME ASPECTS OF AFTER LIFE IN EARLY RABBINIC LITERATURE[1]

by SAUL LIEBERMAN

I

Posthumous Divine Retribution

THE BABYLONIAN TALMUD STATES (*Shabbath* 30b): The sages wished to suppress the book of Ecclesiastes, because its words are self-contradictory. However, they did not do this, because the beginning and the end of the book are the words of the Torah etc., as it is written (Eccl. 12:13), *the end of the matter, all having been heard: fear God, and keep His commandments.* In the *Midrash* we read:[2] The Sages wanted to suppress the book of Ecclesiastes, because they found in it ideas which leaned towards heresy etc. Is there

---

[1] We are mainly concerned with Palestine of the first five centuries C.E., and the relevant non-Jewish literature is therefore Greek and Latin, irrespective of what the ultimate origin of their contents may be.

We deliberately avoided detailed discussion of the nature of the soul, its immortality and the resurrection of the flesh. Jewish and Christian views in this domain are mostly identical. Those problems must be treated separately, with an eye on Jewish-Hellenistic and Christian apologists who were well acquainted with Greek philosophy.

Abbreviations:
BT = Babylonian Talmud.
JQR = Jewish Quarterly Review.
MGWJ = Monatsschrift für Geschichte und Wissenschaft des Judenthums.
PG = Patrologia Graeca.
PT = Palestinian Talmud.
REJ = Revue des Études Juives.
SB = H. L. Strack and P. Billerbeck, Kommentar zum Neuen Testament aus Talmud und Midrasch.

[2] Vayyikra Rabba XXVIII, 1, ed. Margulies, p. 649, and parallels referred to ibid.

neither justice nor judge? When, however, he (i.e. Solomon, the author of Ecclesiastes) said (ibid. 11:9), *but know thou, that for all these things God will bring thee into judgment*, they admitted that he had spoken well.

This is indeed a cardinal principle of ancient rabbinic Judaism: "Fear God and keep His commandments," "God will bring thee into judgment." If a man does not believe in posthumous divine retribution he is a heretic. However, the form of this retribution is open to different interpretations. The *Mishnah* teaches: The judgment of the wicked in Gehenna shall endure twelve months (*'Eduyyoth* II.10). The disciples of Balaam the Wicked will inherit Gehenna, and go down into the pit of destruction etc., as it is written (Ps. 55:24), *But Thou, O God, shalt bring them down into the pit of destruction* etc. (*Aboth* V.19). The very grave sinners, like משומדים, apostates, etc. will remain there for ever.[3]

These earlier rabbinic sources and many others do not portray the topography of Gehenna in its details, its dimensions, compartments, divisions and subdivisions. They do not mention the refined tortures of Gehenna, their minutiae, and the ramified penal code which governs Hades. The rabbis certainly lacked neither the imagination nor the legal mind required for such descriptions.[4] Indeed the great Nachmanides was at a loss as to how to treat the later traditions, but he finally concluded that we should accept them.[5]

Some of the rabbis deny the very existence of Gehenna as an objective reality.[6] There is also no agreement among the sages (who accept the existence of Gehenna) about its location as we shall presently demonstrate. The prevalent Jewish opinion is that Gehenna is located in the depths of the earth. This is the

[3] Comp. *Tosefta Sanhedrin* XIII. 5, and parallels.

[4] On rabbinic sources dealing with Gehenna see Lieberman, *Louis Ginzberg Jubilee Volume*, Hebrew part, p. 249 ff.; idem *Shkiin* (Hebrew), p. 33 ff.

[5] See *Torath ha-Adam, Sha'ar ha-Gemul*, ed. Venice 1595, 97 c.

[6] See *Bereshith Rabba* VI.6, ed. Theodor, pp. 46–47 and parallels. From BT *'Abodah Zarah* 3b and *Nedarim* 8 b it appears that the rabbis have in mind the Messianic era only.

most ancient and the most wide-spread view among all other nations. Some of the rabbis mention its exact location in the subterranean world.[7] But in the Palestinian Talmud there is no indication that Gehenna is placed in the depths of the earth.[8]

Two views on this subject are reported in the Babylonian Talmud (*Tamid* 32b). One places Gehenna above the *Rakiʿa* (see below), and the other behind the Mountains of Darkness. The *Rakiʿa*, according to the rabbis, is the second heaven where the sun and the planets are inserted.[9] It can not be argued from this that the rabbis were aware of the system of the interplanetary inferno of the Greeks.[10] It was probably a popular belief of Oriental origin.[11] A later *Midrash* (cited in *Yalkut Shimeoni* I. 44) mentions the virgin Istahar (איסטהר) who became a star in reward for her resistance to sin.[12] The name Istahar is most probably identical with that of Ištar, the Assyro-Babylonian goddess associated with Venus. Similarly a fragment of an epitaph with Jewish symbols preserves the inscription ACTHP.[13] I accept Cumont's conjecture[14] that ἀστήρ is not a proper name, but the *Greek* "star," i.e. that the dead person became a star, as in our *Midrash* (which is of a late origin). There is no reason to assume that the rabbis were really familiar with the details of "catasteristic" immortality.[15] It is merely a popular belief which they learned from their pagan neighbors, or a remnant of a Jewish apocryphon. Moreover, the

[7] See BT *ʿErubin* 19 a. Comp. L. Ginzberg, *Legends of the Jews*, v, p. 19, n. 55.

[8] See PT *Ḥaggigah* II. 2, 77 d and parallel; ibid. *Sanhedrin* x. 3, 29 b. Comp. ibid. *Ḥaggigah* II. 1, 77 c and BT ibid. 15 b. For non-rabbinic Jewish sources, see SB, *Exkurse* etc., p. 1030 ff.

[9] See *Aboth de R. Nathan* XXXVII, ed. Schechter, p. 110; *Bereshith Rabba* VI. 6, ed. Theodor, p. 45; BT *Ḥaggigah* 12b.

[10] See F. Cumont, *Lux Perpetua*, p. 181, n. 3; ibid. p. 345.

[11] See Test. of Levi III: 2; 2 Enoch 7:1 ff., 18:1 ff. Comp. also Cumont ibid., p. 344; idem, *Recherches sur le Symbolisme Funéraire etc.*, p. 130–131 (hereafter = *Symbolism*).

[12] Comp. S. Spiegel, *L. Ginzberg Jubilee Volume*, p. 341, n. 1. On Ištar's "chastity" see *Gilgamesh* VI, 44 ff.

[13] Frey, *Corp. Ins. Iud.* I, p. 241, No. 306.

[14] *Symbolism*, p. 395 ff.

[15] See Cumont ibid. pp. 116, 183, 496; idem *Lux Perpetua* p. 183.

idea that the just and the pious will shine as the stars in heaven is already found in Daniel (12:2–3) and in many Jewish Hellenistic writers.[16] The transition from "like a star" to "an actual star" is quite natural.

We shall now turn to the other view that Gehenna is located behind the Mountains of Darkness.[17] From many sources it is obvious that the rabbis placed the Mountains of Darkness at the end of the earth[18] which they situated somewhere in Africa.[19] There, behind the gates of the earth, beyond its limits, the rabbis placed both hell and paradise.[20] Or as Homer puts it (*Od.* IV.564): But to the Elysian plain and *the bounds of the earth* will the immortals convey thee.[21]

Now the medieval authorities[22] quote from a lost *Midrash* that "Rebecca saw Isaac walking [like in a mirage] with his head down and his legs up, just as those who come from paradise." Another medieval source[23] puts it: "And he (i.e. Isaac) was coming like the dead who walk with their legs up." This belief apparently goes back to early sources,[24] as indicated by the above mentioned medieval books.

We may therefore assume that "behind the Mountains of Darkness" (where the rabbis placed hell and paradise) is nothing else than the astronomic ὑπόγειον. In this *hypogeion* some "philosophers" located Hades.[25] The learned men who peopled

---

[16] *Symbolism*, p. 494 ff. Comp. also P. Volz, *Die Eschatologie d. jüdischen Gemeinde* etc. p. 399 ff.

[17] Comp. I Enoch 17:7 and below n. 19.

[18] See my notes to the *Pesikta deR. Kahana*, ed. Mandelbaum, p. 474. Comp. Budge, *The Egyptian Heaven and Hell* (London, 1925), III, p. 88 ff.

[19] See BT *Tamid* 32 a, and Theodor's notes in *Bereshith Rabba*, p. 301.

[20] *Tamid* 32 b, Comp. Budge *l.c.* Comp. also A. Heidel, *The Gilgamesh Epic* etc., p. 171 (see p. 157 ibid.).

[21] ἀλλά σ' ἐς Ἠλύσιον πεδίον καὶ πείρατα γαίης ἀθάνατοι πέμψουσιν.

[22] מושב זקנים on Gen. 24:65, ed. Sassoon, p. 35, and *Pa'aneaḥ Raza* to the same verse.

[23] *Tosafoth* Rabbi Judah ben Rabbi Eliezer in דעת זקנים to Gen. 24:65.

[24] See BT *Sanhedrin* 65 b, *Vayyikra Rabba* XXVI. 7, ed. Margulies, p. 601.

[25] See F. Cumont, *Lux Perpetua* p. 191 ff., p. 195. Comp, however, Budge

the *hypogeion* with living creatures (antipodes) were often ridiculed for assuming that men walk with their legs up and heads down (with regard to our position on earth), like our shadows in water.[26] But if the living antipodes were not accepted by the masses, the learned rabbis had no objection to the belief that the *hypogeion* was partly inhabited by the antipodes[27], and in its more distant regions, by the dead. They could easily portray Rebecca seeing Isaac coming from the *hypogeion* with his head down, in the manner of the dead who walk this way[28] (from the perspective of people in the upper hemisphere).

Finally we shall cite another opinion of the early rabbis regarding posthumous punishment. It is stated in *Aboth de R. Nathan*:[29] *And the souls of thine enemies, them shall he sling out as from the hollow of a sling* (I Sam. 25:29) etc., so too the souls of the wicked go זוממות (see below) and roaming in the world, and they do not know on what they will rest. The word זוממות which we left untraslated was completely misunderstood by the commentators and translators. However, this word is pivotal for the full understanding of the text. The souls of all dead were often roaming in the world[30], but they subsequently returned to their resting places, whereas the souls of the wicked, "do not know on what they will rest." The text makes sense, yet its connection with the verse in Samuel (which mentions the slinging of the souls) lacks the usual pointedness of rabbinic *Haggadic* interpretation. According to some

(above, n. 18), p. 87 ff., but the rabbinic views may not be identical with the Egyptian beliefs.

[26] Lucretius, *de rerum nat.* I. 1060 ff.; Lucianus, *Demonax* 22. See Cumont, *Symbolism*, p. 57 ff. p. 58, n. 8.

[27] See Plin., *hist. nat.* II. 65, 161.

[28] This has nothing to do with the punishment of the dead to walk head downward, see J.H. Breasted, *Development of Religion and thought in Ancient Egypt* (N.Y. 1912), pp. 283-284.

[29] XII, ed. Schechter, p. 50; Comp. *Midrash Tannaim*, ed. Hoffmann, p. 226. BT *Shabbath* 152 b quotes it in the name of Rabbi Eliezer (flourished at the end of the first and the beginning of the second centuries).

[30] See *Aboth de R. Nathan* III, ed. Schechter, p. 16 ff., BT *Berakoth* 18 b, *Pirkei de R. Eliezer* XXXIV, ed. Rabbi David Lurie 79 b.

versions of the Babylonian Talmud (*Shabbath* 152b), the verse in Samuel implies that "one angel stands at one end of the world and another at the other end, and they sling the souls back and forth." Something similar is implied in our text.[31] The punishment therefore is slinging and whirling the souls in the air.

It is almost certain that the Hebrew verb זמם[32] is the exact equivalent of the Greek βομβεῖν, to buzz; one might almost suggest, to zoom. Porphyrius[33] mentioning the Nymphs, souls which the ancients called bees, quotes Sophocles: βομβεῖ δὲ νεκρῶν σμῆνος ἔρχεται τ' ἄνω, "A swarm of dead buzz and ascend."[34] The buzzing of the bees is rendered in Syriac: איך דבורא זאמין הוו, like bees did they hum[35]. In our case the souls are being hurled by a sling, and they produce a humming noise when they fly in the air.[36]

The text should be translated accordingly: "So too the souls of the wicked go on *zooming* and roaming etc." The rabbis wanted to emphasize that the souls are forcefully slung and hurled in the air, and they produce a humming noise as they fly in the air; they are punished by being handled in this way. It appears that the rabbis were thinking of the purgatory in the air where the soul is rolled and tossed by the whirlwinds, whose fierce vortex cleans and rubs off the soul's impurity, enabling it to ascend to heaven.[37] The defiled soul is subject to this punishment "until the days of

---

[31] *Aboth de R. Nathan* l.c. (above n. 29) which states: he tosses them from place to place. Comp. also *Midrash Tannaim* l.c.

[32] The reading זוּמְמוֹת is absolutely sure, for it is found in all the manuscripts of BT and *Aboth de R. Nathan* and in *Midrash Tannaim* l.c. — The reading of Rabbi David Kimhi to Sam. 25:29 is a "doctor's" substitution for the misunderstood word. Comp. *Midrash Koheleth Rabba* III. 21 (ed. Romm 12 c).

[33] *De antro Nymph.* 18.

[34] See the notes to the *Fragments of Sophocles*, 879, ed. Pearson (1917), p. 75–76.

[35] See Payne Smith, *Thesaur. Syr.*, p. 1132, s.v. זם and s.v. זממא Comp. also *Aruch Completum* s.v. זמזום and s.v. זמזומי. See the variants in *Bereshith Rabba*, ed. Theodor–Albeck, p. 969, line 2, and Lieberman, *Tarbiz* v, (1934), p. 99.

[36] Comp. Homer *Od.* VIII. 189: This with a whirl he sent from his stout hand, and the stone zoomed (βόμβησεν δὲ λίθος) as it flew.

[37] See the sources cited and referred to by F. Cumont. *Symbolism* p. 129.

her *purification* are fulfilled,[38] or as Rabbi Elijah ben Solomon Abraham puts it[39]: "until the days of her *punishment* are completed."[40] Yet there is no sufficient ground to place this purgatory mentioned by the rabbis into the context of the Greek speculations.[41]

[38] Solomon ibn Gabirol, *Keter Malkuth* 30 (Selected Rel. Poems of Solomon Ibn Gabirol, ed. I. Davidson, Philadelphia, 1923, p. 105).

[39] *Shebeth Musar* 17, end.

[40] Those rabbis have in mind the *Mishnah* (*'Eduyyoth* II. 10) which limits the punishment of the wicked in Gehenna to twelve months only.

[41] Prof. I. Baer (Hebrew quarterly *Zion*, vol. XXIII–XXIV, 1958–1959, p. 9, n. 14) deduced from the passage cited above (in the text) that the rabbis knew the theory of *metempsychosis*. His reasoning is beyond the scope of my comprehension. Prof. G. Scholem is undoubtedly right (ראשית הקבלה, p. 45 ff.) in his postulation that the doctrine of the transmigration of the soul is not to be found in early rabbinic literature.

There is no ground whatever for the assumption of Prof. Baer (*Zion* ibid., p. 18, n. 42) that the rabbis were aware of the thesis of the cycle of eternal generation (κύκλος γενέσεως). The context of the Talmud cited by Baer (*Yebamoth* 62 a and parallels) disproves such a conclusion. It states: "The Son of David will only come when all the souls of the reservoir (גוף) will be exhausted". Each new born child receives a new soul, and even if he died in infancy, he already fulfilled a certain function (see BT *Yebamoth* ibid.). Hence, according to the Talmud, a fixed number of souls were created from the beginning of time, which will last until the advent of the Messiah. There is therefore no need for cycles. This belief goes back to the Apocalypse of Baruch XXIII. 4–5, as observed by many scholars. I also find it in the *Recognitiones* of Ps.–Clemens (III. 26).

It is a well established fact that many Jews accepted the doctrine of the pre-existence (προ-ύπαρξις) of the souls (see Freudenthal, *Hellenistische Studien* I, p. 72, passim), but those pre-existing souls were unused ones, and none of them was used twice. On the other hand, some rabbis claimed the truth of creationism, and they, accordingly, modified the formulation about the relation between the exhaustion of the souls and the advent of the Messiah, see *Bereshith Rabba* XXIV. 4, ed. Theodor, p. 233, and parallels.

Our reservoir (גוף) of unused souls mentioned above is not identical with the *promptuarium, habitaculum*, θησαυρός of the souls found in the *Pseudepigrapha* (see Charles, p. 567, n. 35), or the אוצר of the rabbinic literature (*Sifre* Num. 139, ed. Horovitz, p. 185, ibid. Deut. 344, ed. Finkelstein, p. 401, and parallels). The latter refer to the souls which came from dead bodies, whereas the גוף is the receptacle of unused souls. Baruch l.c. (XXIII. 4) calls the latter

We conclude with the primitive belief that the human soul could be incarnated in an animal as a punishment for sins commited in this world.[42] The Palestinian and the Babylonian Talmuds[43] record the thesis that the backbone of the human body turns into a serpent, if the man did not bow (did not bend his spine) at prayer.[44] However, this passage has nothing to do with the incarnation of the soul. The man will not be resurrected from the dead, because his spine will disappear. According to the very popular tradition, the "almond-shaped" bone (*Luz*) which forms the end of the spine will serve as the nucleus of the new body at the time of resurrection.[45] Hence if the backbone will turn into a snake, no starting point will remain for resurrection, as correctly understood by "some commentaries" cited in *Tosafoth, Baba Kamma* 16 b, s.v. והוא. This is also the opinion of the *Zohar, Bamidbar* 164 a and elsewhere.[46]

Dr. Julius Preuss[47] correctly recalls heathen authors who record this opinion. Ovidius (*Met.* X. 389) remarks: There are those

"a place where they dwell" (אתרא איכא דנעמרון) and the former "[a place] where they are guarded" (ואיכא דנתנטרון). Comp. also ibid. xxi. 23 and xxx. 2 where he refers to the place of the souls of the dead as אוצרא, treasures. Gregory of Nyssa (*de anima et resur.*, *PG* XLVI, 125 a) states: "for if we were to grant that the soul has lived previous to the body in some special residence of its own nature" etc. (ἐν ἰδιαζούσῃ τινὶ καταστάσει). Augustinus (*epist.* CXLIII. 9, end) expresses himself: "Or if they (i.e. the souls) were created previously and stored up with the Lord (apud deum constitutae) and given to each individual body". For some reason all these writers use vague language avoiding the terms frequently employed to designate the receptacles of the souls of the departed. Comp. also A. Marmorstein, *Metsudah* (London, 1943), p. 94 ff.

[42] See Cumont, *Lux Perpetua*, pp. 196 ff., 354.

[43] PT *Shabbath* I. 3, 3 b, BT *Baba Kamma* 16 a.

[44] See BT *Berakoth* 28 b, 12 b. PT ibid. I. 8, 3 d.

[45] See *Bereshith Rabba* XXVIII. 3, ed. Theodor, p. 261 ff. and notes ibid., *Vayyikra Rabba* XVIII. 1, ed. Margulies, p. 394; comp. also L. Ginzberg, *Legends of the Jews*, vol. v, p. 363, n. 345.

[46] It seems to me that the connection between the failure to bow at the time of prayer and human resurrection can be found in *Bereshith Rabba* LVI. 2, ed. Theodor–Albeck, p. 597. The exegesis in the *Midrash* has its roots in an existent popular belief.

[47] *Biblisch-Talmudische Medizin*, Berlin 1911, p. 150.

who believe that when the spine of a man has decomposed in the narrow grave, its marrow is transformed into a snake.[48] Plinius (*Hist. nat.* X. 66, 188) likewise reports: We have it from many [authors] that a snake is produced from the spinal marrow of a man[49]. Plutarch (Agis et Cleomenes, end) contends (in the name of the wiser men among the Alexandrians) that this is a natural phenomenon, like bees generating from the corpse of an ox and wasps from that of a horse. The Palestinian Talmud suggests the same view;[50] this is the normal course of nature. Only a man who bowed at the time of his prayer was exempt from this transformation.

However, some two hundred years later (i.e. than Ovidius and Plinius) Aelianus (De *nat. anim* I, 51) states the same with some reservation (ἢ τοίνυν τὸ πᾶν μῦθός ἐστιν): The spine of a dead man, they say, changes the putrefying marrow into a snake... but it is from the spine of the wicked that those (i.e. snakes) are begotten even after life.[51] The transformation of the spine marrow into a snake[52] now becomes a special punishment of the wicked, but has nothing to do with the incarnation of the soul in an animal.

[48] Sunt qui, cum clauso putrefacta est spina sepulcro, mutari credant humanas angue medullas.

[49] Anguem ex medulla hominis spinae gigni occipimus a multis. Comp. J. Bergel, *Studien über die Naturw. Kenntn. d. Talmudisten*, pp. 52–53.

[50] Comp. M. Sachs, *Beitraege zur Sprach- und Alterthumsforschung* etc. II, p. 92 ff., L. Lewysohn, *Die Zoologie des Talmuds* p. 375. Add the numerous references of Ziegler in his edition of Plutarch (1915) ibid. and Porphyrius, *de antro Nymph.* 15, 18.

Aptowitzer (*MGWJ*, 69, 1925, p. 356) also associated the passage in Plutarch with the rabbinic legend about a snake garding the caves where some famous rabbis were buried. However, the latter seems to be a popular motif among many nations, see Plinius, *hist. nat.* XVI, 44 (85), 234 (subest specus, in quo manes eius custodire draco traditur). It has nothing to do with Plutarch's anecdote.

[51] Ῥάχις ἀνθρώπου νεκροῦ φασιν ὑποσηπόμενον τὸν μυελὸν ἤδη τρέπει ἐς ὄφιν... πονηρῶν δὲ ἀνθρώπων ῥάχεις τοιαῦτα τίκτουσι καὶ μετὰ τὸν βίον.

[52] The rabbis, of course, talk about the backbone itself and not of its marrow. The transformation of the marrow would, in their opinion, not affect the resurrection of the dead. *Midrash Tehilim* XI, ed. Buber, p. 102, states that the soul is attached to the *spinal marrow* (חוט השדרה) thus replacing the

Nevertheless it appears that the rabbis knew *something* of the various opinions current among the heathen philosophers regarding the human soul and its adventures after it departs from the body. But the general impression is that they got their information by hearsay only. The rabbis explicitely instruct:[53] You must pronounce eulogies over the dead of the Gentiles, you must comfort the mourners of the Gentiles, and you must bury the dead of the Gentiles. The Jews followed this command. So, for instance, Rabbi Meir (flourished in the second century C.E.) came to visit the philosopher Oenomaus of Gadara[54] when he mourned over his mother, and a second time after the death of his father.[55]

Conversations during such visits can be readily surmised. It is related in *Bereshith Rabba*[56] that Rabbi Jose (second century C.E.) visited one of the magnates of Sepphoris (in upper Galilee) who mourned the death of his son. According to one opinion, the mourner was a heretic, according to another, a heretic was present there, and a discussion arose regarding the resurrection of the dead.[57] An exchange of opinions on such occasions was unavoidable. In course of time certain views regarding life and death become international property.

"almond shaped" bone of the spine by the spinal marrow, and its disappearance would therefore prevent the resurrection of the dead. But this passage is a very late interpolation in the *Midrash* and is missing in the printed editions and in most of the manuscripts, see Buber's note ibid., p. 101, n. 46.

[53] *Tosefta Gittin* v, end, ed. Zuckermandel 328$_{22}$, PT ibid. v. 9, 47 c, *Demai* IV. 6, 24 a (Comp. BT *Gittin* 61 a), Maimonides, Laws of Kings, x, end.

[54] See Schürer, *Geschichte* etc. II[4], p. 55, n. 1. There can be no question of his identity notwithstanding Schürer's slight reservations. A variant in *Bereshith Rabba*, ed. Theodor–Albeck, p. 734, has twice the spelling אבנימוס.

[55] *Ruth Rabba* II. 8, ed. Romm 5 c.

[56] XIV. 7, ed. Theodor, p. 131.

[57] The Rabbi quoted Genesis 2:7 as proof for the possibility of resurrection of the dead. He maintained: "If a vessel of glass, made with breath blown by a human being, can be reshaped if it is broken, how much more true is this of a human being made with breath blown by the Holy One, blessed be He, as it is said, *and He breathed in his nostrils the breath of life* (*Midrash* on Psalms II. 11, ed. Buber, p. 30). Comp. *Bereshith Rabba* ibid., BT *Sanhedrin* 90 b. Comp. H. A. Wolfson, *Religious Philosophy* (Cambridge, Mass., 1961), pp. 90–91.

Let us examine an additional instance of a *consolatio* which illustrates how certain sentiments have no geographical boundaries. We read in Scripture: *And the day of death [is better] than the day of one's birth* (Eccl. 7:1). The rabbis saw (*Koheleth Rabba* a.l. and parallels) a source of great comfort in this verse. When a child is born he is like a ship which has left port (למן, λιμήν); nobody knows what seas and storms it may encounter; there is no cause to rejoice over it. When a man dies he is like a ship which enters the harbor. It is an occasion for rejoicing since the ship has safely entered the harbor. The man departed from the world with a good name and in peace. Epicurus[58] asserts: οὐ νέος μακαριστὸς ἀλλὰ γέρων βεβιωκὼς καλῶς. ὁ γὰρ νέος ⟨ἐν⟩ ἀκμῇ πολὺς ὑπὸ τῆς τύχης ἑτεροφρονῶν πλάζεται· ὁ δὲ γέρων καθάπερ ἐν λιμένι τῷ γήρᾳ κατώρμικεν. "It is not a young man who is the happiest but an old man who has lived a good life. For the young man in his bloom is confused and is tossed around by fortune. But the old man has come to anchor in old age as though in harbor." The rabbis, of course, could not accept Epicurus' sentence verbatim. An old man as long as he is alive has not yet reached the harbor (see *Mishnah Aboth* II. 4); he arrives there only at the moment of his death.[59] But the reasoning of the rabbis and the philosopher is almost identical. However, there is no real need to assume that the former lifted their argument from Epicurus. Comparisons of this sort were probably current among all intelligent people of the Mediterranean world. The house of mourning was the proper place of exchange of this kind of sentiments.

Problems of the soul and its state after death were of personal interest even to the common man; mere curiosity prompted any intelligent individual to make inquiries into the matter, and even the more sophisticated views of the philosophers reached the

---

[58] *Sent. Vat.* XVII, ed. C. Bailey (Oxford 1926), p. 108. Comp. Commentary ibid., p. 378.

[59] See Sirach 11:28, Joseph. *Bell.* etc. v. 11 3, 461. This notion was also common among the Greeks (see Herodot. I. 32), and it was especially popular with the tragedians. Some heathens extended it until after burial, see Ovid. *Metam.* III. 137. Comp. below chap. III, n. 16.

masses in a popular form. But there is absolutely no evidence that the rabbis read philosophic treatises, or attended regular courses given by philosophers. All information to this effect came to them from second hand sources, or, at most, from the discussions of cynic philosophers who preached in the streets.

Their knowledge in this domain was probably no more than that of the middle class Jew in general. Imagination mixed with information from the outside fertilized the creativity of the *Haggadists*. The variety of opinions and their contradictions (with regard to the soul and its adventures) is typical of this kind of literature, and must be treated accordingly.

II

"Life" in the Grave

The prevalent view in rabbinic literature is that the corpse of the deceased does not lose its sensitivity for a certain amount of time. The dead hear what is said about them in their presence.[1] According to one opinion they know what is said about them until their tombs are closed; according to another they know it until the flesh of the body is wasted away.[2]

For the first three days after death the soul hovers over the body in the hope that it may reenter it,[3] but after the body begins to decompose, the soul finally leaves it.[4]

The atonement of man for his sins starts from the moment the body begins to feel the pains [of the pressure] of the grave,[5] and

---

[1] PT *'Abodah Zarah* III, 42 c, *Bereshith Rabba*, ed. Theodor–Albeck, p. 1237 and parallels referred to ibid. Comp. also PT *Berakoth* II. 3, 4 d, BT ibid. 18 a, 19 a, *Shabbath* 153 a passim. Comp. however the dissident opinion in BT *Berakoth* 19 a.

[2] BT *Shabbath* 152 b.

[3] A Persian belief. See the literature cited by S. Klein, *Tod und Begräbnis* etc. Berlin 1908, p. 13, n. 3; L. Ginzberg, *Legends of the Jews*, vol. v, p. 78, n. 20, end, p. 128, n. 140, end.

[4] PT *Mo'ed Katan* III. 5, 82 b, *Yebamoth* XVI. 3, 15 c, *Bereshith Rabba* C. 7, ed. Albeck, p. 1290, *Vayyikra Rabba* XVIII. 1, ed. Margulies, pp. 397–398, ibid., p. 875.

[5] BT *Sanhedrin* 47 b. According to a late source (*Bet ha-Midrasch*, ed.

the worms are as painful to the dead as a needle to the flesh of the living.[6] Just as the suffering of the dead body in the grave partly atones for the sins commited in life, so the degradations of the body in any way whatever produce the same effect.[7] A *Tannaitic* source[8] states that king Hezekiah dragged the bones (גרר עצמות) of his dead father Ahaz in a bier of ropes. In this way the rabbis reconciled the seeming contradiction between II Kings 16:30 and II Chronicles 28:27. The former records that Ahaz was buried *with his fathers* in the city of David, whereas the latter maintains that "*they brought him not into the sepulchres of the kings of Israel.*" The rabbis concluded that Ahaz was exhumed from his ancestral tomb, his bones dragged, and reinterred somewhere else.[9]

The significance of this passage was not fully understood by the earlier commentators and the modern scholars. In our context the word גרר is a technical term, the exact equivalent of *trahere* (σύρειν),[10] i.e. to drag the corpse of a man who was subjected to *damnatio memoriae*.[11] In the case of king Ahaz the rabbis portray a posthumous *damnatio memoriae* of a king. In the year two hundred twenty two the dead body of the Roman emperor Elagabalus was dragged all over the city of Rome and thrown into the Tiber.[12] He was dubbed the "Dragged" (*Tractatitius*) because this was done to his corpse.[13] Thirty years earlier the Roman Senate

Jellinek I, p. 151, Appendix to *Semaḥoth*, ed. Higger, p. 259), even pious men and innocent babies are subject to these pains.

[6] BT *Berakoth* 18 b, *Shabbath* 13 b passim.

[7] *Sifre* I, 112, end, ed. Horovitz, p. 122, BT *Sanhedrin* 47 a.

[8] Interpolated in some editions of the *Mishnah Pesaḥim* IV, end. See PT ibid. IX. 1, 36 c, and parallel, BT ibid. 56 a and parallels.

[9] See Gersonides on II Kings a.l. and *Tosafoth Yom Tob* on *Mishnah Pesaḥim* ibid. Comp. *Rashi* on BT *Makkoth* 24 a, s. v. שגררו.

[10] See below nn. 12–14.

[11] Disgrace of the memory of a criminal. See also *Koheleth Rabba* I, 15, ed. Romm 6 a, *Ruth Rabba* III. 3 6 c. Comp. Jerem. 22:19. We shall treat this subject in detail below Chapter III, n. 33.

[12] Herodianus v. 9; Lampridius, *Vita Heliog.* XVIII. 1–2.

[13] Lampridius ibid. XVII. 5.

demanded that the body of the emperor Commodus (which was already buried) be exhumed and dragged.[14] The rabbis maintained that Hezekiah dishonored the body of his father Ahaz in the way the Romans disgraced the bodies of their wicked emperors.[15]

In this manner king Hezekiah achieved a double purpose. The *damnatio memoriae* of Ahaz made it clear to the people that Hezekiah has cancelled his father's decrees regarding idolatry. It is stated in *Seder ʿOlam Rabba*[16] that Evil-merodach exhumed Nebuchadnezzar from his grave and dragged his body in order to cancel his decrees. Prof. Louis Ginzberg correctly associated[17] this passage with the text in *Aboth deR. Nathan*[18] which records the same act by Evil-merodach with the additional explanation: No king may abolish the decrees of a [previous] king, unless he takes him out [from his grave] and drags him! In the judgment of the rabbis, the dragging of a king's corpse indicated the abolition of his decrees by his successor.

Secondly, the posthumous insult inflicted on the body of Ahaz, the ἀτιμία to which he was subjected after his death, was considered by king Hezekiah as an act of expiation of his father's sins. The son rendered his father a great favor by dishonoring him after his death.[19] His enormous sins of idolatry would soon be wiped out by virtue of the ignominy he suffered after death.

---

[14] Idem, *vita Commodi* xx. 2: *sepultus eruatur, trahatur.* Comp. Jerem. 8:1–2. See also Plinius, *hist. nat.* vii. 54, 187.

[15] The body of Ahaz was probably partly disintegrated after it was disinterred, and, therefore, could not be dragged in the usual manner by rope and hook. For this reason the rabbis contended that it was dragged in a bier of ropes.

[16] xxviii, ed. Ratner, p. 125. The Rabbis, perhaps, superposed a Roman legal explanation on a general practice of royal revenge. Ashurbanipal boasted that he had exhumed the bones of the Elamite Kings etc. See D. D. Luckenbill, *Ancient Records of Assyria and Babylonia* ii. 810, p. 310.

[17] *Legends of the Jews* vol. vi, p. 428, n. 116. However, he missed the essence of the legend.

[18] Second version 17, ed. Schechter, p. 37.

[19] Our case has nothing to do with the debated question whether there

However, although many of the rabbis admitted the actual sensitivity of the dead body (at least until the flesh was consumed), they never believed that the dead must be provided with food, or other necessaries. Since there is no doubt that the ancient Jews engaged in these superstitious practices,[20] the rabbis, who were not able to uproot them, had to reinterpret the meaning of the customs and impart to them a reasonable significance. It was permitted to place the personal belongings of the deceased beside his body, not because he is in need of them, but because the scene arouses the grief of the onlookers.[21]

It is therefore natural to place a woman's personal articles, even her tube of eye-paint, in her grave. The scene will certainly arouse the grief of the spectators. In fact, the tombs of Bet She'arim in Palestine contain many ornaments of women and, especially, tubes of eye-paint[22] which prove that this custom was also accepted among the Jews of Palestine.[23]

However when the comb and the tube of eye-paint were not inserted in the tomb during the burial, why deliver it by hand

---

is "expiation after death." The dragging of the corpse is an actual punishment inflicted upon the deceased, like all other sufferings imposed upon the dead in their graves.

[20] The heathen customs in this respect are well known, see Maspero, *The Dawn of Civilization* (London 1922) pp. 115, 192, 686; Cumont, *Lux Perpetua*, p. 26, n. 7. On the Jewish practices, see Perles, *MGWJ* x (1861), p. 377, A. Lods, *La Croyance à la Vie future* etc., p. 167 ff., 190. A. Parrot, *Refrigerium* pp. 59–60. The sprinkling of wine and oil on the dead (See *Semaḥoth* XII. 9, and *Tosefta ki-Fshuṭah* IV, p. 673) was tolerated by the rabbis, because of their odoriferous properties.

[21] *Semaḥoth* VIII. 7. See G. Allon, מחקרים, II, p. 103 ff. Comp. Perles l.c., n. 23.

[22] B. Mazar, *Beth She'arim, Report* etc. (Jerusalem 1957), pp. 143, 150. An abundance of lamps were found in the tombs (ibid., p. 143). Lamps were used to honor the dead (see *Mishnah Berakoth* VIII. 6 and parallels. PT ibid. IV. 1, 7 b, *Bereshith Rabba* XXXVII. 4, p. 346: בלא נר ...שהם מתים). Since, according to Jewish law, no benefit could afterwards be derived from those lamps, they were buried together with the dead.

[23] It is unlikely that those findings belong only to the dead who were brought from outside of Palestine.

of another dead messenger? No such contingency would follow from the explanation offered by the rabbis. Yet, the Babylonian Talmud[24] presented such a case. It tells that a rabbi who was visiting a cemetery received the following message from the tomb of his dead landlady: "Tell my mother to send me my comb and my tube of eye-paint by so-and-so who is coming here next day."

This, of course, reminds us of the famous mockery of Lucian (*Philops.* 27) about the dead wife of Eucrates who personally appeared to her husband and rebuked him for not having burned one of her gilt sandals on her funeral pyre. It was, she said, under the chest where it was thrown. It is very surprising that the rabbis related a story which is so flagrantly in the nature of the "ways of the Amorites," the heathen superstitions.

But here, again, the anecdote has its roots in rabbinic reinterpretation of popular superstitions. The Babylonian, and some of the Palestinian Rabbis maintained that at the time of resurrection, the dead would arise in the same clothes which they wore when they were buried,[25] and would therefore appear in proper attire. The Babylonian sage Rabbi Jeremiah[26] asked in his last will that he be buried near a public road with cane in hand and sandals on his legs etc.[27] The burial on a public road was at one time a typical heathen practice.[28] But the rabbi gave the reason for the details of his will: "When the Messiah will come, I shall be ready",[29] or: "When I am wanted, I shall stand ready" (אוטמוס ἕτοιμος).[30]

---

[24] *Berakoth* 18 b.

[25] PT *Kil'aim* ix. 4, 32 b and parallel (in the name of the Babylonian Rabbi Nathan), BT *Kethuboth* 111 b, *Sanhedrin* 90 b, *Semaḥoth* ix, end, ed. Higger, p. 179, and parallels referred to in the notes ibid.

[26] Immigrated to Palestine in the third century c.e.

[27] *Bereshith Rabba* C. 2, ed. Albeck, p. 1285 ff., PT *Kil'aim* ibid. and parallel. The correct reading of PT is recorded by the medieval authorities. See Lieberman, *On the Yerushalmi* (Jerusalem, 1929), p. 25, and Albeck's notes on *Bereshith Rabba* a.l.

[28] See Cumont, *Lux Perpetua*, p. 53. Such practice was unacceptable to the Jewish mind. Comp. *Bereshith Rabba* LXXX. 10, p. 988 and parallels.

[29] PT ibid.

[30] *Bereshith Rabba* ibid., p. 1286.

[17]   AFTER LIFE IN EARLY RABBINIC LITERATURE   511

The poor woman in her grave wanted her comb and tube of eye-paint not for immediate use, but for future service. She expected the advent of the Messiah any day, and, after all, you cannot welcome him with your hair disheveled, and eyes not painted! This kind of folk-lore could, therefore, be admitted into the *Haggada* (narrative part) of the Babylonian Talmud.

Again the rabbis rule:[31] "One may go out to the cemetery for thirty[32] days to visit the dead[33] and have no fear of following the Amorite practices, for it happened that a man was visited (שפקדו אחד) [and found alive], and he went on living for twenty five years etc". Here the rabbis explicitely mention the "Amorite practices." They were well aware of the heathen custom to visit the dead at certain periods after their death[34]. Yet they permitted these visits, because once a supposedly dead man was found alive and rescued by such a visit. The practice has a reasonable basis, and there is therefore no objection to the custom. Comp. also above, n. 20, end.

However, although the Jews were permitted to visit the dead during the first thirty days, they did not feast at the grave,[35] the funeral meal being served either in the street,[36] or at the home of

---

[31] *Semaḥoth* VIII. 1, ed. Higger, p. 148 ff.

[32] This is the reading of the best manuscript of *Semaḥoth*. This is also the reading of *Raban*, ed. Prague 84 c and *Sefer Rabiah* 841, vol. II, p. 565 (The immediately following remark in the two books does not invalidate the reading "thirty", as will be shown somewhere else). Comp. also the *Geonic* source quoted in *Tur Yoreh De'ah* 344 end. All other manuscripts read: three. Comp. J.N. Epstein *Introduction to the Text of the Mishnah*, p. 471.

[33] ופוקדין על המתים See the remark of Rabbi Judah Najar in his *Simḥath Yehudah* a.l. in the name of Rab Hai Gaon.

[34] See Rhode, *Psyche*, English translation, p. 196, n. 87, Cumont, *Lux Perpetua*, p. 36. Comp. *Tur Yoreh de'ah* l.c. (above, n. 32) and the wording of Rabbi Isaac ben Gayyat, p. 44.

[35] See Rhode ibid., p. 195, n. 82, Cumont ibid., p. 35. Comp. also *Pap. Oxy.* 494, l. 24 (second century C.E.): a feast which they shall hold beside my tomb (πλησίον τοῦ τάφου μου) every year on my birthday. On the Roman custom see Daremberg et Saglio *Dictionnaire des Antiquités* etc. II, p. 1380 b, s.v. funus.

[36] See *Tosefta Mo'ed Katan* II. 17, and parallels.

the mourners. The rabbis knew that the heathen behaved differently. A fragment of a thirteenth century manuscript[37] reports (most probably from a lost *Midrash*): "At that time they were burying Job, and it was their (i.e. the Amorites') custom to eat at the tomb,[38] and they were at that moment eating at the grave of Job etc."[39]

To summarize, the Jews shared many customs (regarding the dead) with their pagan neighbors. Some of them probably have their source in the world of the old Semitic tribes. The Torah forbade a number, and the rabbis added their own prohibitions. However, it is easier to fight wickedness than to combat the superstitions of pious people. Whenever the rabbis could provide a loftier justification for some of the practices, they tolerated them regardless of their heathen origin. The Jews were commanded by the law to participate in the funerals of their pagan neighbors.[40] They read the inscriptions on the monuments of the graves again and again,[41] they saw their symbols and often imitated them. The heathen mythological significance of the symbols was long since dissipated, but the practice remained; fashion and art prevented its disappearance.

Not only in the diaspora do the epitaphs of the Jews display plain heathen symbols,[42] but even in Palestine the tombs at Beth She'arim also preserve typical figures of the heathen graves.[43] The numerous boats on the Jewish graves in Palestine[44] most prob-

---

[37] Published by Schechter in *Semitic Studies in Memory of A. Kohut*, p. 492.

[38] See above, n. 35. Comp. A. Lods, *La Croyance à la Vie Future* etc. p. 157, n. 7; P. Stengel, *Opferbräuche der Griechen* (Leipzig, 1910), p. 144; E.S. Drower, *The Mandaeans of Iraq and Iran* (Oxford, 1937), p. 196, p. 224.

[39] Comp. BT *Sotah* 35 a.   [40] See above chapter I, n. 53.

[41] The very reading helped them to forget the advice of the rabbis in BT *Horayyoth* 13 b. The belief recorded ibid. was also current among the Gentiles, see Goldziher, *Festschrift etc. Berliner's*, pp. 132 ff., 134.

[42] See Cumont, *Symbolism* etc., pp. 485 ff., 492 ff.

[43] Horses, winged creatures etc. See Mazar, *Beth She'arim, Report* etc. (Jerusalem, 1957), pp. 50 ff. 56, 58. Comp. Lieberman, *Hellenism* etc., p. 214.

[44] See Mazar ibid., table xx, No. 2. I saw a great number of them on Jewish graves in Palestine.

ably represent the ferry to the other world,[45] i.e. either the divine bark of the ancient Orientals,[46] or Charon's ferry of the Greeks. The women of Shekhanzib (first half of the fourth century C. E.) probably employed (see above n. 45) a standard dirge and elegy of the Persian wailing women. The former completely ignored the heathen substance of the lamentation. The Rabbis would certainly not approve of such expressions and symbols,[47] but the masses had their own ways.

III

ἄταφοι βιαιοθάνατοι ἄωροι [1]

The ancient pagans considered the souls of the dead who were not buried (or cremated), or who were buried (or cremated)

---

[45] BT *Mo'ed Katan* 28 b: "And for the ferry he borrows [the fare]". See *Variae Lectiones* a.l., p. 105, n. 40, *Otzar ha-Geonim* ibid. pp. 72–73, and Rabbenu Hananel a.l. See Perles *MGWJ* x (1861), p. 385, n. 52, who hit the mark. It appears that this ferry-fare was known in Persia, see *Etym. Magn.* 247, 41, s. v. δανάκη (a Persian coin), and see Perles l. c.

[46] See Maspero, *The dawn of Civilization*, London 1922, p. 196 ff., Breasted, *Development* etc. (above ch. I, n. 28), p. 105 ff. (Egypt); A. Heidel, *The Gilgamesh Epic and Old Testament Parallels*, pp. 171–172, and n. 121 ibid. (Babylonia).

[47] On the painting reproduced by Maspero (ibid., p. 197) we see the ferry entering the "cleft" of the mountains. According to the version in BT *Tamid* 32 a, one could reach the other world, by way of dry land (through the mountains). Some sages maintained that the soul had the form of a bird (See Aptowitzer *MGWJ* 69, 1925, p. 150 ff.), and this was also the belief of the Egyptians (See Maspero ibid., p. 108, n. 5). If the ferryman was adamant in his refusal to transport the dead, the latter could commit himself to the air, using either his own wings (See Breasted, *Development of Religion and Thought in Ancient Egypt*, New York, 1912, p. 109), or those of one of the gods (ibid. p. 107).

Thus the other world could be reached by land, sea and air. Contradictory superstitions existed side by side, and even when the ancient doctrines were discarded the old practices remained (see, for instance, Breasted ibid. p. 340, n. 1). One belief passeth away, another belief cometh; And the image abideth for ever.

[1] See the sources on this group cited and referred to by Rhode, *Psyche*, English translation, pp. 210–211, n. 148, p. 215, n. 176, 594–595. Comp. also

without the proper religious rites, and those who did not die a natural death, and those who died before their time (this included bachelors, spinsters and the childless), as dangerous to their relatives, neighbors and to the whole city.[2] In murder the *biothanatus* (= *biaeothanatus*) will not be satisfied unless his blood is avenged, or propitiatory sacrifices are offered to his spirit.[3]

The rabbis took pains to stress the point that the breaking of the neck of the calf (Deuter. 21:1–9) was performed only in the case of a man who was found slain, and not if he was found strangled or drowned etc.[4] Hence, it has nothing to do with a quasi-chtonic sacrifice to appease the spirit of a *biothanatus*.[5] The Babylonian Talmud[6] reports that the Evil Impulse (*Yetzer ha-Ra'*) and the nations of the world challenge the reasonableness of the law which requires the breaking of a calf's neck in case a slain man was found in the field. However, all other rabbinic parallels[7] (including our editions of the Talmud) do not mention this law. The heathen did not question it; they understood it well, in their own way, of course.

F. Cumont, *Lux Perpetua* pp. 306, 309 ff., 312, 319 ff. 328 passim; J. H. Waszink's commentary on Tertullian, *de anima*, pp. 564–567; Idem, *Vigiliae Christianae* III (1949), p. 107 ff.; A.D. Nock, ibid. IV, (1950), p. 132 ff.

[2] See Maspero, *Life in Ancient Egypt and Assyria*, (New York, 1892), p. 242 ff. Rhode ibid. p. 215, n. 176. Comp. also A. Parrot, *Refrigerium*, pp. 9, 10, 15, 16, 18. See also Heidel (above n. 46), p. 156.

[3] Rhode ibid., Cumont ibid., p. 319. Comp. Parrot ibid.

[4] *Sifre* Deut. 205, ed. Finkelstein, p. 240, and parallels referred to in the notes ibid.

[5] See the commentary of Nachmanides and that of Recanati to Deuter. a.l. Ps.–Jonathan a.l. quotes a legend which gives a "rational" explanation of the law. A similar legend to this effect is cited by a medieval commentary on the Pentateuch, published by Schechter (*Semitic Studies in Memory of A. Kohut*, p. 493). Comp. also Maimonides, *Guide* etc. III. 40.

[6] *Yoma* 67 b (in most mss., see Rabbinovicz a.l. p. 189, n. ש). This is also the reading of *Midrash Tanḥuma Mishpatim* 7 (*editio princeps* and the following editions. It is not found in Buber's edition).

[7] *Mekilta*, interpolated into the *Sifra*, ed. Weiss 86 a, *Pesikta de R. Kahana* ed. Mandelbaum, p. 71, and parallels referred to in the notes ibid. As for the red heifer, see *Pesikta* ibid., p. 74. Comp. Athenaeus, *Deipnosophistai* IX, 409 b (the ashes of sacrifices used for purification).

The pagans viewed as one group all the men who did not die a natural death, those who died before their time, and those who were not buried. Originally they did not discriminate between innocent victims and those who were justly executed by the arm of the law. All of them were *biothanati*. All these embittered and revengeful souls were enrolled into the service of the magicians. In many of their adjurations we find the formula:[8] Ὁρκίσζω ὑμᾶ δέμονες πολυάνδριοι κὲ βιοθάνατοι κὲ ἄωροι κὲ ἄποροι ταφῆς.[9] The men who were thrown in the common ditch (πολυάνδριοι, see below) and those who were not buried at all (ἄποροι ταφῆς) are treated alike. Even soldiers (at least of the enemy) fallen in battle were at a certain time considered *biothanati*.

In the later periods the *biothanati* were more or less limited to the suicides and to executed criminals.[10] Both of these classes were deprived of burial (or at least of religious funeral rites) by the legislation of many nations.[11] In Rome the criminals executed in prison were dragged by rope and hook and thrown into the Tiber[12]; in other places they were thrown into the common ditch (πολυάνδριον). The *Tosefta*[13] mentions: "fossa (פוסה) where men that had been slain were thrown." The Latin fossa (φόσσα), which is not found anywhere else in early rabbinic literature, indicates that the rabbis speak of a Roman practice.[14] As late as the second half of the eighth century C.E., executed criminals were thrown into the pit of the *biothanati* (ἐν τῷ τῶν βιοθανάθων λάκκῳ).[15]

The absence of proper burial was considered a horrible punish-

---

[8] A. Audollent, *Defixionum Tabellae* No. 22, l. 30 (p. 41).

[9] See Rhode ibid. (above n. 1), pp. 604–605; Cumont, *Lux Perpetua*, p. 320, n. 1 (read: 26, 20, instead of: 26, 30); Waszink, Commentary ibid. (above, n. 1), p. 574 ff.

[10] See Cumont ibid., p. 339 ff., Waszink, *Vigiliae Christianae* ibid. (above, n. 1), p. 110–111.

[11] See Cumont l.c. and ibid. p. 340.

[12] See Mommsen, *Strafrecht*, pp. 987–988.

[13] *Ahiloth* XVI. 13, p. 614$_{34}$.

[14] Comp. *Mishnah* ibid. XVI, end.

[15] Theophanes, *Chronographia*, PG CVIII, 880 b. See Cumont, *Lux Perpetua*, p. 340, n. 6, ibid. p. 444.

ment by many nations, including the Jews.[16] From II Kings (9:34) we may infer that queen Jezebel would be left unburied were she not a king's daughter. However, in rabbinic times, no human being in the world would intentionally be left unburied by a religious Jew. The verse in Deuteronomy 21:23 allows no exceptions.[17] Josephus considered the behavior of the Idumeans as an abominable sin. They cast out the corpses of the men whom they had slain without committing them to burial in flagrant disregard of Jewish law.[18] This law, according to Josephus,[19] applies even to suicides (τοὺς ἀναιροῦντας ἑαυτούς, those who destroy themselves). The tractate Semaḥoth (II. 1) rules that he who destroys himself deliberately[20] is not to benefit from any funeral rites,[21] but burial is not denied to him.[22] All human beings — slaves, pagans[23] and criminals[24] are entitled to burial.[25]

[16] See I Kings 14:11–13; Jer. 8:2; 16:4, 6; 22, 19; Ps. 79:2 passim. Comp. A. Lods, *La Croyance à la Vie Future* etc. p. 184 ff., A. Heidel (cited above ch. II, n. 46), p. 155 ff., A. Parrot, *Malédictions et Violations des Tombes*, p. 55, 166, n. 3.

[17] See BT *Sanhedrin* 46 b. Comp. Joshua 8:29, 10:27.

[18] *Bellum Iud.* IV. 5. 2, 317.   [19] Ibid III. 8, 377.

[20] המאבד עצמו לדעת which probably means ὁ ἀναιρῶν ἑαυτὸν ἐκ προνοίας. Comp. *Bell.* l.c. ibid. 331 (end), ibid. 368.

[21] I.e. no proper eulogy is pronounced, no prescribed funeral cortege is permitted etc. Comp. Rhode ibid. (see above, n. 1), p. 187, n. 33, Cumont, *Lux Perpetua*, p. 335.

[22] On the Jewish attitude towards suicide, See *Bereshit Rabba* XXXIV, 13, ed. Theodor, p. 324. Comp. Lieberman הלכות הירושלמי by Maimonides, p. 21, n. 23, and commentary ibid. Comp. also II Macc. 14: 41 ff., Josephus *Bell.* III. 7, 331, ibid. 8, 365 ff., *Bereshith Rabba* ibid., BT Taʿanith 29 a, *Kethuboth* 103 b, *Kiddushin* 40 a passim. The rabbis reported (BT ʿ*Abodah Zarah* 18 a) that when Rabbi Ḥanina ben Teradion was consumed by fire (during the Hadrianic persecutions) he refused to open his mouth which would have hastened his death. He said: Let Him who gave it (i.e. the soul) to me take it away. Comp. Cicero, *Somn. Scip.* 3, cited by Cumont, *Lux Perpetua*, p. 336.

[23] *Semaḥoth* I. 9, and see above, Chapter I, n. 53. Comp. however PT *Shabbath* X. 6, 12 c, and the books cited in גליון הש״ס ibid., ed. Romm (x. 5), 64 a. Comp. also the commentary of Rabbi David Kimḥi to Joshua 8:29.

[24] *Semaḥoth* II. 6, 8, in accordance with Deut. 21:23. This is in contrast to Assyrian law, see Heidel l. c. (above, n. 16), p. 155–156.

[25] One medieval sage (quoted by Rabbi Isaac ben Moshe of Vienna in his

The Roman practice of depriving the executed criminals of the right of burial, and exposing the corpses on the cross for many days, an atrocity often inflicted on the Christian martyrs,[26] horrified the Jews. This practice was not limited to the Romans, it was performed by many nations, including the Semites. The law of Deuteronomy 21:23 indicates that the heathen did expose the corpse of the executed man on the gibbet for many days. The Gibeonites demanded that the old heathen practice be applied to the descendents of king Saul, and king David complied with their request (II Samuel 21:9–10). The rabbis[27] claimed that it was an exceptional case of "sanctification of the Name": Princes were hanged and exposed for the whole summer to avenge the innocent blood of serfs shed by a king. The Maccabeans acted in a similar manner (I Macc. 7:46), and the action was apparently approved by the rabbis.[28] Even the total deprival of burial was sometimes inflicted by the ancient Semites[29] on certain criminals, but such a practice would not be permitted by the rabbis.

The lack of burial horrified the ancient man more than death itself. Seneca remarked to this effect: Those who had not feared

אור זרוע II, 422, 86 c) ruled that suicides and certain sinners are not to be buried. But no other authority supports him. The phrase of *Semaḥoth* אין מתעסקין means that no funeral rites are administered to him (see above, n. 21), but the burial itself is never denied, as is obvious from the *Mishnah* (*Sanhedrin* VI. 5) when compared to the language of *Semaḥoth* (II. 6), as already observed by other medieval authorities. The story recorded in PT *Terumoth* VIII. 5 (and parallels) does not disprove this law. The death happened on Shabbath (according to one version), or on the Day of Atonement (according to another), and for this reason the rabbi did not permit to remove the corpse. In a week day, the body would be commited to burial without delay.

26 Frequently recorded by Eusebius in his *Hist. Eccl.* and in *de mart. Palest.* and in many Christian *acta martyrum*. Comp. also Petronius, *Satyricon* 111–112. The crucified were exposed until their flesh entirely wasted away, see *Semaḥoth* II. 11.

27 PT *Kiddushin* IV. 1, 65 c; BT *Yebamoth* 19 a.

28 *Meggilath Taʿanith* XII (thirteenth of Adar), PT *Taʿanith* II. 13, 66 a and parallels, BT ibid. 18 b.

29 See above, nn. 16, 24. Comp. Cumont, *Lux Perpetua*, p. 444.

death might fear something after death.[30] We shall cite an interesting passage to this effect. We find in the *Midrash*[31] an allegorical story about two friends who "stole together and robbed together," but one of them repented and changed his mode of life. After death, they met in the other world. The man who repented was treated as if he had been pious and just. His friend challenged the justice of such a treatment. Thereupon it was disclosed to him: "Your colleague repented, because he saw what happened to you. After your death, you were disgraced (מנוול היית) for three days,[32] your corpse was not put into a coffin, but was dragged to the grave by ropes[33] (ובחבלים גררוך), [as it is said], *the maggot is spread under thee and the worms cover thee*" (Isa. 14:11). The man was obviously thrown without a coffin into a πολυάνδριον, into a common ditch.[34] In this case he was immediately immersed into a heap of maggots and worms which swarmed beneath and below the corpse.

The man who "stole and robbed" was obviously apprehended and executed, but the rabbis stressed that it was the posthumous degradation of the corpse and the lack of proper burial that horrified the partner who survived. The execution itself is not even mentioned[35] by the rabbis. A robber knew in advance what

[30] *Suas. et controv.* VIII. 4, end, cited by Cumont, ibid., p. 340.

[31] *Koheleth Rabba* I. 15, ed. Rom. 6 a; *Ruth Rabba* III. 3, 6 c.

[32] Theophanes (*Chronographia*, PG CVIII, 848 a) reports that the head of the decapitated Bactagius (executed c. the middle of the eighth century C.E.) was exposed (suspended, ἐκρέμασεν) for three days (ἐπὶ τρεῖς ἡμέρας). A rabbi of the third century C.E. accuses (PT *Yebamoth* XVI. 3, 15 c) King Abijah of putting up guards to maintain a three-days watch over the Judeans who fell in battle (so that nobody approached them).

[33] It was the regular Roman practice, see Mommsen, *Strafrecht*, pp. 987–988; Cumont, *Lux Perpetua*, p. 340. See above, chapter II, nn. 11–18. The rabbis certainly did not have in mind the verse in Jeremiah 22:19 which they did not quote.

[34] See above nn. 13, 15.

[35] It is, of course, not impossible that the rabbis referred to an actual occurrence in Palestine of which the people were well aware. The rabbis had a special predilection for utilizing current events in their sermons, for exploiting facts with which their audience was well familiar, see Lieberman, *Hellenism*

may eventually happen to him. But "he who had not feared death might fear something after death,"[36] especially when he had the occasion to watch the "after death" of his partner with his own eyes. Niger the Peraean, the intrepid, fearless fighter for Jewish freedom, before he was murdered by the Zealots, asked for one thing, for a grave (περὶ ταφῆς ἱκέτευεν), which the impious murderers did not grant.[37] The latter punishment was harsher than the former.

There is no wonder, therefore, that among several nations it was considered a sacred duty for each individual to bury the dead whenever one came across a neglected corpse. The Jewish high priest who is commanded *"not to defile himself for his father and mother"* (Lev. 21:11) must contaminate himself through the act of burying any stray corpse.[38] The same law was current among the Romans. "For whereas it was unlawful for the high priests to see a corpse, it would be still more sinful, if they neglected an unburied corpse, when they happened to see it."[39]

Whenever, by the order of the government, a corpse was not to be buried, it was naturally a grave risk to violate this order. When Rizpah, the daughter of Aiah, protected the exposed corpses of the princes (including the bodies of her two sons) from the birds of the air and the beasts of the field (II Sam. 21:10), she probably gambled with her life.[40] Tobit (2:4–8) risked his head,

---

in Jewish Palestine, p. 4 ff. In this case, they might have referred to an actual event when the criminal was either executed in prison, or died before he was condemned. In both cases, his corpse would be posthumously disgraced (see Mommsen referred to above, n. 33), but the execution could not be mentioned by the rabbis as a deterring factor. However, even this possibility does not invalidate our general interpretation of the *Midrashic* passage.

[36] See above, n. 30.
[37] Josephus, *Bellum* IV. 6. 1, 360.
[38] *Mishnah Nazir* VII. 1.
[39] Servius *ad Aeneid*. VI. 176: unde cum pontificibus nefas esset cadaver videre, magis tamen nefas fuerat si visum insepultum relinquerent. Comp. also Lieberman, *Hellenism in Jewish Palestine*, p. 165, n. 12.
[40] According to the rabbis (*Bemidbar Rabba* VIII. 4), King David was moved by her behavior. Rabbi David Kimḥi in his commentary to II Samuel

when he buried the dead.[41] Pagans,[42] Christians[43] and Jews[44] staked their lives[45] for the sake of rescuing the corpses of the *biothanati* in order to commit them to the earth. The proper authorities had the right to grant the permission to inter the corpse of the executed individual,[46] which was often bought for a great amount of money.[47]

However, in many cases, the petition for the delivery of the corpse to the interested party was denied,[48] and the latter resorted to stealing it.[49] The rabbis issued a stern warning against this practice. They ruled[50]: From what time does one begin to count the days of mourning for men who were executed by the government? From the day one gives up hope of asking (i.e. of petitioning the authorities, see above n. 46), even if not of stealing (i.e. they

---

(21:11) reports in the name of a *Midrash* that upon hearing what she did, king David married her (comp. PT *Yebamoth* II. 4, 3 d). The men who informed David about Rizpah's act (II Samuel ibid.) probably did not intend to praise the woman.

[41] The strangled man was probably a *biothanatus*, a man executed by the government, and having been exposed, the government did not permit to bury him. The story has nothing to do with Hadrian and the Jews fallen in the war of Bettar (See Graetz, *MGWJ*, vol. 28, 1879, p. 514 ff.). We have seen above that the cruelty of exposing the corpses of the executed criminals was practised by several nations in hoary antiquity. This punishment would have no sense, if the relations had the right to bury the corpses. The pious Tobit was in the habit of burying those dead which nobody dared to bury, i.e. the *biothanati*. No conclusions can be drawn from Tobit's burying the dead regarding the place and the time of that book.

[42] See Petronius, *Satyricon* 112.

[43] Le Blant, *Les Actes des Martyrs*, p. 223.

[44] Tobit (see above). According to *Midrash Mishle* (IX, ed. Buber, p. 62) the body of Rabbi ʿAkiba was stolen from the prison of Caesarea in Palestine (during the Hadrianic persecutions).

[45] See above, n. 42, Mommsen *Strafrecht*, p. 989, Le Blant ibid., p. 222.

[46] Mommsen, ibid., Le Blant, ibid. p. 220 ff.   [47] Le Blant, ibid. p. 221.

[48] See Mommsen, ibid., p. 988 ff. It is reported in PT * Taʿanith* IV. 8, 69a (about the Jews who fell in the battle of Bettar): ולא גזר עליהם שיקברו which means: And he (i.e. Hadrian) gave no permission to bury them. The prohibition of the burial was automatic and required no special decree.

[49] See the sources referred to above, nn. 42–45.

[50] *Semaḥoth* II 9.

still hope to be able to steal the corpse); [but] he who steals (i.e. a corpse of a man executed by the government) is shedding [innocent] blood etc.[51] How far the masses listened to this warning is an open question. They feared the "after death" more than death itself.[52]

Jew and Gentile alike shared the fear of lack of burial, but rabbinic literature has preserved no trace of the heathen belief that the *insepulti* are barred from Hades.[53] On the other hand, it appears that the rabbis took cognizance of the pagan superstition that both guilty and innocent *ahori* and *biothanati* are not admitted to that place.[54] The rabbis of Caesarea remark[55] that the minors of the Gentiles and soldiers of Nebuchadnezzar[56] will not be resurrected, nor will they be tortured (נידונין)[57] [in Gehenna][58]. This means that the heathen will get what they designated for themselves.[59] The same fate was allotted by the rabbis to the sinful idolatrous generation of the Flood and to the men of Sodom[60] who respectively perished by water and fire.[61] The sages added[62] to this group the generation that died in the wilderness[63], i.e. they

[51] I.e. innocent people may eventually pay with their head in such a case, see above, n. 45. The rabbis liked to add to the gravity of the sin of murder that of adultery and idolatry.

[52] See above, n. 36.

[53] Comp. *The Gilgamesh Epic* XII. 151, and for the western beliefs see Cumont, *Lux Perpetua*, p. 84, 393.

[54] See Cumont ibid., p. 306, J.H. Waszink's commentary on Tertullian's *de anima*, p. 565 ff.

[55] PT *Berakoth* IX. 2, 13 b, *Shebi'ith* IV, end, 35 c. Comp. *Tosefta Sanhedrin* XIII. 1, BT ibid. 110 b.

[56] I.e. those who repented and thereby wiped out their crimes, as is evident from the context of PT *Berakoth* ibid.

[57] See Lieberman, *Jewish Quarterly Review* vol. 35, 1944, p. 15, n. 99.

[58] The rabbis evidently put no time limit on their exclusion from Hades.

[59] See BT *Gittin* 57 a.

[60] According to Rabbi Nehemiah: Both groups "will not face judgment".

[61] *Mishnah Sanhedrin* X (XI). 3.

[62] *Mishnah* ibid. 4.

[63] I.e. the men who were present at the Revelation on Mount Sinai and witnessed all the miracles performed for the sake of Israel, yet they accepted the evil report of the spies.

will share the portion of the old heathen *biothanati*. But the rabbis clearly stated that the men who died in the wilderness were not ἄωροι; they died ὡραῖοι, and the Talmud applied to them[64] the verse of Job (5:26): *Thou shalt come to thy grave in ripe age, [like as a shock of corn cometh in its season]*.

However, we should always bear in mind that the heathen notion of not being admitted into Hades may not have been fully comprehended by the Jews. The Jewish ideas about the pagan concepts of the fate of the *biothanati* and *ahori* were probaly quite vague. However, the rabbis themselves were concerned with the destiny of certain *ahori*. In their earlier writings they apparently connected the fate of the *ahori* in the world to come with the respective laws regulating the disposition of their corpses.[65] So, for instance, according to the opinion of some rabbis, the corpses of still-born babies (including those of infants who could not survive thirty days after their birth) are disposed by simply throwing them into a pit.[66] The *Mishnah*[67] mentions: "A pit into which still-born children,[68] or men that had been slain were thrown," i.e. a ditch into which *ahori* and *biothanati* are plunged. Those *ahori* have certainly no right to be interred in the ancestral tombs.[69]

If the child died after thirty days of his life, or if, regardless of his age, it can be proved that he (or she) was viable, but died by accident, "he may be considered by his father and mother and

---

[64] PT *Bikkurim* II. 1, 64 c. Comp. *Tosafoth* to BT *Mo'ed Katan* 28 a, s.v ומיתה.

[65] Comp. the judicious remarks of A.D. Nock in *Vigiliae Christianae* IV (1950), pp. 132–133.

[66] See *Tosefta Ahiloth* XVI. 12–13, BT *Sanhedrin* 48 a, *Semaḥoth* XIV. 4. Comp. also *Mishnah Niddah* VII. 4 (regarding the custom of the Samaritans). Comp. Eccl. 6:3–4.

[67] *Ahiloth* XVI, end.

[68] נפלים. This term includes infants who died without living thirty days after birth. See also above nn. 13–14.

[69] *Sifre* Deut. 188, ed. Finkelstein, p. 227. Comp. Lieberman. *Tosefta Ki-Fshuta*, vol. v, p. 1337.

all his kinsfolks as a full bridegroom."[70] He may be buried (if they choose to do so) with all the pomp of funeral rites.[71]

However, the love of parents was not satisfied with arranging a full funeral procession for their infant. What about the life of the baby in the world to come? The author of the *Sapientia Salomonis* records an interesting pagan custom with regard to the death of an *ahorus*. He informs us (14:15) that when a heathen father was afflicted with untimely mourning (ἀώρῳ πένθει), he used to make an image of the child taken away too soon, and would worship it as a god. This was a good consolation[72] to a heathen father. The Jew comforted himself in a Jewish manner.

The rabbis assert[73] that the Lord Himself teaches Torah to the babies [who died in their infancy]. According to another version[74] the angel Metatron teaches them. This formulation was accepted by all the later *Midrashim*. The age of the dead children, taught by the angel, is not specified by the Talmud. A manuscript of a late *Midrash*[75] contends that the angel teaches all the infants who

---

[70] *Mishnah Niddah* v. 3, *Semaḥoth* III. 1.   [71] See *Semaḥoth* III. 2–7.

[72] From a book on Egyptian antiquities Fulgentius quotes (Th. Hopfner, *Fontes Hist. Relig. Aegypt.*, p. 685) the custom of an Egyptian father to erect an image of his dead son. The poor father was searching for a remedy to relieve his pain of grief (filii sibi simulacrum in edibus instituit dumque tristitiae remedium quaerit etc.). This is well understood in the light of the ancient Egyptian belief that the dead man retained some form of life as long as his image, or statue, existed (see Maspero, *The Dawn of Civilization*, London 1922, p. 193, n. 9, 194, 232 b ff., A. Parrot, *Refrigerium* p. 87). The destruction of the statue was considered by them a second death. Comp. also *Pg* CXVI, 624ᶜ, and Lieberman *JQR* xxxv (1944), p. 26, n. 166.

The rabbis similarly, state (*Mekilta, Pisḥa* XIII, ed. Lauterbach, p. 100. Comp. *Mekilta deRASHBI*, ed. Epstein–Melamed, p. 29): When the first-born of one of the Egyptians died, they would make a statue of him and set it up in the house. On that night such statues were crushed, ground and scattered. And in their eyes that day was as sad as though they had just then buried their first-born.

[73] BT ʿ*Abodah Zarah* 3 b. Comp. v. Aptowitzer, *Hebrew Union College Annual* III, (1926), p. 126 ff. See also *REJ* III, (1881), pp. 44–45.

[74] Ibid. Comp. the *Gemara* of the minor tractate *Kalla* II, ed. Higger, p. 203.

[75] Cited by Steinschneider in a note to his Introduction in תגמולי הנפש by Rabbi Hillel of Verona, p. 19.

died before the age of thirteen years and one day.[76] On the other hand the *Midrash Othiyyoth deR. ʿAkiba*[77] states that the angel gathers all the souls of the embryos that died in their mother's wombs, of the sucklings who died on the breasts of their mothers, and of the school children who died [during their study] of the five books of the Pentateuch. He arranges them into separate classes and teaches them Torah, wisdom (i.e. *Halacha*), *Haggadah* etc. In short, he gives them a complete Jewish education.

This seems to be an old belief. Clemens of Alexandria cites[78] the Apocalypse of Petrus which in its turn asserts: "The Scripture saith (ἡ γραφή φησι) that the children who have been exposed are delivered to a care-taking angel[78a] by whom they are educated and brought up.[79] And they shall be, it saith, like the faithful in this world aged one hundred years." The same fate is allotted to the abortive babies.[80] The Apocalypse limits the education of the dead infants to the knowledge of a learned Christian a hundred years old. This is, of course, in accordance with the heathen beliefs,[81] or, as Prof. A. D. Nock aptly puts it,[82] "moralistic sophistications" adapted to these beliefs.

The rabbis put no limit to the education of the dead youngsters, nor to its duration. According to all rabbinic sources, the age of the children who benefit from the education supplied by the angel cannot exceed thirteen years and one day, the official time of

[76] I.e. the official age of maturity according to Jewish law. In *Kalla* ibid. the education in confined to infants up to four, or five, years old who did not taste the pleasure of sin.

[77] Ed. Wertheimer, Jerusalem, 1914, p. 11. Comp. Aptowitzer ibid. (above, n. 73), p. 126, n. 21.   [78] *Eclogae Proph.* 41.

[78a] This reminds us of the legend about the children exposed by the Israelites (*Debarim Rabba*, ed. Lieberman, p. 14, and parallels), but that legend speaks of living children.

[79] ὑφ' οὗ παιδεύεσθαί τε καὶ αὔξειν.

[80] Ibid. 48: τὰ βρέφη ⟨τὰ⟩ ἐξαμβλωθέντα.

[81] See F. Cumont, *Lux Perpetua*, p. 328. I find this span of human life in *The Brooklyn Mus. Aram. Papyri*, ed, Kraeling, No. 4 (dated 434 B.C.E.), ll. 17–18. Comp. also PT *Berakoth* II. 8, 5ᶜ and parallel; Is. 65:20.

[82] *Vigiliae Christianae* IV, (1950), p. 133, n. 15.

maturity. To the parents and near kin, any man who died before fulfilling all normal functions of life was an *ahorus*. In an epitaph from Egypt[83] a man forty-five years old is called ἄωρος.[84]

Yet the posthumous education of the dead young could not completely satisfy their near kinsfolk. Did those unfortunate infants entirely disappear from this world just as if they had never existed, or will they be resurrected in the world to come? The rabbis disagree as to the age of babies who will be resurrected in the world to come. Some fix the age at the time the infant is able to talk, and some lower it to the moment of conception.[85] Apparently the latter opinion considers that the soul enters the body at that moment.[86]

Some Babylonian rabbis link the resurrection of boys to their circumcision.[87] It appears that this last view appealed to the masses in particular. Rab Nahshon Gaon[88] reports the custom of circumcising a dead baby on the tomb and of giving him a name etc. in order that he may recognize his father at the time of resurrection.[89] M. Grossberg quotes[90] a manuscript according to which Rab Nachshon claims that this custom goes back to the time of the sages of the Talmud, and he offers the explanation "in order that the baby should not come to the other world without the *seal*." Similarly, Rabbi Joshua ibn Shuʻaib reports[91] the same

[83] Frey, *Corp, Insc. Iud.* II, p. 400, No. 1484.

[84] Comp. *Semaḥoth* III. 7.

[85] See PT *Shebiʻith* IV, end, 35 c, BT *Sanhedrin* 110 b. Comp. also *Kethuboth* ibid. 111 a.

[86] See BT *Sanhedrin* 91 b. Comp. Ginzberg, *Legends of the Jews*, vol. V, p. 80, n. 25; Aptowitzer ibid. (above n. 73), p. 126, n. 21, end.

[87] PT *Shebiʻith* ibid., BT *Sanhedrin* 111 b.

[88] Fl. in the ninth century C.E.

[89] See Lewin, *Otzar ha-Geonim, Shabbath* I, p. 138; Aptowitzer l.c. (above, n. 73), p. 127, n. 22.

[90] חצי מנשה, p. 19.

[91] In his *derashoth* (וירא Cracow, 7 a). All the sources mentioned by Lewin and Aptowitzer ibid. do not name the "seal." The sign of circumcision is termed "seal" in *Tosefta Berakoth* VI (VII). 13 (BT *Shabbath* 137 b) and many other sources. Comp. the *Intern. Critic. Commentary* on *Ad Romanos* IV. 11, p. 107. A ms. *Midrash* (Cambridge T–S, Box C 2, 24) on Deut. 7:17 asserts that this

custom in the name of the *Geonim* with the same explanation "in order that he may bring the *seal* with him" (שיוליך עמו החותם).

The assertion that this custom goes back to the time of the Talmud is highly questionable, and it is hardly likely that Rab Nahshon ever claimed it. In fact some rabbis challenged the very custom.[92] They contended that this was the conduct of women of their time.[93] The Karaite Judah Hadassi[94] reports that the midwife is the one who circumcises the dead infant, in order that he be resurrected with the other dead.

It is very plausible that altogether the custom is based on the excessive solicitude of parents for the child's future fate.[95] The mention of the "seal" in our context, which will help the dead infant to be resurrected[96] reminds us of the Christian σφραγίς[97]

sign is the *seal of the Holy One* and the ζώνη (symbol of office) of Israel. Comp. *Or Zaru'a* I, 3 d, 12, where this *Midrash* is cited (it reads "והיא זוני שלו", instead of "והוא זונין של ישראל"). In *Midrash Shemoth Rabba* XIX. 5 this seal is paralleled to σημαντήρ (סימנטיר). On σφραγίς as a mark of a slave (in this case a slave of the Lord), see Lieberman, *Tosefeth Rishonim* II, p. 168, *Tosefta Ki-Fshutah* III, p. 75.

[92] See *Kelale ha-Milah* of Rabbi Gershom ha-Goser in *Sichron Berith Larischonim* ed. Glassberg p. 126 ff.

[93] ודאי נהוג נשי דידן למיחתכה.

[94] *Eshkol ha-Kofer* 113 b.

[95] See Aptowitzer l.c. (above n. 73), p. 127, n. 23.

[96] The sign of circumcision protects the man from the fire of hell and permits him to enter paradise, see the sources cited in *Sichron* ibid. (above, n. 92), p. 92 ff.

[97] It should he noted that all the numerous medieval rabbis who quoted Rab Nahson did not mention "the bringing of the seal with him." The only exceptions are the manuscript (of an unknown date and origin) published by M. Grossberg and the Spanish rabbi (who was also a famous *Kabbalist*) in the fourteenth century. It is almost certain that the formulation of "bringing the seal with him" is of late origin, and it was not uttered by the great Babylonian Gaon. The Christians, of course, were well familiar with the seal of salvation and with the signet which enables the deceased to be admitted to certain regions in the other world (the latter notion was not foreign to the *Kabbalists* either). The sources referred to above, n. 96, avoid the word "seal," although in essence they are not far apart from our source. Comp. also above, n. 91.

and the similar hope connected with it.[98] It is obvious from the older rabbinic sources that dead infants were not circumcised in this world.[99]

The Jews were concerned with the problem of the resurrection of not only the *ahori*, but also of certain *biothanati* and *insepulti*. The heathen believed that the souls of the latter lose their immortality (see below), and the Christians were afraid that they will not be resurrected. M.E. Le Blant devoted[100] a long article to the fears of the Christians that the martyrs who were consumed by fire, or devoured by wild beasts will not be resurrected. He further refers[101] to various texts which indicate the anxieties of the heathen lest they perish in water, a superstition already alluded to by Homer.[102] Servius[103] explains this as a fear which has its origin in the notion that water extinguishes the soul which is of fire.[104] Le Blant also calls attention to the letter of Synesius which portrays[105] the scene of the soldiers, standing with their swords drawn, ready to stab themselves in order to be saved from death by water.[106]

---

[98] See H. Grégoire et M.A. Kugener, *Vie de Porphyre*, pp. 118–119. Comp. F. Cumont, *Lux Perpetua*, p. 443.

[99] See *Bereshith Rabba* III. 8, ed. Theodor–Albeck, p. 483. Comp. *Sichron* ibid. (above, n. 92), pp. 92, 93, and the novellae by Rabbenu Nissim Gerundi on BT *Mo'ed Katan*, p. 64.

[100] *Académie des Inscriptions* etc., *Mémoires* XXVIII. 2, 1875, pp. 75–95.

[101] Ibid. pp. 80–81.

[102] *Od.* IV. 511; *Il.* XXI. 281.

[103] *Ad Aeneid.* I. 98.

[104] The rabbis asserted that the almond-shaped bone of the spine (which will serve as the nucleus in the resurrection) can be destroyed neither by fire, nor by water, nor by mill stones, nor by hammer (see above chapter I, n. 45). The only exception was the water of the Flood which wiped out that bone (*Bereshith Rabba* XXVIII. 3, p. 262). Consequently the generation of the Flood will not be resurrected nor face judgment. See above, n. 61.

[105] *PG* LXVI, 1333 c. Comp. Juster, *Les Juifs dans l'empire Romain* II, p. 324, n. 5.

[106] Le Blant, naturally, omitted the Jewish element in this letter, for it really has no direct bearing on the subject. The majority of the crew and the captain of the boat were Jews. During the frightful panic of all the Gentiles, only the captain, Amarantus the Jew, remained in a good mood (ibid. 1333 a: μόνος 'Αμάραντος εὔθυμος ἦν). Synesius accounts for it by explaining: "For

Thus, in the beginning of the fifth century C.E. this superstition was still approved[107] by the future bishop[108] of Ptolemais (in Cyrenaica).

The Jews were gripped by the same fears. The rabbis relate[109] that a great number of children were captured by the Romans who intended to use them for shameful purposes. They decided to throw themselves into the sea in order to avoid their abominable fate, but they were apparently worried lest they will not be resurrected after having drowned in water. The oldest of them quoted the verse of Psalms (68:23): *I will bring back from Bashan, I will bring back from the depth of the sea*. From *Bashan* ("Mib-bashan") means from between the teeth[110] of lions, *I will bring back from the depth of the sea* refers to those who were drowned in the sea. The Christians quote the Apocalypse of John (XX. 13) to this effect, and in their medieval paintings they portray monsters, each belching out the body of a man.[111]

In spite of the assurances of the rabbis, the Jewish masses of the tenth century C.E. were still haunted by the fear that those who perished by water might not share in the resurrection of the dead, as is obvious from the story told in the *Sefer ha-Qabbalah* by Rabbi Abraham ibn Daud.[112]

---

now he will finally defraud his creditors." This is a very lame excuse for being in good spirits. From the beginning of his account, Synesius aims to make fun of the financial stress of the captain, and he remained true to his literary style. It is more likely that Amarantus remained cheerful not because he saw a chance to perish and thereby defraud his creditors, nor because he believed in resurrection even if he should vanish in water (he was a very pious Jew, as Synesius described him above, ibid.), but because he was an experienced captain (see ibid. 1332 a). He appraised the situation better than his passengers, and he must have been genuinely amused by watching "those natural descendants of Homer" (τούτους αὐτοφυεῖς Ὁμηρίδας) in a state of deathly panic.

[107] Ibid. 1333 c.   [108] At that time he was still a heathen.

[109] BT *Gittin* 57 b, *Midrash Eka* (to Lam. 1:16).

[110] I.e. מבין שני, see also *Sifre* Deut. 317, ed. Finkelstein, p. 360, line 4.

[111] See Le Blant ibid. (above, n. 100), p. 86, n. 1.

[112] Ed. Neubauer, p. 68. Comp. M. Stein, *Tarbiz* IX, 1938, p. 273, and G. Cohen, *Proceedings of the American Academy of Jewish Research* vol. XIX (1960–1961), pp. 59–60 and notes ibid.

An interesting *Midrash* is quoted by Raymund Martini[113] in the name of Rabbi Moshe ha-Darshan.[114] This *Midrash* contends that the Messiah offered to accept voluntarily all suffering provided "that the dead [who were deceased] in my time be resurrected as well as those who died from the time of Adam until now. And not only those should be saved, but even those who were devoured by the wolves and lions, and those who were drowned in the waters of the sea[115] and in rivers. And not only those should be saved, but even the abortions,[116] and not only they, but even those whom Thou hadst planned to create, but they were not created."

It is evident that this late *Midrash*[117] asserts that the Messiah asks for the resurrection of the *biothanati, insepulti* (devoured by wolves and lions, drowned in water) and *ahori* (abortions). Moreover, the Messiah adds a new class: Those whom the Lord had in mind to create but He did not do so.

I am certain that this is based on a tradition recorded in the *Midrashim*[118] and in the Babylonian Talmud.[119] We read there (i.e. in the Talmud)[120] that all the generations [that the Lord intended to create but] which were never created, were driven out (וטרדן) from their place in heaven[121] and amalgamated in the fire of the "fiery stream" (literally: the fiery stream is emptied, or poured, on those generations) mentioned in Daniel 7:10. This

---

[113] *Pugio Fidei*, ed. Carpzov, p. 416.

[114] Flourished in the first half of the eleventh century C.E.

[115] The Hebrew reads: במים, but in the Latin translation ibid., p. 417, he quotes: *in aquis maris*; hence the Hebrew should read: במי ים.

[116] In the Latin ibid.: sed etiam abortivos.

[117] On its authenticity see Lieberman, *Shkiin* (Hebrew), p. 58.

[118] *Bereshith Rabba* XXVIII. 4, pp. 262–263. There are many variations of this tradition, see Theodor's notes to the *Midrash* a.l. Apparently, according to one tradition the Lord destroyed the souls of the generations He intended to create together with the generation of the Flood, when he saw the crimes of the latter.

[119] *Ḥaggigah* 13 b–14 a.

[120] According to the reading of *'Ein Jacob* (comp. also cod. Monacencis ibid.), *Rashi and Tosafoth* a.l. in the first tradition of the Talmud. The words איכא דאמרי report another version.

[121] See BT ibid. 12 b.

was not a punishment for souls which had never been in a body; they were simply discarded. This is why the above mentioned *Midrash* quite reasonably counts those souls among the *biothanati*, *insepulti* and *ahori*. This is also well understood in the light of the different tradition recorded above, n. 118.

The early and genuine rabbinic tradition claimed that the violent premature death of the ordinary sinner, or his lack of burial, will serve as atonement and help him to gain his portion in the world to come.[122] The Christians subsequently adopted similar notions, and in late medieval times some of their pious men went to the extreme of asking that their dead bodies be thrown out into the field, or into the river, like the corpses of animals.[123] Among Jews such a will would not be executed,[124] for the degradation and the disgrace of a human body are contrary to Jewish law.

---

[122] *Sifre* Num. 112, ed. Horovitz, pp. 121–122. Comp. the reading in BT *Sanhedrin* 47 a, and see 47 a – 47 b ibid. The opinion in שאילתות, 14, and other medieval books that total lack of burial is a bad sign for the deceased is to be understood as meaning that such drastic punishment indicates that the dead man was a grave sinner. But the posthumous dishonor of ἀταφία serves as an atonement for serious transgressions of the Law, as is obvious from BT *Sanhedrin* 46 b and 104 a.

[123] Le Blant ibid. (above, n. 100), p. 88.

[124] See BT *Sanhedrin* 46 b, PT *Kethuboth* XI. 1, 34 b. In the latter source we find a hypothetical question of a person asking in his last will to be cremated and the ashes to be used as manure. The expression עבוד עבודה in this context is a technical term for work in the field. Comp. *Mishnah Shebi'ith* III. 1, and PT ibid. III. 1–2, 34 c. According to one version (Diog. Laert. VI. 79), Diogenes the Cynic left instructions that his dead body be thrown into the Ilissus in order that he might be useful to his brethern (ἵνα τοῖς ἀδελφοῖς χρήσιμος γένηται).

ADDITIONAL NOTE

On p. 496 I quoted the word משומדים from the *Tosefta*. This is the reading of all the parallel sources.[1] The word מומר never occurs in any ancient manuscript of the Talmud and earlier rabbinic sources; nor is this word to be found in any of the ancient uncensored printed editions of the above mentioned sources.

R. Rabbinovicz in his *Variae Lectiones* to the Babylonian Talmud did not always record the true reading משומד (instead of the emended מומר) from the manuscripts and the early printed editions. Moreover, by sheer habit he sometimes erroneously quoted מומר from cod. München. So, for instance, in his work to BT *Horayoth*, p. 34, he cites מומר twice from that codex. However, both cod. München and all ancient printed editions read משומד in these two instances as well. Our printed edtitons of BT *Hullin* 4b record the word מומר nineteen times in this one single page. In the *Variae Lectiones* a.l. there is not one variant of this word. However, cod. München and all ancient printed editions invariably read משומד. Similarly, in BT *Pesaḥim* 96a the manuscripts read משומדות instead of המרת דת of the censored printed editions.[2] The same can be said about BT *Succa* 56b. The manuscripts, the ancient printed editions and the parallel passages read שנשתמדה instead of שהמירה דתה of our censored editions of the Babylonian Talmud.

As a matter of fact the *Geonim* were at a loss with regard to the explanation of the word משומד.[3] This bears witness to the antiquity of the term.

Rab Saadia Gaon in his Book of Doctrines and Beliefs (translation of A. Altman, p. 130–131) states: "As to the disobedient

---

[1] *Sder 'Olam Rabba* III, end, ed. Ratner, p. 9 b, BT *Rosh Hashanah* 17a in the uncensored editions of the Talmud and all the mss., see R. Rabbinovicz, *Variae Lectiones* a.l., p. 32, n. 50.

[2] The ancient editions mistakenly read משמרות instead of משמדות.

[3] See *Aruch Completum* s.v. שמד and the *Additamenta* by S. Krauss etc. s.v. שמד.

he is one who singles out one particular law which he makes it a rule always to transgress. Our ancient teachers call him משומד (an apostate)".[4] We have here explicit testimony that the word משומד is not a later invention.[5]

---

[4] Rab Saadia's remark is correct. It is based on PT *Kiddushin* I. 10, 61d. Comp. also *Tosefta Horayoth* I. 5, BT ibid. 11a. Rab Saadia's statement has nothing to do with the divergence of opinions as to whether a משומד לדבר אחד, an apostate with regard to one commandment, is considered a thorough apostate. Rab Saadia talks about a man who made it his principle *always* to violate a certain commandment. The context in PT *Kiddushin* l.c. certainly supports his view.

[5] As to the original meaning of the word see Lieberman, *Tosefta Ki-Fshutah* III, p. 402, n. 45. I subsequently found that E. Levitas had already explained the origin of the word in his תשבי s.v. שמד. However, he offered no proofs for his thesis.

SPINOZA ON THE RAINBOW AND ON PROBABILITY

by RICHARD MCKEON

THE FRIENDS OF SPINOZA who published his Posthumous Works in 1677, the year of his death, in both a Latin and a Dutch edition, expressed in their Preface the confidence that their collection was inclusive and that no other work of Spinoza would be found which added to what he had said more than once in the published writings. One possible exception was mentioned — a *Treatise on the Rainbow*, which he composed a number of years ago as many people knew, and which was hidden somewhere, unless he burned it, as was probable. Early biographies and biographical sources mention the treatise and differ in their conjectures or certainties about its fate. In the middle of the nineteenth century, a short treatise which had been published in the Hague in 1687, ten years after Spinoza's death, without name of author but with the title "Algebraic Calculation (*Stelkonstige Reeckening*) o fthe Rainbow, a Contribution to the Closer Connection of Physics and Mathematics," came into the possession of an Amsterdam bookdealer, Frederik Muller. J. van Vloten reported the discovery as recent (*aliquot jam ante annos*) in 1861 in the Preface to his *Ad Benedicti de Spinoza Opera quae Supersunt Omnia Supplementum* (1862) in which the treatise is included. A few years later a second copy was found, bound with another work, eight pages long, entitled "Calculation (*Reeckening*) of Chances." The two works were published by J.P.N. Land in 1883 and by the mathematician D. Bierens de Haan in 1884. Van Vloten and Land included them in their edition of Spinoza's works, *Opera Quotquot Reperta Sunt* (1st ed. 1882, 1883; 2nd ed.

1895; 3rd ed. 1914), and they were continued in C. Gebhardt's critical edition in 1923.[1]

Apart from some discussion of reasons for crediting or doubting their ascription to Spinoza, the two works have received little attention since their republication. Yet they have a significant bearing on several interrelated problems: they present incidents from important stages in the history of modern mathematics; they permit a concrete reconstruction of the work and communication of a group of Dutch mathematicians with whom Spinoza was acquainted; and they provide explicit reminders concerning conceptions of the methods of mathematics and the relation of mathematics to other disciplines, which were widespread in the seventeenth century but are often ignored in interpretations of Spinoza's application of the geometric method to ethics. They are worth reading for the light they throw on these questions, whether or not Spinoza wrote them, but attention to the contents of the works increases rather than diminishes the probability that Spinoza was their author.[2]

In the Sixth Part of the *Discourse on Method* Descartes recounts the misgivings aroused by the condemnation of Galileo, which led him to abandon the publication of the principles of his physics and to publish instead illustrations of his method to enable others to follow a course similar to his. In 1633 he wrote to Mersenne that he was "almost resolved" to burn all his papers,[3] but instead he

---

[1] The documents bearing on the early history of the *Treatise on the Rainbow* are published in J. Freudenthal, *Die Lebensgeschichte Spinozas* (Leipzig, 1899): Lucas, p. 25; Kortholt, p. 28; Colerus, p. 83; Rieuwertsz, p. 227. The history is recounted in Carl Gebhardt, *Spinoza Opera* (Heidelberg, [1923]), IV, 431–34.

[2] J. Freudenthal finds reason to accept the authenticity of the *Treatise on the Rainbow* because a statement in the opening paragraphs accords with expressions found in the *Tractatus Theologico-Politicus*, but he questions the authenticity of the *Treatise on Chances* (*Das Leben Spinozas*, 2nd ed. edited C. Gebhardt, Heidelberg, 1927, pp. 292–3, 347). Gebhardt undertakes to refute the judgment of Bierens de Haan that the two treatises are set in different type (*Spinoza Opera*, IV, 433–434).

[3] Letter XLIX, *Oeuvres de Descartes*, ed. C. Adam and P. Tannery (Paris, 1897), I, 270–1.

reworked a portion of *Le Monde* into a treatise on *Dioptrics*, part of which he read in Amsterdam in 1635 to a group which included Constantyn Huygens.[4] Later that year he wrote, "As for telescopes (*lunettes*) I will tell you that, since the condemnation of Galileo, I have reviewed and entirely completed the treatise which I had earlier commenced on that subject; and, now that I separated it entirely from my *Le Monde*, I propose to have it printed separately in a short time."[5] In November 1635, he wrote to Huygens that he proposed to add the *Meteors* to the *Dioptrics* and to join to them a "preface."[6] In March 1636 he projected work was to consist of four "treatises" brought together under the title "The Project of a Universal Science which can Raise our Nature to its Highest Degree of Perfection, also the Dioptrics, the Meteors, and the Geometry, in which the most Curious Matters which the Author was able to Choose are explained in such Fashion that even those who have not Studied are able to Understand Them."[7] The figures, drawn by the son of Frans van Schooten, who was later to succeed his father in the chair of mathematics at Leyden,[8] were not yet ready in October.[9] In February 1637 Descartes replied to Huygens' objection to the use of the word "Discourse" in the title.[10] During the same year, the work was published in Leyden, anonymously, under the title *Discourse on the Method of Conducting one's Reason Well and Seeking the Truth in the Sciences, also the Dioptrics, the Meteors, and the Geometry which are Essays of this Method.*

The three treatises repeat the emphasis of the *Discourse*. Descartes brings the Geometry to a close by remarking that the method is adapted to transforming the problems of one class into an infinity of others and thus to solving each in an infinite number of ways.[11]

[4] Letter LIX to Golius I, 315.   [5] Letter LXI to ***, I, 322.
[6] Letter LXIII to Huygens, I, 329–30.
[7] Letter LXVI to Mersenne, I, 339.
[8] Letter XI, Descartes to Huygens, *Correspondence of Descartes and Constantyn Huygens 1635–1647*, ed. L. Roth (Oxford, 1926), p. 25.
[9] Letter XIII, pp. 27–29.
[10] Letter XVII, 34–35.
[11] *La Géométrie*, III, *Oeuvres de Descartes*, VI, 485.

Moreover, the ideal of providing a method for many men to use was realized in the group of Dutch amateurs and mathematicians which continued the discussions occasioned by the composition of the *Discourse on Method*. Frans van Schooten, the younger, translated the Geometry into Latin. The translation was published in 1649 with the *Notae Breves* of Florimond Debeaune and van Schooten's *Commentarii*. The second edition, 1659–1661, was expanded to two volumes by the addition of two letters of John Hudde to the original volume, *The First Letter on the Reduction of Equations* (pp. 401–506) and *The Second Letter on Maxima and Minima* (pp. 507–516) and by the constitution of a second volume made up of a redaction of van Schooten's lectures *Principles of Universal Mathematics or Introduction to the Method of the Cartesian Geometry* prepared by his pupil Erasmus Bartholinus; two treatises of Debeaune *On the Nature and Constitution of Equations* and *On the Limits of Equations* edited after his death by Bartholinus; John de Witt's *On the Elements of Curved Lines* in two books; van Schooten's *Treatise on Forming Geometric Demonstrations from Algebraic Calculation*, and a short Preface by Hudde. A third edition appeared in 1683 and a fourth in 1695. Men who were not professional mathematicians, in accord with the Cartesian ideal, contributed to the elaboration of the Cartesian method — de Witt was Grand Pensionary of Holland, Hudde studied medicine and became Burgomaster of Amsterdam, Bartholinus was a distinguished physician[12] — to such an extent that the commentaries assembled by van Schooten are an indispensable step in the development of Analytic Geometry. Christian Huygens, son of Constantyn Huygens, studied Descartes' *Geometry* under van Schooten.[13] Huygens began work on what was to become his *Dioptrics* in 1652. Van Shooten urged him, in 1654, to publish his work in a projected new edition of a Latin translation of the *Discourse on*

---

[12] J. L. Coolidge includes two of the group in *The Mathematics of Great Amateurs* (Oxford, 1949): Chapter IX is devoted to Jan de Witt and Chapter X to Johann Heinrich Hudde.

[13] Letter XCVIII Huygens to Descartes, *Correspondence of Descartes and Constantyn Huygens*, p. 235.

Method and the *Dioptrics* and *Meteors* of Descartes.[14] In 1657 he wrote to René-François de Sluse that it would appear shortly and that all the demonstrations were elaborated according to the Euclidean method.[15] He acknowledges in a letter to Leibniz in 1692 that there were many things still to be straightened out in the *Dioptrics*. It was published in his *Opuscula Postuma* in 1703.

Some of the chief figures in the history of the development of the Cartesian method in geometry, dioptrics, and meteorology are important in the life of Spinoza. Christian Huygens' name appears several times in Spinoza's letters, and Spinoza is mentioned in Huygens' letters. Huygens is prominent in the correspondence of Spinoza and Oldenburg in 1665. Spinoza wrote to Oldenburg (Letter 26) that Huygens has told him about Boyle's work on colors, thermometers, and microscopes because Spinoza was unable to read English, and Oldenburg asked (Letter 29) about Huygens' treatises on *Dioptrics* and *On Motion* and (Letter 31) for information concerning Huygens' work on pendulums. Spinoza supplied some information about Huygens' views on Descartes' laws of motion and on polishing lenses (Letter 32), which Oldenburg repaid (Letter 33) with information about Huygens' visit to London. Spinoza corresponded with Schuller in 1675 about Tschirnhaus' meeting with Huygens (Letters 70 and 72). Huygens was interested in the problem of sizes of lenses and of apertures and several of his letters of 1667 and 1668 to his brother Constantyn refer to Spinoza in treating these problems: he reproaches Constantyn for leaving Spinoza in error concerning Huygens' technique of polishing large lenses; he asks him to find out what size aperture Spinoza and Hudde use for 40 feet; he recalls that the "Jew of Voorburg" had lenses of admirable polish in his microscopes; he asks Constantyn to find out how well Spinoza is succeeding with large lenses; he is convinced that experience will refute "our Jew's" theory of apertures; he asks for information concerning what "our Israelite"

---

[14] Letter 201 van Schooten to Huygens, *Oeuvres Complètes de Christiaan Huygens*, I (The Hague, 1888), 301. Huygens' reasons for refusing are in Letter 203, p. 303.

[15] Letter 414, *Oeuvres Complètes*, II (1889), 66.

does; he is convinced that if the objectives of the Israelite are not good in his telescopes of 3 and 6 feet, he is still far from doing anything with those large apertures he worked up with Hudde; he acknowledges that experience confirms what Spinoza said, that small objectives in a microscope represent objects more distinctly than large, with proportional apertures, and then sets down measurements for a Campani eye-piece, enjoining his brother to say nothing about this to the Israelite, lest he or Hudde or others push on in this speculation which has still other utilities.[16]

Spinoza and Hudde are associated in the letters of Huygens. There are evidences of that association in Spinoza's letters. In 1671 Leibniz sent Spinoza *A Note on Advanced Optics* and asked him to get Hudde's judgment on it (Letter 45). Spinoza expressed his doubts concerning Leibniz' *pandochal* lenses, and reported that he had sent the copy to Hudde who had not had time to examine it (Letter 46). Three letters in the Spinoza collection (Letters 34, 35, and 36) illustrate the problems of the communication of ideas, despite occasional secrecies, in this circle of Dutch seekers of the truth. The three letters are concerned with problems of geometrical proof in the *Ethics* and in the *Principles of Descartes' Philosophy*, but the third goes on to a problem of polishing lenses, with a reference to the recipient's "small *Dioptrics*." The letters appear in the *Opera Posthuma*, without the name of the recipient, as Letters 39, 40, and 41. Van Vloten and Land supply the name of Christian Huygens in their edition but add a footnote that the figure (Figure 1) is not found in the 1703 edition of Huygens' *Dioptrics* and conjecture that an earlier version might have been communicated to Spinoza. Gebhardt makes the recipient John Hudde, but gives no evidence that Hudde wrote a small *Dioptrics*. They are published as Letters 1513, 1531 and 1541 in the *Complete Works of Huygens*, with a note that Huygens may have sent Spinoza some manuscript notes on his *Dioptrics*. The question Spinoza raised has to do with polishing convex-plane lenses. He proposed

---

[16] Letters 1601, 1603, 1606, 1608, 1611, 1615, 1633, and 1638, *Oeuvres Complètes de Christiaan Huygens*, vi (1895), 148, 151, 155, 158, 164, 168, 205, and 213–215.

to put the index of refraction at 3 to 2 for glass and to use small letters to designate the lines, such as z for NI. In 1653 Huygens had discovered that the spherical aberration of a convex-plane lense is less when the convex surface is opposite to the incident rays than when the plane surface is, and in 1666 he had completed the second part of the *Dioptrics* on the aberration of rays from the focus. In the fourth proposition of this work he considered convex-plane lenses, taking 3 to 2 as the index of refraction and using small letters to represent lines. His problems are different, but his equations are consistent with those Spinoza constructs.[17] The letter of Spinoza was written in 1666.

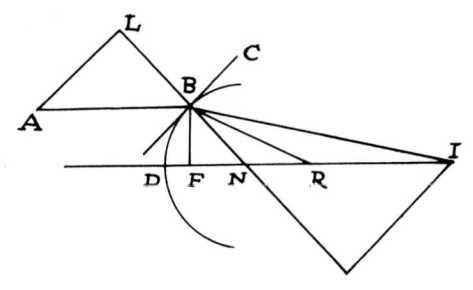

Figure 1.

This is not the only case in which Huygens and Hudde change roles. The editors of the *Complete Works of Huygens* call attention to the fact that van Schooten, when he was preparing the second edition of the *Geometria* of Descartes, asked Huygens to communicate to him any corrections or modifications he thought should be made. In 1654 Huygens sent him the annotations he had made in the margin of his copy. Van Schooten used these, sometimes without acknowledging their source. The editors quote Uylenbroek who proposed the conjecture that *Huddenius* should be changed to *Huygenius* on page 367 of the 1659 edition of the *Geometria*. They support this conjecture by pointing out that in 1655 Huygens had

[17] *Oeuvres Complètes de Christiaan Huygens*, VI, 281–296; see particularly the figure and equations on page 297 where he is concerned with the case of incident rays falling on the curved surface.

proposed the method used there to resolve the equation, but they also add that Hudde used an analogous method in his *Letter on the Reduction of Equations*, written in 1658, and may have explained his method verbally to van Schooten at an earlier date.[18]

The name of John de Witt does not appear in the correspondence of Spinoza. It appears, often in association with John Hudde, in the letters of Huygens. According to Lucas' biography of Spinoza, de Witt wished to learn mathematics from him and consulted him on important matters. De Witt gave him a pension of 200 florins which Spinoza relinquished when de Witt's heirs made difficulties about it after de Witt's death.[19] Spinoza was profoundly shocked by the murder of de Witt.[20] His name is mentioned in pamphlets against de Witt in 1672, the year of de Witt's assassination.[21] Leibniz wrote that Spinoza told him that he wanted to go out the day of the massacres of John de Witt and his brother to post a sign consisting of the words *Ultimi barbarorum* near the place of the crime, but his landlord had locked the door to prevent his going out and running the risk of being "torn to pieces."[22] There is no evidence that Spinoza did or did not know de Witt personally; but he did own one of de Witt's mathematical treatises, he might have had further information about his mathematical interests from Hudde, and he must have been profoundly interested in de Witt's political administration and policy.[23]

The brief Preface to the *Treatise on the Rainbow* places it in the midst of this tradition.[24] The treatise is published to aid the

[18] *Oeuvres Complètes de Christiaan Huygens*, XIV (1920), 412–415.

[19] *La Vie et Esprit de Mr. Benoit de Spinosa* (J. Freudenthal, *Die Lebensgeschichte Spinozas*), pp. 15–16.

[20] *Ibid.*, p. 19.

[21] *Ibid.*, pp. 194–195. [22] *Ibid.*, p. 201.

[23] For a survey of scholarly opinions concerning the relations between Spinoza and de Witt, see M. Frances, *Spinoza dans les Pays Néerlandais de la Seconde du* XVIIe *Siècle* (Paris, 1937), pp. 92–104. For de Witt's theories and policy and for the relation of the social and political milieu to Spinoza's thought, see L. S. Feuer, *Spinoza and the Rise of Liberalism* (Boston, 1958).

[24] The author of the Preface is unknown. He was probably a friend whom Spinoza had asked to read it and who had it in his possession when Spinoza

unlearned, but with the hope that it will not displease the learned. Three good examples of excellence in the art are cited for the youths of the Provinces: Hudde in his Reduction of Equations and his Maxima and Minima, Huygens in his many ingenious and no less perfect works, and de Witt in his Description and Calculation of Conic Sections.[25] The author of this work wants to ascend from the things known by a beginner and to make a beginning in his treatment of the Rainbow from principles, using only the first six books of Euclid. (Huygens in his letter to Sluse had also proposed to make his *Dioptrics* depend only on propositions from Euclid.) He had followed the recommendation of Horace to put these notes away for "more than ten years," and they have been published only to teach youth the utility of principles and the use of knowledge of algebra.[26]

died. Van Vloten suggests that it might have been John van der Meer to whom Letter 38 (*olim* 43) is addressed in 1666. We know nothing about van der Meer except that he asked Spinoza a question about the calculation of probabilities which is answered in that letter.

[25] Spinoza owned copies of the works of these men. See A. J. Servaas van Rooijen, *Inventaire des Livres Formant la Bibliothèque de Bénédict Spinoza* (The Hague, 1889); the list is reproduced in Freudenthal, *Die Lebensgeschichte Spinozas*, pp. 160–164. Spinoza had a copy of "Renatus Descartes *de Geometria*" (Quarto 20, pp. 149–150). He also had a copy of "a Schooten *Principia Matheoseos 1651*" (Quarto 38, p. 159), which appeared in Volume II of the second edition of the *Geometria* in 1661. If Spinoza's copy of the *Geometria* was also the second edition, it contained the two works of Hudde referred to in the Preface and the second volume contained de Witt's work. Spinoza had "Hugenii Zulichemii *Horologium Oscillatorium*, Paris, 1673" (Folio 16, pp. 130–1).

[26] *Spinoza Opera*, ed. C. Gebhardt, IV, 347. The reference to Horace was doubtless intended to identify the anonymous author to readers who knew Spinoza. Even the casual reader who was acquainted with Horace or Descartes would be likely to notice that Horace's rule had been changed from *nine* years to *more than ten years*. The change draws attention to the ten years which separated the date of publication from the death of Spinoza and it also covers the slightly longer period since the composition of the work. Horace had said *nonumque prematur in annum* (*Ars poetica* v. 388), and Descartes quoted the line in his letter to Mersenne concerning his reaction to the condemnation of Galileo, quoted above, reminding Mersenne that he had been the source of the advice, which Descartes now used to justify another year's delay in sending him the manuscript of the Treatise. This letter was included in the edition of

Spinoza states the problem which he thinks worthy of the attention of youthful lovers of learning (*de jonge liefhebbers der Wiskonsten*) in terms of the discoveries of "their great predecessor Descartes." Descartes had demonstrated not only that the primary or lower rainbow is caused by two refractions and one reflection, but also that the secondary or upper rainbow is caused by two refractions and two reflections. Moreover, he had proved that the maximum angle at which the lower rainbow can be observed, or its radius, can not be greater than 41°47′ and that the minimum angle at which the upper rainbow can be observed, or its radius, can not be less than 51°37′. But he does not state for lovers of algebra, as is customary, how he found the two rules of refractions which he used in computing his table. Spinoza proposes to give a brief algebraic demonstration of them.[27]

Descartes used an enlarged model of a waterdrop, a glass ball filled with water, to discover the refractions and reflections and to determine the angles of the two rainbows,[28] and then proceeded to the construction of his tables. The figure Spinoza used (Figure 2) is a reproduction of Descartes' figure[29] except for the addition of points L and V and of the lines extended to them, as well as the addition of the letters, M, T, and Y, and, since S is used for the line drawn to L, the substitution of X for Descartes' S. FY is the incident ray of light from the sun. In the primary rainbow, it is refracted at F, reflected at K, and refracted a second time at N; the observer is located at P. In the secondary rainbow, it is refracted at F, reflected at K and at N, and refracted a second time at Q; the observer is located at R. Since the calculation of refractions is based on the sines of angles rather than on the angles themselves, the angle of refraction of the incident ray is FH/HC. To avoid

the *Lettres de Descartes* published by Clerselier in three volumes, 1657, 1659, and 1667 (vol. II, pp. 349–351). There was a copy of the Dutch edition, "Descartes, Brieven," in Spinoza's library (Quarto 7, p. 140), of which the first volume appeared in 1661.

[27] *Ibid.*, 348–349.

[28] *Les Météores. De L'Arc-en-Ciel. Discours Huitième. Oeuvres de Descartes*, VI, 325–327.

[29] *Ibid.*, 337.

[11] SPINOZA ON RAINBOW AND PROBABILITY 543

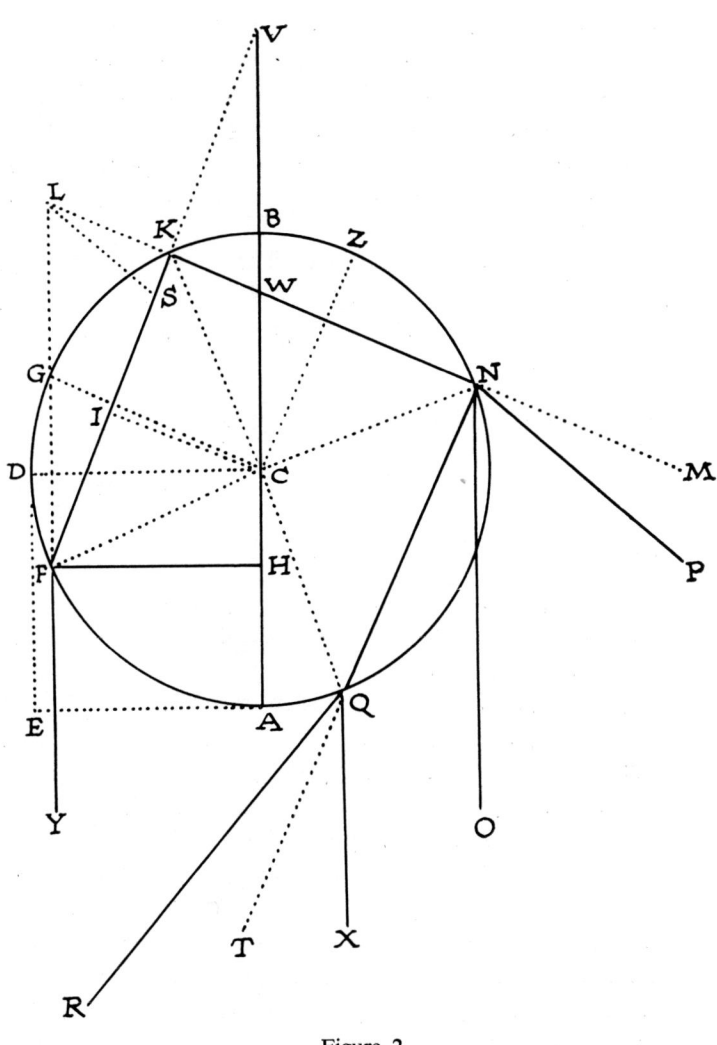

Figure 2.

fractions Descartes made the radius of the drop of water 10,000 units and constructed his first table by taking the ten lengths of HF which differ by 1,000 units between 1,000 and 10,000. He found a cluster of rays for the primary rainbow near 40° and for the secondary rainbow near 54°. He therefore constructed a second table by taking the nineteen lengths of HF which differ by 100 between 8,000 and 9,8000.[30] This gave him a maximum angle for the primary rainbow of 41°47′ and a minimum angle for the secondary rainbow of 51°37′.

The organization of the tables determines the three algebraic problems which Spinoza must treat. The two tables are composed of six columns: when HF is composed of 9,000 units the values are as follows:

Line HF	Line CI	Arc FG	Arc FK	Angle ONP	Angle SQR (or XQR in Spinoza's figure)
9,000	6,732	51°41′	95°22′	40°57′	54°25′

The three problems are to find the equations which determine, when HF is given, (1) the line CI, (2) the arcs FG and FK, and (3) the angles ONP and XQR.

The first problem is concerned with determining the index of refraction. Spinoza takes the index of refraction for water used by Descartes, 250:187, and sets up the proportion between HF and CI when the length of HF is 9,000 units, namely, $250:187 = 9,000:x$; or, $x = CI = 6,732$. But this proportion requires a proof that the ratio HF:CI is the index of refraction. Spinoza begins his proof by reference to the *Dioptrics, Discourse II*, where Descartes establishes the law of sines. In the figure which he constructs (Figure 3), beginning with the ratio of OP to RL as the index of refraction, he demonstrates by equal triangles (and a reference to Euclid, Bk. I, prop. 26) that $OP = HF$ and $RL = CI$. Therefore HF:CI is the index of refraction.[31]

---

[30] *Ibid.*, 338 and 339.
[31] Spinoza does not refer to *Discours* VIII, but Descartes there uses a similar

[13]   SPINOZA ON RAINBOW AND PROBABILITY   545

The second problem is solved by trigonometry. If the lengths of HF and of CF, the radius, are known, the sine of the arc FD can be found by the Pythagorean theorem. For HF = 9,000, Spinoza obtains .4358. If this is looked up in Lansberg's, van Schooten's

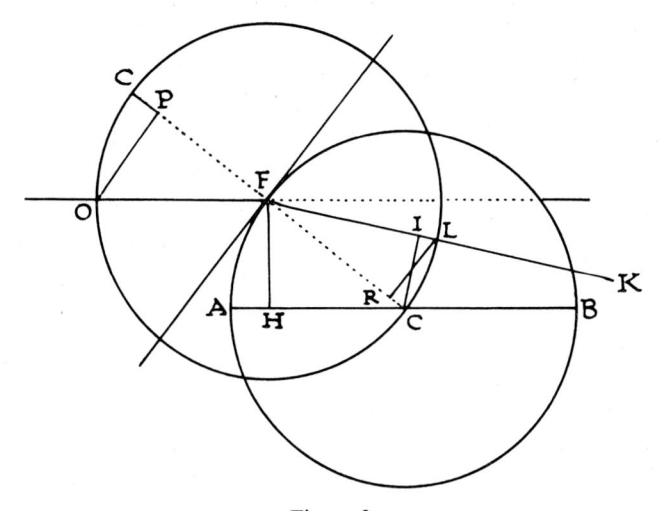

Figure 3.

or any other tables,[32] angle FCD is found to be 25°50′, or more precisely 25°50$\frac{1}{2}$′. Arc FG is double arc FD or 51°41′, and Descartes' value for arc FK, 95°22′, is found in the same way.

The third problem is the formulation of the rules for determining the altitudes of the two rainbows. Spinoza states the first rule,

method to equate the index of refraction of an elliptical lense with the ratio between the diameter through the foci and the line joining the foci. With appropriate changes from ellipse to circle, the figure which he uses (*Oeuvres de Descartes* VI, 170) is the figure used by Spinoza in Letter 36. (Figure 1 above.) In treating this problem, Spinoza and Huygens state the index of refraction as a ratio of lines drawn along the diameter of the circle. G. Milhaud makes use of this figure to prove that Descartes had discovered the sine law long before Snell wrote his paper and therefore was not guilty of the plagiarism he was charged with by Huygens (G. Milhaud, "Descartes et la Loi des Sinus," *Nouvelles Etudes sur l'Histoire de la Pensée Scientifique* [Paris, 1911], pp. 190–192).

[32] Spinoza had a copy of "Lansbergii Cyclometria nova" (Quarto 42, p. 163).

for the primary rainbow, "to find the angle ONP or the radius, that is, the altitude of the lower rainbow, add the arc FG to 180° and subtract twice the arc FK."[33] This rule, Spinoza observes, is stated clearly enough for those who want only to use it,[34] but it remains obscure to those who wish to know the principle of everything. Spinoza therefore states the rule in algebraic terms, as he did the problem treated in Letter 36. He uses a for a right angle, b for arc FG, c for arc FK, x for angle ONP, and y for angle GFK. The formulation of the rule is $x = b + 2a - 2c$, which Spinoza undertakes to "discover and demonstrate" (*uyt te vinden ende te bewyzen*) by the relations among the lines, angles, and arcs established in the first three books of Euclid. The second rule, for the radius or altitude of the upper rainbow, is angle XQR = arc FK − angle ONP, or $y = c - x$, which is also established by means of propositions from Euclid.

When Spinoza has completed the task of explaining the proportions and equations which Descartes used in the construction of his tables, he goes on to a more general formulation of the problem of the two rainbows in terms of maxima and minima. The starting point of his new line of inquiry is a reference to René-François de Sluse, canon of the Cathedral of Liège, Counselor of the Prince-Bishop of Liège, and a man learned in all the sciences,[35] who "demonstrated that all these lines, arcs, and angles can also be discovered mathematically." Spinoza's source for this statement is Isaac Barrow's *Lectiones Opticae*, Lectio XII. There Barrow quotes the judgment of the "distinguished Master Sluse, which a friend had communicated to him," in support of the conclusion Barrow draws "that Descartes could have determined his angle of the rain-

---

[33] *Spinoza Opera*, IV, 352.

[34] *Oeuvres de Descartes*, VI, 338: "Puis, ostant le double de l'arc FK, de l'arc FG adiousté à 180 degrés..."

[35] Sluse made contributions to mathematics, linguistics, history, medicine, chemistry and botany. His *Mesolabum*, in which he analyzed cubics and quartics, was published in 1659. Many of his demonstrations are found in his extensive correspondence with men like Oldenburg and Huygens. One set of curves to which he drew attention came to be known as the "pearls of Sluse."

bow without constructing tables."[36] Sluse had described a simple experiment, which he says he had performed many years ago, to determine the angle of the radius of the iris or bow of any refracting substance. If the rays of the sun are permitted to fall on a globe filled with a given liquor, the arc of the great circle cutting the illuminated area on the opposite side of the globe will have the same number of degrees as the radius of the bow. For water Sluse measured approximately 40°, which he found to correspond to the maximum value for ONP in Descartes' tables,[37] and he concluded that the tables are unnecessary, since the arc can be determined geometrically. Sluse's letter to Oldenburg was written in November, 1667; ten years earlier Huygens had written to Sluse concerning his use of the method of maxima and minima some time ago (*olim*) to determine, given the index of refraction of any diaphanous liquor, the angle under which the iris or bow should be seen, "without the construction of tables such as Descartes gives in his Meteors."[38]

Descartes had determined that the maximum angle ONP for the rainbow, that is, the angle at which light is most concentrated in the direction NP, is 41°30′, and that the minimum angle XQR is 51°54′.[39] What was in question in the changes introduced by Sluse, Huygens, and Barrow, was not the determination of the values of

[36] *The Mathematical Works of Isaac Barrow, D.D.* ed. W. Whewell (Cambridge, 1860), *Lectiones Opticae* XII, 14, p. 106. The friend was Henry Oldenburg. The passage of Sluse's letter concerned with the rainbow is quoted in Oldenburg's letter to Boyle, Nov. 25, 1667, *The Works of the Honorable Robert Boyle* (London, 1772), VI, 251. Oldenburg adds that Boyle will doubtless wish to communicate this to Wallis. The *Correspondance de René-François de Sluse* was published by M. C. Le Paige in the *Bullettino di Bibliografia e di Storia delle Scienze Mathematiche e Fisiche*, XVII (Rome, 1884), 427–554, 603–726. The letter to Oldenburg is No. 83, 662–623.

[37] Sluse, *op. cit.*, 623. Descartes *Oeuvres* VI, 339.

[38] *Oeuvres Complètes de Huygens*, Letter 397 (July 27, 1657), vol. II, 41. His method of measuring refractions is expounded in Letter 153 to G. van Gutschoven (March 6, 1653), vol. I, p. 226.

[39] *Les Météores*, p. 340. Descartes adjusted for the radius of the sun by adding 17′ to the maximum and subtracting from the minimum, giving ONP=41°47′ and XQR = 51°37′.

those angles nor the statement of the proportions which enter into that determination, but rather the choice of mathematical methods for the treatment of the problems. Descartes had used the index of refraction and the law of sines to schematize the values of angles ONP and XQR for all angles of incidence and had found the maximum ONP for the primary rainbow among the values calculated for ONP and the minimum XQR for the secondary rainbow among the values for XQR. His successors sought a mathematical determination of those angles without recourse to tables. Their methods continued to differ, and the differences throw light on the history of the development of analytic geometry. Barrow recognized that the angle described by Sluse is angle KCZ in Figure 3, and gave a geometric solution to the problem of its relation to ONP in the *Lectiones Opticae*, the first edition of which appeared in 1669.[40] Huygens set himself two problems in the Appendix to Book I of the *Treatise on Refraction and Telescopes* (written in 1652): if the index of refraction is given, to find the angle of the primary rainbow, and if the angle of the rainbow is given, to find the index of refraction of the refracting medium. He accepted the maximum ONP found by Descartes, 41°30′, demonstrated that ONP = 2 KCB (or KCZ) and then used Fermat's rule for maxima and minima to find the length of CH for which the angle KCB becomes a maximum, which can be calculated by means of the angles FCA and FCK.[41] In 1667 he undertook the solution of the same two problems concerning the index of refraction and angle of the secondary rainbow.[42] Spinoza's small treatise is of interest because he assumes that the "beginners," to whom the work is addressed, will be able to make the transition from a geometrical solution similar to Barrow's to a solution based on the maxima and minima of Hudde.

Spinoza undertakes to prove that angle ONP is always equal to 2 KCB and that XQR is equal to FK—KCB. Angle KCB or arc

---

[40] *Lectiones Opticae*, Lectio XII, 9–15, pp. 104–107.
[41] *Oeuvres Complètes de Huygens*, XIII (1916), 146–150.
[42] *Appendix viii au Premier Livre du "Tractatus de Refractione et Telescopiis," Oeuvres Complètes*, XIII, 163–168.

KB is designated by z. Two proofs are given for $x=2z$. The first proof consists in showing that, since ONM had been shown to be equal to $x+y$, AWN and KWV are also equal to $x+y$, and $KVW=y$. Angle FKC is then shown to be equal to $x+2y$ and to $2z+2y$; if $2y$ is subtracted from both sides of the equation $x=2z$. Spinoza says that the second proof was shown to him by a great amateur (*een groot liefhebber*). It had been proved in the first rule of Descartes that $x=2a+b-2c$. But arc KB or $z=a+1/2b-c$, for $BD=a$, $DF=1/2\ b$; if FK or c is subtracted from their sum, the result is KB or $z=a+1/2b-c$. Therefore $2z=2a+b-c$, and $2z=x$. The proof that $XQR=c-2z$ is reduced to substituting the value found for x in the equation already established in the second rule, that is, that $XQR=c-x$. Spinoza applies his two formulas to the arcs which he had used to illustrate his earlier proof: $KN=FK$; if FK is $95°22'$, angle ONP or arc $KZ=2a+b-c$, or $40°57'$, and angle XQR or arc $ZN=c-2z$, or $54°25'$.

Spinoza goes on to point out that KN, which is equal to c and which is the same in the two rainbows, is divided into two equal parts by Z. KZ or $1/2\ c$ is equal to two half radii and KB or z is the half radius of the lower or primary rainbow, or of the angle ONP. BZ, or $1/2c-z$ is half or the upper of secondary rainbow, or of the angle XQR. From this follows the solution of the two "delightful questions" mentioned in the beginning, namely, how to find the maximum lower rainbow, determined in its amplitude by the shadow above, and the minimum upper rainbow, determined in its smallness by the shadow below. Since the index of refraction was included in the questions, and since the maximum sine of the arc KB and the minimum sine of the arc BZ were found by algebra and by Hudde's rule, students of this art determining arcs on paper, inquire concerning the maximum altitude in the heavens at which the lower rainbow appears and the minimum altitude at which the upper rainbow appears. This and many other questions which could be added are left for the reader to seek and discover with trigonometric and logarithmic tables.

The *Calculation of Chances* is a short unfinished work.[43] It

[43] *Spinoza Opera*, IV, 360–362.

begins abruptly with the statement of five problems of probability, presents the solution of the first, and stops as abruptly as it began. The five problems with which it is concerned relate it to the same circle of theoretical inquirers that formed the background to the *Calculation of the Rainbow* and to a related development of mathematical method.

In 1654 the Chevalier de Méré asked Pascal a question concerning games of chance which led to a correspondence between Pascal and Fermat concerning the calculation of probabilities. Christian Huygens, who was then 26 years old, visited Paris in 1655. He did not meet Pascal, Fermat, or Carcavy, but he established connections with Claude Mylon and Roberval who had taken part in the discussion of de Méré's problems. The problems were of two kinds: "the problem of points" raised by de Méré (if several players put up stakes on the condition that the one who makes a given number of points in the game will win, how much of his stake should a player recover if he wishes to withdraw at any given stage of the game before any player has made the designated number of points?) and "the problems of dice" (the calculation of the odds of specific games or bets). When Huygens returned to Holland he started work on his *Treatise on the Calculation of Games of Chance* (*Tractaet handelende van Reeckening in Speelen van Geluck*). He sent the portion on the problems of dice to van Schooten, who suggested the problem which became Proposition xiv, the final proposition of the treatise, and urged Huygens to publish the work. Later van Schooten suggested that it be included as an appendix in his *Exercitationum Mathematicarum Libri Quinque*, and he undertook the preparation of the Latin translation. It was published in the Latin edition in 1657, under the title *De Ratiociniis in Aleae Ludo*, and in the Dutch edition in 1660.[44] Huygens explained in the letter to van Schooten dated April 27, 1657, which

---

[44] A detailed history of the development and influence of Huygens' treatise is given in the *Avertissement* to the edition contained in *Oeuvres Complètes de Huygens*, xiv (1920), 3–48. I. Todhunter, *A History of the Mathematical Theory of Probability from the Time of Pascal to that of Laplace* (Cambridge, 1865), places it in a larger, but less clearly developed, context of history.

was printed as preface to the treatise that some of the most celebrated mathematicians of all France have for some time been occupied with this sort of calculation, and the honor of first discovery therefore does not belong to him. But these learned men, although they have tested each other by proposing many difficult problems, have hidden their methods. He has therefore had to examine and establish the entire matter himself beginning with the elements, and he is unable to say whether they agree in their first principle. So far as the results are concerned, his solutions do not differ from theirs.[45] The first three propositions state Huygens' basic principles in calculating chances: (1) when a player has equal chances of gaining two sums a or b, (2) when he has equal chances of gaining a or b or c, and (3) when he has p chances of gaining a, and q chances of gaining b (his expectation is then $\frac{pa + qb}{p + q}$). The fourth to the seventh propositions treat the problem of points when there are two players, while the eighth and ninth propositions go on to the problem of points when there are three players. The tenth to the fourteenth propositions treat "problems of dice." The treatise closes with the statement of five problems, which are not solved, although the answers to problems 1, 3, and 5 are given. In the Prefatory letter Huygens explains that he did not give the resolutions to these problems because the statement of the reasoning that led to the answers would be too laborious and because it seemed useful to leave something for the reader to work out as exercise and pastime.[46]

The *De Ratiociniis in Aleae Ludo* had a wide influence, and many readers did work out the terminal five problems. P. R. de Montmort included the solution of the five problems in his *Essay d'Analyse sur les Jeux de Hazard*, Paris, 1708, (2nd. edition, 1713). A. de Moivre solved the second, fourth, and fifth in his *The Doctrine of Chances: or a Method of Calculating the Probabilities of Events in Play. The Second Edition, Fuller, Clearer, and more Correct than*

[45] *Oeuvres Complètes*, XIV, 57–59.
[46] *Ibid.*, 59. We know that problems 1 and 3 were suggested by Fermat in June 1656. *Oeuvres Complètes de Huygens*, I, 433–434.

the First, London, 1738 (the first edition appeared in 1718). The *Ars Conjectandi* of James Bernoulli, published posthumously in 1713, reprinted Huygens' treatise with a commentary by Bernoulli as the first of its four parts. Bernoulli gives the solution of four of the five problems there, but postpones the treatment of the fourth problem as well as a second solution of the third problem to Part III because it depends on the calculation of combinations, and he makes important departures from Huygens' method. Nicolas Struyck gives solutions to the five problems in his *Uytreekening der Kansen in het Speelen*, published in 1716.

Other members of the circle of Spinoza's acquaintances were deeply involved in the history of probability calculation. In 1665 Hudde wrote to Huygens about probability problems. Hudde submitted solutions for the second and fourth problems, for which no answers had been published. Huygens' solutions differed from those of Hudde. Bernoulli was later to point out that the second problem could be interpreted in three different ways: it is a problem of drawing balls from a set of eight white and four black balls — (1) the ball drawn may be returned after each play, (2) it may not be returned, or (3) each player may have his own set. Huygens gave the problem the first interpretation, Hudde gave it the second. From these problems they went on to the discussion of the advantages of the first turn under different conditions. They also discussed the fifth problem, which is likewise subject to two interpretations.[47] In 1671 Hudde wrote to Huygens concerning the method used by John de Witt in calculating life annuities. The States of Holland had in the past granted such annuities; using the facts made available by these annuities relative to the average life duration of persons who had received them, de Witt prepared a report and treatise concerning such transactions. In 1671 the States General passed a resolution to negotiate funds by life annuities.[48] Leibniz tried without success to obtain a copy of de Witt's

---

[47] *Oeuvres Complètes de Huygens*, XIV, 10–11, 31–48.

[48] An English translation of de Witt's treatise was published in 1852 by Frederick Hendricks, "Contributions to the History of Insurance and of the Theory of Life Contingencies, with a Restoration of the Grand Pensionary de

treatise.[49] He returns to the question when he treats probability in the *New Essays on the Human Understanding*. After having observed that lawyers treat of probabilities in their proofs, presumptions, conjectures, and indices, and doctors in their signs and indications, he proceeds to the mathematical treatment of probability.

> The mathematicians of our time have begun to estimate chances in relation to games. The Chevalier de Méré, whose *Agrémens* and other works have been printed, a man of subtle wit, and who was a gamester and philosopher, gave a start to the matter by framing questions about stakes, to ascertain how much the game was worth if interrupted in such and such a state. By this he induced his friend M. Pascal to examine a little into these things. The question spread and gave M. Huygens occasion to compose his treatise *De Alea*. Other learned men entered upon the subject. Certain principles were established, which were also made use of by the Pensionary de Witt, in a short

Witt's Treatise on Life Annuities," *The Assurance Magazine*, II (London, 1852), 232–249. The treatise is followed by a certification "that the method employed for that effect is perfectly discovered, and that the conclusion made therefore... depends on solid and incontestable mathematical foundations" signed by J. Hudde. (249–50). Hendricks traces the history of later references to de Witt's treatise, including citations from Leibniz, de Montmort, Condorcet, de la Lande, and Struyck.

[49] Hendricks, *op. cit.*, 250. Hendricks' authority for this statement is Montucla's *Histoire des Mathématiques*. He also quotes Leibniz's reply to the *Reflexions* of Bayle written about 1694, in which Leibniz places de Witt and Hudde in the historical sequence of inquiries started by the Chevalier de Méré. Leibniz notes that the Pensionary de Witt has pushed the reflections *de Alea* of Pascal, Fermat, and Huygens even further and has applied them to other more considerable uses, such as life-annuities, adding, "and Mr. Huygens has told me that Mr. Hudde has had still other excellent meditations on the question and that it is too bad that he has suppressed them together with so many others." (*ibid.*, 250–251). Todhunter quotes the same passage from Montucla more fully (*A History of the Mathematical Theory of Probability*, pp. 38–39), including the opening statement that Hudde and de Witt had worked on the problem of life-annuities, referring to the title of de Witt's treatise, but noting that he does not know the title of Hudde's work.

discourse printed in Dutch, upon life annuities. The foundation on which he builds consists in prostapheresis, that is to say, in taking an *arithmetical* mean between several equally admissable suppositions, and our peasants have made use of this for a long time in their *natural mathematics*.[50]

Leibniz states the principle as the axiom, *aequalibus aequalia*, for equal suppositions we must have equal considerations, and reiterates the judgment he has often made that a *new kind of logic* is needed to treat the degrees of probability, since Aristotle fell short of nothing more in his *Topics* than in undertaking only to set certain popular rules in some order, distributed according to commonplaces, without providing a balance necessary to weigh probabilities and to form a solid judgment on them.

Spinoza was obviously acquainted with the problems of probability on which his acquaintances were at work. In his letter to van der Meer (Letter 38) he found the question proposed to him very simple. The "universal demonstration" depends on this principle: that the fair player is he who makes his chance of winning or losing, or his expectation, equal to that of his opponent. Spinoza explains this equality in terms which recall Huygens' first three propositions. It is established by the prospect and the stake. If the prospects are the same for two players, the stakes must be the same; if the prospects are unequal, one player must stake as much more as his prospect is greater. In the case of a game in which three players play with equal chances, each stakes an equal sum and risks a third to gain two-thirds. If he withdraws before the game begins, he may take back one-third of the total stake, and another player may buy his chance by putting up the same stake. Spinoza then applies the rules for one guess of one of two numbers, for one guess and two guesses of one of three numbers, for three guesses of one of four numbers, and finally for four guesses of one of five numbers. He sums up by running the sequence of one, two, three, four, and five guesses of one of five numbers,

---

[50] *Nouveaux Essais sur l'Entendement Humain*, IV, 16. Quoted by Hendricks, *op. cit.*, 251.

and by remarking that the rule is the same whether it is applied to one man making a given number of guesses or the same number of men making one guess each.

The five problems with which Spinoza's treatise *On the Calculation of Chances* begins are Huygens' five problems. Spinoza had a copy of Huygens' treatise.[51] His edition seems to have been the Latin edition of 1657, but the problems are stated precisely, word for word, in the formulation of the Dutch edition of 1960. The form of the statement of the problem which he solves follows that of the statement of the rules in the *Treatise on the Rainbow*. Spinoza uses headings in both treatises, and in the customary pair, "rule" or "proposition" and "demonstration," Spinoza substitutes, for the second, "operation and demonstration" (*Werking en Bewys*),[52] a change which is in accord with his interpretation of geometric demonstration. The first problem is, "A and B play with a pair of dice on this condition, that A will win if he throws 6, and B if he throws 7. A is to take one throw first, then B two throws together, then A two throws, and so until one of them wins. The question is, what is the ratio of A's chance to B's. Answer: as 10,355 is to 12,276." Spinoza divides the problem, following the second rule of Descartes' Art of Thought,[53] into two propositions. The first proposition states the condition, that B will win if he throws 7, and A if he throws 6, provided that each makes two consecutive throws and that B throws first. The problem is simplified by omitting A's first turn in which he has a single throw. The ratio of A's chances to B's is 8,375 to 14,256. A's chance is called x, and the stake is a; therefore B's chance is $a-x$. When B throws, A's chance is x, but when A throws it is larger or y. Since B throws first, and since he can throw 7 in 6 of the possible 36 combinations of two dice, he has in the first two throws 11 chances to win a and 25 chances to miss his number, in which case A has his turn. Therefore, at the beginning A has 11 chances to lose, and 25 chances

---

[51] Quarto 27 "a Schooten *Exercitationes Mathematicae*," p. 154.
[52] *Spinoza Opera*, IV, 352, 355–356, 361, and 362.
[53] *Discours de la Méthode*, II, *Oeuvres* VI, 18.

to have y, or $x = \dfrac{25y}{36}$, and $y = \dfrac{36x}{25}$. The value of y can also be calculated when it is A's turn to throw. He can throw 6 in 5 of the 36 possible combinations of two dice. In two throws he has 335 chances to win a, and 961 to miss his number, in which case B has his turn and A's chance returns to x. Therefore $y = \dfrac{335a + 961x}{1296}$. But it has been shown $y = \dfrac{36x}{25}$, therefore $x = \dfrac{8{,}375a}{22631}$ which is A's chance, and consequently B's chance $= \dfrac{14256a}{22631}$ The ratio of A's chance to B's is as 8,375 to 14,256. Q.E.D. The second proposition adds A's initial turn of a single throw to the conditions set by the first proposition, and by means of a similar calculation establishes the ratio of A's chances to B's under these conditions as 10,355 to 12,276.

Spinoza's short treatises *On the Rainbow* and *On the Calculation of Chances* present a treatment of problems which throws light on the history of mathematics in the seventeenth century and gives body and significance to a group of men who influenced his thought. The treatises make no pretense to contributing to the solution of mathematical problems, for the first is an elementary treatise in which many of the proofs are explicitly attributed to other men, and the second is an effort to solve a problem raised by Huygens, using Huygens' method. They do, nonetheless, call to our attention questions of mathematical method which are of great importance in the development of mathematics and in the application of mathematics to other subjects, including ethics and philosophy in general, which was a widely held objective in the seventeenth and eighteenth centuries and which was then based on other presuppositions, and led to other consequences, than are attached to twentieth century efforts toward an objective similarly stated.

Spinoza's emphasis on the importance of principles, of algebraic rules, and maxima and minima, in the *Treatise on the Rainbow*, echoed the purpose of Huygens and Barrow to derive mathematically the angles of the rainbow and other optical laws. This may seem to historians a few hundred years later to be a difference between an empirical and a formal method. A. Wolf writes,[54] "Descartes tabulated the deviation of a ray passing through a drop against its angle of incidence on the surface, and showed from his table that, for a certain angle of incidence, this deviation was a minimum." Descartes doubtless used a globe filled with water to establish his theory that the primary rainbow is explained by two reflections and one refraction. But he did not *tabulate* observations of the behavior of a series of rays passing through the globe or through a drop; he constructed his tables mathematically. Descartes had made algebraic calculations and expressed his results in geometric lines, arcs, and angles. Spinoza sought, first, to state and prove the algebraic rule employed in those calculations and, second, to derive the angles directly from the mathematical calculations. In these calculations he, like Huygens, depended only on propositions from Euclid. The difference is more akin to that between the two manners of demonstration which Descartes distinguished in the geometric method, analysis and synthesis, than to the difference between empirical and formal demonstration. His successors did not add maxima and minima to his method: he found maxima and minima in his tables, while they generalized the formulae which he used in constructing his tables to find maxima and minima without tables. The same difference of method entered into the early history of analytic geo-

---

[54] A. Wolf, *A History of Science, Technology, and Philosophy in the 16th and 17th Centuries* (New York, 1935), pp. 269–270. Wolf makes a similar error in his interpretation of Descartes' law of refraction when he writes (p. 252), "His supposition that light increases its velocity upon passing into a denser medium met with much opposition from contemporary physicists." He goes on to treat Fermat as one of Descartes' critics on this point. Descartes distinguished between the velocity and the determination or direction of motion, and Fermat made the same distinction. G. Milhaud has pointed out that Fermat's criticism of Descartes was based, not on a refusal to make this distinction, but rather on Fermat's rejection of Descartes' postulate that the determination parallel to the surface of separation remains constant (*Nouvelle Etudes sur l'Histoire de la Pensée Scientifique*, pp. 186–188).

metry: Fermat laid its foundations in the calculation of maxima and minima, Descartes laid them in the solution of geometric problems, but the difference between them cannot be stated properly as a difference between an algebraic and a geometric method, for algebra and geometry entered into both methods, and analytic geometry in its later text-book sense emerged in methods generalized from both beginnings in the treatises of Debeaune and de Witt in van Schooten's edition of the *Geometria*.

The calculation of probabilities is a branch of applied mathematics, and a similar attention to principles directs attention to additional hypotheses as well as purely mathematical postulates. Huygens explained that he had examined the whole subject himself in order to begin with the elements, and he expressed doubts concerning whether his principle was the same as that used by the French mathematicians. At the beginning of his treatise he stated his non-mathematical hypothesis: "in a game, the chance which one has to win something has a value such that if one possessed that value one could get the same chance for oneself by an equitable play."[55] Having stated that principle, he proceeds immediately to the solution of particular problems, much as Descartes did in the *Geometry*, and it was left to his successors to discover the advantage of stating the general case and calculating combinations.

In Spinoza's treatises these differences carry some tinge of the philosophic consequences which appear in his discussions of geometric method. The difference between analysis and synthesis was not a difference between discovery and proof. Both methods were methods of discovery *and* of proof. Spinoza combines the two terms several times in his statements in the *Treatise on the Rainbow*, and the meaning of the method of discovery is further elucidated by his combination of the term "operation" (*Werking*) with "proof." Descartes and many of the other mathematicians of the seventeenth century sought to define conic sections according to the processes by which they are constructed; they sometimes

[55] *Oeuvres Complètes de Huygens*, XIV, 61.

justified such definitions by the continuity of the process of defining the figure and deducing its properties; and some of them held that axioms were deduced from definitions. Spinoza stated a preference for definitions which express the efficient causes of figures in the *De Emendatione Intellectus* as well as in his letter to Tschirnhaus (Letter 60), and Tschirnhaus (who was an outstanding mathematician) expressed all three of these convictions about the geometric method in his *Medicina Mentis, sive Tentamen Genuinae Logicae, in qua Disseritur de Methodo Detegendi Incognitas Veritates*. They are convictions which are important to the interpretation of Spinoza's use of the geometric method in the *Ethics*, and of his proof that the order and connection of ideas is the same as the order and connection of things.

ASPECTOS FILOSOFICOS DE LA POLEMICA JUDAICA EN TIEMPOS DE ḤASDAY CRESCAS

por J. M. Millás-Vallicrosa

BIEN PUEDE DECIRSE que el Judaismo en la España cristiana alcanzó sus más altas cotas en el siglo XIII, con Mošé ben Naḥmán, con Šĕlomó ben Adret, con Don Profeit Tibbón, con los colaboradores del rey Alfonso el Sabio: Don Abraham, Don Zag, Yĕhudá ben Mošé ha-Kohen, con el mismo Zóhar; en cambio, el siglo XIV ya inició el principio de una decadencia, con el enrarecimiento de los bandos judaicos y los grupos familiares, a fin de lograr la hegemonía, con los ecos que hallaron en España, las persecuciones desatadas con motivo de la Peste Negra y de los *Pastoureaux*, para encontrar un trágico epílogo en los saqueos y crímenes desatados en el mes de junio de 1391, en la ciudad de Sevilla, y propagados por gran parte de España.

Pero no por ello dejó este siglo XIV de presentar altos valores intelectuales y espirituales entre los judíos españoles. Y quizá fué en la España del Noreste, especialmente en Cataluña, donde hallamos estos valores hebraicos más distinguidos. En Barcelona encontramos, en la segunda mitad del siglo XIV, la escuela de R. Nissim Gerundí,[1] con sus alumnos o continuadores Ḥasday Crescas, En Profeit Durán (Efodi), Yosef Albó y otros, la cual supo polarizar un gran movimiento teológico y filosófico y supo remozar las bases en que se asentaba la antigua tradición filosófica. En verdad, con esta escuela o núcleo de estudiosos en

---

[1] Aparte los estudios y citas de H. Gross en *Gallia Judaica*, pag. 407 y de S.A. Horodezky en *Enzyklopaedia Judaica*, VII, 304–307, se pueden ver las numerosas citas que hacen a nuestro autor en I.F. Baer, *Die Juden im christlichen Spanien*, I, 306 sigs., 406, 417, 450, y *Toledot ha-yehudim bi-Sĕfarad ha-noṣrit*, pag. 243 sigs (2a edicion).

torno de R. Nissim, ya barruntamos como un cambio de cuadrante en las viejas doctrinas medievales para orientarse hacia nuevas posiciones,[2] Pero esta generosa corriente fué azotada en Barcelona por los vandalismos de agosto de 1391, eco de los iniciados en Sevilla, y con el saqueo del Call bercelonés se provocó la muerte, el exilio y la defeccion o aparente conversión de tantos judíos españoles. Fué un movimiento demagógico, subversivo, en el que las autoridades fueron desbordadas casi completamente. El mismo Ḥasday Crescas perdió un hijo en aquel *pogrom*, y es emocionante constatar la serie de documentos emanados de la Cancillería Real de Barcelona, en los cuales el Rey dicta medidas interesándose por la salvación de su respetado y querido R. Ḥasday Crescas.[3] Pero aquella explosión de vandalismo, con sus terribles consecuencias, habría de ahondar un abismo que dificilmente se podría salvar, y cuyas consecuencias llegaron hasta la expulsión de 1492.

Todo ello produjo en la España de finales del siglo XIV y principios del siglo XV un enrarecimiento, una tensión en la convivencia de los espíritus, que encontró sus válvulas en la polémica judaicocristiana, la cual si casi siempre fué dura, ergotista y poco humana, a lo largo de toda la Edad Media, ahora se manifestaba con una violencia por ambas partes, casi al rojo vivo. El grupo de intelectuales del sector judaico en Cataluña y Aragon: Ḥasday Crescas, En Profeit Durán o Efodi, Yosef Albó y otros, casi todos ellos polemizaron en medio de su ulterior actividad filosófica, científica o literaria, preludiando o coreando las grandes polémicas abiertas por el Papa Benedicto XIII en San Mateo, cerca de Tortosa, (1413–14).[4] No pretendemos en modo alguno internarnos por la

---

[2] Cf. la obra del Prof. H.A. Wolfson: *Crescas' Critique of Aristotle* (Cambridge 1929).

[3] Cf. en la citada obra del Prof. I.F. Baer *Die Juden im christlichen Spanien*, I, 660 y sigs., la serie de medidas que el rey Don Juan I tomó para proteger a los judíos que ya se veían amenazados; ya en la pag. 669 aparecen las medidas del rey para proteger a los familiares de Ḥasday Crescas y a otros judios, y para impedir que se les forzara al bautismo.

[4] Aparte las referencias hechas a esta celebre controversia en las dos obras citadas del Prof. I.F. Baer, véase la edicion y estudios que de la misma ha hecho el Dr. A. Pacios: *La disputa de Tortosa*, vols. I y II (Madrid, 1957).

enmarañada selva de tales polémicas, pero sí desearíamos ofrecer al lector algunos puntos de vista filosóficos o teológico-filosóficos que afloraron en alguna de tales polémicas. Sea ello como una modesta contribución al Homenaje ofrecido a mi muy querido y admirado amigo el Prof. H. A. Wolfson, quien tanto ha ilustrado el pensamiento filosófico de Ḥasday Crescas.

Hay que tener en cuenta que la Apologética entre los judíos españoles siempre estuvo sensiblemente vigilante en pro del legado de la fe, tanto de la fuente de la Revelación como de la Tradición. Pensemos en R. Abraham ben David con su obra *Emuná Ramá* luchando contra los caraitas en pro de los títulos de la tradición rabínica; en Yĕhudá ha-Leví quien su obra *El Kuzarí* levanta una verdadera fortaleza en pro de un Sionismo teológico,[5] y donde hace une acerba crítica — como un nuevo Algazel — contra las teorías filosóficas paganizantes. El mismo Maimónides en su *Moré nebukim* no duda en cercenar su adhesión y pleitesía a Aristótcles en diversos puntos concernientes a la Metafísica. Y si bien luego, con las luchas entre maimonistas y antimaimonistas, se exacerbaron los ánimos y se compartieron dos corrientes: racionalista la una y conservadora la otra, no puede negarse que, al fin, se impuso una posición de compromiso, la de R. Šĕlomó ben Adret de Barcelona, posición que podemos considerar influyó en la Escuela de R. Nissim Gerundí. Claro está que siguió, más o menos vivaz, la posición racionalista con un averroismo hebraico, bastante parecido al averroismo latino, del que encontramos un buen ejemplo en Isaac Albalag.[6]

Pues bien, deseamos captar ecos de tales posiciones filosóficas en algunas polémicas judaicocristianas, de la generación subsiguiente a la de R. Nissim Gerundí, o sea, la generación de Ḥasday Crescas, en las cuales polémicas sus autores tuvieron que aguzar sus armas en aquel momento tan crítico, de fines del siglo XIV y principios del siglo XV, cuando el judaismo peninsular se enfren-

---

[5] Cf. mi obra: *Yĕhuda ha-Levi como poeta y apologista* (Madrid-Barcelona, 1947).

[6] Cf. la reciente obra del Prof. G. Vajda: *Isaac Albalag, averroïste juif, traducteur et annotateur d'Al-Ghazālī* (Paris, 1960).

taba con una de las pruebas más duras de su historia. Hay que tener en cuenta que en aquella época tan torturada, los judíos españoles y singularmente los de Cataluña, Mallorca y Aragón tenían una gran preparación filosófico-teológica, se había ya digerido y comentado todo el legado de Aristóteles, se habia hecho no sólo la crítica de su Metafísica sino incluso la de su Física[7] y se ensayaban nuevas posiciones; además, los judíos catalanes y los mallorquines están entonces muy impuestos en las diversas ciencias matemáticas, astronómicas, cosmográficas, gracias sobre todo al impulso comunicado por los reyes Pedro el Ceremonioso y su hijo Juan I el Cazador. De modo que ellos se creían facilmente los auténticos representantes de un frente científico, filosófico, y por esto hemos de constatar en algunas de sus polémicas la conciencia de tal privilegiada posición, que a un lector moderno podrá parecer desorbitadamente extremada.

Nos vamos a fijar primeramente en la más célebre de tales obras polémicas, en la *Iggéret "Al těhi ka-aboteka"* de Isaac ben Moše ha-Leví, más conocido con su nombre catalán *En Profeit Durán*, con cuyas iniciales se hizo el anagrama *Efodi*, en latin, *Ephodeus*. Nacido en Perpiñán, capital del Rosellón, que entonces pertenecía a la Corona de Aragón, o quizá, cerca de Montpellier, se formó, segun era costumbre en su época, en toda la vasta enciclopedia cultural que podía presentarse ante un estudioso judío: Filosofía, Astronomía, Medicina, Gramática, Literatura; al parecer, mantuvo estrechas relaciones con Ḥasday Crescas y con su familia. Seguramente se beneficiaría de aquel crepúsculo de saber y cultura que había ido perdurando especialmente entre los judíos de la Corona de Aragón, sobre todo en Barcelona, gracias a la decidida protección de los reyes Pedro el Ceremonioso, su hijo Juan I, y la reina Violante. Nuestro Efodi había estudiado, quizá bajo la guía de Ḥasday Crescas, la Filosofía y conocía a fondo las doctrinas sustentadas por Yěhudá ha-Leví en *El Kuzari* y las de Maimónides en la *Guia de los vacilantes*; pero los puros conocimientos científicos y filosóficos se interferían en la mente de nuestro autor con

---

[7] Cf. la citada obra del Prof. H.A. Wolfson: *Crescas' Critique of Aristotle*.

cuestiones de caracter astrológico y aún místico-mágico, sobre las propiedades del numero 10 o del número 7, en lo cual se reconoce la influencia del gran Abraham ibn ʿEzra. En todo caso, nuestro autor se movia en el círculo intelectual judaico de Barcelona y, en general, de Cataluña, a finales del siglo XIV. Ello se echa de ver en sus respuestas a unas cuestiones astronómicas que le formuló Šealtiel Gracián Ḥen, que florecía en Barcelona; nuestra obra es de hacia el año 1383. En el año 1393 nuestro Efodi dirige una epístola de pésame a En Joseph Abraham, hijo de Don Abraham ben Isaac ha-Leví, rabino que había sido de Gerona. Aun en el año 1395 Efodi escribía su obra sobre calendario judaico *Ḥešeb ha-efod* escrita en verso, por razones mnemotécnicas.

Pero mientras tanto habían ocurrido sucesos muy graves para nuestro autor, asi como para muchos de sus compañeros de comunidad israelita de Barcelona; la ola de estragos antisemitas que habia empezado en Sevilla llegó a Barcelona hacia finales de julio del 1391, y a pesar de las medidas de las autoridades, de las diligencias del rey Don Juan I, ausente de la ciudad, el furor popular se desbordó contra el Call barcelonés, de modo que sólo el bautizo pudo salvar a muchos judíos en aquella hora cruelmente fatídica. Uno de estos conversos forzados fue nuestro Efodi. Segun parece, a base del prólogo a la edición que de nuestra obra se hizo en Sabionetta (1554) y luego en Constantinopla (1577) por medio de Isaac ben Abraham ben Yĕhudá Aqrish,[8] nuestro autor Efodi junto con otro converso Bonet ben Gudán,[9] decidieron dirigirse a Tierra Santa, como en viaje de penitencia y perdón por su apostasía, y allí volverían a profesar su antïguo Judaismo.

[8] La obra fué muy pronto comentada profusamente por diferentes autores judaicos, los cuales aparecen en la mencionada edición de Constantinopla, 1577. En los tiempos modernos ha sido editada por A. Geiger en *Melo ḥofnayim* (Berlin, 1840), y aun se ha editado acompañado de diversos comentarios o traducciones. En el *Oṣar ha-wikkuḥim* de J.D. Eisenstein (New York, 1928), figura en las pags. 94–98.

[9] Al parecer, era descendiente del astrónomo En Bonet Bonjorn, cuyas Tablas estudiamos ultimannente. Cf. *Sefarad*, XIX (1959), 365–371: "Una traducción catalana de las Tablas astronómicas (1361), de Jacob ben David Yomtob, de Perpiñán," artículo que luego reproducimos en nuestra obra

Primero, hizo el viaje nuestro Maestre Profeit, mientras que su amigo Bonet se retrasó unos días en Avignon, y en tal coyuntura llegó a la ciudad papal el célebre converso Pablo de Santa María, —antes llamado Don Šelomó ha-Leví— quien llegó a ser Obispo de Burgos y Canciller del reino de Castilla;[10] allí en Avignon, hablaron largamente los dos conversos Pablo de Santa Maria y Bonet ben Gudán, y éste, ganado por las razones apologéticas del primero, renunció a su judaismo, y en este sentido escribió a nuestro Efodi. Renunciaba, pues, a su ulterior readmisión en la religión judaica. Puede comprenderse la penosa impresión que esta decisión produjo en el Maestre En Profeit Durán. Contestación a la misiva de Bonet a Efodi es la Epístola *Al tĕhi ka-aboteka*, que éste envió al primero, en la cual, el autor, lleno de despecho, de pena, se produce en estilo como sarcástico, irónico, pero manteniendo bien altas las posiciones que el Judaismo de su época postulaba en orden a una superior racionalidad de sus doctrinas, a una auténtica armonía de su doctrina religiosa son los principios de la Filosofía y de las Ciencias entonces imperantes. Se comprende que aquel escrito apologético sólo pudo salir de la pluma de un científico, que se ufanaba de sus conocimientos filosóficos y científicos, y que seguramente el recipiendario En Bonet tambien debía de ser otro científico — quizá hijo del astrónomo Yaqob ha-Poel, tambien conocido con el nombre de Maestre Bonet[11] —, para que pudiera calibrar adecuadamente tales razones filosóficas y científicas empleadas por Efodi en su carta apologética.

La epístola que Efodi envió a su amigo David Bonet ben Gudán — despues de su conversion, conocido por Maestre Astruc Francisco Deuscorones(?)[12] — está redactada en estilo de prosa rimada,

Nuevos estudios sobre historia de la ciencia española, pag. 271 sigs. (Barcelona, 1960).

[10] Cf. el estudio del P.L. Serrano: *Los conversos Don Pablo de Santa María y Don Alfonso de Cartagena* (Madrid, 1942), y el del Prof. F. Cantera: *Alvar García de Santa María. Historia de la Judería de Burgos y de sus conversos mas egregios* (Madrid, 1952) (ambas obras publicadas por el Instituto Arias Montano de Estudios Hebraicos y Oriente Próximo).

[11] Cf. nuestra anterior nota 9.

[12] Encontramos dudosa la exacta transcripción de la grafía hebraica de

según era el gusto de la época, con acopio de expresiones rebuscadas, de citas y alusiones bíblicas, pero todas ellas destilando una cierta amarga ironía por el abandono que ha hecho David Bonet respecto de la fe de sus padres y antepasados. Para nuestro autor las razones y excusas alegadas en la carta de David Bonet explicando su conversión decidida al cristianismo, son razones algo veladas y especiosas, pero que se percibe en el fondo de las mismas el desahucio que David Bonet hace de las creencias de sus padres. Y muy pronto ya asoman puntos de vista filosóficos en la respuesta de Efodi. Para su contendiente David Bonet es un absurdo o una quimera suponer que la razón y la fe religiosa son dos luces, pues la razón sería del todo extraña a la creencia religiosa, así como ésta no tiene nada que ver, ni nada que ganar, con los argumentos y pruebas que pueda aportar la razón. Esta no conoce el camino donde mora la Luz. Este sería el sentido del pasaje bíblico: "El justo en su fe vivirá."[13]

A base de tal razonamiento por parte de David Bonet, podemos inducir que su posicion era la típica en muchos espíritus de la época, entre ellos Abner de Burgos — o sea, el converso Alfonso de Valladolid — y seguramente Pablo de Santa María,[14] en el sentido de que en la vivencia de la fe religiosa había un elemento de gracia, un don carismático, una inefable iluminación que superaría en mucho los medios de la prueba razonadora. Al parecer, para un tal científico, filósofo, como era Efodi, esto era inaceptable, y lo expone sólo a título de amarga e irónica decepcion — segun se desprendería, tambien "la razón sería tortuosa de caminos" — pero sin entablar polémica sobre ellos. La buena intención de su amigo le induce también a ello. Pero no quiere renunciar a exponer y subrayar a su amigo David Bonet toda la gran diferencia que va de la doctrina religiosa judaica, sobre todo

este nombre. Desde luego que no puede admitirse la transcripcion que se había sugerido: *Dios Carne.*
[13] Habacuc 2:4.
[14] El prof. I.F. Baer probó en su artículo publicado en *Tarbiz*, XI (1940), 116–87, que incluso tales ideas encontraron cierto eco en la obra teológico-filosófica de Ḥasday Crescas.

en sus relaciones con la filosofía y las ciencias, respecto a la nueva fe cristiana profesada por su amigo David Bonet. Y así empieza la larga e irónica requisitoria, cada una de cuyas partes empieza con el *Leitmotif*: *al tĕhi ka-aboteka* "No seas como tus padres."

En la primera de estas injunciones Efodi insta irónicamente a su antíguo hermano en la fe mosaica que no siga creyendo en el Dios de la unidad absoluta, האחדות הפשוטה, incompatible son toda idea de pluralidad, הרבוי, unidad entendida por sus antepasados a tenor de lo que se desprende de su propia definición. De modo que Efodi entiende que la unidad adscrita por el Judaismo al Dios bíblico se adecua perfectamente con la unidad lógica o filosófica. En cambio, le insta a su amigo, siguiendo el tono amargo y mordaz, para que, al tenor de la fe cristiana, entienda que este Dios es unidad y tres al mismo tiempo, o tres y unidad; pero esta trinidad no supone una entidad relativa, צרופיי, o sea —, por lo que entendemos de la expresión tan rápida y alusiva del autor — una simple yuxtaposición matemática de unidades, sino que es una entidad substantiva, עצמיי, que se unifica, מתאחד, de un cabo a otro cabo. Y remata el autor su ataque a fondo diciendo interjectivamente que una tel doctrina, tan contraria a la razón, ni la boca puede expresarla ni el oido puede alcanzar a percibirla bien. De modo que la polémica antitrinitaria la centra nuestro autor no en bases bíblicas que chaquen con las aportadas por los cristianos,[15] sino en la absoluta irracionalidad filosófica de tal doctrina. La polémica es de pronunciado y casi exclusivo carácter filosófico.

En la siguiente requisitoria Efodi insta a su amigo, converso al Cristianismo, que no imite a sus antepasados, los cuales creyeron en un Dios no afecto a ninguna variación, tal como dice la expresión bíblica: "Yo soy Yahwé, no cambio."[16] Ellos negaron rotundamente de su Dios la corporeidad, pero le atribuyeron un simple פשוט y puro Intelecto, a tenor de lo que les enseñaba la Filosofía cuyas enseñanzas siguieron acérrimamente. Sólo a modo de condescendencia admitieron otra interpretación, más proclive a lo

---

[15] Como era lo corriente en la gran parte de las polémicas judaicocristianas en la Edad Media.
[16] Mal. 3:6.

sensible, para los débiles y limitados de espíritu.[17] Seguidamente dirige a su amigo converso una dura sátira contra los excesos antifilosóficos y antirracionales de su nueva fe: le dice irónicamente que él no actue a tenor de la conducta correcta de sus antepasados, sino que no excluya de Dios la corporeidad y la composición, y, además, que afirme de El que revistió carne en una de sus formas o personas,[18] si bien ello no afectó a toda la Trinidad. A continuación sigue una pintura rápida, pero muy despectiva, de la doctrina de la redención de los pecados humanos, ¡no habría encontrado Dios otro modo para la salvación de los hombres!; de la doctrina de la concepción virginal de la segunda persona de la Trinidad en María, desde luego que el autor niega la supuesta base bíblica[19] para defender tal doctrina.

En el párrafo siguiente Efodi encomia en gran manera los esfuerzos de los antepasados judaicos para profundizar en el relato de *Ma'aše Bĕrešit*, Obra de la Creación,[20] a fin de encontrar sus arcanos y sus objetivos científicos "de modo que se armonizara con la Filosofía." Ellos idearon diferentes explicaciones, siete hipótesis, sobre el tema del Paraíso Eden, los ríos, el árbol de la ciencia del Bien y del Mal, y aún sobre Adám y Eva y sus túnicas de piel. El autor alude aquí a las diferentes exégesis filosóficas del relato de la Creación, a base de las cuales a menudo quedaba más o menos desnaturalizado el relato bíblico. Y acto seguido se dirige acerbamente a su amigo converso, diciendole que él no recurra a tales exégesis sino que — a la usanza de su nueva fe — interprete el relato bíblico de un modo literal, y aún añada la doctrina del pecado original, el cual sólo podía ser redimido y

---

[17] Es la exégesis tan socorrida, sobre todo entre los filósofos, del sentido traslaticio, alegórico, que hay que dar al texto sagrado, huyendo de los antropopatismos de la interpretación literalista.

[18] El autor emplea la expresión תואר que en este contexto tiene el valor y sentido que le damos.

[19] Especula sobre el sentido de la palabra עלמה, empleada en Isaias 7:14 y en otros pasajes bíblicos.

[20] La *Obra de la Creacion* y la *Obra de la carroza*, מעשה מרכבה, aludida en Ezequiel, I, constituian dos centros capitales de la problemática exegética, con vertiente cosmológica y teológica.

borrado por el Redentor. Esta doctrina del pecado original, sigue diciendo Efodi, fué innovada por el príncipe de los apóstoles, cuyo nombre es como el del maestro de David Bonet. Como quiera que éste fue influído por Pablo de Burgos, no hay duda que Efodi alude al apóstol San Pablo.

En la requisitoria siguiente Efodi presenta un verdadero despliegue de sus doctrinas y teorías filosóficas, las que coteja irónicamente con la nueva fe de su amigo converso: Sus antecesores judaicos fueron llevados por los fundamentos del intelecto a reconocer o aceptar necesariamente los principios o fundamentos lógicos, físicos, metafísicos, lo mismo que las consideraciones o teorías matemáticas; todo lo cual, y segun sus categorías, reporta sus consecuencias. Y con el estilo poético de la prosa rimada encomia Efodi cómo los autores judaicos, a base de aquellos fundamentos científicos edificaron en el palacio del intelecto altas torres, y supieron profundizar para alcanzar las vías y categorías de la reflexión, y a fin de distinguir entre las diversas clases de argumentación lo que es demostrativo y lo que no lo es. Los autores judaicos supieron hacer honor a Aristóteles y a sus *Ocho libros*;[21] pusieron toda su atención en las nobles Matemáticas, supieron descubrir secretos dignos de todo elogio, y de las profundidades del mar de la ciencia del numero (Aritmetica) y de la Geometría supieron extraer valiosas perlas; en la mesa de la ciencia astronómica, חכמת התכונה, comieron manjares deliciosos, y en la cúspide del monte de la ciencia Física levantaron altas estelas, y en lo referente a la Metafísica alcanzaron secretos escondidos, inestimables.

De esta manera, el científico que era Efodi, dotado de una cierta cultura casi enciclopédica, tiene conciencia de todos lo merecimientos de la aportación judaica en la ciencia medieval, y no deja de prorrumpir como en un canto o elogio, de carácter

---

[21] O sea, la enciclopedia lógica conocida con el nombre de *Organon*, incluida la Retórica y la Poética; sobre la recepcion por los autores judaicos, de los libros del Organon, a través de traducciones hechas del árabe al hebreo, cf. M. Steinschneider, *Die Hebraeischen Uebersetzungen des Mittelalters*, pag. 43 sigs.

[11] POLEMICA JUDAICA EN TIEMPOS DE CRESCAS 571

apologético en este caso. Pues para Efodi la aportación científica de los cristianos no sólo no puede parangonarse con la judaica, sino que quiere ver en la doctrina cristiana un impaliable irracionalismo, una contradicción con los principios del razonamiento lógico. Para Efodi es una piedra de tropiezo lógico, una muestra de este impaliable irracionalismo la simple enunciación de la doctrina de la Trinidad; ella ya es una conculcación de los principios lógicos. Además, esta doctrina cristiana tambien choca con los principios de la ciencia matemática, de que lo grande y lo pequeño se han de diferenciar, de que el número es un conjunto de unidades.

La doctrina de la Eucaristía en modo alguno puede compaginarse con los postulados y axiomas de la ciencia matemática y física. ¿Cómo es posible que el cuerpo del Mesías se encierre en el tamaño pequeño de una hostia? ¿Y que los miles y centenares de cuerpos del Mesías correspondientes a los miles y centenares de hostias, en los diferentes santuarios, sean una y única cosa? A los cristianos no les hacen mella los principios de la ciencia física, de que todo movimiento se da en un tiempo, y que es imposible que el movimiento y el reposo se den al mismo tiempo en un objeto dado. Estos principios físicos se ven contradichos por la doctrina cristiana que admite al Mesías estar en paz en el cielo, y al mismo tiempo, descendiendo a los altares para revestir las hostias consagradas por boca del sacerdote, sea cual fuere la ciencia o la virtud o la dignidad de éste, pues dichas palabras consagratorias actuan no por la dignidad del que las dice sino por su origen, ya que remontan a la última Cena del Mesias con sus apóstoles y discípulos.

Desde luego que este estilo de polémia judaicocristiana, ofrecida en este opúsculo de Efodi, no es el corriente en la Polémica medieval. Efodi se nos presenta teniendo una alta conciencia del valor de la aportación científica judaica, lo cual redundaría en mayor prestigio y mérito de su fe religiosa; en cambio, silencia del todo la aportación científica o filosófica cristiana y aún se empeña en defender la obvia incompatibilidad de la Lógica, de la Matemática y de la Física con algunas doctrinas cristianas. Comprendemos bien la alta conciencia que Efodi tiene de la aportación judaica a las

Ciencias y a la Filosofía, pero no atinamos a comprender su desconocimiento o su silenciamiento de la aportación cristiana, del gran esfuerzo que las escuelas cristianas llevaban a cabo, precisamente en aquella segunda mitad de siglo XIV, desde los maestros en Artes, nominalistas muchos de ellos, de la Universidad de Paris, hasta la misma Barcelona, en la cual, bajo el mecenazgo real de Pedro el Ceremonioso, tanto se esforzaron cristianos y judíos en diversas ciencias, desde la Astronomía y Astrología hasta la Medicina y Agricultura. ¿No habían calculado las nuevas Tablas astronómicas del rey Don Pedro el Ceremonioso, después de largas observaciones con ayuda de grandes aparatos astronómicos, dos sabios cristianos, los maestros Dalmau de Planes y Pere Gilbert, y estas no fueron después reducidas a la 8a esfera por el judío Ya'aqob Carsono?[22] De las mismas se guarda texto en catalán, en latín y en hebreo. Pues bien, este paraleismo del esfuerzo científico entre judíos y cristianos en su pais de Blarcelona, no podía pasar desapercibido a Efodi; ¿porqué este silenciamiento suyo de los méritos científicos que tenían los cristianos, como si no existieran? Además, tampoco podemos ocultar que su presentación de las doctrinas cristianas como absolutamente reñidas con la razón, peca de muy superficial y chapucera. Desde los tiempos de los Santos Padres hasta el florecer de las escuelas teológicas, ya dominicana ya franciscana, se había tratado ampliamente de la problemática teológica cristiana, y muchas de las pretendidas dificultades alegadas por Efodi hacía tiempo que ya estaban contestadas y resueltas.

Por desgracia, a continuación el tono empleado por Efodi en su epístola apologética ya toma un tono subido de ironía y de

[22] Hace ya largo tiempo que venimos dedicando nuestra atencion a estas Tablas astronómicas del rey Don Pedro el Ceremonioso; en el año 1953, con ocasion del VII Congreso Internacional de Historia de las Ciencias, celebrado en Jerusalén, leimos una comunicación: "En torno a las Tablas astronómicas del rey Pedro IV de Aragon" (publicada, en parte, en las *Actes* de dicho Congreso, pags. 451–540, y reinserta en mi obra *Nuevos estudios sobre historia de la ciencia española*, pags. 279–85; hoy nos satisface referirnos a nuestra edición crítica y largo estudio de dichas Tablas astronómicas (Barcelona-Madrid, 1962).

caricatura, que supone un verdadero abuso de su pretendida posición científica. Dice que la esfera celeste imposibilita el movimiento recto y que tampoco sería posible el que el cuerpo del Mesías pasara continuamente, durante el dia y la noche, a través de dicha esfera celeste, horadándola o trepanándola, para encerrarse en el cuerpo de las hostias consagradas. Desde el dia de su ascensión a los cielos hasta el dia presente ya han transcurrido 1360 años,[23] y tantas serían las veces que el Mesías habría pasado a través de la esfera celeste, que su cuerpo estaría casi como una criba (!).

Asimismo se encarniza contra el misterio de la Eucaristía, sosteniendo que entraña una negación de los principios de la ciencia Metafísica, segun los cuales es imposible que al mismo tiempo se predique de una cosa la afirmación, חיוב, y la negación, שלילה, y que es imposible que se transforme el accidente en substancia y la substancia en accidente; tambien se opondría dicho misterio al principio metafísico que afirma que la substancia existe en su substancialidad, mientras que el accidente se da en el soporte o substrato que existe en dicha substancialidad. Así aceptando dicho misterio eucarístico, tendríamos que el Mesías en el Cielo no sería afectado de movimieto, mientras que el Mesías que se contendría en el cuerpo de la hostia, en el altar, sería capaz de movimiento, de modo que se predicaría del Mesías, al mismo tiempo, el movimiento y la carencia de movimiento, en contra de aquel principio metafísico. Del mismo modo tenemos que la substancia de la hostia antes de las palabras de la consagración es la substancia del pan, mientras que después de las palabras de la consagración aquella substancia de pan queda transformada en simples accidentes, sin soporte o substrato en su substancialidad. Asimismo, elle se opone a los principios de la ciencia Física, segun la cual nuestros sentidos, en estado de normalidad, no pueden engañarnos.

Asimismo este misterio eucarístico se opondría (פלילות)[24] al

---

[23] El autor computa desde el año de la muerte de Jesus y de su ascensión a los cielos, que solía calcularse como el año 33 o 34 de la Era cristiana, lo cual coincide casi con el año 1396 que se atribuye a la fecha de radaccion de nuestra obra.

[24] No se registra esta valencia terminológica de tal palabra en el *Thesaurus*

principio lógico de que el todo es mayor que la parte, pues con dicho misterio tenemos que el todo es igual a la parte y viceversa, puesto que el cuerpo del Mesías lo mismo se encuentra en la hostia entera que en una partícula de la misma, y contra ello no vale el ejemplo, aducido por los cristianos, del espejo roto en diversos fragmentos, en cada unode los cuales se refleja la misma imagen. Otras muchas razones de indole física se podrían aducir contra tal misterio cristiano, pero, dato su número, Efodi renuncia a exponerlas, pues ya basta con las razones aducidas.

En los párrafos siguientes ya no se encuentran argumentos de índole filosófica, sino más bien Efodi quiere probar en ellos sus conocimientos en la primitiva historia de la Iglesia, y cómo en un principio se practicaban en ella los antiguos ritos de la Sinagoga. Antes de terminar, dedica Efodi una amarga alusión al maestro de su amigo Bonet, o sea, Pablo de Santa María, muy querido y celebrado por su alumno: dice que, segun Bonet, Pablo Burgense recuerda la imagen de Jesucristo y casi se equipara al Papa. Efodi habla de Pablo de Santa María como con cierta reticencia: dice que no sabe si se encuentra entonces en Roma o en Avignon, y que tambien le son conocidas sus diversas actividades tanto en la Astronomía — cuestiones de las excéntricas y de los epiciclos — como en otras ciencias. Siguiendo en el mismo estilo, dice Efodi que no en vano el Rey — de Aragón (?) — dió a Pablo de Santa María valiosos dones, y tampoco en vano eligió al hombre único en Israel, el cual es Rabi Ḥasday Crescas, y a quien honró en gran manera, invitándole a palacio, teniéndole siempre consigo, por el gran amor que le profesaba.[25] Siguen algunos detalles sobre la actuación de Pablo de Santa María, el maestro de su amigo David Bonet, tanto en España como en Avignon; y ratificando su sentimiento por la conversión cristiana de David Bonet y, en cambio, certificando su perenne fidelidad a la fe judaica, termina su carta nuestro Efodi.

Tanto o más que por su estilo irónico se caracteriza nuestra

philosophicus linguae hebraicae et veteris et recentioris, de J. Klatzkin, III, 191.

[25] Ya vimos anteriormente, cf. la nota 3, las muy buenas relaciones de la corte real aragonesa con Maestre Ḥasday Crescas.

obra por el especial carácter filosófico, científico, de sus argumentos apologéticos, por la acusada conciencia de los méritos científicos y filosóficos del Judaismo, de la ardua exégesis de sus escrituristas y teólogos, los que supieron concordar la fe revelada con los principios científicos y lógicos. En esto se diferencia profundamente no sólo de la restante apologética y polémica judaica de su tiempo, tan densa, prolífica y torturada, sobre todo en los países de la Corona de Aragón,[26] sino también se distingue de la otra obra polémica de Efodi, el *Séfer kĕlimat ha-goyim* "Libro de la confusión de los gentiles," obra escrita algo posteriormente a la anterior, hacia el año 1397, dedicada a Ḥasday Crescas, distribuída en doce capítulos,[27] y en la que se hace una dura crítica de los principales dogmas y doctrinas cristianas, pero partiendo principalmente de un estudio de los datos evangélicos y bíblicos. Se notará en dicha obra la formación filosófica del autor, pero su apologética ya no se centra especialmente en puntos de vista filosóficos y científicos como en la Epistola que hemos estudiado. En la obra *Séfer kĕlimat ha-goyim*, Efodi, se produce análogamente que Ḥasday Crescas en la obra casi contemporánea, escrita en lengua española — hoy perdida — y traducida posteriormente (1451) al hebreo por Yosef ben Šem Tob, con el nombre *Biṭṭúl ʿiqqeré dat ha-noṣerim* "Refutación de los fundamentos de la religión cristiana,"[28] o sea, a base de una crítica porfiada y despiadada del texto evangélico y de la exégesis cristiana. La obra de Efodi supera, al parecer, a las de sus contemporáneos, y logró una larga influencia, pues el *Séfer kĕlimat ha-goyim* influyó en las obras apologéticas de Šem Tob ben Isḥaq ben Šaprut *Eben boḥan* y de Šimeon ben Ṣemaḥ Duran, *Qéšet w-magén*, todas ellas índices, algo más tardíos, del clima de la polémica judaicocristiana en el Noreste de España.

---

[26] Cf. en especial el conspecto bibliogràfico que presenta Y. Rosental en su articulo "Sifrut ha-wikkuaḥ ha-anti-noṣrit ad sof ha-mea 18" en *Aréset*, II, 130–179 (Jerusalén, 1960).

[27] Cf. la edición de A. Poznanski en la rev. *Ha-zofé* (Budapest, 1913–14), III, 99–113, 143–180; IV, 37–48, 81–96, 115–132.

[28] Cf. la edic. de Eisenstein en su mencionado *Oṣar*, pp. 288–310.

BURIDAN AND A DILEMMA OF NOMINALISM

by ERNEST A. MOODY

I

JEAN BURIDAN, REMEMBERED through the centuries for the story known as "Buridan's Ass," was the most able and influential philosopher of the university of Paris during the fourteenth century. His achievements in the field of mechanics, brought to light some fifty years ago by Pierre Duhem, have made him known to students of the history of science, and recent studies by Anneliese Maier have drawn attention to his remarkably advanced discussions of some problems in the philosophy of science.[1] But in logic and metaphysics Buridan's work was no less impressive, although up to the present time it has not received the attention it deserves. The distinctive feature of his work in metaphysics is the use of the method now known as "logical analysis," whereby philosophical problems are formulated as questions concerning the meaning and reference of terms and the truth conditions of sentences. This method, known in the late Middle Ages as the *via moderna*, was used by Ockham in his theological and philosophical writings, but it was applied by Buridan to many problems which Ockham had not treated or on which he had only touched.

---

[1] Pierre Duhem, *Etudes sur Léonard de Vinci*, III (Paris, 1913); and Anneliese Maier, *Metaphysische Hintergründe der Spätscholastischen Naturphilosophie* (Rome, 1955), pp. 273-338. Relevant texts, with critical discussion of Buridan's contribution to mechanics, are translated in *The Science of Mechanics in the Middle Ages*, by Marshall Clagett (Madison, Wisconsin, 1959), pp. 505-682. Buridan's mechanical theories are also discussed in two articles of mine: "Laws of Motion in Medieval Physics," *The Scientific Monthly*, LXXII, 1 (January 1951), 18-23; and "Galileo and Avempace: The Dynamics of the Leaning Tower Experiment," *Journal of the History of Ideas*, XII, 2 (April 1951), 163-193, and XII, 3 (June 1951), 375-422.

One such problem, which has been much debated in recent decades by philosophers concerned with formal semantics and the foundations of logic and mathematics, affords a striking illustration of Buridan's use of this method as a tool of philosophical inquiry. This is the problem of the analysis of statements in indirect discourse, containing such verbs as 'knows,' 'believes,' 'desires,' 'promises,' or other verbs which take as grammatical objects expressions specifying what it is, in the given case, that is said to be known, believed, desired, or promised. The peculiar difficulties involved in the analysis of such sentences were brought to light by Frege in 1892, and they have given rise to a variety of proposed solutions, none of which seems to be fully adequate.[2]

This problem is far from being an idle dispute about words. It involves one of the fundamental issues of metaphysics and theory of knowledge, debated since the days of Socrates. Since the terms occuring in the subordinate clauses of sentences in indirect discourse purport to designate what it is that is said to be known or believed, the question of what such terms denote is the question of what kinds of entities constitute the objects of knowledge or of belief. Are the objects of knowledge the individual things existing in the world of space and time? Are they timeless essences of an abstract nature, as Plato supposed? Are they the words themselves or, as Berkeley supposed, ideas in the mind of the person said to have the knowledge or belief? The problem of analysis of sentences of this sort has revived the ancient controversy over

---

[2] Cf. Gottlob Frege, "Über Sinn und Bedeutung," *Zeitschrift für Philosophie und philosophische Kritik*, 1892; translated under the title "On Sense and Nominatum" by H. Feigl, in *Readings in Philosophical Analysis*, ed. by H. Feigl and W. Sellars (N.Y., 1949), pp. 85–102. The problems raised by Frege in this essay have given rise to an extensive literature of discussion: by Bertrand Russell, *An Inquiry into Meaning and Truth* (London, 1940) ch. 12–15; by Rudolf Carnap, *Meaning and Necessity* (Chicago, 1947), pp. 96–144; by W.V. Quine, *From a Logical Point of View* (Cambridge, Mass., 1953), pp. 102–129 and 139–170, and *Word and Object* (N.Y., 1960), pp. 141–156 and 191–216; and by many other authors concerned with the "logic of belief."

universals among contemporary philosophers of mathematics and of language.[3]

Before considering Buridan's treatment of this problem, we may illustrate the nature of the difficulty involved in it with an example adapted from Frege. Consider this sentence: 'Peter believes that the evening star is a planet.' What does the expression 'evening star,' occurring in the subordinate clause of the sentence, denote? If it denotes the object ordinarily named by the phrase 'evening star,' then it must likewise denote the object named by the phrase 'morning star,' since the two phrases name the same object. Now it is a general logical principle that when two expressions have the same denotation, one can be susbtituted for the other in any sentence without altering the truth value of that sentence. If, then, in the above sentence the phrase 'evening star' denotes the celestial body ordinarily named by it, we should be able to substitute 'morning star' for 'evening star' in this sentence without changing its truth value. But such is not the case, for it may well be that although Peter believes that the evening star is a planet, he will stoutly deny that the morning star is a planet, claiming that it is a fixed star. It would seem, then, that what Peter believes to be a planet is not the object ordinarily denoted by the phrase 'evening star,' for if it were, we would face the paradoxical conclusion that Peter both believes and does not believe that this object is a planet.

Because of this difficulty Frege concluded that when a term occurs in a clause following on a cognitive verb such as 'believes,' 'knows,' or the like, the term does not denote its ordinary referent, but denotes another entity which Frege described as the "sense" (or meaning) associated with the term in its ordinary usage. Frege thus distinguished between two types of entity, or between objects of meaning and objects of reference. His distinction has been adopted and developed by C. I. Lewis, Alonzo Church, and in an in-

---

[3] This has been pointed out by Quine, "On What There Is," *Review of Metaphysics*, 1948; reprinted in *From a Logical Point of View* (Cambridge, Mass., 1953), pp. 1–19.

direct way by Rudolf Carnap. It has however been criticized by Quine insofar as it involves commitment to a Platonist ontology of intensional entities duplicating the universe of concrete particulars. Those who, like the mediaeval nominalists, repudiate such an ontology, are faced with the task of finding an alternative analysis of sentences in indirect discourse which will not involve commitment to any objects other than those belonging to the domain of individuals. Let us consider how Buridan, the leading nominalist of the university of Paris, employed the techniques of late mediaeval logic in facing this dilemma of nominalism.

II

Although Buridan takes account of the problem in discussing various issues raised in Aristotle's *Metaphysics*, his most direct treatment is found in a work entitled *Sophismata*. This work, containing eight chapters, is extant in an edition published at Paris during the last decade of the fifteenth century, although one manuscript version has been identified in the Amplonian collection at Erfurt.[4] The work is devoted to a group of problems of a logical or semantical nature, formulated in the manner of paradoxical statements which seem to be both true and false. One such problem, generating a certain type of paradoxical sentence known as the *insolubile*, involves the reflexive use of the terms 'true' and 'false,' as in the classical Paradox of the Liar.[5]

It is in the fourth chapter of his *Sophismata* that Buridan takes up the problem of sentences in indirect discourse, in connection with what he calls 'appellative terms.' These are terms which,

---

[4] The present study is based on this edition, printed at Paris by Antoine Denidel and Nicolas de la Barre under the title *Sophismata Buridani*, a copy of which is in the Harvard College Library, through whose courtesy I have obtained a photostatic copy of the work.

[5] The significance of this paradox for the philosophy of language was made evident by A. Tarski, "Der Wahrheitsbegriff in den formalisierten Sprachen," *Studia Philosophica* I (1936), 261–405. In my book, *Truth and Consequence in Mediaeval Logic* (Amsterdam, 1953), pp. 101–110, Buridan's analysis of this type of paradox is presented.

when used in a sentence, involve an oblique or indirect reference to some thing or things other than those which the term directly denotes, or for which it stands. The term 'father,' for example, occurring in the sentence 'Tom is a father,' directly denotes the individual named by the word 'Tom,' but the condition of it being applicable to denoting Tom is that there is or has been another individual of whom Tom was the male parent. Similarly, if we say 'Socrates was an Athenian,' the word 'Athenian' is appellative of the city of Athens, and its applicability as a designation of Socrates, in this sentence, implies the condition that Socrates was born in Athens. Yet the sentence does not affirm this condition, but it affirms the identity of the object named by the proper name 'Socrates' with one or another of the objects denoted by the term 'Athenian.' How, or on what conditions, this latter term specifies the objects it denotes is not what the sentence affirms, although the truth or falsity of the sentence is conditioned by whether or not there is an object denoted by the term. An appellative term, in Buridan's use, corresponds to what Ockham called a connotative term, and to what Aristotle, in the *Categoriae*, called a denominative term.[6]

This theory of extensional connotation, or of oblique reference, was used by Ockham as a means of eliminating the Platonist or "realist" doctrine of intensional connotation — i.e., the doctrine that general terms have indirect reference to abstract or universal *objects of meaning* distinct from the concrete particulars which they directly denote. Although, for Ockham and for Buridan,

---

[6] *Sophismata Buridani*, cap. IV: "Primo enim sciendum est, quod terminus innatus pro aliquo supponere dicitur appellare omne illud quod ipse significat vel consignificat preter illud pro quo supponit.... Tertio notandum est quod secundum diversos modos positivos adiacentie rerum appellatarum ad res pro quibus termini supponunt, proveniunt diversi modi predicandi, ut in quale, in quantum, in ubi, in quomodo se habet hoc ad illud, etc. Ex quibus diversis modis predicandi sumuntur diversa predicamenta." As J. Bochenski remarks, *Formale Logik* (Freiburg-München, 1956), p. 205, Buridan's analysis of appellative terms involves the principle of multiple quantification, at least implicitly. As we shall see, this principle becomes explicitly involved in his analysis of sentences in indirect discourse.

general terms may connote or consignify things other than those for which they stand, the things so consignified are of the same logical type (or belong to the same domain of entities) as those directly denoted by the terms. If Socrates is a father, this does not imply that there is an abstract entity called 'fatherhood' which inheres in, or is participated by, the individual Socrates. The only entities signified or consignified by a term are individual or singular things; connotation is construed extensionally, not intensionally. This is indeed the thesis of nominalism, as a thesis of the philosophy of language: that all cognitively significant statements can be analyzed, or paraphrased, in a purely extensional language whose sole domain of reference is the domain of concrete singulars.[7]

Nominalism is not committed to materialism in the sense of holding that the domain of individuals is limited to those individuals which are material bodies. A nominalist can admit angels into his universe, provided that they are individual angels; it is not angels, but angelhood, that he finds repugnant to his ontology. He may also admit that there are thoughts, or concepts, on the same condition that they are particular entities or events. What distinguishes the nominalist from the realist or conceptualist, with regard to concepts, is his denial that the *objects* of thought or of conception are abstract or universal entities; *acts* of thought or of conception, as psychic events associated with the usage of words in speech or in reading or writing, are denizens of the universe of concrete particulars, however obscure their nature may be in other respects.

The extensional analysis of appellative terms encounters no

[7] Cf. W.V. Quine, "Designation and Existence," in *Readings in Philosophical Analysis*, ed. cit., pp. 50–51: "As a thesis in the philosophy of science, nominalism can be formulated thus: it is possible to set up a nominalistic language in which all of natural science can be expressed." Ockham's detailed procedures of nominalistic reduction of the significations of general terms, for each of the modes of signification distinguished by Aristotle in his *Categoriae*, are found in his *Summa logicae, Pars prima*, ch. 1–62 (edited by Philotheus Boehner, St. Bonaventure, N.Y., 1951, pp. 8–175). They are also discussed in my book, *The Logic of William of Ockham* (N.Y. and London 1935) pp. 53–175.

great obstacles in the ordinary contexts of discourse about physical objects and occurrences. But when we turn to statements containing such words as 'knows,' 'believes,' 'is aware of,' and the like, this analysis runs into the difficulties raised by Frege. Buridan, after discussing appellative terms in general, takes up these difficulties. He introduces them with a few *sophismata* which are strikingly similar to the examples adduced by Frege. The first, originally propounded by Aristotle in the *De sophisticis elenchis*, is the sentence, 'You know the person approaching' (Tu cognoscis venientem). We assume that the person is at some distance away, and that when you are asked if you know that person, you reply, 'I do not know him.' Despite your disclaimer, we argue that you do know him, as follows: The person approaching is your father; you know your father; therefore you know the person approaching. The analogy of this sophism to the case of Peter and the evening star is obvious.

Buridan's second sophism is the following sentence: 'You know that the pennies in my purse are of an even number.' It is assumed that you have not looked in my purse, and that in fact you believe there is only one penny there. Yet we argue that the sophism is true, as follows: You know that two is an even number; the pennies in my purse are two; therefore you know that the pennies in my purse are of an even number.[8]

After stating several sophisms of this type Buridan proceeds to discuss the source of the difficulty involved in them. Because we can apprehend or specify what is one and the same object, in more than one way, we can institute different words for designating that same object, corresponding to these diverse ways of identifying

[8] The first of these sophisms is drawn from Aristotle, *De soph. elen.* ch. 24, 179a 33 ff.; the second is suggested in Aristotle's *Anal. Post.* I, ch. 1, 71a 30–33. This latter sophism is similar to an example used in many recent discussions of the problem: Copernicus knew that $9 > 7$; the number of planets is 9; therefore Copernicus knew that the number of planets is greater than 7. In all of these cases, the arguments rest on the substitution of expressions denoting the same object, within the clauses following on the verb 'knows' or 'believes,' just as in the case of the 'evening star' and 'morning star' example.

it. These differences in the ways a thing may be denoted reduce, in general, to differences in connoted conditions of applicability of the word to the object it denotes; as, for example, in the case of the two expressions 'author of Waverly' and 'author of Ivanhoe.' When we use words *for* their objects, in sentences formed by means of the verb 'is' or by the extensional operators of universal or particular quantification, the truth or falsity of the resulting sentence is conditioned only by whether the denoted objects satisfy its syntactical form. How, or by what means of specification, these objects are denoted, is not part of the truth condition of the sentence. On this account, terms which denote the same object or objects, regardless of the ways in which they may do so, are interchangeable in such a sentence without alteration of its truth value.

But such verbs as 'knows,' 'believes,' 'understands,' and the like, determine that the terms falling within their scope, in sentences, denote their objects only according to the connected modes of specification according to which the terms were instituted to designate. The cognitive verbs thus constitute a special type of variable-binding operator. Like the extensional operators, they determine an identification of objects denoted by the terms governed by them; but unlike the extensional operators, they condition this denotation by the further requirement that these objects be denoted in just the ways in which these terms can denote them. Thus when it is said, 'Tom is aware of something white,' the sentence is true only if Tom is aware of something as being white; if he is aware of that thing, but not in that way, the sentence is false. For example, he might with his eyes shut become aware of a lump of sugar by tasting it; he is then aware of something sweet. And though this object of which he is aware is in fact white, he is not aware that it is white; hence, properly speaking, it should not be said that he is aware of something white (quod cognoscit album).

As Buridan puts it, the cognitive verbs determine that the terms following on them connote determinately and explicitly the *rationes* according to which they denote their objects. On this account substitution of another term denoting the same object, but according to a different way of specifying it, is not valid within the scope of these cognitive verbs. If however the term occurs *outside* the scope of the cognitive verb, by preceding that verb in the sentence, its denotation is not thus conditioned by its connoted mode of specification, and it may be replaced by any other term which can denote the same object. Thus, in the case of Tom and the lump of sugar, we may truly say that something white is such that Tom is aware of it, even though Tom is not aware of it as something white. Here the expression 'something white' occurs outside the scope of the verb 'is aware,' and it is not necessary that we, in referring to the object of which Tom is aware, specify that object in the same way that Tom does.[9]

According to Buridan's analysis, then, the principle that expressions having the same denotation are interchangeable without altering the truth value of the sentence in which they occur, is not valid for expressions falling within the scope of the cognitive verbs. To this extent Buridan's analysis is in accord with that of

---

[9] *Sophismata Buridani*, cap. IV (*post sophisma* 12): "Propter ista sophismata sciendum est quod ista verba 'intelligo,' 'cognosco,' 'scio,' et huiusmodi de quibus post dicemus, et participia et nomina inde descendentia ut 'intelligens,' 'cognoscens,' 'intellectio,' 'cognitio,' etc., faciunt in terminis cum quibus construuntur quosdam modos speciales appellationum. Nam quia eandem rem possum cognoscere secundum multas diversas rationes, et isti rei secundum diversas rationes diversa nomina imponere ad significandum eam, ideo talia verba faciunt terminos cum quibus construuntur appellare rationes secundum quas imposita sunt nomina ad significandum, et non solum res cognitas ad extra sicut faciunt alia verba. Aliter tamen a parte ante et a parte post; nam a parte post illi termini appellant determinate et precise suas rationes proprias, sed a parte ante appellant eas indifferenter sub disiunctione ad alias rationes quibus res significate possunt significari et intelligi. Propter quod ista propositio non est vera, 'Cognosco venientem,' proprie loquendo, nisi cognoscam eum secundum eam rationem secundum quam dicitur veniens, licet cognoscerem bene secundum alias rationes. Et sic non sequitur, 'Cognosco Sortem, et est veniens, ergo cognosco venientem,' quia licet cognoscam illum secundum illam rationem secundum quam dicitur Sortes, non tamen cognosco ipsum secundum illam rationem secundum quam dicitur veniens. Sed a parte subiecti bene sequitur, 'Sortem cognosco, et Sortes est veniens, ergo venientem cognosco.' ...Non ergo sequitur, 'Venientem cognosco, ergo cognosco venientem,' immo est possibile quod ignoro venientem. Sed bene sequitur, 'Cognosco venientem, ergo venientem cognosco.' "

Frege. But in an important respect his analysis differs from that of Frege, and also from that of most other recent logicians. Buridan does not admit a shift of denotation on the part of the term occurring in the cognitive context; the term continues to denote what it ordinarily denotes, and it does not denote (though it explicitly connotes) the mode of specification which constitutes its "sense." Nor is the occurrence of terms in such contexts non-designative, as Quine contends.[10]

Because terms occurring in cognitive contexts are held by Buridan to denote the objects ordinarily denoted by them, Buridan can, and indeed must, admit the operation known as existential generalization with respect to a term occurring within the scope of the cognitive verb. Thus this consequence is held to be valid: 'Peter believes that the evening star is a planet, therefore there is something such that Peter believes it to be a planet.' This something, which Peter believes to be a planet, may be specified *outside* the scope of the verb 'believes' by any expression which denotes this object, and hence by the expression 'the morning star.' We may therefore infer the following sentence, 'The morning star is such that Peter believes it to be a planet.' But the further inference, 'therefore Peter believes that the morning star is a planet,' is invalid because this sentence implies not merely that the object, which we who state the sentence are specifying as the morning star, is believed by Peter to be a planet, but it carries the further implication that this object is specified by Peter as the morning star. And this is not the case.[11]

---

[10] Cf. W. V. Quine, *Word and Object* (N.Y., 1960), pp. 141–156. What Quine calls a "not purely designative" occurrence of a term is suggestive of the mediaeval *suppositio materialis* or *suppositio simplex*, as contrasted with its "significative" use in *suppositio personalis*.

[11] The contrast between 'A is such that Peter believes that it is B,' and 'Peter believes that A is B,' is analogous to that drawn by Quine (*Word and Object*, pp. 149–150) between 'Tom believes Cicero *to have* denounced Catiline,' and 'Tom believes *that* Cicero denounced Catiline.' Quine calls the first construction *transparent*, and the second *opaque*, with respect to the position of the term 'Cicero' in each sentence. Failure of substitutivity in the opaque construction is taken by Quine as evidence of non-referentiality on the part

Up to this point Buridan's discussion has been concerned with the special case of the non-interchangeability of singular terms of diverse connotations within the scope of cognitive verbs. While admitting non-interchangeability he does, as we have seen, admit existential generalization with respect to such terms in such occurrences. This is to admit the validity of quantification from outside a belief context, binding a variable within the scope of the modal operator, this bound variable being of the ordinary type whose range of values is the extensional domain of individuals. Thus Buridan's admission of quantification into modal contexts does not involve any ontological commitment to a domain of intensional entities of abstract character constituting objects of meaning distinct from objects of reference.[12] In relation to recent treatments of the problem, which have either denied the possibility of quantification into modal contexts or have admitted it only with respect to special variables ranging over a domain of intensional entities, Buridan's analysis offers an interesting alternative. It has, moreover, an intuitive plausibility in this respect: it is in accord with our normal interpretations of such statements as these, 'The man of whom you are thinking is the one who murdered his wife,' or 'The thing that seems green to you looks blue to me.'[13]

of the occurrent term (*ibid.*, p. 151). Although Buridan admits the failure of substitutivity in such a construction, he does not take this as evidence of non-referentiality, but as evidence of restriction of the condition of referentiality to the connoted mode of designation.

[12] Alonzo Church admits quantification into modal contexts only with respect to a special type of variable taking intensional entities as values; cf. his "A Formulation of the Logic of Sense and Denotation," in *Structure, Method and Meaning*, ed. by Paul Henle, Horace M. Kallen and Susanne K. Langer (N.Y., 1951), pp. 3–24. A somewhat similar method is developed by Carnap (*Meaning and Necessity*, ed. cit., pp. 173–204), though Carnap seeks to avoid any metaphysical commitments by construing intensions and extensions as properties of language expressions rather than as entities named by them.

[13] An obvious counter-instance to this claim of intuitive plausibility is afforded by those cases in which the subject term of the subordinate clause of the belief sentence happens to be a fictitious name, as in the sentence 'Tom believes that Pegasus was a winged horse.' Buridan, in the first two chapters

III

While it is plausible to suppose that if Peter believes the evening star to be a planet, there is something such that he believes it to be a planet, it is less plausible to suppose that if Peter knows that every man is mortal, every man is such that Peter knows that he is mortal. For if every man is known by Peter to be mortal, then Oscar Twiddledee, of whom Peter has never thought, is nevertheless known by Peter to be mortal. When sentences of indirect discourse contain universal or existential quantifiers within their subordinate clauses, new problems are encountered in the analysis of such sentences. The last three *sophismata* taken up by Buridan in his chapter dealing with belief sentences, extend his general method of solution to these cases — cases which bear more directly on the traditional formulations of the problem of universals.

The first of these sophisms is the following: 'If someone knows that every triangle has three angles equal to two right angles, then every isosceles figure is known by him to have three angles equal to two right angles.' The argument for the truth of this sophism has the following form: If P knows that every A is B, then every A is such that P knows that it is B; but every C is A; therefore every C is such that P knows it to be B. Aristotle, Buridan remarks, touched on this problem in the *Posterior Analytics*, saying that a person knowing the universal statement that every triangle has angles equal to two right angles in a way knows, and in a way does not know, that this particular figure inscribed in the semicircle has this property. He knows it, says Aristotle, in the universal, but not in the particular instance until he has recognized the latter as an instance of the universal. But Aristotle's statements, Buridan says, do not meet the arguments, for they fail to deal

---

of his *Sophismata*, provides a method of analysis of fictitious terms, by reduction to descriptive phrases whose referentiality is impeded by the falsity or impossibility of an implied condition, though the terms of which the descriptive phrase is composed are, taken separately, designative of non-fictitious entities. He does not apply this to the case of fictitious terms occurring in belief sentences, but such application would appear to be quite possible.

with the crucial question — whether, from the sentence, 'I know that every A is B,' there follows the sentence 'Every A is such that I know it to be B.'[14]

As in the previous sophisms discussed, Buridan does not admit interchangeability of terms within the cognitive context; thus he does not admit that if every C is A, and if P knows that every A is B, than P knows that every C is B. As formulated, however, the sophism involves interchangeability only *outside* the cognitive context, and for this reason Buridan concedes its validity. The whole issue reduces to whether, from the sentence, 'P knows that every triangle has three angles equal to two right angles,' we can validly infer the sentence, 'Every triangle is such that P knows it to have three angles equal to two right angles.' And this, says Buridan, is a hard question.

Because of the difficulties involved in admitting this inference, Buridan adds, many people had held that knowledge is not of the things which exist in the world of nature, but that it is only of propositions or of the terms of which they are composed. On this view it would be said that Peter knows that the statement, 'Every triangle has three angles, etc.' is true, or that the subject term, 'Every triangle', is known by Peter to be such that the predicate term, 'has three angles, etc.', is truly predicable of it. But it would be denied that Peter's knowledge is in any literal sense *of* the individual things for which the subject term, of the proposition he is said to know, is distributed.

But this view, Buridan says, is hard to accept. For it would follow that although a mathematician knows that every triangle has angles equal to two right angles, there is no triangle which he knows to have angles equal to two right angles. And although

---

[14] *Sophismata Buridani*, cap. IV: "Et Aristoteles satis superficialiter loquitur de hoc, primo Posteriorum, dicens quod sciens omnem triangulum habere tres quodammodo scit iscoscelem, vel figuram in semi-circulo descriptam, habere tres, sed simpliciter non scit... Tamen illa dicta Aristotelis non satisfaciunt argumentis; quero enim questionem difficilem, non ponendo in conclusione totum a parte post, sed ponendo subiectum dicti a parte ante et predicatum a parte post. Verbi gratia, utrum sequatur 'Scio omne B esse A, ergo omne B scio esse A'..." The reference is to *Anal. Post.* I, ch. 1, 71a 19–30.

the physicist knows that every body is movable, there is no body which the physicist knows to be movable. This follows, because on whatever grounds it can be argued that one body is such that the physicist knows it to be movable, it can be argued that every other body is such that he has this knowledge of it; hence it is of all bodies that he has this knowledge expressed in the universal proposition, or it is of none. But to say that there is nothing of which he has this knowledge is odd indeed. Yet this view has plausibility, Buridan concedes, because in general we cannot infer a modal sentence *in sensu diviso* from the corresponding modal sentence *in sensu composito*. For example, from the sentence, 'It is necessary that every ass is an animal' it does not follow that 'Every ass is necessarily an animal.'[15]

While conceding that in the case of such modal operators as 'necessary' and 'possible' this type of inference is invalid, Buridan says that in other cases there is nothing to prevent such inferences; for example, from the sentence, 'It is true that every A is B', we may validly infer the sentence, 'Every A is such that it is true that it is B.' So, on account of the considerations already indicated, he concludes that it is "probable" that the inference is valid from the sentence, 'I know that every A is B', to the sentence, 'Every A is such that I know it to be B.' And if this type of inference is valid, then the *sophisma* is true.

In reply to the arguments against the sophism Buridan invokes the same analysis used in the other cases. Interchangeability of

---

[15] Buridan, *loc. cit.*: "Tota difficultas videtur stare in hoc, utrum sequatur 'scio omnem triangulum habere tres, ergo do omni triangulo habeo scientiam scilicet quod habeat tres.' Unde propter hanc difficultatem dixerunt quidam quod de solis conclusionibus demonstratis habemus scientiam et non de rebus aliis, ut nec de lapidibus, animalibus, et sic de aliis. ...Sed videtur hec responsio dura valde, quia sequeretur quod de nullo triangulo haberem scientiam, quia qua ratione de aliquo, eadem ratione de omni, ideo de omni vel nullo. ...Et tamen ista opinio habebat apparentiam, quia ex modali composita non videtur sequi divisa. Verbi gratia, non sequitur 'necesse est omnem asinum esse animal, igitur omnem asinum necesse est esse animal,' quia Aristoteles concederet primam et negaret secundam, eo quod omnis asinus potest non esse, et per consequens non esse animal."

co-designative terms within the scope of the cognitive verb is not allowed; but replacement of the universally quantified term occurring within the context, by a variable bound by a universal quantifier from outside the context, is permitted.

The next sophism deals with the case in which a particular or existential quantifying prefix occurs within the scope of the cognitive verb. The sophism is the following: 'Socrates the astronomer knows that some stars are over our hemisphere.' It is supposed that Socrates is in a dark room, unaware of the time of day, but that as a good astronomer he is prepared to assert this statement, 'Some stars are now overhead.' It is then argued that he does not know that some stars are overhead, because if he did, it would follow that there are some stars such that he knows them to be overhead. But this consequent is denied on the ground of the following inductive procedure: If Socrates is asked whether the stars of Aries are overhead, he will say that he does not know; if asked whether Betelgueuse is now overhead, he will again say that he does not know; and similarly in the case of each star, mentioned one by one. Consequently there is no star such that Socrates knows it to be overhead, and hence the *sophisma* is false.

Buridan rejects this argument and the induction on which it is based. He says that the case is similar to that of the good logician who, concerning a given pair of contradictory sentences, is said to know that one of the sentences is true and the other false. Can we infer from this that one of the sentences is known by him to be true? Buridan says that we can infer this, and that if it is the affirmative sentence which is true, then it is the affirmative sentence which the logician knows to be true, even though the logician does not know that the affirmative is true. It is known by him to be true only by way of the statement, 'Of the contradictories one is true,' and not according to the statement, 'The affirmative is true.' Nevertheless, since the affirmative is that member of the pair of contradictories which is true, it is the affirmative which is known by the logician to be true; for the negative, which is false, cannot be known by him to be true, and yet one of the contradictories is such that he knows it to be true. In the same way, if Socrates the astronomer knows that some stars are overhead, then whatever stars are in fact overhead are such that Socrates knows them to be overhead; and if Betelgueuse is overhead, Betelgueuse is such that Socrates knows it to be overhead despite the fact that Socrates does not know that Betelgueuse is overhead. The case is entirely similar to that of Peter and the evening star, except that in the present case the star Betelgueuse is specified by Socrates only under the general designation 'some star,' whereas the morning star was specified by Peter according to the singular designation 'evening star.'[16]

Paradoxical as Buridan's solution to these last two sophisms may appear, the alternatives seem no less odd. The realist or Platonist solution, which would infer from the sentence, 'Tom knows that every man is mortal', the sentence 'The attribute *human* is such that Tom knows that anything having it has also the attribute *mortal*,' not only appears to say something that the original sentence did not seem to say, but it leaves the original question unanswered — namely, whether there is anything (i.e., any individual) such that if it has the attribute 'human,' Tom knows that it has the attribute 'mortal.' If there is, then existential generalization with respect to an individual variable occurring within the scope of the cognitive verb is valid; and if so, the additional quantification for a domain of "attributes" would seem superfluous. The other alternative, however, of denying that there is anything which Tom knows to be mortal (or which he knows to have the attribute

---

[16] Buridan *loc. cit.*: "Et tunc respondetur ad rationes in oppositum, per quod arguebatur quod Sortes nullum astrum scit esse supra nostrum emisperium. ...quia nec solem scit esse supra terram nec lunam et sic de aliis. Ego nego inductionem, immo illa astra que sunt supra terram ipse de illis scit quod sunt supra terram, et hoc non scit secundum istam propositionem 'Stelle Arietis sunt supra terra,' sed hoc scit secundum istam propositionem 'Alique stelle sunt supra terram.' Similiter alteram partem illius contradictionis scio esse veram, et aliam scio esse falsam; et si affirmativa est vera et negativa falsa, tunc affirmativam scio esse veram et negativam falsam, sed non secundum istam propositionem 'Affirmativa est vera et negativa falsa,' immo dubito de illis; sed secundum istam propositionem 'Una pars contradictionis est vera et alia falsa.'"

'mortal') is more a refusal to face the dilemma than a method of resolving it. The paradoxical appearance of Buridan's solution can perhaps be explained by the fact that our ordinary linguistic habits, established in extensional discourse, do not take account of the difference between a sentence of the form, 'A is known by Tom to be B,' and one of the form, 'Tom knows that A is B.' Because the second sentence is normally taken to imply the first, we tend to suppose that the first implies the second; and because this seems odd in many instances, we are led to cast doubt on the converse implication as well. In a well-formed language whose syntax is adequate for scientific usage the non-equivalence of these two sentences is made evident, and the air of paradox attaching to Buridan's solution is dissipated to a large degree.

IV

The concluding sophism propounded by Buridan, though not originated by him, receives a treatment which makes it a worthy companion piece to the case of Buridan's Ass, and deserving of the title of "Buridan's Horse." It constitutes something of a pragmatic validation of Buridan's nominalistic solution to the problem of indirect discourse, and a somewhat humorous *reductio ad absurdum* of the realist or Platonist solution. The sophism is this sentence: 'I owe you a horse.' It is supposed that in return for services you have rendered to me, I promise to give you a horse, and I go before a judge and solemnly declare that I owe you a horse, and that I will deliver a horse to you by Easter. But I, being a clever sophist, go before the judge at Eastertide and argue as follows: If no horse is such that I owe it to you, then I do not owe you a horse. That no horse is such that I owe it to you, I establish by questioning you on the witness stand. Is the horse Morellus such that I owe it to you? If you say yes, I will then say that since my debt can be paid by delivering Favellus to you, or by giving you Brunellus, or some other horse, it cannot be said that Morellus is owed to you. To this you will no doubt agree, unless you are pretty sharp. Then I ask if Favellus is owed to you, and by the same reasoning you are forced to concede that

Favellus is not owed to you. And so for each horse. Nor is it necessary that I run through all the horses that there are; for if I can establish that there is one horse which is not such that I owe it to you, by the same course of reasoning I can establish this for every other horse. Hence it follows that if any horse is such that it is not owed to you, no horse is owed to you. And surely if you admit to the judge that no horse is owed to you, the judge will rule that I do not owe you a horse.

But if the judge has listened carefully to my argument, and if he is a just and reasonable man, he will not let me off by reason of this argument. If he is a good logician as well, he will realize that he cannot give a verdict requiring me to give you a horse, unless existential generalization with respect to a term occurring within the scope of the cognitive verb 'owes' or 'promises' is valid. Furthermore, such existential generalization must be of the ordinary extensional type, since a just judge would not demand that I deliver to you a concept or an abstract universal. He must therefore hold that if I owe you a horse, there is a horse such that I owe it to you.

Still, the judge must respond to the crafty argument which I have offered. And he has only one way in which to do so. Since he can give no reason why one horse is owed to you, that does not apply equally to every other horse, and since he cannot admit that no horse is owed to you without admitting that I do not owe you a horse, he must prove that if I owe you a horse, then every horse is such that I owe it to you. And this he can do, according to Buridan, by the following argument.

Let us suppose that there are just three horses in the world, and cannot be any more; for the problem remains the same whether the number of horses is three, four, or an infinite number. Let the three horses be named Morellus, Favellus, and Brunellus. Given this condition, the sentence, 'Some horse is owed to you' is equivalent to the disjunctive sentence, 'Morellus is owed to you or Favellus is owed to you or Brunellus is owed to you.' If at least one of these disjuncts is true, then some horse is owed to you; but if all are false, then no horse is owed to you.

[19] BURIDAN AND A DILEMMA OF NOMINALISM 595

Buridan now argues that if any of these three disjuncts is true, all are true, and if any of them false, all are false. For there is no more reason that any one of them should be true rather than another, or that one should be false rather than another. Therefore, if some horse is owed to you, every horse is owed to you; and if some horse is not owed to you, then no horse is owed to you. That every horse is owed is argued on several grounds. First, if anything is such that, when delivered to you, it satisfies my debt, that thing is such that I owed it to you. But each of the horses satisfies this condition; therefore all of them are owed to you. Second, if you were to concede to the judge that no horse is owed to you by me, he would rule that I did not owe you a horse. Finally, all the arguments developed in the previous sophisms apply to this case; if, as was argued, it is false to say that if someone knows that every man is mortal, then no man is known by him to be mortal, by the same token it is false to say that if someone owes you a horse there is no horse that is owed to you. Consequently, if I owe you a horse, every horse is such that I owe it to you.

If it be objected that I did not promise you every horse, and that I do not therefore owe you every horse, the judge can willingly concede that this is so. Although every horse is such that I owe it to you, and such that if I give it to you I am absolved of my debt, it does not follow from this that I owe you every horse. Nor does it follow from the fact that Morellus is owed to you that I owe you Morellus. But as the arguments showed, if I owe you a horse, then everything that is a horse is such that I owe it to you.[17]

[17] The foregoing is a free rendering of Buridan's much longer discussion of this sophism, which is numbered *Sophisma 15*, concluding the fourth chapter of his *Sophismata*. The same sophism is introduced in Buridan's *Quaestiones in Metaphysicam Aristotelis*, Lib. VII, Qu. 16 (ed. Paris, 1518, fols. 51r–52r), where it is used as an argument for the realist doctrine of universals, and then resolved in the same manner as above. The realist use of the sophism occurs in this form: "Item Sortes promittit tibi dare bovem vel equum, et non promittit tibi omnes boves vel equos, nec promittit dare istum vel istum, quia dando unum alium bene tibi solvet; ergo ipse promittit tibi bovem vel equum communem." In another argument, in similar vein, the Buridanic Ass appears as follows: "Item asinus sitiens appetit aquam, et non appetit omnes singu-

The logical affinity of Buridan's solution of the sophism of the promised horse, to his solutions of the preceding sophisms concerning objects of knowledge and belief, is evident. But it is characteristic of Buridan to give weight to the practical consequences of a theory. The Platonic realist, however enamoured he may be of his theory that the objects of knowledge or of desire are abstract universals distinct from the particulars of sense experience, is likely to protest if his theory is used to deprive him of a horse that has been promised to him. He turns nominalist in action, and demands an individual horse on which he can ride, in payment of the debt. The pragmatic test of belief, as that on which a person is prepared to act, is in this way invoked by Buridan as a final argument *ad hominem* against the partisans of abstract essences as objects of human cognition.

It has been the purpose of this study to expound Buridan's analysis of sentences of indirect discourse, rather than to evaluate or to criticize this analysis. Whether or not his resolution of the problem can stand the test of criticism, by contemporary standards, may well be doubted. But to have discerned the problem, and to have faced it with such tools of analysis as were available in the fourteenth century, was a significant achievement.

lares aquas... nec appetit determinate istam vel istam, ita quod non aliam... igitur appetit aquam communem." One is moved to pity for this Platonic ass, the object of whose thirst, being an abstract universal, is undrinkable; the nominalistic ass, for whom every bucketful of water is such that he desires it, can have his thirst slaked by whichever bucketful he encounters.

ABRAHAM ZACUTO HISTORIOGRAPHER

by ABRAHAM A. NEUMAN

ABRAHAM ZACUTO, born in Salamanca about 1450, was a distinguished figure in a momentous age. His contemporaries referred to him as "Famoso médico e insigne mathematico."[1] A famous astronomer in the revolutionary era of Spanish and Portuguese explorations at the end of the fifteenth and during the sixteenth century, he played a significant role in the currents of world history. His prestige as astronomer and astrologer assured for him a place in the royal courts of Spain and Portugal. In the royal Council in Spain, his opinions were weighted in favor of Columbus' expedition. Some years later as a refugee in Portugal, he encouraged King Don Manuel to further the exploits of Vasco da Gama. He was also favorably known among the higher ranks of the Church. He enjoyed the friendship of the Bishop of Salamanca, Don Gonzalo de Vivero to whom he dedicated his celebrated work, the *Almanach Perpetuum*,[2] and who in turn remembered him in

[1] Harry Friedenwald, "Abraham Zacutus," in *Bulletin of the History of Medicine*, VII, 458.

For biographical data regarding Zacuto, see Francisco Cantera Burgos, *Abraham Zacut SIGLO XV* (Madrid, 1935); *Idem, El Judio Salmantino Abraham Zacut* (Madrid, 1931); M. Kayserling, *Christopher Columbus* (New York, 1894), *passim*; Alexander Marx in *A.S. Freidus Memorial Volume* (New York, 1928); *Idem* in *Essays and Studies in Memory of Linda R. Miller*, (New York, 1938), pp. 167–170; Cecil Roth in *Sefarad*, IX (1949); Raphel Levy, *J.Q.R.*, XXVI, 385 ff.

[2] The *Almanach Perpetuum* is the popular title under which Zacuto's classic astronomical work ס׳ החבור הגדול is generally known. The *Almanach Perpetuum* is an abridged Latin translation by one of Zacuto's disciples, José Vizinho, more popularly styled Joseph Vechino. The complete translation in Latin of the original Hebrew version, *Magna Compositio*, was the work of another

his will.[3] At no time was he personally troubled by the Spanish Inquisition during the most fateful period of its anti-Jewish persecution.

This Jewish courtier, like so many others of his religious compatriots, lived in two worlds: the outer sphere of world affairs and secular interests, and the inner sanctum of the medieval Jew in exile: his religion and the spiritual heritage of his people. Zacuto treasured his Hebrew heritage above the gifts and glamour of the outer world, His scientific treatises were written in Hebrew although Spanish was his native tongue and Latin was the natural medium of scientific writing.[4] In the religious sphere in which Zacuto had his being, Hebrew lore, biblical and rabbinical, ranked higher in value than secular learning. Even to this renowned astronomer, rabbinical tradition was of primary importance; secular science was secondary. His major contribution to rabbinical literature — the *Sefer Yuḥasin* — was as distinctive a pathfinder in the field of rabbinics as was the *Almanach Perpetuum* in tracing the course of the stars in the celestial spheres. In the perspective of time, Zacuto's scientific contributions are but a passing memory in the progress of science, and his very existence is known only within the specialized coterie of historians of medieval science. By contrast, his Hebrew work, *Sefer Yuḥasin*, has continued an important reference work to this day. This historic perspective was not shared by Zacuto's contemporaries. For history was held in light esteem among the Jews in Spain,[5] and *Sefer Yuḥasin* is primarily an historical work. Zacuto felt called upon to explain apologetically the reasons that led him to write his remarkable chronicle as if the record of the past was not worthy of serious study.[6]

disciple, Augustin Riccius. This rendition was in turn translated into Spanish by Juan de Salaya.

[3] See A. Marx in *Essays and Studies in Memory of Linda R. Miller* (New York, 1938), pp. 167–170.

[4] Zacuto assisted Juan de Salaya in the Spanish rendition of the Latin *Magna Compositio*, Levy, *JQR*, XXVI, 387.

[5] Cf. A.A. Neuman *Landmarks and Goals* (Philadelphia, 1953) pp. 82–104.

[6] See author's *Introduction* to *Sefer Yuḥasin*.

Zacuto, as we shall see, lived chiefly during the latter part of the fifteenth century. It was only during the following century that the historic consciousness forced itself upon some of the survivors of the tragedy of the Jewish expulsion from Spain. Zacuto was only dimly aware of the importance of history. That a philosophy of history was needed for the survival of the Jewish people was revealed later to the succeeding generations.[7] Intuitively, however, Zacuto was impelled to record at least what seemed to him most important in the history of his people, its religious and literary personalities, a record of the "stars" that illumined the history of the Jewish people. To justify his work, he resorted to artificial semantics in the opening of his book. For, said he, did not the Bible compare the righteous to the stars? Therefore, the history of the righteous is comparable to the science of astronomy whose theme are the stars in the skies above, the science which the sages of old agreed was a sacred fount of wisdom. However artificial this reasoning may appear to us, and perhaps to the author himself, what really prompted him to devote the greater part of his life to this composition was the relevancy of this treatise to the stability of Jewish tradition and to his conception of Jewish law and doctrine.[8]

The inspiration for the *Sefer Yuḥasin* dawned upon Zacuto when he completed his major astronomical *opus* in 1478.[9] For Zacuto, the transition from the stars of the heavens to the divine luminaries of the terrestrial world was a logical transference of ideas, not a verbal metaphor of speech. Zacuto seemed to believe there existed an affinity between astronomy and history. He showed this in an interesting account of Alfonso X, the Wise, which may well be quoted here: "He (Alfonso) loved the sciences, especially astronomy. He designated the (Jewish) sage R. Isaac ibn Cid, the precentor of Toledo to draw up astronomical tables with great exactitude. They have become known as the Alfonsine

---

[7] See note 5 above.
[8] *Yuḥasin*, ed. Filipowsky (1924), p. 3b. Cf. below pp. 628–9. Paginal references to *Sefer Yuḥasin* will be noted in the text in parentheses.
[9] Cf. Freimann, Introduction, p. X, *Yuḥasin*, ed. Filipowski (1924).

Tables. From the rising of the sun to its going down, in Germany, France, England, all of Italy and Spain, they destroyed the former charts, replacing them with these (Alfonsine) Tables to this very day.... Alfonso then assembled all the learned scholars to set them to write a major historic work from Adam to his own time. *And this was an amazing accomplishment"* (221b–220a).

One should not defer the composition of the *Sefer Yuḥasin* to the later period of Zacuto's exile merely because the dates 1500, 1504 occur in the completed text. To do so is to overlook the time element which alone explains the uneven structure of this work. It is fair to assume that the concept of a spiritual "astronomy" matured in his mind during the decade and a half prior to the Spanish Expulsion, when he still enjoyed a sense of security as the celebrated "Man of Salamanca."(57a). It was during these years of relative well-being that he wrote most of what appears in the first two chapters of his book. It is in these sections, comprising the biblical narratives, as seen through midrashic legend, and the firmer periods of the Tannaim and the Amoraim, that Zacuto displayed encyclopedic talmudic knowledge and keen dialectic powers. These chapters, by contrast with the disjointed parts that followed later, give evidence of intense concentration and thoughtful organization of the wide range of rabbinic material, which could best be accounted for in his well ordered life in Spain.

All signs point to the conclusion that the major part of Book I which is devoted to the period of the Tannaim and Amoraim was written shortly after he completed the חבור הגדול, the *Almanach Perpetuum*, while his mind was still soaring among the stars and planets in the upper spheres.

It was this first section of the *Yuḥasin* in which he gloried and which from his viewpoint fully justified his labors on this encyclopedic work. Indeed, it may well be that his original plan did not envision the inclusion of the later generations of the Middle Ages; these were relatively unimportant. His major goal was to establish a proper sequence and interrelationship among the "stars" within the orbit of the Mishnah and the Talmud.

This aspect of his work appealed not only to his poetic conception of astronomy and Jewish wisdom: it was vitally significant for Jewish law and tradition. In the chain of Jewish tradition, the chronological sequence of the Fathers of Jewish law and the respective authority that was accorded to the individual sages within each generation, these were decisive factors in the determination of legal principles and practices.

These early chapters commanded his greatest efforts. They were obviously written during the years of comparative personal tranquility prior to the tragedy that overwhelmed him and his people in the course of the expulsions from Spain and Portugal. During these years, there were still available to him all the tractates of the Babylonian and the Jerusalem Talmud, all the Midrashim and the entire rabbinic literature.

Zacuto's mastery of the contents of this literature enabled him to reconstruct the generations of the inspired teachers, of Palestine and Babylon, who fashioned the law of Judaism during the early centuries of the present era. With thoughtful planning, he first arrayed the Tannaim in chronological sequence and then rearranged them in alphabetical order. This two-fold treatment was reversed in the case of the Amoraim, where the alphabetical order was more practicable and the generations had to be sketched selectively because of scant information. However, under both headings, Tannaim and Amoraim, Zacuto devoted much attention toward clarifying outstanding issues among the authorities within each generation and indicating whose views were declared authoritative.[10] In this area, Zacuto displayed vast erudition, sparked by keen dialectic reasoning. By contrast, the immediate post-talmudic period, embracing the Babylonian Geonim no longer bears the stamp of creative research for the reason that this section

---

[10] In support of his detailed characterization of the individual Tannaim and Amoraim, Zacuto cited Naḥmanides' letter to his son as well as Rabbi Isaac Campanton's teaching that in talmudic study it is important to know, "who is the Tanna etc.," and then concludes: "All the more can this be said in support of our small book, since in the course of our chronicle, we occasionally offer novel explanations of the law (under discussion) or whatever new idea can be usefully brought (to bear on the subject)."

was written in 1500 in the anguish of the double exile from Spain and Portugal. Haunted by misfortune, bereft of all wordly possessions and books, the greatest of all treasures, Zacuto fell back for this period upon the well-known chronicle of Abraham Ibn Daud, which he copied literally, content to make occasional additions to the Ibn Daud text. Zacuto freely acknowledged his full use of the older chronicle; "But", said he firmly, "that which I have written of the earlier period and all that concerned the sages of the Mishnah and the Talmud, is the result of my independent intense labors. I am far from satisfied with the result, as much has been left in doubt; but I could not do more for the present. Perhaps I may perfect it, if God spares me in the years to come. For the present, my writing is limited by the books that are available to me. When more (books) will reach me, with God's help, I shall make further additions" (216b).

From the standpoint of Jewish historiography, Zacuto's *Sefer Yuḥasin* marks a transition from the older types of family records and traditions, or literary chronicles which were prevalent in rabbinic literature to wit: the chronicle that properly belonged to halakic methodology, such as *Seder Tannaim va-Amoraim*; or the chronicles of polemical genre, as the *Seder ha-Kabbalah* of Abraham Ibn Daud; or the literary chronicles which consisted chiefly of a listing of eminent rabbis, scholars, poets, and other literary personalities and their writings. Zacuto incorporated all these latter types in his *Sefer Yuḥasin* but he stretched his subject on a broad canvas from the period of Creation to his own lifetime about the year 1500 or 1504. He drew upon a wide variety of sources, Jewish and non-Jewish, to establish historical facts. He drew broad lines of demarcation in Jewish history, especially in the ancient section. By applying dialectic reasoning to the earlier classical period, he determined critically some of the religious issues that were discussed and resolved in the ancient academies from the Sanhedrin to the close of the talmudic schools. Under this heading was included the fixing of the line of succession of the religious authorities. Into the circle of rabbinic characters, as we shall see, he introduced the names of non-Jewish contemporaries, especially astronomers and mathematicians. Furthermore, without any particular relevancy, he incorporated a number of unrelated documents of historic value.

Zacuto had no clear plan or outline for the *Sefer Yuḥasin*. In its composition, he betrayed neither the systematizing clarity of the astronomer-mathematician nor the language simplicity of the narrator. The *Yuḥasin* is, strictly speaking, neither chronicle nor history. It seems rather to be the unique product of a mind steeped in talmud, midrashic legend and lore colored by mysticism and supernaturalism. Intellectually, his mind steered a strange course in the labyrinth of Talmudic reasoning. The *Sefer Yuḥasin* mirrors the Talmud itself in style and methodology or the lack of both, as it must appear to a modern reader. Nevertheless, as we shall see, the book marks an advance on the road to historiography.

In the early period of the Mishnah and the Talmud, Zacuto set an example of independence in the use of rabbinic sources. In the loose intermediate section of the book which is not talmudic in content, Zacuto incorporated miscellaneous historic documents of considerable importance. In his own contemporary period, the incidental references to his experiences in exile subsequent to the expulsion from Portugal is not only biographically interesting, but mirrors, if only dimly, the anguish of his compatriots in exile, and the mournful loss of their treasured sacred books. From this record, for instance, we know that even so large a community as Tunis was woefully lacking in important talmudic texts (22a). It would be hopeless, however, to try to reconstruct a continuous narrative out of this medley of themes, arguments, and casual allusions, notwithstanding the flashes of thought and sentiment that fitfully illumine this work.

To compensate for the author's failure to divide the *Yuḥasin* into subdivisions or chapters, the modern editor, H. Filipowski (1857) divided it into five uneven chapters, with a supplementary sixth chapter which does not properly belong in the scope of the *Sefer Yuḥasin*. It purports to be "a history of the Kings of Judah and Israel and the other nations according to Greek authors." In Filipowski's arrangement, Chapter One includes a chronological account of persons and events from Creation to the end of the Tannaitic period; and thereafter, a series of unconnected documents dealing variously with the heads of the Sanhedrin, Rashi and his spiritual successors, the schools of Sura and Pumbeditha, passages relating to Jesus; Simon Duran's kabalistic interpretation of the nature of the soul, etc., etc., ending finally with the sensational story of Moses de Leon's alleged authorship of the *Zohar*. After this conglomeration of topics, the following chapters are, by comparison, quite orderly: The Ammoraim (Chapter Two); the Saboraim and Geonim (Chapter Three); the post-Geonic Rabbis (Chapter Four); the "later generations" (Chapter Five). The sixth chapter, as indicated above, is extraneous to the theme of the *Sefer Yuḥasin*.

Zacuto's sources were many and varied. Over eighty sources are named in the *Sefer Yuḥasin*.[11] Strangely enough, the Bible does not stand out as a primary source. For the biblical period, Zacuto drew upon the Aggadah and Midrash, where the biblical stories were changed into homiletical or fanciful legends, and chronological problems were resolved by arbitrary rules of rabbinic hermeneutics. The most important and comprehensive source was the entire range of rabbinic literature, comprising the tannaitic compilations, the Talmud, in both the Babylonian and Jerusalem versions, and the earlier and later Midrashim. Of lesser importance were the post-talmudic works of the Geonim and the medieval Rabbis down to his own time.

Zacuto was more skeptical of non-rabbinic authors, and outspoken in his negative attitude to non-Jewish sources. Among Hebrew writers, he drew variously on chroniclers and annalists, halakists and commentators, philosophers and poets, philologists and exegetes.

In rabbinic and talmudic literature, Zacuto was conscious of complete mastery, and he displayed independence of viewpoint. It was a world in which he lived spiritually, and in which his faith was anchored. Every utterance in the earlier sacred writings was

---

[11] *Yuḥasin*, pp. XI–XVI.

truth, and brooked no contradiction from whatever source. This conviction colored all his writings, including even his approach to the scientific works in astronomy; but nowhere was it more pronounced than in the *Sefer Yuḥasin*. In this sphere, the non-Jewish sources had no validity for him. Even the book of *Yosippon*, which enjoyed a high degree of reverence was swept aside when its testimony was opposed to his understanding of a talmudic passage.[12] Time and again, he contradicted the views of Maimonides who was the supreme authority among Jews of Spain.[13]

Zacuto's application of the early rabbinic sources was directed to three chief objectives: to fix the order of the Fathers of Jewish tradition in correct chronological sequence and, wherever possible, to do the same for the important Amoraim: to contribute original ideas of his own ingenuity to elucidate the meaning of equivocal talmudic texts and to clarify and reconcile debatable views of the early authorities; and finally to abstract biographical and historical data from the pages of the Talmud on contemporaneous events and personalities.[14] In these areas, he also utilized a knowledge of geography and lexicography. Zacuto was successful in attaining the first two objectives. His results have stood the tests of centuries of critical study. The same cannot be said of the historical abstracts because of his uncritical acceptance of every passing utterance of the ancient sages to be found in talmudic and midrashic literature. Despite this shortcoming, however, Zacuto's imperfect results stimulated a new interest in historical writing among the Jews.

Zacuto's treatment of talmudic sources presents strange contrasts. In matters related to religious law and ideology, directly or indirectly, he was a keen dialectician; on the other hand, talmudic passages that contained what purported to be facts or imaginary legends were accepted as authentic historic statements literally and uncritically. Typical was Zacuto's repetition of the legend of Jezdegered III, King of Persia, who decreed the compulsory abandonment of the Sabbath by the Jews of his kingdom,

---

[12] See below p. 639.   [13] *Idem* pp. 639–640.
[14] Cf. *Sefer Yuḥasin*, pp. 628–629.

to wit: "Rabbi Mar-bar R. Ashi, spiritual head of the Sura Academy, prayed unto God, and his prayer was answered. A monstrous snake, or dragon, attacked the King at midday and swallowed him as he was lying on his couch. Thus the decree was nullified, thank God."

Likewise, a passage in the Tractate of *Abodah Zarah* accounted for the legendary history of Ancient Rome: "In the days of Hezekiah, Romulus and Remus built the city of Rome. They ruled until the days of Nebuchadnezzar. Then their rule declined until the period of the Hasmoneans, 180 years before the destruction of the Temple (248 B.C.E.). Formerly they were under the Greeks. Julius Caesar was the Roman king who conquered the world mightily. After him, Augustus Caesar ruled the whole world for fifty-two years. He paved the Tiber River, on whose banks Rome is situated, with heavy copper plates for two miles. But according to the Book of Ben-Gurion this (the above) occurred during the time of King David, peace be with him" (202b).

Occasionally, Zacuto introduced into the rabbinic annals the names of general historic figures. Thus, "In those days there lived the famous scholar, the astronomer Ptolemy sixty-five years after the destruction of the Temple (133 C.E.)" (83a). He named Galen as a contemporary of Rabbi Judah ha-Nasi (198b). He was less fortunate in following the authority of Rabbi Simon Duran (*Magen Abot*, Chapter 2), and placing Constantine "who made Rome and Italy accept the religion of Jesus in the year 402 (162 C.E.)."

In the Saboraic, pre-Geonic period, Zacuto, following his source with slight modification, introduced tangentially the rise of Mohammed and the two Califs Omar and Ali, thus: "Rabbi Isaac was of the fourth generation (of Saboraim). In his time, the Moslem kingdom grew in power and the Persian kingdom was utterly destroyed. And there came to Babylon Ali Ibn Abu Talab, king (Calif) of the Moslems, as the Moslems had already conquered Persia some years past. The Persian empire had been vanquished in the days of Omar Ibn Alkhatab, king (Calif) of the Moslems. The daughters and the sons of Jezdegered, the Persian monarch, were led into captivity. The Moslem ruler gave the daughter of Jezdegered[15] to Bostanai the Exilarch who proselytized and married her. In the year 4382 (622 C.E.) Mohammed began to preach his doctrine."

"We find, moreover, that it happened in the year 4382 (622 C.E.) on the fifth day of the week, on the second day of the (Hebrew) month of Ab."[16] At this point Zacuto departed from his source in the *Sefer ha-Kabbalah* and inserted passages taken from another text:

"And in the year 387 (627 C.E.)[17] the Moslems captured Jerusalem which had been in the power of Rome five hundred and sixty years since the destruction of the Temple.[18] Thereafter the city was in the power of the Moslems for seven hundred and two years [sic] after which in the year 859 (1099 C.E.) on the sixteenth of Ab, the thirtieth day of August, the Christians recaptured Jerusalem.[19] It occurred in the days of Rabbi Abraham bar-Ḥiyya, ha-Sefardi."[20]

Zacuto then reverted to his previous source: "When Ali made his entry to Babylon, Rabbi Isaac, head of the Academy (the spiritual leader of the Jewish Community) received him with honor and the Calif elevated him (over all the Jews) in the year 4420 (660 C.E.)" (204 b).

As in the case of Mohammed, allusions to Jesus are introduced

---

[15] A mistake for Chosroes II.

[16] The Hegira took place in Sept. 622.

[17] Omar occupied Jerusalem 637–638, not 627.

[18] This would be roughly in accord with an assumed date of 627 or 628 for the capture of Jerusalem by the Arabs.

[19] Cf. 212a: "And in the year 787 (1027 C.E.) the year in which Rabbi Samuel he-Nagid, was appointed Nagid, Jerusalem was conquered by the Romans, and the Moslem rule was overthrown. But I, Abraham Zacut, present author and writer, have seen in the book of Rabbi Abraham bar-Ḥiyya (ha-Sefardi), the great astronomer, that in his time, in the year 859 (1099 C.E.), the Christians took Jerusalem." The correct date of the capture of Jerusalem by the Crusaders was July 15, 1099.

[20] The exact dates of Abraham b. Ḥiyya's lifetime are not known. He is presumed to have died in 1036.

in the *Sefer Yuḥasin* in tangential manner, without intrinsic relevancy or continuity. In one instance, the subject which elicited a reference to Jesus was Hillel the Nasi, or President, of the Sanhedrin. Zacuto stated that Hillel became Nasi one hundred years before the destruction of the Temple (32 B.C.E.) and remained in office until his death forty years later (8 C.E.). There followed this remark: "If so, then it follows from the viewpoint of the Christians that the man whom they believe to be God was born eight years before the death of Hillel" (82b).

Many pages prior to this section, allusion is made to ישו הנוצרי = Yeshu ha-Noẓri (Jesus the Nazarene) in a totally different setting. Here he appears in a story about Rabbi Joshua b. Peraḥya who fled from Jerusalem to Egypt to escape the anti-Pharisee persecution, and Yeshua ha-Noẓri, (Jesus the Nazarene), we are told, accompanied him to Egypt. At this point Zacuto records also a parallel passage in the Jerusalem Talmud, where the same story with a different motif is told of Judah b. Tabai who fled from Jerusalem to Egypt, accompanied by a disciple, Jesus the Nazarene. (ישו הנוצרי). As Joshua b. Peraḥya lived during the second and first centuries B.C.E., and was recalled to Jerusalem in the year 88 B.C.E., there is a discrepancy of about a century between the Jesus of talmudic traditions and the Jesus of the Christian records. This discrepancy helped to defend the Talmud against the charges of having cast aspersions upon the Founder of the Christian religion. Medieval rabbis, who were forced into religious disputations, argued that the character known in the Talmud as Jesus, had no relation to his namesake in Christian writings as he lived a century later.

Zacuto repeated the rabbinic contention, for he never doubted the absolute truth of ralmudic tradition: "The truth is that the Nazarene was born in the fourth year of the reign of John Hyrcanus, which is the year 263 of the Second Temple, the fifty-first year of the Hasmoneans, the year 3678 of Creation (82 B.C.E.), although the Christians say he was born in the year 3760 A.M. (the first year C.E.). They say that he was executed when he was thirty-two years old, thirty-eight years before the destruction of the

Temple so that they can scoff at us and say that in less than forty-years (after the crucifixion) the Temple was destroyed, because of the sin which we committed against him. Verily this is falsehood, for he was born eighty-nine years earlier than they claim: the truth is that he was born in the year 3678 A.M. (82 B.C.E.), and that he was seized in the year 299 of the era of the Temple, when he was thirty-six, in the third year of the reign of Aristobulus, son of John (Hyrcanus). Thus the Jewish sages, in their disputations with the Christians, stated that there is nothing written in the Talmud about the Nazarene of whom they speak."[21] Zacuto added the following: "in the Christian chronicles too there are differences of opinion as to when he was born" (15a–b).

Still another Talmudic reference to Jesus was adduced elsewhere in the *Sefer Yuḥasin* (86b–87a), without any attempt to relate it to the passages quoted above. The Talmudic point of reference here was the subject of magic or witchcraft discussed by Rabbi Eliezer and the sages, in which the names of Ben Stada, Ben Pandera (allegedly a pseudonym for Jesus) occurred.

The starting point for Zacuto was the statement of Rabbenu Tam, that "Ben Stada was not Jesus the Nazarene, for he (Ben Stada) is referred to as a contemporary of Pappos b. Judah, who lived in the time of Rabbi Akiba (Second Century C.E.) while Jesus was a contemporary of Joshua b. Peraḥya who lived long before Rabbi Akiba." To this Zacuto responded: "And I Abraham say that there was another Pappos ben Judah a century earlier, a contemporary of Rabbi Eliezer, Akiba's teacher, in whose period Jesus lived according to the Christians."[22]

This view that the Nazarene lived in the time of R. Eliezer, Zacuto reasoned, was supported in the talmudic passage that

---

[21] ובעבור זה כתבו חכמי ישראל בויכוח שהיה להם עם הנוצרים כי בתלמוד אינו כתוב הנוצרי שהם אומרים (15b).

[22] There was an opinion that this Pappos might have lived for more than a hundred years and spanned the lives of both Rabbi Eliezer and Rabbi Akiba, each of whom lived an extraordinary long life; but Zacuto could not accept the incredible conjecture, quoting from the Talmud, "We cannot rely on miracles."

"Rabbi Eliezer discoursed with Jacob, a disciple of Jesus the Nazarene.' 'Therefore, I say that there were two persons (by the name of Pappos b. Judah) one who lived during the Second Temple, and the other at the time of Rabbi Akiba's death." Hence it appeared to Zacuto that, contrary to Rabbenu Tam, Ben Stada was the Nazarene (86b).

For added support, he turned to Rashi, grandfather of Rabbenu Tam, who stated that "Ben Stada was the well-known Nazarene, and they hanged him in Lud (Lydda) on the eve of Passover." Zacuto reinforced his opposition to Rabbenu Tam's view by citing talmudic references to "disciples" who performed miracle healing in the name of Yeshu (Jesus) son of Pandera (Stada). At no point did Zacuto attempt to reconcile this position with the previous assertion that there was no mention in the talmud of the "Nazarene of whom they (the Christians) speak" (86b). Nor did he show any awareness of the contradiction.

Immediately following upon the above passage, another reference to Rabbenu Tam led to a different subject, which ends with the characteristic conclusion. "Although these discussions do not properly belong to the theme of this book, I wrote them down because they are novel (חדוש) and it is good to record them here" (87a).[23]

It was by means of interpolations that Zacuto introduced valuable historical records and personal insights. Thus, for example, a talmudic passage, quoted in the *Sefer Yuḥasin*, ended with the phrase, "was rewarded with eternal life in the world to come." Like a trigger, these words propelled Zacuto far from his theme to a glorification of martyrs and martyrdom: "The conditions prevailing in our time, when we have witnessed saintly men take their own lives and their children's in order to save them from being forced to abandon the religion of their God, make it fitting to state clearly that this (act of immolation) is not only permissible,

---

[23] It may be noted, although Zacuto's loose manner of writing and his rambling style in general is disconcerting, he always returns to the previous point of departure with the naive remark, ונחזור לענינו "and now let us return to our subject." 31a, 51b, 60b, *et passim*.

but is a holy act." A series of talmudic statements corroborating this opinion were then cited. "All the more is this true in times of persecution when we must not only refrain from defiling but must sanctify the Holy Name (with our lives). This act of sanctification was performed by the saintly Rabbi Judah son of the Princely Rabbi Asher in Toledo when he, his wife and her mother, the wife of Rabbi Jacob, author of the *Turim*, died for the glorification of the Holy Name during the persecution of 1391. And thus acted the sage Isaac B. Zahin of Boñilla de la Sierra, both he and his sons, during the persecutions in Portugal in 1497." Zacuto concluded: "Thus acted Samson, son of Menoah; and he was rewarded with eternal life in the world to come" (51a–b).

Zacuto's unaccountable methodology also reflects an ambivalent attitude to the authors whose writings served him as sources. Aside from the Bible, the Talmud, and the related collections whose writings were sacred, Zacuto treated the later scholars and religious authorities with pious deference but exposed their views to analysis, criticism and at times to opposition.

His treatment of Maimonides is a good example. In his Introduction to the Mishnah, Maimonides listed in chronological sequence the Tannaim of that period. Zacuto prefaced his own treatment of the same subject as follows: "But first, I must review briefly, the account given in Maimonides' Introduction, and point out the difficulties I find therein. For it appeared to the Master, of blessed memory, that the successors who followed him would accept his views without further searching. But at times a small candle can pierce with its light into a hole or a crack better than a luminous light or a torch. My predecessors left room for me to distinguish myself. Perhaps another will follow me who will excel me in research. Let him have his reward. For it is all labor in the name of Heaven" (22a).

Zacuto entered into the fray forthwith, subjecting Maimonides' chronological sketch of the Tannaim to sharp analytical criticism. Suffice it to say, the "little light" pierced into the holes and crevices of the structure Maimonides erected, a procedure too minute and detailed to follow here with profit. One instance may be noted, however, in which Zacuto the pietist, appeared more liberal than the famous philosopher and rationalist. Elisha ben Abuya, whose religious philosophy was regarded with suspicion by his contemporaries, was eliminated from the ranks of the sacred teachers in Maimonides' listing; but Zacuto stated: "I am prepared to accept him." Finding good ground for doing so, he included him among the chosen teachers of the Law, contrary to Maimonides' more rigid views (22b). Elsewhere, when Maimonides made application of a general principle, we read: "And I Abraham say that in this instance he is correct but this is not true in all cases" (54a).

In these critical remarks, Zacuto expressed independence of thought, rather than adverse reflections on Maimonides, whom he held in highest esteem and reverence.[24] The saintly Rabbi Moses ben-Naḥman (Naḥmanides), Zacuto tells us, was inclined to name Maimonides *Mosheh Rabbenu*. He refrained from doing so only because the appellation *Mosheh Rabbenu* belonged to Moses of the Bible, Moses the Lawgiver. This was high praise, indeed, especially as it was attributed to Naḥmanides, the mystic, whose philosophic sympathies were anti-Maimonist.[25]

In the pursuit of truth, Zacuto was no respecter of persons, not even of a Gaon, although in the chain of tradition, the Geonim followed directly after the talmudic rabbis. The *Aruk* (talmudic dictionary) composed at the close of the ninth century by the Gaon of Pumbeditha Ẓemaḥ b. Paltai was freely consulted and generally followed by Zacuto; nevertheless, he had no hesitation in bluntly rejecting the Gaon's views when he disapproved of them: "This is in the *Aruk* but it is not correct" (33a); "it is not acceptable" (55b); "it is not true" (63b).

[24] 229a: ואו״כ לא עלה זה על דעת הרמב״ם ז״ל אלא שנפל שבוש בספרים. Cf. 181a, where Zacuto defended Maimonides against the harsh attack of Rabbi Abraham b. David of Posquiere (RABaD). To RABad's attack: אמר אבל אני אומר שמא סמך יש : Zacuto retorted אברהם זה לא היה ולא נברא להרמב״ם ז״ל. See also 198a–b where Zacuto attributes certain errors in Maimonides' works to incorrect texts: זה שקר בספרים כי לא עלה בדעתו של הרב ז״ל.

[25] והרמב״ן שנקרא הרב הנאמן לא היה קורא להרמב״ם רבינו משה מפני כבוד משה רבינו (221a).

The book which served Zacuto as a major source was the *Sefer ha-Kabbalah* of Abraham Ibn Daud, referred to by Zacuto as *Sefer Dorot Olam*. He copied this source verbatim, page after page, without troubling to change even the personal pronoun. This is true of the sections dealing with the Geonic period and the North African and Spanish schools. Zacuto acknowledged his indebtedness. "Be it known that most of this, (the record of the Saboraim), I have taken from the *Sefer Dorot Olam*, which is the *Sefer ha-Kabbalah* of the saintly Levite, which I corrected and supplemented" (204b). Somewhat later in the text he was more revealing. "Till here — aside from some of my supplements, the text is from the *Dorot Olam*, i.e. the *Sefer ha-Kabbalah* of the saintly R. Abraham ha-Levi ibn Daud ha-Levi (the memory of the righteous is for a blessing) who died in Toledo for the Unity of the Holy Name. What I have said pertains only to the events of the period concerning the Saboraim and the Geonim. But the earlier sections concerning the sages of the Mishnah and the Talmud is the result of my own great labor. My goal has not been fully attained, for much has been left in doubt, but I could not do more now. If the Holy One, blessed be He, will grant us life, we shall perhaps bring everything into order" (216b).

However, Zacuto's indebtedness to Ibn Daud was more extensive than he thus indicated. For Ibn Daud's chronicle covered also the earlier period of the Mishnah and the Talmud. Ibn Daud arranged the sages of the Mishnah in chronological sequence. He succeeded in the more difficult task of classifying the talmudic generations in numerical series. Zacuto followed the pattern set by Ibn Daud, without necessarily following the content within the framework. Clearly, Zacuto's major pride was in his contribution to the period of the Mishnah and the Talmud. This area he guarded jealously, as if it were his own special domain. We have seen above his resistance to Maimonides within this period. Even more so was he outspoken in his refutation of Ibn Daud. (30b, 31a, 33a, 35b, 200a–b, 201a). His vehement attitude was revealed in a comparatively minor question concerning the date of the death of R. Yohanan.

Said Abraham Zacuto: "Here I want to attack and to refute all that was said by the writer of the *Dorot Olam*, i.e. the *Sefer ha-Kabbalah*, of the saintly author. I refer to his statement that Rabbi Yoḥanan died in the year 39 A.M. (279 C.E.), eleven years before the death of Rav Huna, which occured in the year 50 A.M. (290 C.E.)" (169b).

Although Ibn Daud's chronicle filled a prominent place in the *Sefer Yuḥasin*, Zacuto assigned a modest space to him personally among the scholars and sages whom he listed in the *Sefer Yuḥasin*. In a brief sketch of a few lines, Zacuto outlined the writings of Ibn Daud. Referring to the *Sefer ha-Kabbalah*, he stated simply that it extended from Moses to Joseph ha-Levi. He glorified the author on having given his life for the Unity of the Holy Name (220a).

The manner in which Zacuto utilized the *Book of Yosippon* invites special attention. This book was the most popular Hebrew historical work, universally read and accepted among the Jews, learned and unlearned, during the Middle Ages. Rabbinical authorities and Bible exegetes, such as Rashi, Abraham ibn Ezra, David Kimhi, Isaac Abravanel and other celebrities turned to this work as a classic of unquestioned authority.[26] All the references of those writers to *Yosippon* are readily found in the existing recensions in the Mantua and Constantinople editions and their derivations. Even anonymous quotations from *Yosippon* are easily traceable to their source.[27]

In contrast, Zacuto's attitude to *Yosippon*, the book and the author, is variable and critical. It ranges from complacent acceptance to outright rejection, bordering on hostilily. When Yosippon's narrative accords with the Talmud and Midrash or Zacuto's

---

[26] Neuman, *op. cit.*, pp. 27, 35.

[27] Note, however, Judah Rosenthal in *Studies and Essays in Honor of Abraham A. Neuman* (Hebrew), pp. 30–31. When the apostate Abner Burgos cited Joseph b. Gorion, his respondent, R. Joseph Shalom, replied as follows: דע כי חפשתי כל דברי יוסף בן גריון ולא מצאתי שאמר זה הפסוק בשום ענין, ואפילו אודה לך שאמרו לא היה יוסף בן גריון נביא ולא חכם מחכמי התלמוד. ואם לא נאמין לדבריו לא יחסר ולא יוסיף שום דבר בתורה ולא בדברי חכמים ז"ל

interpretation of these sources, or if it records a sympathetic Jewish legend, Zacuto cited the passages as authentic testimony.

Thus he quoted the following story: When the first Temple was destroyed, the sacred fire on the altar was not extinguished. The prophet Jeremiah hid the fire in a secret cave. When the Second Temple was built and the sacrifices were laid on the altar to be offered up, there was great distress among the priests, for the sacred fire of old could not be found. But miraculously an aged priest recalled the pit in which Jeremiah had sequestered the liquid flame of the ancient altar. When the liquid was poured on the new altar, it burst into a fierce flaming conflagration. The altar was cleansed by the flames, the sacrifices were consumed, and the Temple was purified. With this story taken from Yosippon,[28] Zacuto embellished the narrative of the dedication of the Second Temple and authenticated it under the name of Joseph b. Gorion.[29] Zacuto's acceptance of this narrative from Yosippon is especially noteworthy because he realized that the legend exceeded the limits of an early tradition recorded in the *Sifra*, which stated that "the sacred fire descended (from heaven) on the copper altar in the days of Moses; it vanished when the sacred fire again descended (from heaven) in the days of Solomon, when he built the altar; and it vanished therefrom in the days of Manasseh." "But," added Zacuto, "the fire still survived, for Joseph b. Gorion stated that Jeremiah hid the fire, and the Men of the Great Synagogue found it" (24b).

In another context, however, Yosippon is described as one "who indulges in exaggerations with a tongue that speaketh proud things (Ps. 12:4) and who draws calculations that are not in accord with the plain meaning of the Torah." Zacuto introduced this characterization of Yosippon in the course of a diatribe against the historical writers of other nations "whose mouth speaketh falsehood and their right hand is a right hand of lying" (Ps. 144:8). In this connection he added that all those writers "lean on Joseph

---

[28] See *Yosippon* (Jerusalem, 1956), pp. 21–22.
[29] See S. Zeitlin, *Decline and Fall of the Judaean State* (Philadelphia, 1962), pp. 103, 250; II Mac. 1:18–24.

ben Gorion the Priest" whom he disparaged with the above characterization (231a).

This harsh repudiation of Joseph ben Gorion was inconsistent with the high regard in which Yosippon had then been held for centuries among the highest Jewish authorities. It was also out of tune with Zacuto's use of Yosippon in other instances (cf. 244b, 245a).

The explanation is to be found in the confusion which existed in the mind of Zacuto about the identity of Yosippon in relation to Josephus. Zacuto accepted Yosippon's self-representation as Josephus; that the self-same person wrote a history of the Jewish people in Hebrew, for Jewish readers, under the name of Yosippon; and another version for the Romans in their language under the name of Josephus. Zacuto quoted from both versions interchangeably. The biblical theme of Samuel and King Saul, for instance, had no place in Yosippon's narration, but it does form an integral part in Josephus' *Antiquities*. Zacuto, drawing the passage from *Antiquities* attributed it to *Yosippon*, where it is non-existent.[30]

Another clear case of a substitution of Yosippon for Josephus is illustrated in the story connected with the building of the Temple by Onias in Leontopolis, Egypt. The story is not mentioned in any existing version of *Yosippon*. It is, however, related at length in Josephus' *Antiquities*, XIII, 62–79. While the Zacuto account (241a–b) in the name of Yosippon is abbreviated and differs in some details from the Josephus text, their identity can hardly be questioned. Furthermore, the juxtaposition in both narratives of the controversy between the Samaritan spokesman for the Temple on Mt. Gerizim and the representatives of the Judean Temple in

---

[30] Zacuto obviously used the Latin translation of the *Antiquities*. According to the Greek text Saul outlived Samuel by twenty-two years, which raises Saul's reign to forty years. This agrees with Acts 13:21. Marcus (*Ant.* VI, 378, note f) suggested that the reading in the present Greek texts was an emendation by a pious Christian scribe. The Latin translation goes back to an earlier Ur-text and reads two years, as stated in *Sefer Yuḥasin*. It is interesting to note that Zacuto was aware that "in the story of Jesus and in the writings of his disciples" they stated that Saul reigned forty years.

Jerusalem adds more evidence — if any were needed — that Zacuto's narrative was drawn from the pages of Josephus. In both passages, Zacuto refers to *Yosippon* as an authentic source. While in the first passage, Yosippon's chronology differed from the rabbinic tradition, and was therefore to be rejected out of hand, Zacuto stated simply that the talmudic chronology negated the view of Joseph ben Gorion. לאפוקי is an expression which occurs frequently in talmudic discussions to denote that the negated view was that of a minority or was otherwise unacceptable. No reflection of integrity was thereby implied.

In another passage concerning the years that the Hasmonean brothers reigned in Judea (12b), Zacuto assigned six years to Judah, six years to Jonathan, and eighteen years to Simon. "But," said he, "according to the Roman chronicles, Judah ruled four years, Jonathan nineteen and Simon eight years. And thus also the Book of Ben Gorion." In the existing texts of Yosippon and Josephus the figures do not agree with the above quoted figures. Nor did Zacuto agree with his own version in a later passage (90a): "A summary according to Joseph ben Gorion of the period of the Hasmoneans, 213 years after the building of the Second Temple. Matathias ruled one year, and after him, his son Judah six years, and Jonathan his brother six years, and Simon his brother seven years". The significant feature that stands out in the above quotations is the linking of the Book of *Yosippon* (Josephus) with the Roman chronicles. Finally, in Book VI (ed. Filipowski) which was written as a supplement to the *Sefer Yuḥasin* in 1504, Zacuto adopted without further ado the figures he had attributed earlier to the Roman chronicles and the Book of Ben Gorion. Zacuto's linking of the Roman Chronicles with the Ben Gorion book would indicate that he referred to the version supposedly written by Yosippon for the Romans under the name of Josephus.

Why then did Zacuto cast such aspersions on Yosippon in connection with the non-Jewish historical writers "whose mouth speaketh falsehood" etc. and who lean on Joseph ben Gorion? Obviously because he felt that the history which Yosippon supposedly wrote for the Romans in their tongue, as Josephus, was slanted to be pleasing to Roman readers to the detriment of the Jewish people. Zacuto sensed the influence of Josephus in Roman and later Christian chronicles. To him, Joseph ben Gorion represented a double personality under two names, Yosippon and Josephus, with dual shaded loyalties.[31] This was sufficient to cause the resentment which Zacuto expressed so tartly. Zacuto's leanings in this respect became transparent in his account of the destruction of the Temple. There were two conflicting dates for the destruction of the Temple: the ninth of Ab according to Yosippon, the tenth of Ab according to Josephus, who furthermore dramatized the play of Fate in the timing of the destruction of the Temple. Zacuto, of course, could not do otherwise than follow Yosippon's dating, as this date had been the established fast-day for well over a millenium. But it is significant that Zacuto passed over the Josephus passage in silence.

Notwithstanding his high regard for Yosippon the historian, his opinion even in an historical matter could not stand up against a statement of Rashi, in Zacuto's judgment. Thus he accepted Rashi's comment that Queen Alexandra, wife of John Hyrcanus, was the sister of R. Simon ben Shetaḥ, "which is not according to Joseph ben Gorion" (13a).

Strange to say, the author of the *Book of Yosippon* appeared to overlook the contradiction in the paternal names of the alleged Joseph son of Gorion and Josephus son of Mattathias. Zacuto did not face this problem squarely; he casually alluded to a Mattathias whom he called the "last high-priest," and added "he appears to have been the father of Joseph son of Gorion." A few lines later, Zacuto actually added the name Mattathias to Joseph ben Gorion and described him thus: Joseph ibn Gorion son of Mattathias, the high-priest. He evidently assumed the name Gorion to be a patronymic.[32]

The sources that were examined thus far comprise the major works from which Zacuto drew much of his information. He also

---

[31] Neuman, *op. cit.*, pp. 1–34.   [32] *Ibid.*, p. 29, n. 14.

drew upon an astonishing number of other works for occasional reference for varied items of historic interest. We are stymied however, in our investigation of other major sources after the end of Ibn Daud's period and chronicle.[33]

No vivid picture emerges from his pages in the subsequent centuries of the massacres, the mass conversions, the terrors of the Inquisitions, all of which led inexorably to the catastrophe of the Spanish Expulsion. The freshness and independence of mind which Zacuto displayed in the earlier chapters concerning the Mishnaic and talmudic sages is lacking in the later period. The *Sefer Yuḥasin* takes on the form of the literary chronicles of the Provencal school; it becomes a register of the names of scholars, their writings, the dates of their death and at times the year of birth.

However, the monotony is relieved occasionally when the person recorded is one of special interest, Maimonides, for example (219 a–b). Zacuto paid special regard to scholars, poets and exegetes who distinguished themselves in Jewish lore and in the sciences of mathematics and astronomy, such as Abraham ibn Ezra (218a), Levi ben Gershon (224b). Zacuto always revealed his predilection when he discussed the scientific exploits of himself or others in the field of astronomy (221b–222a). Even in this section one meets occasionally flashes of interest. Thus, a bare line mentioned the persecution of Jews in the kingdom Leon; but it led to a highly important discourse about the fate of the famous Bible codex known as the Hillel Codex. The description of the manuscript is detailed and first-hand; its age, its migration from country to country is described; the origin of the name — the Hillel Bible — is explained; namely, the scribe of that beautiful and meticulous manuscript was one, Moses ben Hillel (220b).

The personality of Naḥmanides peers through Zacuto's brief

---

[33] Isidor Loeb (R.E.J. XVII): suggested that Zacuto and Joseph ben Zaddik may have utilized a common unknown source. This is neither helpful nor plausible. The outlook of their authors and the contents of their chronicles differ too widely to assume a common origin. Cf. Neubauer M.J.C. I, pp. XIV, 85 ff.

description. He was known as the Faithful one (הנאמן). A human touch was this comment: So profound was the dialectic power of Naḥmanides that at times, he himself had doubts about the reasoning in his own *novellae* (221a). The mystic Naḥmanides did not know the *Zohar* (224b).

A short note about the French expulsion of the Jews in 1306 led Zacuto to make the following remark: "And thus, owing to our sins, I have personally witnessed the Jewish expulsion from Spain, Sicily and Sardinia in 1492, and again from Portugal in 1497. But from France, in 1306, flight was possible, for my great grandfather fled hitherto. My ancestors remained steadfast in their faith in God and His Torah. And I too have been privileged by God, blessed be His Name, to sanctify His Holy Name together with my son, Samuel. We reached Africa after having been taken captive two times. May God, in His grace and mercy, reward me and my son that we may continue to the end to serve His blessed Name, Amen."

"Mayest Thou grant our portion to be among the righteous in Heaven. May we live through resurrection and behold the rebuilding of Thy Holy Temple. May this be Thy will, Amen" (223a).

Rabbi Asher ben Yeḥiel occupied a place of high honor in Zacuto's gallery of Jewish immortals, "our teacher Rabbi Asher, the holy one (הקדוש)". All his works were enumerated and highly praised. At seventy, Rabbi Asher expressed a wish to study astronomy, "which rated highly in those days as a wondrous science." To fulfill his desire, Isaac Israeli wrote two astronomical books, *Yesod 'Olam* and *Sha'ar ha-Shamayim*. Playing on the number twenty-two, which was the number of years that Rabbi Asher lived in Toledo, he applied the verse "In thee shall Israel be blessed" (the Hebrew for "in thee" בך spells 22) (223b).

Comparing Rabbi Asher to Maimonides, Zacuto indulged in surprising sarcasm directed at Maimonides when he stated: "As for us, we rely more on Rabbi Asher, for Maimonides writes as if his words were prophecy and needed no proof. By contrast, Rabbi Asher's decisions are profound and thorough. It is not that I feel personally competent to evaluate their relative degrees of greatness. I am passing on a generally accepted opinion and tradition. In his generation, Rabbi Asher was looked upon not as a mortal but as "an angel of the Lord of Hosts" (223b).

More restrained but highly eulogistic was Zacuto's appraisal of R. Asher's sons, particularly the younger son, Jacob, author of the famous code *Arba Turim* (The Four Rows),[34] who succeeded his father. He completed this work, said Zacuto, immediately after his father's death. "It covers all the laws which are still in vogue in our time. It is useful for the learned and the unlearned alike, because of its excellent arrangement, better than any work of its kind that has ever appeared. This sage excelled all other scholars, for everybody studied his code" (224a). But the community of Toledo did not support him adequately. He languished most of his life in poverty (224a).

A few scattered references to the disciples of Rabbi Asher and his sons are followed by sketchy allusion to the tragedy that befell the Jews of Castile as a result of the civil war between King Pedro and his brother Henry. Zacuto's account, meager and sketchy as it is, is worth quoting. "The year 1370, was a time of anguish for all the Jewish communities of Castile, and, more grievous still, for the Jews of Toledo. This city was under a distressful siege, so that the people were reduced to eating the flesh of their children. Twenty-eight thousand Jews perished in consequence of the fratricidal war in which Don Enrique killed his brother King Pedro. He (King Pedro) himself had killed under *torture in prison* R. Samuel ha-Levi who built the synagogue in Toledo and other synagogues in Castile and had rendered great service to Israel. The Holy One, blessed be He, visited quick vengeance upon King Pedro when his brother killed him at Montiel in 1370" (224a).[35]

From this emotional recital, Zacuto dropped again into a bare enumeration of Jewish scholars and their writings, paying little

---

[34] The "four rows" is a reference to the four rows of jewels on the breastplate of the High Priest.

[35] Cf. Neuman, *The Jews in Spain*, II, 253 ff.; Baer, תולדות היהודים בספרד הנוצרית I, 244 ff.

regard to any sequence of content or chronology. With his penchant occasionally to introduce wordly events into his religio-literary chronicle, he interpolated at this point that "in 1381, the Christians abolished the Augustine Calendar which was thirty-eight years behind the Christian reckoning and they began to count (time) from the birth of the Nazarene" (225a).[36]

The fearful events of 1391, the year which was the precursor to the final tragedy one century later under Ferdinand and Isabella followed immediately upon the changeover to the Christian Calendar. No numerical figures of the martyrs who met death are given by Zacuto but he named two famous rabbis who died in Toledo for the "sanctification of the Holy Name: Rabbi Judah b. Asher, a descendant of the famed Rabbi Asher, and R. Isaac b. Shoshan and others." The persecution, we are told, extended to Toledo, Sevilla, Lerida, Barcelona, Majorca and Minorca. "The population rose up against the Jews, killed them with the sword, seized their children and their women, and carried them off to sea to sell them. Over four thousand changed their faith." In the confessional mood of Hebrew martyrdom, Zacuto wrote: "According to our tradition, these sufferings were the just punishment of divine wrath.[37] For many had taken gentile women into their homes; children were born of the illicit unions and they later killed their own fathers. Although their own (legitimate) children were righteous, we all bear joint responsibility for one another, especially in sins of immorality. God visits stern retribution (upon the sinful generation). God is just and who can say to Him, 'What dost Thou?'" (225a).

From this pitiful declamation Zacuto returned for a brief period, to record the scholars, such as Isaac Barfat and Simon Duran who were part of the exile that settled in Algiers, Oran, Bugia, Tunisia and Constantine.

As he crossed over into the fifteenth century his annals of both

---

[36] Cf. *Catholic Encyclopaedia*, III, 739 s.v. Chronology.

[37] The disastrous character of 1391 was expressed mnemonically in the Hebrew phrase אל קנא "God Avengeth." The numerical value of the latter word signified 1391 (151 plus 1240).

the scholars and public events were no longer reflective of bookish sources, detached and detailed. Freedom from following slavishly a written source did not liberate Zacuto from its restrictions. His writing, if anything, became more diffuse and less organized.

Zacuto, the mathematician and astronomer, the Talmudist and chronicler lacked the power of historic imagination so essential for unifying historic threads. He lacked the capacity of literary portrayal, so that the closer he approached the period in which he was a living witness and participant the more glaring became his inability to portray whole that which he felt so deeply and passionately.

Occasionally however, a stir of spontaneity, an outburst of indignation, a cry of pious exultation, or a quaint episode, unexpectedly breaks through the closing pages of Zacuto's chronicle. Such passages, often irrelevant, reflect the spirit of the age, as well as the spirit of the many faceted author.

Thus Zacuto opened the destined drama of the fifteenth century: "In the year 1400, the Chief Rabbi of the Kingdom of Castile was the sage Don Meir Alguades; great in the knowledge of Torah, physician to the King, and famed astronomer, he translated into Hebrew the ספר המדות; a disciple of the martyr Rabbi Judah b. Asher, he was noted for his saintliness." A brief note about Judah b. Asher followed.

Immediately thereafter, Zacuto introduced the subject of the Disputation of Tortosa, which had such dire consequences. "In the year 1412, a persecution, the like of which had never been known before, broke out in Aragon and Castile, instigated by the priest Fray Vincente, supported by King Don Ferdinand, King of Aragon, grandfather of King Fernando who ordered the expulsion of the Jews in Spain in our time: and aided also by the dissolute and widowed Catalina, Queen of Castile. They brought about the conversion of more than two hundred thousand Jews."[38]

"And in the same year," he continued, "a great storm broke out on the sea, during which many ships were wrecked, epidemics

---

[38] Cf. Baer, *op. cit.*, 407 ff.

and plagues ensued, but not like the plague of the years 1345–46 and 47 when two thirds of the world's inhabitants died, and when they killed all the lepers for fear that perhaps they poisoned the atmosphere. And in various kingdoms, they rose up against the Jews and killed them as never before. It was then that they burned the Jews in Germany, saying that they had poisoned the waters with deadly poison. But the scholars of that time attributed the fatal events to the juncture of the planets, caused by heavenly forces" (225b).

Without any apparent connection in time or cause, Zacuto slipped back to 1365 when the King of Portugal captured the province of Sabata on the African shores. He said that he seized it "because they received the 'forced converts' and the Jews who fled from Castile." He concluded: "This Sabata is a big city which was built by Shem the son of Noah. Joab b. Zuriah lived there" (225b–226a).

Approaching the period of his birth about the mid-century his impressions became reminiscences. The scholars whom he included were not numerous but they were introduced with a feeling of greater intimacy. In this manner, he described the Benveniste family, of his own time and their support of the "three major Yeshibot." The heads of the three talmudic academies were personally known to him. One, Isaac Aboab was his teacher; another, Isaac Campanton, "Gaon of Castile," made a profound impression on Zacuto when he was only six or seven years old. "He who saw his face was as one who beheld the glory of God's presence." Still another, Samuel Valensi was his relative on the maternal side; his family boasted a long uninterrupted scholarly tradition" (226a-b).

The paragraph following reads: "Constantinople, the capital city of the Byzantine Empire was conquered by the Turkish king, the ruler of Persia[39] (מלך פרס) on Tuesday, May 29, [5] 213 A.M.,

---

[39] The reference is to the Turkish Sultan Mohammed the Conqueror.

[40] Daughter of Edom בת אדום equals 453 in Hebrew mnemonics, to which is added one thousand, thus furnishing the date 1453. This is one of the few cases in which Hebrew symbolism is applied to non-Jewish dates.

1453 in the Christian calendar symbolized in the verse 'Rejoice and be glad oh daughter of Edom' (Lam. 4:21).[40] Four days thereafter, the chief of the Castilian army was executed by decree of the King, an example followed by the kings of France and Tunis toward their respective chiefs of the army. In that year, they burned in Contantina (Constantinople) the tree on which, the Christians say, their Messiah, the Founder of their faith, was hanged.... There being no Caesar left, they appointed the king of Germany as Emperor (Caesar).... In the year 1479 an assembly of Christian theologians of Italy, France, and Spain was held in Alcada, a distance of one and a half days from Toledo, concerning a book by Master Diazma of Salamanca, Master of Theology. They burned the book because of heresy.... In the year 1482, the city of Alhama was conquered by Marcus Diclos, because the Moslems had captured the city of Zara. This was unfortunate (loathsome) for Ishmael (Moslems).[41] and to the children of Israel because of our sins.[42] With the capture of Alhama, the war against the Ishmaelites began and in ten years the entire kingdom of Granada fell to the Christians" (226b).

"In that year an inquisition was begun concerning the religion of the Conversos and they were sentenced to burning and their property was confiscated to the king. In the same year they separated the Jewish quarters and their homes from the Christians" (226b).

At this climactic point, the historic thread is snapped. We are given precise dates for the rainfall which, "fell upon our country unceasingly for six months in 1486," the famine of the year following and the inundation of the "beautiful city of Malaga on the shores of the ocean, west of Granada" to which the king of Castile laid siege one hundred days. A Moslem left the besieged city with the intention of slaying the king and the queen in the Roman camp. But the attempt failed. It was a prince and a great lady who were in the royal tent, whom he attacked, and the Moslem

[41] This was a play on the word Zara, as in Numbers 11:20 where זרא means loathsome. בעבור שלקחו ישמעאל לעיר שמה זרא, זאת היתה לזרא לישמעאל.
[42] *ibid.* (226b) ובעוונותינו לבני ישראל.

was killed. Desperate battles were fought for the duration of the siege. The attacking Romans surrounded the city with fourteen thousand men. Within the city, besieged by enemy ships on the sea and the army on land, hunger ravaged among the inhabitants till they surrendered the city. "The city fell on the Sabbath, the twenty-ninth of Ab, which was August 18th. Twelve thousand were taken captive, among them four hundred Jews, who were ransomed by the Jewish communities of Castile" (227a).

The final tragedy from 1492 to 1497, which was now at hand, was thus described by Zacuto: "In the year 1492, after the Christian New Year, January 1st, Granada was captured, and the expulsion of the Jews from Spain was then decreed. After four months, at the end of April, a public proclamation reached every province announcing that the Jews must leave the country within three months extending to the seventh day of Ab. The decree included Castile, Aragon, Granada, Sicily, Sardinia, Majorca and Minorca, comprising all the provinces of the kingdom. Some of the Jews emigrated to Turkey, others to Africa, to the cities of Fez and Oran whither they were pursued by hunger and pestilence, so that almost all perished. But the bulk of Castilian Jewry, unable to reach the sea in quick time, emigrated to Portugal after giving up a tithe of all their possessions. In addition, every person paid one ducat besides a fee of one ducat for a transit permit. They also surrendered one quarter to one third of all the possessions that they brought into the country. Even for those who had no money the sum of eight ducats had to be paid for every soul or else they were taken as captives. Time without limit would not suffice to relate the happenings in Portugal where over one hundred and twenty thousand souls entered the country and only a small remnant survived the ravages of the plague. Of these some were taken captive, their children seized and taken away to distant islands; others, overwhelmed by suffering, changed their religion." (227a).

The successor king (Manuel) "persecutor of Jews", decreed the expulsion of the Jews from Portugal on Sunday, Dec. 24, (1497), during the week of Ḥanukkah on the 29th of Kislev at Presmona

[31] ABRAHAM ZACUTO — HISTORIOGRAPHER 627

near Santarem, the decree to go into effect in eleven months.[43] A terrible persecution was enacted that year, the like of which had never happened before. On the eve of the Great Sabbath (the Sabbath preceding Passover), a decree went forth that the entire Jewish youth, boys and girls, of Evora and of the entire kingdom of Portugal, should be compelled to renounce the Jewish religion. Great was the outcry in Evora in the presence of the King as never before.

"On Passover, they seized the boys and the girls — and the decree was expanded, so that they made even aged people to give up their religion against their will. Many gave up their lives for the sanctification of the Holy Name" (227 a–b).

"In that year, there was an expulsion of Jews from the kingdom of Navarre so that no Jew was left in all of Spain, save fifty who fled to Seville and were imprisoned there for two years till the month of Ab, 1499, when they were taken out to be sold. They were taken to Algiers which is in Africa between Oran and Bougie on the shores of the sea and belonged to the king of Bougie. There had dwelt Simon Duran, and his family is still living there to this day. This community small in number, but great in spirit, ransomed them with the payment of seven hundred ducats. May the Holy One reward them richly in this world and in the world to come. Also the holy congregation of Bougie aided in the ransom. May God their Rock and Creator preserve them."

"And then there was no Jew left in all of Spain. May God gather together our exiles, and rebuild His Sacred Temple, hastily in our time. Amen, May this be Thy Will" (227b).

Thus ends the chronicle of Abraham Zacuto. Factually it is not the end, for it still continues with an apparently irrelevant discussion of a Talmudic question.[44] Zacuto then appended the abstract of an obscure communication which R. Isaac ibn Alfara of the city of Malaga sent to R. Simon Duran in 1441 and to his son R. Solomon[45] of what he saw in the Land of Israel, sup-

---

[43] Cf. M. Kayserling, *Gesch. der Juden in Portugal* (Leipzig, 1867), p. 128, n 4.
[44] (227b) אם אסור לגלות אם נתערבה משפחה פסולה עם מיוחסת.
[45] The text (228a) should read שלמה בנו instead of שלמה בני.

plemented by a further communication dated 1443, and another document of similar content, all of them constituting a strange travelogue among the graves in the Holy Land of the saintly personages in Jewish history.

It would seem that Zacuto was incapable of forming a suitable conclusion for his nobly conceived chronicle. The theme of his work as he planned it in the happier days of his life in Salamanca centered around the luminous heroes of his religion whom he compared to the stars in the heavens. But the overwhelming sufferings of his latter days forced him into detours of dungeons, wanderings filled with horrors of human cruelty and the worst pestilences of nature; expulsions, treachery and betrayals. In these dark surroundings his soul lost its bearings.[46] He no longer saw or mentioned the stars among his own contemporaries, not even the most heroic figure of his own generation, Isaac Abravanel. He did not bring to light the great rabbis who were then setting up new centers of Torah in the Turkish Empire where he himself finally found shelter and security.

Stranger still, Zacuto with his deep strain of mysticism did not find room in the latter pages of his chronicle for those great spirits who then laid the foundations for the famous schools of mysticism in Safed, Jerusalem and elsewhere in the Holy Land. His eyes were no longer focused on the rabbis and scholars who continued the sacred traditions from generation to generation.

The *Sefer Yuḥasin* may therefore be said to have come to an end without reaching its planned conclusion. Strong in faith, defiantly loyal to God and His Torah, Zacuto in the latter days lost touch with the immediate present and faith in the near future. But his work, in the main, stands forth as a testimonial of his belief in the ultimate — in God and in the indestructability of His people and the Torah.

A fitting conclusion for the author of the *Sefer Yuḥasin* — the

---

[46] See (1a): כי בעונותי מרוב השמדות והשביה וצורך המזונות אין בי כח ולא חכמה ודעת ולא עמד טעמי בי וריחי נמר.

man and the book — is the avowal which he made prayerfully at the end of his Introduction:

"I implore God that He lead me in the way of truth, that I may be privileged to complete this work and to write (with the Psalmist 119):

'Happy are they who are upright in the way...
For I trust in Thy word...
I understand more than my elders
Because I have kept Thy precepts...
Turn Thou toward me and be gracious unto me
As is Thy wont to do unto those that love Thy name. Amen'."

THE SYNAGOGUE MURALS OF DURA-EUROPOS

by ARTHUR DARBY NOCK

1. HARRY AUSTRYN WOLFONS'S services to scholarship are so great that one who seeks to pay homage to him on this happy occasion may be pardoned for falling back on the apologetic phrase with which Ovid accompanied a gift, *in quo censendum nil nisi dantis amor.*

Mine is a modest postscript to the splendid publication by Carl H. Kraeling of the synagogue which the Yale excavators, under the direction of Michael Rostovtzeff, found at Dura-Europos on the Euphrates, and investigated with minute and most rewarding skill.[1] One or two details might be mentioned as bearing on the Jewish community in this outpost between two cultural worlds,[2] but our present concern is with the wall paintings, and in particular with the pageant of Jewish history set forth before the eyes of the congregation and of any outsiders who might find themselves within the building. Those who were responsible for these paintings wished to "magnify God," just as did the men who gave portions of the mosaic floor-decoration in the synagogue of Apamea, "for the wellbeing (*soteria*)" of their nearest and dearest.[3] Their

---

[1] *Excavations at Dura-Europos, Final Report* VIII, Part I (1956). This includes contributions by C.C. Torrery, C.B. Welles, and B. Geiger.

[2] The fragment of a prayer in Hebrew after meals is reproduced in *Final Report V, Part I* (1959), 74 f., no. 11. For Jewish names on pottery at Dura cf. Du Mesnil du Buisson, *Mél. Univ. St. Joseph* (Beyrouth) XXXVI (1959), 19 f., 24. On the decorations of the Torah shrine cf. now A. Grabar, *Cahiers archéologiques* XI (1960), 60 ff., to which Kraeling drew my attention.

[3] Mouterde-Mondésert, *Inscr. Gr. Lat. Syr.* nos. 1320 ff., with my remarks, *Am. J. Arch.* LXII (1958), 339 f. Cf. the commemorative inscriptions at Dura: Kraeling 263 f., 277 f.

place of worship must not be inferior to pagan shrines in the city.

We cannot ascribe to them any conscious deviationism. Recent discussion has made it clear that in different times and places there has been a considerable range of variation in the interpretation and application of the "Second Commandment."[4] Further, Kraeling has shown that, just as the design above the Torah shrine reflects the Messianic and eschatological Hope of Israel, so also these scenes from the sacred story are closely related to Palestinian and Babylonian interpretation. Thus it is here that we have our earliest dated evidence for the figure (commonly called Hiel) inside the altar of the prophets of Baal who was ready to take steps to produce the fire for which they were praying.

2. On one detail this view cannot indeed be pressed. Kraeling (176 f.) remarks that the scene of the finding of Moses differs from the Biblical account in that it shows the daughter of Pharaoh actually retrieving the child from the river herself in contrast with Exod. 2:5, "she sent her maid to fetch it," and relates this detail to the reading of the Hebrew homograph 'mh as meaning "arm," "hand," in accordance with a Tanna of the second century C.E. recorded in the Babylonian Talmud, Sota 12 b, whereas the LXX and other Jewish sources (see Sota, *ibid.*) took the homograph to mean "maid." Since then J. Gutmann, *Eretz Israel* VI (1960), 17 has observed that the Hellenistic Jewish dramatist Ezekiel says "she saw the babe straightway and seizing it took it up."[5]

---

[4] On the neutral character of the female heads and zodical signs in the ceiling decoration, cf. *Gnomon* XXXII (1960), 731 adding *Am. J. Arch.* LXIV (1960), 65 (heads, e.g. of Demeter, on ceiling-slabs of theater at Side), L. Ginzberg, *Legends of the Jews*, IV, 401 (signs of zodiac protest against Haman's plot to slay the Jews), 415 (Sun and Moon put on mourning), F.H. Colson, *Philo*, 8,352. Josephus does indeed (*B.J.* V, 214) note the absence of zodiacal signs from the representation of the heavens on the veil of the Temple. In general cf. J. Gutmann, *Hebrew Unio nCollege Ann.* XXXII (1961), 161 ff.. (Were not the statues of Herod Agrippa's daughters, for which he quotes Jos. *A.J.* XIX, 357, set up by the citizens of Caesarea and Sebaste rather than by the monarchs?)

[5] ἰδοῦσα δ'εὐθὺς καί λαβοῦσ' ἀνείλετο l. 21 of the citation in Eus. *Pr. Ev.*

Now this Ezekiel is clearly dependent on the LXX, and I venture to suggest that there is no need to suppose that the painting implies the pronunciation of *'mh* in the sense of "arm." After all, Exodus 2:10 proceeds to say "she named him Moses, for she said, Because I drew him out of the water" (ἀνειλόμην in the LXX),[6] and that is the heart of the story, as recalled in Acts 7:21 "and when he was exposed, Pharaoh's daughter took him up." (ἀνείλατο here is, I think, "took him up," as the A.V. gives, and not "adopted him," as the R.S.V. has it. The verb ought to have the same meaning as in Exodus; otherwise it can indeed indicate that some one sets about rearing a foundling, but does not indicate the foundling's destiny, which may be adoption or something like it, but may also be slavery:[7] here the meaning is made clear by the following words, "and brought him up as her own son.") Furthermore, in the LXX, 2:5 reads, somewhat awkwardly, "seeing the ark in the marsh, sending her maid, she picked it up (ἀνείλατο)": the handmaid's part is a subsidiary detail. Pictorially the young princess, standing in her unselfconscious innocence[8] and displaying the young Moses to the world, is most effective.

IX, 28. J. Wieneke, *Ezechielis Iudaei Poetae Alexandrini fabulae quae inscribitur* ΕΖΑΓΩΓΗ *fragmenta* (1931) is excellent.

[6] Ezekiel 30 f. ὄνομα δὲ Μωσῆν ὠνόμαζε, τοῦ χάριν ὑγρᾶς ἀνεῖλε ποταμίας ἀπ' ἠόνος. The fact that Ezekiel speaks of Jacob as bringing 70 souls to Egypt, as against the 75 of the LXX, can hardly be taken to show knowledge of the Hebrew original: metre has its exigencies. With his freedom in handling the story, cf. that of Josephus, *A.J.* II, 224, where the princess does not go down to the river to bathe but sports on its banks (which almost looks like a reminiscence of Nausicaa) and, seeing the ark, sends divers to bring it to her.

[7] Cf. Bauer-Arndt-Gingrich, *Greek-English Lexicon of the New Testament* (1957), s.v. ἀναιρέω. The two possibilities appear side by side in Manetho VI, 53 ff. — In Ezekiel, as Wieneke remarked, the child has his tokens, *gnorismata*, like Ion in Euripides and foundlings in the New Comedy. Contrast Paolo Veronese's picture described by Giles Robertson, *Burlington Magazine* XCI (1949), 100 as "a gay record of a contemporary picnic in fine modern clothes set in a local landscape;" cf. K.E. Maison, *Themes and Variations* (1960), p. 96 ff.

[8] Cf. Cabrol-Leclercq, *Dict. arch. chrét. lit.* XII, 1801 ff. (on baptism);

3. In making this suggestion about the picture of the infancy of Moses I do not for one moment wish to give the impression that I believe that the illustrations of the Dura synagogue are related to any ideas specifically proper to Hellenistic Judaism. It has been suggested that they reflect a type of thinking such as has been thought to be found in Philo. Against this Kraeling (351) rightly notes Philo's much narrower range of interest in Scripture. Apt and far from obvious are some of Philo's Biblical quotations from outside the Pentateuch, their proportionate number is astonishingly low,[9] and the only episodes from other writings on which he dwells relate to Hannah and Samuel.[10] Moreover, the paintings do at least suggest a greater interest in episodes as concrete events than we usually find in Philo.[11]

Now I. Heinemann has observed that other Hellenistic Jews show familiarity with more of the Old Testament:[12] the fragments of the older Philo's hexameter poem and the various historical writers quoted by Alexander Polyhistor[13] furthermore take

E.R. Goodenough in *Greek and Byzantine Studies*, I (1958), 73 (Jewish-Gnostic amulet: Adam and Eve just before eating the forbidden fruit); Gutmann, *Studies in Bibliography and Booklore*, III (1957), 35 (on nudity in Spanish medieval Jewish manuscripts), and *Eretz Israel, 1. c.*

[9] To the references in A.C. Sundberg, *Harv. Theol. Rev.*, LI (1958), 210 f. add E. Bickerman, *Alexander Marx Jubilee Volume* (1950), 163 f. It may indeed be remarked that a glance at L. Ginzberg's *Legends of the Jews* will show that the story down to the entry on Canaan provided much more stimulus to the imagination than did later events.

[10] Otherwise we have *Q. d. immut.* 136 on the widow in I Kings 17:10, as bearing the same interpretation as Tamar — and the sequel (138) shows that Philo has in mind the full context of her speech with Elijah; *Conf. ling.* 128 ff. on Gideon and the tower of Penuel.

[11] Cf. R.P.C. Hanson, *Allegory and Event* (1959), p. 49 ff. To be sure, Philo's thought has a great fluidity. In *De agric.* 96 the serpent of Moses (Num. 21:8) and the serpent that spoke to Eve, if taken literally, "are like prodigies and marvels": in *Q. Gen.* I, 32 ff. the speaking of the serpent is accepted and explained.

[12] *Philons griechische u. jüdische Bildung* (1932), p. 528.

[13] Conveniently accessible in Wallace N. Stearns, *Fragments from Graeco-Jewish Writers* (1908); Jacoby, *Fragm. gr. Hist.* III C (1958) nos. 722 ff. Cf. R. Marcus in *The Jews*, ed. L. Finkelstein, (1949), p. 749 ff.

a matter of fact view of the sacred story. From a later period, probably the second century of our era, we have evidence for a wide range of interest in Scripture and for a literal reading of it which is highly significant and which in fact furnishes a remarkable parallel to the themes of the Dura paintings.

I refer to two of the prayers in *Constitutiones Apostolorum* VII/VIII in which Bousset found reworked products of Greek-speaking Jews. We must not indeed push this inference too far,[14] but, apart from one exception to be noted later, Bousset's conclusions, with his reservations, seem to me assured. Could there be clearer evidence than VII, 36, a thanksgiving to God for ordaining the Sabbath, the Sabbatical year etc.? What is said about Christ and Sunday and Sunday's superiority is clearly secondary, and all

[14] *Nachr. Gött. Ges.* 1915, 435 ff., reinforced by H. Lietzmann, *Messe und Herrenmahl* (1926), p. 122 ff. and E. Peterson, *Ephemer. Liturg.* LXI (1947), 339 f. The texts are translated and discussed by E.R. Goodenough, *By Light, Light* (1935), p. 306 ff.: he seems to me to go too far. Cf. *Gnomon* XIII (1937), 162 f. Let me add three points. (1) In the prayer for the consecration of a bishop (VIII, 5; Goodenough, 330 f.) this Jewish material is used to enrich an earlier formulary (Bousset, 480 f.) now attributed to Hippolytus (cf. R.H. Connolly, *The so-called Egyptian Church Order* [*Texts and Studies*, VIII, iv, 1916], 11 ff.). We therefore cannot use this as an indication of a Jewish rite, any more than we could base any inferences on the O.T. precedents quoted (VIII, 20, 14: cf. 2.9) in the ordination of deaconesses. (2) We have to reckon with the personality of the redactor of *Const. Apost.* G. Dix, *The Treatise on the Apostolic Tradition of St. Hippolytus of Rome* I (1937), lxxiii says of him, "He everywhere fuses the language of his sources with phrases and sentiments entirely of his own devising," and speaks of the works "profuse and ingenious use of scripture, its verbose prayers and its inflated rhetoric." (3) While, as P. Lundberg remarks, *La typologie baptismale* (Acta Semin. Neot. Upsal. X, 1942), 35, Christian prayer in general stems from the Jewish tradition, it remains that the Keduscha was apparently late in showing itself as the Trisagion: cf. Lietzmann, *op. cit.*, p. 164 ff. Since then W.C. van Unnik, *Vigiliae Christianae* V (1951), 204 ff. has proved that I Clem. 34 is no evidence for its use in Eucharistic worship. There has been altogether too much talk of liturgies in times when there could be at most patterns for worship; cf. R.P.C. Hanson, *Vig. Chr.* XV (1961), 173 ff.

[15] Contrast the attitude to the Sabbath of *Didascalia Apostolorum*, p. 236 Connolly (with his comments, lvii ff.).

the rest breathes the spirit of Hellenistic Jewish orthopraxy. Bousset rightly compared § 4, "Thou didst command the observance of the Sabbath, giving them not an excuse for idleness but an occasion for piety," with Philo, *Spec. leg.* II, 60 ff.; it is an answer to Gentile criticism such as Tac. *Hist.* V, 4 *septimo die otium placuisse ferunt, quia is finem laborum tulerit; dein blandiente inertia septimum quoque annum ignaviae datum.*[16]

The first of the two prayers with which we are here concerned begins thus (VII, 38), "We give Thee thanks for all things, O Lord Almighty, for that Thou hast not taken away from us thy mercies and thy compassions, but in every succeeding generation Thou dost save, deliver, help, and protect: for Thou didst help in the days of Enos and Enoch, in the days of Moses and Joshua, in the days of the Judges, in the days of Samuel and Elijah and the prophets, in the days of David and the kings, in the days of Esther and Mordecai, in the days of Judas Maccabeus and his brethren...."

No less to our purpose is the prayer that precedes (VII, 37). We must set aside as Christian the opening words, "Thou who hast fulfilled the promises made through the prophets, and hast had mercy on Zion and compassion on Jerusalem, by exalting the throne of David thy servant in the midst of her, by the birth of Christ, who was born of his seed according to the flesh of a virgin alone."[17] Again, the invocation which follows "Do Thou

---

[16] *finem laborum* refers to the story told at the end of ch. 3, about the six days' march through the wilderness (cf. Virg. *Aen.* I, 10 *tot adire labores*). In general cf. Philo, *Hypoth.* 7.14 (9, 432 Colson): I. Heinemann, *Pauly-Wissowa, Supp.* V, 21. The purpose of the statement in the prayer is, I think, to be explained as V. Tcherikover, *Harv. Theol. Rev.* LI (1958), 59 ff. explains some of the Letter of Aristeas — to make the prescriptions of the Law acceptable to Jews steeped in Gentile culture.

[17] "By the birth... alone" is obviously Christian. Bousset and Goodenough are rather inclined to take the preceding words as Jewish, and so was emphatically K. Kohler, *Jewish Encyclopaedia*, IV, 594 in his pioneer article on this document. But how could any Jew of the period in which these prayers were composed (they show acquaintance with Aquila's version) have thought of the promises made through the prophets as having been fulfilled or of the throne of David as having been exalted in the midst of Jerusalem, except perhaps in a moment of enthusiasm during the revolt of Barcochba? And

Thyself now likewise, O Lord God, receive the prayers that proceed from the lips of Thy people which are from the Gentiles" is clearly Christianized. But what comes next is unmistakably Jewish, "as Thou didst accept the gifts of the righteous in their generations," after which there is a remarkable list of illustrations of the theme: Abel, Noah when he went out of the ark, Abraham after he left the land of the Chaldaeans, Isaac at the Well of the Oath, Jacob in Bethel,[18] Moses in the wilderness, Aaron between the dead and the living, Joshua in Gilgal, Gideon before his sin, Manoah and his wife in the field, Samson before his transgression, Jephthah before his rash vow,[19] Barak and Deborah, Samuel in Mizpeh, David on the threshing floor of Ornan, Solomon in Gibeon and in Jerusalem, Elijah on Carmel, Elisha at the barren fountain, Jehoshaphat in war, Hezekiah in his sickness and before the threat of Sennacherib, Manasseh after his transgression, Josiah at the Passover, Ezra at the return, Daniel in the den of lions, Jonah in the whale, the three young men in the fiery furnace, Hannah before the ark,[20] Nehemiah at the rebuilding, Zerubbabel, Mattathias and his sons, Jael. For the structure you have only to look at the prayers for days of fasting in Mishnah, Taanith 2, 4 (E.T., p. 196, Danby), "May he that answered Abraham our father in mount Moriah...," and the longer lists of parallels in mediaeval liturgies quoted by D. Kaufmann, *Rev. ét. juives* XIV (1887), 246 ff.

how would a prayer composed then have survived the bitter disillusionment which followed, and the exclusion by ordinance of all Jews from Jerusalem? This fulfillment, this exaltation were matters of prayerful hope, as in the fourteenth Benediction of Shemoneh Esreh (E.G. Hirsch, *J. Enc.* XI, 271, 274, 280), Ps. Sol. 17:21 ff. and in Luke 1:32, not of thankful assertion. On the formal side, the *parallelismus membrorum* "Zion... Jerusalem," was well within the compass of a Christian familiar with the Psalms.

[18] The text has "Bethlehem," by an easy error.
[19] Traditionally Jephtha was much blamed: cf. Ginzberg, *Legends*, IV, 43 ff..
[20] Stern, *l.c.*, 253, remarks on Christian *Bilderzyklen*: "Das Wesentliche war, eindringliche Beispiele vor Augen zu führen, nicht aber sie in historischer Folge zu geben." Cf. Morton Smith, *J. Bibl. Lit.* LXXVI (1957), 325. On O.T. *exempla* see also Hanson, *Allegory*, p. 14 ff..

When we turn back to the Dura paintings, we find scenes identified (with a slight margin of uncertainty) as Abraham offering Isaac (over the Torah shrine), Jacob at Bethel, and episodes involving Moses and the Exodus, Aaron, Hannah, Samuel, David, Solomon, Elijah, Esther and Mordecai, Ezekiel (prophecy in the time of disaster), as well as defeat by the Philistines and the miraculous power of the Ark in captivity. It is moreover to be remembered that we have lost more than a third of the murals. This is a pageant of national figures and crucial events distinctly comparable with the prayers just mentioned, and the analogy seems to me to confirm Kraeling's rejection of any schematic interpretation of his material. In fact H. Stern, in his most instructive review in *Theol. Literaturzeitung* LXXXIII (1958), 249 ff. noted the prominence in the paintings of God's interventions to bless his People or an individual or to chastise the People's temporary disobedience, and remarked "Die Aufzählung solcher Paradigmen der jüdischen Geschichte scheint nun (zumindest seit dem Beginn des 4. Jahrhunderts v. Chr.) eine charakterische Besonderheit des jüdischen Denkens gewesen zu sein." He refers to Sirach 44 ff. Box and Oesterley in their note thereon (R.H. Charles, *Apocrypha and Pseudepigrapha of the O.T.* (1913), I, 479) illustrate the antiquity of this theme, and M. Simon, *St. Stephen and the Hellenists* (1958), 40 f. has observed that it is followed with "a very different emphasis" in Stephen's speech in Acts 7 and reappears in Paul's speech at Pisidian Antioch in Acts 13. If the pageant could be presented as a chronicle of *magnalia Dei*,[21] it could also be presented as an honor roll of men of God, e.g. in Sirach and Ep. Hebr. 11: an instance of special interest to us is IV Macc. 18:11 ff.,[22] which

---

[21] Cf. Joseph *A.J.* III, 86 ff. (speech of Moses); *B.J.* V, 376 ff. (occasions on which the Jews had been delivered); M. Dibelius, *Sitz.-Ber. Heidelberg* 1941/2, ii, 19 (ethical application). A. Grabar, *Rev. hist. rel.*, CXXIV (1941), 27 expressed a similar point of view and mentioned the prayers in *C. Apost.*

[22] A. Dupont-Sommer, *Quatrième livre des Machabées*, p. 153 may well be right in regarding this speech (which begins at v. 7) as an interpolation — but a Jewish interpolation of the second century of our era.

ends with Ezekiel as saying "Shall these dry bones live?"[23] Now Ezekiel's Vision fills an entire register on the North wall at Dura and there clearly suggests the national Hope, indicated also, as has been said, above the Torah shrine.

The prayers in *Const. Apost.* speak of the promise of resurrection, but not of this Hope: yet we must not press the point, since we have only fragments in a Christian setting. Philo expresses the Hope seldom, but then with such emphasis that we cannot suppose that it counted for little in his eyes,[24] and from the Greek Dispersion we have also the evidence of *Orac. Sib.* III, 702 ff.; V, 260 ff. and 414 ff.. Hope and retrospect alike were characteristic of most Judaism.

[23] Cf. *Prophetarum vitae fabulosae*, p. 48 Schermann, p. 23 Torrey [*J. Bibl. Lit. Mon.* I, 1946] on Ezekiel as persuading his people "that there is hope for Israel both here and in the future (age)."

[24] Wolfson, *Philo*, II, 407 ff..

— I am indebted to Professors Saul Lieberman, Krister Stendahl and Zeph Stewart for generous help.

IBN AL-MAḤRUMA
A CHRISTIAN OPPONENT
OF IBN KAMMUNA

by MOSHE PERLMANN

SAʿD B. MANSUR IBN KAMMUNA (hereafter I.K.) scion of a well-known Jewish family, distinguished oculist and philosopher, lived in Baghdad in the second half of the thirteenth century, under the Mongols before they embraced Islam. The most interesting of his works is the *Tanḳīḥ al-abḥāṯ fī-l-milal aṯ-ṯalāṯ*, a critique of the investigations into the three faiths (or rather a critical investigation into the three faiths). This work contains an introductory chapter about religion and prophethood in general, followed by three chapters on the three monotheistic faiths respectively. It is written with austere objectivity. Almost a century ago Steinschneider remarked that it was the most interesting work on interfaith polemics in Arabic. Written in the seventies of the 13th century, it evoked Muslim refutations. In 1284 disorders, something like a pogrom, broke out in Baghdad on account of this pamphlet, for rumor had spread about the unusual liberty the author had taken in the discussion of Islam. I.K. died shortly after the event.[1]

---

[1] Cf. Brockelmann, *GAL*, Suppl. I, 768 f, Suppl. III, 1232; (more mss. of I.K.'s are known); M. Zobel in *Encyclopaedia Judaica s.v.* I.K.; W.J. Fischel *Jews in the Economic and Political Life of Medieval Islam* (London, 1937), pp. 134 ff.; M. Steinschneider *Polemische und apologetische Literatur in arabischer Sprache* (Leipzig, 1877), pp. 37–41 (and index *s.v.* Saad), and *Die arabische Literatur der Juden* (Frankfurt a.M., 1902), p. 239 f. The *Tanḳīḥ* is analyzed by D.H. Baneth "Ibn Kammuna" in *MGWJ*, 69 (1925), 295–311 ("an unusually interesting document of the as yet insufficiently appreciated rationalist trend in the middle ages").

An edition of the tract has been prepared.

L. Nemoy published *The Arabic Treatise on the Immortality of the Soul*

One of the mss. of this work has been preserved at the Biblioteca Angelica in Rome. It contains also a Christian author's annotations on Chapters two and three, that is, on the sections dealing with Judaism and Christianity. These notes, twice the length of I.K.'s chapters, form a running commentary, a full-fledged pamphlet of retort to I.K. But they do not appear as a separate work: The text of I.K. is now and then interrupted; with the word *ḥāshiya* an annotation begins, and when it ends, the word *matn* signifies the return to the basic text by I.K. The copyist describes the annotator's work as *taḥshiya*.

The author of these annotations is Abū-l-Ḥasan ibn Ibrāhīm ibn al-Maḥrūma (hereafter I.M.). He lived in Mardin. The notes mention that over thirteen hundred years had elapsed since the death of Christ. Writing in 755/1354 the copyist mentions the annotator as deceased. We are then dealing with a writer of the first half of the 14th century. Possibly he too was a physician.[2]

Presumably, the author had no objections to I.K.'s exposition on religion in general or to his critique of Islam. What he wrote was a Christian critique of I.K. and a polemic against Judaism.

The late author of the annotations said: A certain event occured that urged me to write these notes on the text of the sections on the two religions only, of the Jews and of the Christians, in this book. I pray to God for inspiration that the notes may be accurate (43).[3]

(New Haven, 1945) and translated it in the *Ignaz Goldziher Memorial Volume II* (Jerusalem, 1958), and furnished notes on the treatise on the differences between Rabbanites and Karaites in *Tarbiz*, vol. 24.

S.W. Baron *A Social and Religious History of the Jews*[2], V, 102 f. (New York, 1957).

[2] (Ignazio Guidi) *Catalogo dei condici orientali della Biblioteca Angelica di Roma* (Firenze, 1878), pp. 10–11.

Guidi noted that mss. of Ibn Kammuna's work seem to be connected with Mardin. The data in G. Graf, *Geschichte der Christlichen arabischen Literatur*, II, 70 f. (Citta del Vaticano, 1947) are based on Guidi's catalog.

A Sarīja Zayn al-din is mentioned in these books as connected with the ms. but the name does not seem to appear in this ms. at all.

[3] The ms. has a pagination by leaves. Here the pagination is given by

This may be a literary device, or a reference to a disputation. It may also reflect an imitation of I.K. who begins his exposition with a similar sentence.

What is remarkable is I.M.'s attitude toward I.K. I.M. designates I.K. as *al-muṣannif*, the author, who, he knows was an eminent scholar and thinker. But he maintains that in this particular book, i.e. in the *Tankīḥ*, I.K. did not live up to his standard and reputation; his objectivity was impaired, his truthfulness forsook him, he was overcome by a bias for his native Judaism, and his customary scientific detachment gave way to emotionalism and arbitrariness (*mayl al-muṣannif maʿ al-hawā*). This weakness is revealed especially in his treatment of Christianity. The Gospel quotations are inexact, perhaps distorted on purpose. That such a fine man should take recourse to such methods is most regrettable.

> Empty claims and senseless assertions became the author's (I.K.'s) habit and custom in this book, unlike his wont in his philosophical writings, because in those writings he followed his reason whilst in this book he followed his bias. That is why, by reason of this book, the end of his career is marred after those (earlier) books had established his reputation. It is evident that his discussion here is insufficient to silence his opponent: first, because it is a claim without proof... The author (I.K.) was misled in this book... by empty claims and senseless assertions to such an extent that they became his characteristic and habit. (117–119)
>
> I do not know how the author could permit himself (this) fickleness (*talawwun*) in discussion... This is strange coming from such a man nor does it befit his stature. (173–174).
>
> But he feigns to ignore the truth, and speaks without truth, to carry favor with his coreligionists and to share their bias (185).

pages. Where the ms. counts 100, my pagination counts 200. A selection of passages is attached in the order of my pagination. At the end of a reference or passage the page is indicated, and by it the original can be located among the appended passages. Thus the copyist's note (re date) is at the end of the *Tankīḥ* as a whole pp. 326–327.

The author (I.K.) has in this book so accustomed his tongue to (mere) assertions that they became characteristic of him. Or else, how could he forget that these objections, and more — can all easily occur to Muslim, Christian, Jew? To Muslim or Christian — to demonstrate the abrogation of the Mosaic law; to Jew — to search the innermost recesses of his religion until he either becomes certain of its truth and continues his worship, or else, becomes certain of its wrongness — and abandons it for another faith, in quest of his own (or: his soul's) welfare. (187).

What is said here about the Gospel is incorrect; a lie from such a distinguished man (I.K.) is most reprehensible (218).

I suspect that the author, when he penned this, was either inebriated or somewhat mentally unbalanced. For otherwise how dared he utter this assertion whose falseness is apparent to any child, let alone the mature and the adult? (62)

I.M. makes observations on I.K.'s style and usage. When I.K. cannot rationally accept and argue a point he propounds, he will say "it has been said," or betray his awareness of the weakness of the argument by inserting the innocuous looking *perhaps* (*laʿalla* or *ʿasā ʾan*), (p. 122, 133, 185). Moreover,

A sign of his (I.K.'s) bias is that in his discussion of the Jews he did not take the trouble to mention their sects, whilst here he mentioned each Christian sect separately. Another sign of his bias is that in discussing the Jews he did not separate the queries from the rebuttals but mentioned each objection and answered it immediately; while in (the section on) Christianity he mentioned the objections one after the other without answering any until he had enumerated all of them. I suspect he wanted thereby to heighten vituperation (214).

I.M.'s own polemic often begins with the remarks

"One might say",
"Should one object",
"Suppose we admit",

[5]   IBN AL-MAHRUMA   645

"May it not be that",
"Does it not say in the book".

In the chapter on Judaism which, with I.M.'s notes, is three times the size of that on Christianity, I.M. is on the offensive;[4] in that on Christianity, on the defensive. Indeed, he displays the same features which he decries in I.K., and it, seems, he was *consciously* imitating the show of objectivity so well put on by I.K. Certain Christian views and utterances are to be understood, he says, in the light of Christian interpretation. I.M. wanted to write only on Christianity *in general terms*, and not on behalf of any denomination (215)

> But I do not undertake to satisfy all the factions of the Christian community; I try to satisfy only the Christians in general (205). As my purpose in these annotations is to warn against the mistakes of the attackers of the (Christian) faith as a whole, not of the various sects that belong to it, I refrained here from a rejoinder because volumes had been devoted to that in Arabic, and whosoever desires to acquaint himself with them should seek them and look into them (215).

The subject matter of the polemic runs its usual course: the law and its validity and abrogation; transmission and its deficiencies; anthropomorphism, etc. But I.M. strikes a rather unexpected note. He is anti-Torah; the Torah is not a book of divine origin but a shabby compilation presumably by Ezra replete with contradictions, unworthy tales, etc. Coming from a Christian author of the time, this is a bewildering statement. I.K. quoted such notions from the twelfth century Jewish convert to Islam, Samau'al al-Maghribi (hereafter S.M.).[5] I.M. is fully in support of these ob-

---

[4] For the section on Judaism in I.K., cf. Leo Hirschfeld *Sa'd b. Manṣūr Ibn Kammuna und seine polemische Schrift* (Berlin, 1893); for that on Christianity — Baneth's study, pp. 300 f.

[5] Cf. M. Schreiner in *MGWJ* (1898–9). Edition to appear shortly. On S.M.'s influence cf. M. Perlmann in *Journal of Jewish Bibliography* (New York. 1942), pp. 71–74 and in *Studi Orientalistici in onore di Giorgio Levi Della Vida*, vol. II, (Roma, 1956).

jections, and berates I.K. for ignoring the force of the argument. And yet, I.M. says (not noticing that his remark belittles his own faith) "I.K. criticizes the contradictions in the gospels: the blind reproaches the one-eyed, the cripple blames the lame."

> This is a very powerful objection whose force the Jews cannot escape. One point that indicates the correctness of the assertion of this objector (S.M.) is that Moses, peace upon him, cannot be accused of the compounded ignorance which consists of disbelief in the truth plus belief in its opposite...
> No doubt the Torah the Jews possess contains matters indicative of the ignorance of its author, of his being in error himself and of his being, at the same time the cause of other people's error, e.g. the description of God as regretful, resting when tired, addressing Moses face to face (91).
> ...numerous contradictions the like of which cannot occur in the words of God or a prophet (93).
> What we have quoted — or the like of it — indicates the correctness of the assertion of the objector (S.M.) that the Torah is a book by Ezra, not a book of God. I quoted from it so extensively merely in support of the objector, in order to alert the reader to the author's (I.K.'s) propensity for bias, insofar as he ignored these contradictions in the Torah (105).

I.K. had offered a counter-argument: Ezra, righteous man that he was, would not have tampered with remnants of the divine Scriptures. I.M. disagrees.

> What the opponent (S.M.) claims is the inauguration of the (present) Torah after the disappearance (of the original), not (mere) distortion and substitution (of passages) while (the whole) was extant, as the author's (I.K.'s) wording would indicate. As to Ezra's righteousness and piety — should the opponent (S.M.) admit that — that would not be an argument against him (the opponent) but one in his favour, for he might say that Ezra's piety and righteousness were the greatest stimuli for the concoction of a scripture to substitute for the one that perished; all this — out of anxiety about the community, lest

its affairs should be disrupted, its welfare impaired and lest hearts should be inclined toward following some other nation... until such time as God may send a messenger to inaugurate (*yujaddid*, perhaps *yuḥaddid*, define, lay down) a new religion that will enable them to dispense with this concocted scripture (144).

I.K. (actually excerpting Yehuda Hallewi) mentioned that the divine power (*al-'amr al-'ilāhī*) operated among the children of Israel. I.M. objects.

I say that the word of the author (I.K.) in this passage admits of two interpretations: One is that by 'the Children of Jacob' he refers to Joseph and his brethren; the other — that the reference is to the progeny of Jacob (in general). If the author's reference is to the former, his word is contradicted by what has befallen Joseph at the hands of his brethren, as mentioned in the Torah, by their decision to shed his innocent blood, by their selling him for a trifle and turning him into a slave after he had been a free man, even though had he been a mere slave his price would have been over a thousand *miṭkāls* of gold, on account of his widely-famed beauty (43). If, on the other hand, the author (I.K.) meant by 'the Children of Jacob' the progeny of Jacob (44), then the wrongness of his words is proved by the fact that most of them were rebellious of the worship of God who demonstrated to them miracles through His prophet Moses in Egypt, on the Red Sea, and in the wilderness. And after all they had witnessed they worshipped the calf made of metal... Had any unbelieving people from among the peoples the Jews hold in contempt witnessed the miracles the Jews had witnessed, it would have abandoned its unbelief and would have believed in God, and exerted itself for His sake, and would not have deviated from His worship, even if the emperors of East and West (Rome and Iran) had sought to force it into such deviation (45).

Jews had the tablets of the law for nine hundred years, continues I.K. I.M. retorts:

These people (the Jews), when they disobeyed God, as admitted by the author, were forced into exile by Nebukadnezzar. But the later disobedience the author did not mention is the one that brought about their exile by Titus, King of Rome.... Its seriousness is greater than that of the former.... In the exile by Nebukadnezzar the Divine wrath against the Jews lasted but a fraction of the duration of the exile by Titus.... But the disobedience that preceded the exile by Titus necessitated the continuance of the wrath against them forever because it was extremely evil. How could it be otherwise when they had rejected Jesus and the Apostles.... Had they committed only this great sin it would have been sufficient to deprive them of the bounties God had granted them, and to necessitate their eviction from His noble gate and to preclude their return to the land in which they had been, i.e. the Holy Land. Passages in their prophetic books indicate that there is no return for them to that land forever. [Many quotations follow of passages such as Deut. 28:23; Jer. 14:11, 12; Hos. 1:6; etc.] This is a sample of the prophets' words on the subject. These demonstrate that our assertion is right (55).

I.K. says the miracles of Moses may not be dismissed as a convention among the Jews (*tawāṭu'*), because so many people in so many lands have accepted them. I.M. objects: Christians have even more people and lands and yet the Jews reject the Christian miracles. I.M. finds that abrogation of the Mosaic law occurs many a time in the Scripture itself. Thus, if Jericho was compassed on seven days (Joshua 6:15) it is clear that one of them was a Sabbath; Elijah offered a sacrifice outside the temple, etc. I.M. stresses that even if only one revealed precept is abrogated in the Scripture, that is sufficient to destroy the whole structure of revealed commandments (*al-farā'iḍ al-sam'īya*) (pp. 79–88). The Onkelos version changed words, e.g. the term for revelation (85). The Rabbis further added words and deeds abrogating Scriptural injunctions.

I.K. says that Moses added new precepts but did not abrogate old ones, and the special precepts were to serve as a mark of honor for the Jews. I.M. disagrees. What Moses did add, was new burdens which were a curse. The nations that did not accept the Mosaic law may well consider themselves lucky in avoiding this pitfall and the Deuteronomic execrations...

> As to his assertion "and God added to the precepts some that pertain to the Children of Israel exclusively, not to any other nation" — it is quite true. That is the (gentile) nations should praise and thank God fervently for having delivered them from carrying the burdens of the Mosaic law, and for having released them from being included in the Deuteronomic curse which inevitably affects the followers of the Jewish faith when they violate any of the law's commandments and prohibitions (64).[6]

I.K. introduces the comparison of the prophet as soul doctor to the healer of the bodies. I.M. takes up this analogy but with a negative conclusion.

> The relation of the precepts to the souls is like the relation of the medicines to the bodies (in which the souls dwell). Just as a body that is on the whole sound may need only little medication, light medication at that, so the soul that is on the whole charitable needs only a few light precepts. A multitude of precepts is needed for the wicked souls dominated by evil traits like a body seized with malignant diseases. In treating (them) the physician may have to increase medication, and to prescribe powerful drugs, so that "the addition" mentioned will be not in the nature of an honour, as the author said, but rather in the nature of chains in order to deter the Jews from following evil paths for which they have a natural bent... 'Just as the healer of bodies will treat only the disease present in the body, so the healer of souls, that is the prophet, will attempt to heal

---

[6] The honorific quality of the Mosaic precepts (*tashrīfan lahum*) figures in the *Khazari*, e.g. p. 94, 1. 18, (II, 26). Cf. p. 18, 1. 15–19 (I, 27) as an opening statement of Hallewi's view on the election of Israel. In the *Bustān al-'uḳūl* of Nathanael b. al-Fayyumi, ed. D. Levine (New York, 1908) p. 65 f./104 f. this is even supported with quotations from the Koran.

the human soul disease in accordance with his findings in his own time.' These are his (I.K.'s) own words. It is in accordance with this thesis that we say that had not the soul diseases of the Jews been greater and more malignant than the soul diseases of earlier nations, their physician, i.e. Moses, would not have been forced in treating them to use medication more extensively, than was the case in any earlier treatment. From this, the falsity of the author's (I.K.'s) assertion — that the addition of precepts was to honour the Jews — will be evident (65–67).

Here we have a curious blending of the *ṭibb al-'adyān* versus *ṭibb al-' abdān* motif with Christology and the damning of the Jews.[7]

Torah injunctions are criticized on a moral basis even when they outwardly appear noble.

Beyond doubt, the Torah does not display any truly noble features whatsoever. It does display what outwardly suggests noble traits but is inherently the opposite thereof. Of this kind is the Torah verse in Deuteronomy: 'Thou shalt not lend upon interest (to thy brother): interest of money, interest of victuals, whether much or little;* unto a foreigner thou mayest lend upon interest, but unto thy brethren* thou shall not lend upon interest.' Of this kind is also the Torah verse, again in Deuteronomy:* 'Thou shalt not deliver unto his master a bondsman that is

---

[7] The notion of the prophet as soul doctor, (esp. as social soul doctor) is strongly represented in the *Epistles of the Sincere Brethren*, e.g. (in the Cairo edition of 1927), II, 271; IV, 22 f., 25, 72 f., 84, 105 f., 228 .Cf. A. Awa, *L'esprit critique des 'Frères de la Pureté* (Beirut, 1948) pp. 198 f. If on the one hand it goes back to Fārābī's elaboration of Platonic notions on the role of the philosopher-(king-ranking) legislator, the relativist element can be traced to the stoic theories of introducing social reforms and institutions in a religious guise in accordance with the needs of place and time, in the interests of society, and in order to keep the masses under control. Cf. F. Rahman, *Prophecy in Islam* (London, 1958), pp. 42 ff., 55–64; Jul. Guttmann in *MGWJ*, 78 (1934), 456–464; also Ibn Ḥazm's data in *JQR*, 40 (1950), 279 sq. (from *Fisal*, V, 119 sq); M. Asin Palacios in *al-Andalus*, III (1935), 345–389.

* The Arabic is inexact in the rendering of Deut. 23:20–21, 16–17.

escaped from his master unto thee; he shall dwell with thee, in the midst of thee.' It is clear that true nobility of character would dictate confronting the bondsman and his master, and investigating thoroughly the case: if the bondsman escaped from his master's cruelty, he should be given refuge and not delivered to his master; but if he escaped because of a crime,... he should be delivered unto his master so that the latter might revenge himself upon him.
I shall further reproduce from the Torah some encouragement of evil character traits.... On the other hand, prayer and fasting are not mentioned in the Torah at all (69–70).

I.M. says that we often hear of Jewish tenets that seem attractive only to discover that they were plagiarized by the later Jewish scholars from the bigger and better faiths. Example: the belief in resurrection which is so painfully absent from the Hebrew Scripture. Even before I.M.'s annotations begin there are two marginal notes in the spirit of I.M. but possibly coming from the copyist. They are but rumblings announcing I.M.'s thunder against the lack of reference in the Hebrew Bible to the hereafter (28, 29).

I.M. stresses that when the Jews attempt to improve upon their Scripture they succeed merely in violating the basic command — neither to add to nor detract from the divine law.

> This belief is an accretion to what is in the Torah because the latter does not mention it either by implication or explicitly. A community that believes in what is not in its scripture deviates from its founder's ruling and rejects his law.
> The Torah did say that the reward of obedience is wordly benefits, and the punishment of disobedience — calamities and misfortunes, again wordly in nature.... (72)
> Thus it appears that the Jew who believes otherwise does not follow the Torah. It will not escape an intelligent person that the Rabbis, aware that the Mosaic law misses this important point which every true religion must needs mention, i.e. the notion of the hereafter and reward and retribution in the life to come, set out to supplement the Torah, and in their zeal for

their religion disregard the prohibition of adding to or subtracting from the Torah. Now if this is the revealed Torah, how did Moses permit himself to omit this matter which is of the utmost importance in true religions, though he mentioned matters of no consequence, such as 'And Noah begot three sons* Shem, Ham, and Japheth,' which he repeats somewhat further...*. If he only once mentioned retribution in the hereafter! If, however, this Torah is not the same (as the revealed one), then the Jews' refractoriness is even greater. You, O reasonable and just (reader), know that the Jew who believes in what is not in the Torah and makes it a pillar of his faith, will have abandoned his religion...... What the author (I.K.) has quoted on the authority of the Rabbis and the Jewish traditionalists is just of this nature, and is not based on Mosaic law. Hence, this belief of theirs is an argument against them, not one in their favour (74–75).

All this talk is one of the (illegal) innovations invented by the Jewish scholars or borrowed from non-Jewish sources, for the Torah has not a single word of it all. He who believes that this talk is true must then say that he draws upon the Rabbis, not Moses, and that the Jews in general follow neither the Torah nor Moses but these Rabbis. And he who is bound by this (law) does not follow any prophetic faith, be it of Moses or any other prophet (76–77).

It is amazing that the Jews fail to disown the Rabbis and these innovations (of theirs). But the Jews follow the Rabbis, as one blind man will follow another, and they do not recollect the word of the prophet Isaiah who says on behalf of God: 'O my people, they that lead thee cause thee to err and destroy the way of thy paths' [Is. 3;12. The Arabic here ends thus: and they assert that they are beneficial to you] — (158).

Yes, the Christians do not deny that the Jews postulate resurrection and the hereafter following death. But the Christians

---

* Gen. 5:32 inexact, and Gen. 6, 10.

say, at the same time, that the Jews stole this tenet from another religion, and that it has no place in their Torah (187—188).

The critique of the transmission and tradition is not enough. Anthropomorphisms abound in the text, and these could not be of divine origin. If the Torah prohibits anthropomorphisms, then such passages violate the prohibition, and we arrive at the argument of the contradictions in the Torah (p. 119 f.) The Pentateuch contains improbabilities (where did all the animals for the sacrifices in the desert come from?). The book abounds in senseless and useless stories, genealogies, repetitions. Jacob's love for Rachel shows the power of animal passion. The story of the Egyptians' admiration for the miracles performed by Moses is suspicious: If the Egyptians had believed just as the author (I.K.) says they did, they would have followed Moses in all his commands, positive and negative, even unto getting out of Egypt along with him.

The classical verse, Gen. 49: 10 (*the scepter shall not depart from Judah*) evokes an angry remark to the effect that the passage refers to the transfer of the kingdom from Saul to David at the hands of Samuel.

Some of the Rabbis among I.M.'s contemporaries believed the Messiah would appear soon — before 770 (of the Hijra era).

I.K. stated that one of the objections (the fifth) to Judaism was that the Scriptures have no reference to the notions of a hereafter, nor of reward and punishment therein. He suggested as a (possible) Jewish retort that in the time of Moses, the defect of the Hebrews had been that of pagan trends and temptation, not the rejection or lack of the notion of a hereafter. The soul-healing prophet had to treat the present danger of the time with the proper mental medicine, i.e. by fighting polytheism and strengthening monotheism.

I.M. reacts to this attempt of explaining away a difficulty in no uncertain terms.

> I examined this book from beginning to end, and found in it nothing viler than this point, nor farther from truth. If we grant it, for the sake of argument, I would say (by the same

token): had not polytheism been dominant among the Hebrews, the Torah would not have enjoined monotheism; had they not been anthropomorphists, it would not have prohibited anthropomorphism unto them; and had they not hated God it would not have ordered them to love him; and so on, in the same fashion. How can then a sensible person believe the author (149). The falseness of the author's view becomes clear to anybody in his right senses (149–150).

Two XII century Muslim authors are referred to. When in the discussion of hypostases I.K. mentions an argument of the inadequacy of terms, I.M. says that "though this is mentioned in many books, it is not correct, and it was Shams al-Dīn al-Samarḳandī (*barrada -llāhu maḍjaʿahu*) who pointed out its falsity, and mentioned in his book entitled *Sharḥ al-ṣaḥāʾ if al-ilāhīya* how false it is (206).

I.K. mentioned the Jews' claim that non-Jews failed in their attempts to imitate the Jewish faith, and only Jewish sanctuaries have been visited by divine grace. I.M. retorts:

> Who would like to be likened to a Jew? Would anybody nowadays, if addressed as 'Jew,' whether in earnest or in joke, respond otherwise than in anger, with practical results if possible?

Nor is it true that non-Jewish sanctuaries have not been visited by divine grace. Near Tiflis there is a village Karbi (?) with a well-known monastery where hydrophobia is cured. This miraculous cure is mentioned by a Muslim author, the physician Muhaḏḏib al-Dīn Ibn al-Hubal, in v. IV of his work entitled *al-Mukhtār* (166 f.)[8]

I.M.'s case is strange in that here a medieval Christian of the 14th century, in his polemics against I.K., the Jewish author of the 13th century, rallies gleefully to the support of the 12th century convert to Islam, S.M., in his attack on the Pentateuch, which book I.M., would be expected to consider of divine origin. His notes are copied by another Christian who does not seem to be shocked at I.M.'s assault on the Pentateuch or notice in that

---

[8] For these authors cf. *GAL*, I, 468; Suppl. I, 849 f.; I, 490; Suppl. I, 895.

assault a danger to the faith. However, it is probable that the heretical implications of I.M.'s notes made their wider circulation undesirable. (This is the only copy preserved.)

Of course, a millenium earlier such attitudes had not been unknown among Christians, especially in Marcionite circles that had been echoing Hellenistic biblical criticism.[9] But there is no reason to believe that in I.M. we have a reversal to Marcionism. It stands to reason that I.M. was acquainted with Muslim theological literature of the *milal wa niḥal* genre which prepared him for S.M.'s attack on the Mosaic law as well as on post-Mosaic Judaism.

I.M.'s notes testify once more to the effect of S.M.'s anti-Jewish tract, and to the effect of I.K.'s inquiry, this time in a Christian circle.

I.M. was displeased with I.K.'s section on Christianity. Yet he could not withhold a grudging admiration for the attempt at fairness displayed by the Jewish author. On the one hand he finds I.K. dangerous:

> No doubt, all the calumnies mentioned by the author (I.K.) — and he will mention more of them in the following — have in Christian commentaries their various answers that will eliminate their viciousness. But it would require a large volume to quote them. Know, that the author followed in this book the road of pro-Jewish and anti-Christian partisanship to the extent that, unfairly, he distorted the wording of the gospel which he quotes in this book, sometimes adding to and sometimes detracting from it. All this is excessive calumny against the Christians and reduction, with sophistic tricks, of their case, to absurdity (226).

And in the same strain:

> He is most insistent among the Jews on enmity toward the Christians, on attacking their faith and on destroying their truths (244).

---

[9] Cf. E. Stein *Späthellenistische Bibelkritik* (Lwow, 1931); J. Bergmann *Jüdische Apologetik im neutestamentlichen Zeitalter* (Berlin, 1908).

But then he arrives at I.K.'s remarks:

[From Ibn Kammuna's treatise]: Most of these retorts [to critique of Christianity] I did not find in the expositions of the Christians but I replied in them (the retorts) on their (the Christians') behalf, in supplementing the consideration of their creed (249).

This touches I.M. to the quick, and his reaction is positive.

These words show that the author (I.K.), may God have mercy on him, sought to amend his previous wrong exposition concerning the Christians. For had he not been certain of partisanship having occurred against them he would not have helped them by mentioning some rebuttals on their behalf. Therefore we, Christian people, should pray God Almighty for forgiveness, for what this man had displayed toward us by heaping upon us (abuse) and seeking to mislead us in this book of his.

This is the end of the annotations which I wanted to write in the course of (reading) this book. Praise be perpetual to the Lord of Lords, the cause of causes; praise to Him; He is above the speech of the infidel, the liar (250–251).

The copyist includes both I.K. and I.M. in his eulogy:
kaddasa-llāhu anfusahumā wa-nawwara darīhayhuma bi-'afwihi wa-rahmatihi, amīn. May God sanctify their souls and illumine their graves in His forgiveness and mercy, Amen.

APPENDIX

TITLE PAGE

كتاب تنقيح الابحاث تاليف المولى العلامة عز الدولة المعروف بابن الكونة وتحشية الحكيم الجليل ابو الحسن ابن ابراهيم المعروف بابن المحرومة المارديّ قدّس الله انفسهما ونوّر ذريحيهما بعفوه ورحمته امين

28 اذا كان الامر هكذا فلما ذا خلت توراة المصنّف عنه بالكلية ولم يذكر فيها من هذه الكلمات؟ وكفى بذلك تبكيتا للمصنّف وتسكيتا له وردّاً عليه وعلى كل من يوافقه غير الوحدة ونفى التشبيه وكفى.

29 فلم خلت توراتك عن ذكر الصلوة والصيام وغيرهما كالمعاد؟

43 قال صاحب الحواشي، قدسه الله تعالى: Text (Margin).
وقعت واقعة اقتضت ان اكتب هذه الحواشي في اثناء الكلام على ملّتى اليهود والنصارى، دون غيرهما من هذه الكتاب. والله استلهم، اصابت الصواب. [Cf. I. K.'s opening in the Tankīḥ قد جرت مفاوضات اقتضت ان عملت هذه المقالة في تنقيح الابحاث للملل الثلاث]
فاقول ان كلام المصنّف هاهنا يحتمل وجهين: الوجه الواحد ان يكون مراده باولاد يعقوب، —يوسف واخوته؛ والوجه الآخر ان يكون مراده ذرية يعقوب. فان كان مراد المصنّف هو الوجه الاول — ينتقض كلامه الذى جرى فى حق يوسف من اخوته، على ما هو مذكور فى التوراة، من تصميم عزمهم على سفك دمه ظلماً وبيعهم اياه بالثمن البخس وجعله عبدا بعد ان كان حرّا، حتّى لو انه كان عبدا لكادت قيمته تنيف على الف مثقال من الذهب لعظمة جماله المشهور ذكره بين الناس

44 واما ان كان مراد المصنّف باولاد يعقوب ذرية يعقوب

45 فيدلّ على فساد كلامه ما جرى من اكثرهم عددا من الخروج عن عبادة الله الذى اظهرهم الآيات على يد نبيّه موسى فى مصر وفى البحر وفى القفر. وبعدما شاهدوا واجتمع ذلك، عبدوا العجل المعمول من المعدن ... لو شاهد تلك المعجزات التى شاهدوا هؤلاء القوم بعض الكفرة من الشعوب المرذولة عند اليهود، لكان قد خرج عن كفره وآمن بالله وبذل نفسه فى سبيله و ما انثنى عن عبادته ولو اكرهَ على الانثناء عنها الاكاسرة والقياصرة.

49 ان كلام المصنف ههنا ليس بصحيح لأن موسى عم لم يمت موتا اختياريا.... وقال الله لموسى: اصعد الى هذا الجبل وهو جبل العبرانيين.... الا ترى انه مات وفى قلبه خسرة من الدخول الى ارض كنعان....

51 ان هؤلاء القوم، لما عصوا الله العصيان الذى اعترف به المصنف،

52 استوجبوا بسببه جلاء بختنصر. واما العصيان الآخر الذى ذكره المصنف فهو الذى استوجبوا بسببه جلاء طيطوس ملك الروم. وخطره اعظم من خطر العصيان السابق... جلاء بختنصر لم يطل عليه زمان الغضب على القوم عشر طول الزمان على جلاء طيطوس. ....واما العصيان السابق على جلاء طيطوس فهو الذى اوجب استمرار الغضب عليهم الى ابد الابدين لأنه كان عصيانا قد بلغ من شدة الرداءة اقصى حدّ. كيف لا وقد اندرج فيه تكذيبهم للسيد المسيح والحواريّين... لو لم يرتكبوا من الذنوب غير هذا الذنب العظيم، لكان هذا الذنب وحده كافيا فى سلب

53 ما منحهم الله من المواهب وموجبا لطردهم من بابه الكريم وقاطعا لهم عن العودة الى الارض التى كانوا فيها اعنى الارض المقدسة.

وفى كتبهم النبوية اشياء تدلّ على انهم لا عودة لهم الى تلك الارض.... ابد الابدين Deut 28, 23 ; Jer 14, 11-12 ; Jer 7, 16 ; Hos 1, 6 etc.

55 هذا انموذج من كلام الانبياء فى هذا المعنى. وقد ظهر منه صدق الذى ادّعيناه. وليس لاحد ان يتأوّل كلام الانبياء تأويلا يخرجه عن فحواه كما قد تاوله بعض علماء اليهود هربا من التزام هذه المحذورات المخوفة، لأنّى اقول للمتأول: انك، ان تاولت ما يتوجه عليك من الزامات طمعا فى التخلص منها،

56 الزمناك ان تتأول جميع الكلام الذى تدّعيه انه حجّة لك كما تأولت الذى هو حجة عليك..
قد غلب على ظنى ان المصنّف، لما سطر هذا الكلام، اما انه قد كان سكران او كان
قد عرض له طرف ماليخوليا. والّا — فكيف تجاسر على التفوّه هذا الكلام الذى فساده
ظاهر لبعض الاطفال، فضلا عن المحنكين والرجال ؟...

64 واما قوله (وزاد عليها ما خصص به بنى اسرائيل دون غيرهم من الامم) فهو
كلام صحيح. ولهذا يجب على الامم الحمد والشكر لله تع بغاية حمدهم لانه اراحهم
من حمل اثقال الشريعة الموسوية واعفاهم من الدخول تحت اللعنة التى فى السفر
الخامس من التوراة التى لا بدّ وان تلزم اهل الملّة اليهودية اذا خالفوا شيئا من
اوامر التوراة ونواهيها.

f 65 ...نسبة التكاليف الى نفوس الناس كنسبة الادوية الى ابدانهم. فكما ان البدن
القريب من الصحة لا تحتاج من الادوية الّا الى السهل اليسير فكذا النفس القريبة
الى الخيرية لا تحتاج من التكاليف الّا

f 66 الى اليسيرة السهلة. واما كثرة التكاليف فانما تحتاجها الانفس الشريرة التى
تمكنت منها الاخلاق الرديئة تمكن الامراض الخبيثة من البدن. فان الطبيب
حينئذ يحتاج فى العلاج الى تكثير الادوية واستعمال القوى منها دون الضعيف.
وعلى هذا لا تكون الزيادة المذكورة تشريفا لهم، كما قال المصنّف، بل انما
تكون قيودا تمنعهم عن سلوك السبل الرديئة التى فى طباعهم الميل الى سلوكها.
.... وكما ان طبيب الابدان انما يعالج المرض الحاضر فى البدن لا غيره فكذا
طبيب النفوس الذى هو النبى انما يداوى مرض نفوس الناس على حسب ما يجده
فى زمانه. هذا كلامه بعينه. فعلى هذه القاعدة نقول :

f 67 لو لم تكن امراض نفوس اليهود اكثر من امراض نفوس الامم السالفة
واشدّ رداءة لما كان طبيبها — وهو موسى عم — محتاجا الى تكثير الادوية والمبالغة
فى المعالجة الى حد يزيد على علاج سبق عليه. ومن هذا يظهر فساد قول المصنف
حيث قال ان الزيادة تشريفا لهم

69 ولا شكّ ان التوراة ليس فيها من مكارم الاخلاق الحقيقية شيئا ابدا. لكن فيها ما ظاهره يوهم انه من مكارم الاخلاق وباطنه بخلاف ذلك. فمنه قول التوراة فى السفر الخامس لا يحل لكم ان تأكلوا الربو فضة ولا طعاما لا قليلا ولا كثيرا — فاما من الغريب كل واما من اخوتك فلا تأكل. . . .
ومن ذلك قول التوراة فى السفر الخامس ايضا — اذ القيتم عبدا فارّا من سيّده فلا تحبسوه ولا تدلوا عليه بل اجلسوه معكم حيث من قراكم. ومعلوم ان مكارم الاخلاق الحقيقيه تقتضى ان يجمع بين العبد والسيّد

70 ويستقصى حالهما بالتحقيق، فان كان العبد قد فر من جور سيده فيجار ولا يسلم الى سيده؛ وان كان فرّ بسبب جريمة... فليسلم الى سيده لينتقم منه. وسانقل مما فى التوراة من الحث على سؤ الاخلاق.... واما الصلوة والصوم فان التوراة خالية عن ذكرهما بالكلية...

f 72 هذا الاعتقاد زيادة على ما فى التوراة لانها ما ذكرته لا تعريضا ولا تصريحا. والملّة التى تعتقد ما ليس في كتابها تكون خارجة عن حكم شارعها وقادحة فى تشريعه. والتوراة قد نطقت بان ثواب الطاعة فوائد دنيوية وعقاب المعصية افات وبلايا دنيوية ايضا. . .

f 74 فظهر ان اليهودى الذى يعتقد غير هذا لم يكن تابعا للتوراة. وليس يخفى على لبيب أن الاحبار، لما علموا ان الشريعة الموسوية اعوزها هذا الامر المهم الذى لا بدّ من ذكره فى كل شريعة حقه، اعنى ذكر المعاد والثواب والعقاب الاخرويين، تبرعوا لتتميمها تعصّبا لشريعتهم، وغفلوا عن فريضة النهى عن الزيادة والنقصان. فان كانت هذه f 75 التوراة هى التى انزلت فكيف استجاز موسى عم الاخلال بذكر هذا الامر الذى هو اهمّ مهمّات الشرائع الصحيحة، مع انه ذكر اشياء لا فائدة فى ذكرها، مثل قوله وكان نوح ابن خمس مائة سنة فولد له ثلاثة بنين[1] سام وحام ويافث؛ ثم انه كرر ذلك بعد كلام قليل... فيا ليته ذكر المجازاة الاخروية ولو مرة واحدة. وان كانت هذه التوراة غير تلك فمعصية اليهود اعظم. وانت، ايها

1 t. ثلاث بنون

IBN AL-MAHRUMA

الرشيد المنصف، تعلم ان اليهودي الذي يعتقد ما ليس فى توراته ويجعله ركنا من اركان دينه يكون قد خرج عن شريعته...

والكلام الذي نقله المصنف عن احبار اليهود ونقلة شرعهم انما هو من هذا القبيل وليس من اصل الشريعة الموسوية، فاذن اعتقادهم ذلك حجّة عليهم، لا لهم.

f 76 جميع هذا الكلام هو من البدع التي اخترعوها علماء اليهود من انفسهم او استحسنوها من اقاويل غير اليهود، لان التوراة ليس فيها من ذلك ولا لفظة واحدة. فالذي يعتقد صحّة هذا الكلام يلزمه القول بان الشريعة مأخوذة عن احبار اليهود، لا عن موسى ÷ وان اليهود كافة ليسوا

f 77 بتابعين لموسى ولا للتوراة لكن لهؤلاء الاحبار. ومن يلزمه هذا اللازم فهو غير داخل تحت شريعة نبى من الانبياء لا موسى ولا غيره.

91 هذا اعتراض قوّي جدّا لا نجاة لليهود من التزامه. ومما يدلّ على صدق دعوى هذا المعترض ان موسى عم لا يتهم بالجهل المركب الذي هو عدم اعتقاد الحق مع اعتقاد نقيضه... ولا شك ان التوراة التي بايدي اليهود فيها اشياء تدل على جهل قائلها وعلى انه ضالّ فى نفسه وهو مع ذلك سبب ضلال غيره وذلك مثل وصف الله تعالى باته ندم وانه استراح من تعبه وانه خاطب موسى وجها لوجه

93 اختلافات كثيرة لا يتوهم وقوع مثلها في كلام الله ولا كلام مرسل

105 فهذا الذي نقلناه وامثاله يدل على صدق قول المعترض ان التوراة كتاب عزرا وليست كتاب الله. وانما نقلت منها هذا القدر نيابة عن المعترض لينتبه القاريء على ميل المصنّف مع للهوى من حيث انه تفاعل عن هذه الاختلافات التي في التوراة

106 اعمى يعيب اعور او زمن يعيب اعرج النصارى لا يعتقدون تحريف التوراة بل انما يعتقدون نسخها.

107 الذي ادّعى المعترض هو تجديد التوراة بعد ذهابها، لا تحريفها وتبديلها حال وجودها، كما هو مدلول كلام المصنف.

114 واما خيرية عزرا وديانته فلو سلمها المعترض — لم يكن حجة عليه بل حجة له لان له ان يقول ان ديانته عزرا وخيريته هى من اعظم البواعث على تلفيق كتاب ينوب عن الكتاب الذى ذهب، اشفاقا على الملّة لئلا تضطرب امورهم وتفسد مصالحهم وتميل قلوبهم الى متابعة بعض الامم ... الى ان يبعث الله رسولا يحدد لهم شريعة تغنيهم عن هذا الكتاب الملفق

117 ان المصنّف قد جعل الدعاوى المجردة والتحكمات الباردة دأبه وديدنه فى هذا الكتاب، بخلاف المعهود منه فى مصنّفاته الحكمية، لانه تابع فيها نهاه، وفى هذا الكتاب تابع هواه. ولهذا اساء بسبب هذا الكتاب مآله من بعد ما حسن بتلك الكتب حاله. ومن الظاهر ان كلامه

118 ههنا غير كاف فى تسكيت الخصم. اما اولا فلأنه دعوى من غير دليل ... ان المصنّف قد أفتن فى هذا الكتاب بالدعاوى
119 المجردة والتحكمات الباردة الى حد صارت له ملكة وعادة

149 انى تصفحت هذا الكتاب من اوله الى اخره فلم اجد فيه اسقط من هذا الكلام ولا ابعد منه عن الصواب. وعلى تقدير صدقه اقول لو لم يكن الشرك مستوليا على بنى اسرائيل لما امرتهم التوراة بالتوحيد ؛ ولو لم يكونوا مشبّهين لما نهتهم عن التشبيه؛ ولو لم يبغضوا الله لما امرتهم بمحبته ؛ وعلى هذا القياس ما عداه، ثم كيف يجوز عند عاقل تصديق كلام المصنّف ...

150 ثبت فساد قول المصنّف عند كل عاقل منصف ...

158 والعجب من جمهور اليهود كيف لم ينكروا على الاحبار فى هذه البدع. لكنّهم انقادوا لهم انقياد الضرير للضرير، ولم يخطر ببالهم قول اشعيا النبىّ القائل عن الله تعالى: يا شعبى، رؤساءكم هم الذين اضلوكم وزعموا انهم يحسنون اليكم.

161 نعم، هذا هو الحقّ الذى لا محيد عنه. لكن ليس ذلك من شريعة اليهود، لانّه غير
162 موجود فى توراتهم. ومن ههنا يعلم ان هذا مسروق من شريعة اخرى، هى الشريعة الحقّة لو كانوا يعقلون.

166 من هو الذى يرضى لنفسه التشبّه بهذه الملّة ؟ وهل احد من اهل زماننا يقال له على سبيل الجد او الهزل « يا يهودي » الّا ويغضب على هذا القائل غضباً يوقع به الفعل لو امكنه ذلك.

173 وانا لا ادرى كيف استجاز المصنّف التلوّن في الكلام ... وهذا عجيب من مثله
174 وغير لائق بفضله.

178 قد ظهر من بعض الحواشى السالفة شدة حرص المصنف على التعصب لليهود بالتموّهات والمغالطات ...

لا سيما وهو يعلم قطعا ان جميع المخالفين لليهود من المسلمين والنصارى ليس عندهم من العلم باللغة العبرانية لا قليل ولا كثير.

185 والمصنف خبير بذلك. ولكنه تغافل عن الحق وتفوّه بغير الصدق، تقربا الى قلوب اهل ملّته وميلا مع هوى انفسهم

187 ان المصنّف قد عوّد لسانه التحكمات فى هذا الكتاب حتى قد صارت ملكة له. والّا فكيف لم يخطر بباله ان هذه الاعتراضات يتاتّى ايراد جميعها ــ بل وايراد ما يزيد عليها ــ للمسلم والنصرانى واليهودى؟ اما المسلم والنصرانى ــ فلاظهار نسخ الشريعة الموسوية ؛ واما اليهودى ــ فللتفتيش على خفيّات شريعة حتى اذا تيقّن صحّتها استمرّ على التعبّد بها، واذا تيقّن فسادها ــ انتقل عنها الى غيرها طلبا لمصلحة نفسه.

... نعم، النصارى لا يجددون اقرار اليهود بالقيامة والمعاد
188 بعد الموت، لكنهم يقولون مع ذلك ان اليهود سرقوا هذه المقالة من غير ملتهم، ولا وجود لها فى توراتهم.

204 واعلم ان العبد الضعيف يقتنع بالاجوبة التى سوف يذكرها المصنف ... الا في مواضع قليلة اهملها المصنف او لم يستوف الجواب عنها ...

205 على انى لا التزم رضى جميع فرق الملة النصرانية لكن التزم رضى النصرانى مطلقا لا غير ...

214 من جملة ميله مع الهوى انه عند كلامه على اليهود ما عرّج على ذكر فرقهم وههنا قد ذكر فرقة من النصارى على حدة. ومن ميله مع الهوى ايضا انه، لما تكلم على اليهود، لم يفرد الاجوبة

215 عن الردود، لكنه ذكر الاعتراض، ثم اجاب عنه فى الحال؛ وفى ملة النصارى ذكر الاعتراضات على التوالى ولم يجب عن شىء منها حتى استوفى الجميع. واظنّه اراد بذلك المبالغة فى التشنيع. ولما كان قصدى فى هذه الحواشى التنبيه على غلط الطاعنين فى مطلق الملة، لا فى مذاهب الفرق المنتمية اليها، اضربت عن الجواب ههنا، لان ذلك قد أفرد له مجلدات بلغة العرب، فمن احبّ الوقوف عليها فليطلبها وينظر فيها.

218 المحكى ههنا عن الانجيل ليس بصحيح. وكذب مثل هذا الرجل الفاضل — غاية القبيح.

226 ولا شك ان جميع التشنيعات التى ذكرها المصنف — وسيذكر غيرها فيما بعد — لها عند النصارى فى التفاسير وجوه كثيرة تزيل الشناعة عنها، لو قصد نقلها لاحتاج الى مجلد كبير. واعلم ان المصنف سلك فى هذا الكتاب طريق التعصب لليهود والتعصّب على النصارى حتى انه، لقلّة انصافه، حرف كلام الانجيل الذى نقله فى هذا الكتاب، وزاد عليه تارة ونقص منه تارة اخرى. كل ذلك — مبالغة فى التشنيع على النصارى وسوق كلامهم الى الباطل بالحيل السوفسطانية.

233 ...فى زمان القران الثانى، هذا القران الذى نحن فيه وقد بقى من هذا القران قريب تسع سنين ومدة القران الثانى له جميعها قريب عشرين سنة فيكون المجموع دون ثلاثين سنة وهذا المبلغ يقتضى قبل سنة سبعين وسبع مائة للهجرة.

234 ومعلوم ان المسيح قتل منذ مدة تنيف على الف وثلثمائة سنة

241 وانا اتعجّب من المصنّف كيف يدّعى هذه الدعاوى الفاسدة من غير استحياء مع
242 علمه وعلم كل يهودى ان السيد المسيح حل السبت ولاجل ذلك شنع اليهود عليه فى اكثر الامر.

IBN AL-MAHRUMA

244 ...لانه احرص اليهود على معاداة النصارى وعلى الطعن فى دينهم وعلى تضييع حقوقهم

From J. K.

249 واكثر هذه الاجوبة لم اجدها فى كلام النصارى ولكنى اجبت بها نيابة عنهم وتتميما للنظر فى معتقدهم.

From I. M.

250 هذا الكلام يدلّ على ان المصنّف، رحمه الله، قد استدرك به ما كان اسلفه من

251 الكلام الباطل فى حق النصارى، لانه لو لم يتيقن وقوع التعصب عليهم لما كان انتصر لهم بذكر بعض الاجوبة نيابة عنهم. فإذن يجب علينا نحن، معشر النصارى، ان نسأل الله تعالى فى غفران ما بدا من هذا الرجل فى حقنا بما كال* علينا وغالطنا فى كتابه هذا. وهذه اخر الحواشى التى قصدت كتابتها فى اثناء هذا الكتاب. والحمد الدائم لرب الارباب ومسبب الاسباب. سبحانه وتعالى عن قول الملحد الكذاب.

End

326 انهاها نقلا وتحشية العبد   327 الفقير الى رحمة الله المقرّ بذنبه الراجى عفوه مسعود المعروف بابن ارجوك الماردى مولدا المسيحى معتقدا فى نهار الجمعة ثانى كانون الآخر سنة خمس وخمسين وسبعمائة بمدينة ماردين حماها الله تعالى من الآفات ورحم الله تعالى من وصل اليه هذا الكتات وترحم على كاتبه وعلى جميع المستغفرين امين

والحمد لله رب الارباب واله الآلهة ما دامت السموات والارض اشكرك حين اصبح الاهى وحين امسى هذا الدهر حياً كنت او كنت فى رمسى ارجوا يكن يومى الذى قد بلغته بتوفيقك المعهود اجود من امسى.

For ‏اما‎ in the first line of the poem read ‏مدى‎.
The second should begin

‏ارجو ان يكون‎

* ‏اكال‎ t.

AVICENNA AND ORTHODOX ISLAM:[1]
AN INTERPRETATIVE NOTE
ON THE COMPOSITION OF HIS SYSTEM

by F. Rahman

I

THE NATURE OF THE relationship to orthodox Islam of the philosophical systems — where these impinge on religion — evolved by the great medieval Muslim philosophers, is of considerable importance and interest. A great deal of the understanding of the orthodox reaction to the philosophical movement crucially hinges on an adequate understanding of how seriously the Muslim philosophers grappled with a genuine philosophical interpretation of Islam. In the present article we shall briefly treat of Avicenna (Ibn Sīnā) from this point of view, both because, among these philosophers Avicenna is the only one who has left us a fully worked out system and because his philosophy has been taken most seriously by the orthodox themselves where it was exalted from a philosophy into a philosophical tradition of a durable influence in Muslim society.

Like Muslim tradition, modern Western scholarship has found among its ranks both attackers of and apologists for Ibn Sīnā. There is a very widely prevalent view according to which Avicenna was a pure philosopher who constructed his whole system on entirely rationalistic grounds but who nevertheless, since he was a member of the Muslim society, paid an external lip-service to Islamic beliefs "in order to pass as a good Muslim." The other side asserts that Avicenna's whole philosophical system has been constructed with the conscious purpose, if not of philosophically interpreting Islam, at least of adapting the entire range of philosophy — in

[1] An original version of this paper was delivered as a public lecture at Princeton University on 20 April, 1961.

so far as it impinges upon religious questions — to Islamic beliefs. This thesis has been powerfully argued by Père L. Gardet in his *La Pensée Religieuse d'Avicenne*. In the following we shall attempt to locate, if possible, the real point of contact, if any, between the Islamic tradition and the philosophic system which Avicenna built on Greek bases.

II

A fact that emerges clearly from a careful study of Avicenna's thought is that it has a deeply personal character. He devised a philosophic system which he not merely constructed on paper but which he lived by. It was an operative philosophy. This does not necessarily mean that he entirely acted upon it and lived up to it fully (his over-indulgence in certain sensual practices is underlined by his biographers),[2] but that he had a strong personal faith in it is a fact that may not be doubted. When close to death, he is reported to have said, "The Manager (i.e. the soul) that used to manage me is no more capable of managing me."[3] This is a personal application of his oft-repeated law of mind-body relationship. But even more vividly and strikingly, what he has to say about revelation and its noetics seems intimately related to certain facts of his intellectual life. He tells us in his autobiography: "Whenever I found myself perplexed by a problem, or could not find the middle term in any syllogism, I would repair to the mosque and pray, adoring the All-Creator, until my puzzle was resolved and my difficulty made easy.... If ever the least slumber overtook me, I would dream of the precise problem which I was considering as I fell asleep; in

---

[2] This has been repeated both by Muslim classical biographers and, with none-too-clear insinuations, by many modern scholars. The classical accounts have no hint of licentiousness or impropriety and there is even no suggestion that Avicenna regarded e.g., his sexual indulgence as being necessarily contrary to his principles (where the body is irrelevant after the soul has developed). We have pointed out in the paper that his Sufism was not moral-ascetic but a kind of intellectual illuminationism.

[3] A.J. Arberry *in Avicenna: Scientist and Philosopher*, ed. by M. Wickens (London, 1952), p. 26.

that way (solutions to) many problems revealed themselves to me while sleeping."[4]

From his rather meager autobiography we do not know much about Avicenna's earliest education. It is quite clear that he was a prodigy, an "infant phenomenon." But it is also clear that his specifically Islamic religious education was not very great. By the age of ten he had memorized the Koran and read literature. The only next thing Islamic he acquired was jurisprudence from which he moved to logic and arithmetic and thence to natural sciences and philosophy. He did study Kalām later on (alongside of philosophy) which partly influenced him enough to produce a metaphysical synthesis of the two with regard to the problem of God-world relationship but which was mostly rejected by him. A highly precocious child though he was, one wonders how deep an Islamic education could have been that hardly went beyond the age of ten years. Once his intellectual power was fired under al-Nātilī (who seems to have been more a victim than a teacher), he embarked on the high seas of a purely philosophical and scientific inquiry.

The role of the purely Islamic element, therefore, in the early education of Avicenna does not seem to have been very great. Conspicuously absent are the Koranic exegesis (which, however, he studied later when his own philosophical point of view had been fully formed) and the tradition, that vast science whereby the early generations of Muslims had transformed their understanding of the Koran and the prophetic teaching into a normative system and of which a compatriot of Avicenna, al-Bukhārī, had produced the most authoritative collection about a century earlier. Sufism has left a more immediate and deep impress on both Avicenna's thought and person. But it is a thoroughly intellectually oriented Sufism and is different in character both from the moral-ascetic and emotive Sufism of traditional orthodoxy and the occult-istic-gnostic Sufism of Ismāʿīlī heterodoxy. Whether the stories of his correspondence with the famous Sufi, Abū Saʿīd b. Abu'l-Khayr are genuine or not and if so, how far, his interest in Sufism

---

[4] A.J. Arberry, *op. cit.*, p. 16.

cannot be doubted. The starting point of this interest was most probably his personal intellectual experiences and on the basis of these he constructed a theory of Sufism (e.g. at the end of his *Ishārāt*) which is essentially intellective-illuminative and not ecstatic or gnostic.

Nevertheless, it is his doctrine of prophethood, rather than that of Sufism, that stands in the center of Avicenna's religious thought. It is in order rationally to understand and to explain the Prophetic Revelation and not the utterances of the Sufis that he develops the doctrine of his symbolic character of imagination and its relationship to the prophetic intellect. In fact, the Sufi doctrine of "attaining to God" or even "union with God" requires neither a doctrine of intellectual revelation nor one of imagination. It is here, indeed, that Avicenna comes to grips with orthodox Islam with the dogma of the Prophetic Revelation at its very centre. What impelled the philosopher to devise this theory?

Avicenna found a great many elements of this kind of doctrine among his predecessors. We have shown in a previous study[5] that most of the vital elements of Avicenna's doctrine of Prophecy came from Greek sources. Immediately before him, al-Fārābī had developed a theory of prophethood based on two factors: the Prophetic imagination and the religio-social order established by the Prophet through an imaginative handling of the philosophical truth. It may be said that Avicenna took this picture from al-Fārābī and further supplied the basis of an intellectual revelation and added a rational-psychological explanation of the orthodox doctrine of the prophetic miracles. And this is, in fact, what did happen. Avicenna stands on al-Fārābī's shoulders and stands under an immense debt to him.

But, as we pointed out earlier, Avicenna's philosophy was also his religion, a personal faith. It was not an edifice of which he borrowed elements from others and then constructed it still for others but primarily for himself to live in. The Active Intellect and the World Soul are for him living and operative realities with

[5] *Prophecy in Islam: Philosophy and Orthodoxy* (1958).

which the human mind stands in a living relationship. Such a reality for him, in which he evinces a profound faith, is the Prophet. But the interesting point is that, unlike the Active Intellect and the World Soul, the Prophet, as an object of his faith, is also an object of other Muslims' faith. The question is, what, in his philosophical system, may have constituted a point of definite transition from his purely rational metaphysics — a purely Greek legacy — and led him to take so seriously the phenomenon of Prophethood — a purely Semitic and Islamic legacy? If we can understand this, we shall understand better the inner composition of his system and also, as a second step, we may be in a better position to discover if this Islamic consciousness was serious enough to re-act on his pure philosophy and, if so, how far.

III

Avicenna's theory of Prophethood, though it occupies a central place in his religious thought, cannot be regarded as the starting-point of this thought but is rather a development of his metaphysics and epistemology. If his speculation on the nature and content of Prophecy had been the starting-point of his religious philosophy a very different metaphysics, especially a very different theory of the God-world relationship, would have been the result. Of these two, the metaphysics and the epistemology of the intellectual revelation, the latter is really, when taken alone, not only indifferent to religion but incapable of producing a religious epistemology. The moral insight and the religious inspiration of the Prophet cannot have their basis in a purely intellectual intuitionism. And in his general theory of intellection Avicenna offers us only an intellectual intuitionism. There is no hint of a specifically religious mode of knowledge, of the moral imperative or of conscience. But once having been inspired, as we shall show, by his metaphysics to take into serious account the Prophetic religion, Avicenna, who already had a theory of pure intellection, decided to turn this latter to the service of a prophetic epistemology and to use it as the latter's base. In this he was undoubtedly encouraged by his concept of the mutual relationship of philosophy and religion, which he had gained from his metaphysics and its comparison with religious dogmas. It would, therefore, be vain to look for a genuine point of transition from philosophy to the doctrine of Prophecy in the philosopher's epistemology, which was rather used as a never-too-willing tool for a purpose inspired elsewhere.

The most fundamental idea in Avicenna's doctrine of prophecy is that the prophetic religion is related to philosophy as a figure or a symbol is related to a corresponding reality. This idea could hardly have arisen if the prophetic religion were regarded as the *datum* from which to start; it could hardly have arisen from a purely intellectual epistemology designed to serve a purely philosophic purpose. Where did it arise? A little reflection will show that Avicenna's most basic metaphysical theory, viz. that of the God-world relationship and nature of God would be the most proper place to give rise to such an idea or rather, since the idea was already present before him, should provide the best ground for the adoption of such an idea. This is not the place to give a detailed analysis of this interesting and considerably original theory which we shall state in a brief outline.

The proposition that to each clear and distinct concept in thought there must correspond a distinction in reality is one of the most fixed points in the philosophic thought of Avicenna. This proposition is asserted by Avicenna at different levels and in varied contexts and underlies the great importance attached by him to definitions. To every distinction, however, there does not necessarily correspond a separate existent. The vegetative soul in man, for example — insists Avicenna — although it may be conceptually separated from other human functions, is not existentially separate (this is an Aristotelian doctrine; cf. Aristotle, *De Anima*, Book I, last chapter). But a further specificative re-statement of this proposition involves existential separateness: "If something is a composite of two notions such that one of these is found to exist separately, then the other must exist separately as well."[6]

Avicenna's argument for the existence of God and his view of

---

[6] *Prophecy in Islam*, p. 34.

the God-world relationship is a consequence of the application of this principle. Since everything in the world "becomes," i.e., is a combination of possibility and actuality — is possible-in-itself and necessary-by-the-other —, it follows that the necessary-by-itself (God) must exist. This theory has fundamentally an Aristotelian basis, but it also undoubtedly represents a development from Aristotle. For Aristotle, necessary being and actual being are synonymous in this context and when he says that God necessarily exists, he means that God is eternally actual. But in Avicenna's doctrine there is a clear and definite shift in the meaning of "necessity" from pure actuality to a *logical* necessity. And in so far as God's existence is seen as flowing *logically* from the concept of God it may be regarded as a form of the ontological argument. Also, for Aristotle, God does not produce matter, which exists independently and is only arranged into a hierarchy of forms under the influence of God's attraction. For Avicenna, on the other hand, — who is under the influence of Plotinian emanationism here—the world proceeds from God. And yet the Avicennian theory develops very differently from emanationism as well. Whereas, in emanationism, the world simply proceeds or flows from God, Avicenna tranforms this process into one of "bestowal of existence" by God on eternally existing essences. It is this "bestowal of existence" theory wich renders Avicenna's God — the Bestower of existence — intrinsically different from Plotinus' One.

This doctrine is obviously much closer to the Islamic concept of God and His relationship to the world than is any Greek philosophical theory. Yet there seems no trace upon it of a conscious effort to insert into the philosophic movement of thought a specifically religious motif, and, to all appearance, the theory seems to be worked out entirely on rational grounds. (For our present purpose the possibility of an unconscious Islamic influence is not relevant.) Indeed, this theory, despite its closeness to orthodox Islam from this point of view, was opposed to it on two basic issues, on which account it was rejected. One of these is its relentless theistic determinism. Although the world is not in itself necessary but only possible, it becomes nevertheless necessary when viewed from God's side, who operates by a rational dynamic necessity. The other issue concerns the philosopher's acceptance of the eternity of the world and his rejection of temporal creation.

But it is precisely this half orthodox half anti-orthodox theory which, in our view, could provide Avicenna with the consciousness of his relationship with traditional Islam. On the one hand it convinced him that philosophy and religion were treading the same ground and pursuing the same objectives — the discovery of truth. On the other hand, since the findings of philosophy and religion did not completely tally but ran parallel, so to say, this led the philosopher to think that religion was the philosophy for the masses who could not understand pure philosophy, and that the Prophets were mass-philosophers. This doctrine of the God-world relationship, therefore, offers the most genuine point of transition to Avicenna's doctrine of prophethood. Prophetic religion states there is God, philosophy has established the first cause and the Giver of existence; religion asserts that God has created the world in time and through His Will, philosophy has established an eternal dependence of the world on God; etc. etc. It is after this that the religious attributes of God as formulated by orthodox theology are discussed and given new, philosophic interpretations.

If one does not accept that the point of transition lies here then one may try to hold one of two alternatives. One alternative is to say that in fact no such point exists. On this alternative one will have to say either that Avicenna did not really believe in prophethood and simply tagged it on to his system to pass as a reasonable Muslim. This we have rejected before. Or, one will have to say that Avicenna's philosophy is not in fact a real system. This would be obviously false because whatever its inner weaknessess and inconsistencies may be, it has all the traits of a personal system whose parts thoroughly hang together and Avicenna presents it systematically in *all* of his major philosophic works. The second alternative would be to say: why cannot the point of transition lie in the theory of prophethood itself from where Avicenna then proceeded to his metaphysics. After all, if his doctrine of God is half orthodox and half anti-orthodox, so is his theory of prophethood. This would mean that Avicenna started from orthodox theology but made a transition to philosophy. This too, as we have indicated before, is untenable, for if Avicenna had started from Revelation as a given fact, it would be impossible for him to arrive at a position where Revelation turned out to be a mere symbol and not the reality itself.

The details of Avicenna's theory of Prophecy need not detain us here. The terms of Avicenna's approach to the problem of Prophecy are squarely set by philosophy, as we have shown in *Prophecy in Islam*. The aspect of this theory of Prophecy that is closest and most intimately related to the ethos of historic Islam is its teaching that the Prophet, by virtue of his office, must function as legislator and must found a Community-state.

This idea as such does not come from Greek philosophy. Although there is much in the whole ancient atmosphere of thought which links the state-law with religion, the idea of the Prophet as such does not exist in the Greek tradition. Its more immediate source of inspiration must have been Islam. But it is precisely in its handling of the nature and the status of the *Sharia-Law* that this theory betrays its philosophical bias at its acutest. The *Sharia* and its imperatives are declared to be merely symbolic of a higher philosophic reality which is available only to the philosopher. The idea that religious law can give only a shadow-happiness seems to have also its more immediate source in Islamic mysticism. It is at this point, indeed, that Avicenna's debt to Sufism becomes most clear. But at the same time a fundamental change occurs in this doctrine at the hands of the philosophers. The distinction that the Sufis made between the outer crust of the Law and its inner intention rested on a *moral* basis. Those who practice merely the crust of the Law, the Sufis declared, are deprived of its inner moral intention. But the Sufis regarded the moral-legal distinction as relative. Since the emphasis was on morals rather than on intellectualism, this did not destroy the essential egalitarianism of Islam, since the door to moral improvement is always in principle open to all human beings. Indeed, it is on the moral base that the optimism for humanity's future must be rested. But with the rise of philosophy, the inner-outer duality is shifted from the moral plane to the intellectual plane. And since not all humanity can be expected to be intellectual or nearly equally intellectual, the chasm between the naturally privileged with intellect and the naturally barred becomes in its very nature incurable. According to this theory, then, the letter of the Law was forever for the masses while its inner, intellectual truth was forever the prerogative of the philosopher.

Avicenna's Islamic consciousness left clear marks on the detailed working-out of his doctrine of God, and elsewhere. The most original instance is exhibited in his doctrine of the Divine knowledge where he argued that God, being the First Cause of all things, knows every individual and every particular event — in all its particularity — even though His knowledge is non-perceptual and supra-temporal. But orthodoxy rejected this system and the compromises that it offered between Greek philosophy and the Prophetic religion from the philosophical side. Both the compromise and its rejection are fateful moments in the spiritual history of Islam. This brief paper has only attempted to elucidate the inner composition of Avicenna's religio-philosophical thought and to locate the point of transition from pure reason to historic Islam and the point of contact with the latter. This may help us to assess the terms and extent of this contact and compromise which may, in turn, throw light on and help to evaluate the nature of the orthodox rejection.

THE PROBLEM OF THE *CRITIQUE OF JUDGMENT* AND SOLOMON MAIMON'S SCEPTICISM

by NATHAN ROTENSTREICH

(1) IN THE *Critique of Pure Reason*, Kant establishes sensation and concepts as the two ultimate foundations of cognition, which, while possibly having a common root, are (as regards the structure and prerequisites of cognition) to be clearly distinguished as ultimate. According to Kant, the difference between the two foundations of cognition are both real and methodological. Sensation is passive, dependent upon activation from without, while thinking or conceptualisation is active, spontaneous and self-moving. Thus the factual difference between the two "stocks of cognition" consists in the passivity of the one and the activity of the other. The methodological difference between sensation and concepts is determined by the structure of their tools, i.e. the structure of the forms of intuition on the one hand and of the forms of thinking on the other. This structural difference is manifest in the nature of the relation of particular to universal in the respective domains of intuition and concept. In terms of this relation, the difference between the factors is determined, first of all, by the consideration which of the related terms, the particular or the universal, is primary in their respective domains. Conceptualisation presupposes the particular as the primary datum. Only by proceeding from the particular given datum is it able to arrive, by way of abstraction, at the universal content. On the other hand, the structure of intuition (Anschauung) features a reverse relation, presupposing the primacy of the universal from which it descends, so to speak, to the particular. From the point of view of intuition, the particular is not an independent factor but is rather arrived at through determination (*determinatio*) of the universal. An examination of the

nature of space will illustrate what is meant by the primacy of the universal in the domain of intuition. A specific-particular space is not an independent factor, nor do we arrive at a notion of space in general only by progressive addition of particular spaces. On the contrary — a specific space is but a limitation and determination of space in general. Accordingly space-in-general, or infinite space, is, in Kant's view, primary. In addition to the reverse directions of the particular-universal relation in the domains of conceptualisation and intuition respectively, Kant points to a difference in the internal structure of this relation in these domains. In the conceptual domain, the relation of particular to universal is structured in a scale or hierarchy. At the top of the scale is the universal concept, the content of which includes or enfolds that of the lower, particular concepts. The universal concept subsumes the particular ones and the relation between them is one of graded ascent or descent, depending on the angle of the particular or of the universal from which we examine the contents. This is not the state of affairs in the domain of intuition where the relation of, e.g., universal space to a particular space does not follow a hierarchical pattern. Universal space contains the particular spaces and is not perched, as it were, at their peak. It is thus the duality of the vertical relation between universal and particular prevailing in the conceptual domain, and the horizontal relation between them prevailing in the domain of intuition — that determines the methodological difference between the two domains which together form in turn the foundations of valid cognition.

True, it is precisely within the context of Kant's philosophy that this duality gives rise to difficulties, for Kant asserts that there are concepts other than those arrived at by way of abstraction, to wit, the categorical concepts resulting from independent acts of thinking. Within the domain of the categorical concepts, the primacy of the particular over the universal, the primacy which was established as the criterion of the conceptualisation-intuition duality, does not exist. Yet despite the difficulty of reconciling Kant's criterion of distinction between intuition and conceptualisation with his assertion of concepts, to which this criterion does not apply, we find that Kant never blurs the distinction between the two foundations of cognition. We are therefore permitted to regard this criterion as a basic tenet of Kant's theory of the methodological duality characteristic of the structures of conceptualisation and intuition.

The duality of the foundations of cognition is at once the starting-point and the conclusion of Kant's first *Critique*. There are no compelling grounds for assuming the existence of a third factor from which both might be derived. And even should we posit such an unknown factor, it would contribute nothing towards an account of cognition as we know it. The Ideal, as the totality and substratum of all these positive determinations, lends itself to such a definition as would show the two foundations of cognition to be its by-products. However, in the constitutive domain, in the domain of the foundations of cognition proper, the duality of intuition and conceptualisation is a final datum. The relation established between the two factors is a methodological or functional one. Both factors are assigned a cognitive function; neither factor can fulfill the function of the other. Cognition presupposes both the intuitional datum and the conceptual synthesis, and it is a necessary prerequisite of cognition that these factors are, despite the differences and duality between them, nevertheless mutually related. The unification of these factors in one cognitive framework does not imply that theirs is an ontological unity. Their unity is teleological only, serving to afford cognition its validity as objective cognition. Intuition and concepts unite only to the extent that they fulfill an epistemological function. Beyond that function, their duality and differences stand. The question which arises is whether this functional unity of intuition and concepts within the realm of cognition is not illusory. That is, granting the necessity of this unity for warranting the validity of cognition, can we not say that despite its necessity, its accomplishment is impossible as the differences between the foundations preclude the establishment of a domain where they might meet? Is it not possible that due to its chaotic nature or to the infinite multiplicity of which it is comprised, sensation will not lend itself to organization, to a final and crystallized conceptual synthesis? At any rate, the possibility of a *hiatus* exists as long as we maintain the factual duality of the two factors, confining their unification to the functional aspect. Were we to establish their unity, we would thereby remove the danger of an unbridgeable gulf between them, for such a unity would afford the possibility of discovering the concept in the sensual data and the latter in the former. As a result, the problem of their unification and harmonious inter-relationship within the realm of cognition would be solved of itself. However, both tenets of Kant's doctrine, the one asserting the factual and methodological duality of intuition and concepts, the other asserting their functional unification, imply — at least — the possibility that their synthesis, although necessary, is not realizable. It was in post-Kantian philosophy that the problem of a possible *hiatus* implied by the assumption of an intuition-concepts duality, was brought explicitly to the fore. Yet it can be shown that this problem was already recognized and dealt with by Kant. Taking Solomon Maimon as a characteristic representative of the "Kantian" school, we shall endeavor to show that his problem can be traced to Kant. We shall examine the thematic relation between the treatment of this problem in the philosophies of Kant and Maimon, with an eye to the affinities as well as the differences between them.

(2) The Analytics in the *Critique of Pure Reason*, and especially the chapter on the Principles, presented the specifically qualified contents of the transcendental laws. It is in this section of the first *Critique* that the transcendental unity of the apperception as the condition of the unity of experience, is afforded its concrete meaning. As establishing the supreme laws of the natural sciences, the Analytics is concerned with what is to be considered as the second level of scientific law, the first level being the principle that posits the very existence of transcendental principles, i.e., of a non-experiential domain serving as the grounds of experience. The second level, comprised of the framework of principles, determines the detailed nature of the transcendental domain, its real structure, and its manifestations that afford it its crystallized character; it is here that the transcendental unity in general becomes a set of

[5] CRITIQUE OF JUDGMENT AND MAIMON'S SCEPTICISM 681

principles of real-constitutive validity. The framework of principles determines the nature of the transcendental *laws* within the domain of the transcendental *law* of unity in general.[1]

It is not the purpose of the *Critique* to determine the particular laws of the natural sciences. The purpose of critical philosophy is not to accomplish, or even to endeavor to accomplish, the transition from the transcendental domain to the realm of the sciences in their specific contents. The particular laws of the natural sciences are determined within the framework of these sciences. However, when determining its particular laws, science utilizes the transcendental apparatus presented in the *Critique*. The *Critique, qua Critique*, does not determine the particular laws of science because there is no continuous transition from the transcendental laws to the immanent-scientific laws. What is more, the *Critique* establishes the impossibility of such a transition, of deriving the *particular-substantive* laws from the universal transcendental ones. To put the fundamental impossibility of such a transition another way: the transcendental laws are laws of nature-in-general while the particular laws of, e.g., physics, biology, etc. are laws of specific spheres of nature, of nature as *qualified*. It is impossible to accomplish a transition from nature-in-general to nature as qualified for it is impossible to derive from nature-in-general (nature in its formal aspect) the qualifying component, the component that determines the quality of the spheres of nature. "Pure understanding is not, however, in a position, through mere categories, to prescribe to appearances any *a priori* laws other than those which are involved in a *nature in general*, that is, in the conformity to law of all appearances in space and time. Special laws, as concerning those appearances which are empirically determined, cannot in their specific character be *derived* from the categories although they are one and all subject to them. To obtain any knowledge whatever of these special laws, we must resort to experience; but it is the *a priori* laws that alone can instruct us in regard to experi-

---

[1] Concerning these levels see: B. Bauch, *Kant* (Berlin, 1921), p. 152.

ence in general and as to what it is that can be known as an object of experience."[2]

There are thus two domains: the one — the transcendental domain, which contains the very principle of transcendental unity and the particular transcendental laws in terms of categories, and the other — the domain containing the sensuous component. The latter domain, like the former, features two levels, that of the particular natural law and that of the individual case subject to that law.[3]

There is, as stated, no continuous transition from one domain to the other. Here Kant established the logical status of the particular laws at the same time establishing that critical philosophy is neither required to fill, nor even capable of filling, the empty logical universe with particular material laws. What Kant asserts is, put negatively, that the particular law is not a transcendental law, and, put positively, that the particular law is created by the meeting of the universal law and the datum encountered in experience. The particular laws are immanent laws of science and do not guarantee the very existence of science, *qua* science. However, if we discover a type of law featuring both characteristics, a type of law at once transcendental and particular, then we shall necessarily assign it a position within the epistemological domain, within the critical domain proper, and will not relegate its treatment to the particular sciences proper. The problem of *particular* transcendental law was dealt with in the first and second Introductions to the *Critique of Judgment*. It is here that we find a starting point for our analysis of the meaning and scope of what one may call "Kantian scepticism." This scepticism is witnessed by and manifest in the fact that Kant finds it necessary to posit particular transcendental laws as a mid-stage between the universal laws and the intuitional data.

In itself, establishing the meaning of particular laws and asserting the impossibility of deriving them from the universal laws, does not involve any sceptical tendency whatever. Here, in the *Critique*

---

[2] *Kritik der reinen Vernunft* B, p. 165. (Kemp-Smith's translation [London, 1950], p. 173.)

[3] B. Bauch, *Kant*, p. 152.

of Pure Reason, there is a fundamental division, a basic delineation of domains, connected with the concept — sensation duality, i.e., the duality of the *a priori* and given factors. Here we have a clear-cut distinction between universal and particular laws and are given the criterion of this distinction, namely, the transcendental aspect. However, if there arises a need to posit an additional type of transcendental laws, other than that of the framework of categories and principles, in order to safeguard the validity of the principles themselves, their validity as the domain that builds a unified experience — this need bears witness to a tendency to doubt the validity of the principles, or, more cautiously, their ability to fulfill their function. Let us therefore examine the nature of sceptical motifs in Kant's *Critique of Judgment* and their affinities with the later scepticism of the "Kantian school."

(3) The particular laws, the meaning and status of which are discussed in the *Critique of Judgment*, are from the first assigned a transcendental function, the function of a system which serves as the grounds of science, which is logically prior to science and which therefore is not the result of the technical scientific process. The systematic motive which led Kant to posit this type of law, accounts for its nature and for its function in the domain containing the conditions of experience: "for it is quite conceivable that, despite all the uniformity of the things of nature according to universal laws, without which we would not have the form of general empirical laws of nature, with their effects, might still be so great as to make it impossible for our understanding to discover in nature an intelligible order... out of material coming to hand in such confusion... to make a consistent context of experience."[4]

It was the problem of the possibility of exhausting the given-intuitional content by means of a limited number of universal syntheses that led Kant to posit another type of law in addition to the universal one. In order to overcome the possible breach implied

---

[4] *Kritik der Urteilskraft*, ed. E. Cassirer (Berlin, 1919), p. 254. (English rendering James Creed Meredith, *Kant's Critique of Aesthetic Judgment* [Oxford, 1911], p. 25.)

by the inexhaustibility of content, it is necessary to posit other laws in addition to the universal ones, laws that will bridge the *hiatus* and build one unity of consistent, unambiguous experience, a unity which in turn will overcome the irrationality of the amorphous datum. The laws assigned this in-between position (e.g. the law stating that there is not an infinite multiplicity of forms) are established for a transcendental purpose, to wit, so as to afford the grounds and warrant the unity of science. That by virtue of their function as the grounds of science these laws are assigned a special status, distinct from and superior to that of the particular laws of science proper, follows from the analogy of their function (as regards its logical status) with the function of the categorical laws. Thus there is a functional affinity between the universal and particular transcendental laws, despite the differences in the extent of their validity and necessity. In other words, with respect to their logical priority to scientific work, there is an analogy between the two levels of law; for the laws of reflective judgment enable us to regard individual aggregates of experience as systems. Were it not for this assumption, there could be no unity according to law.[5]

Thus the particular laws of judgment are, in this respect, related to the supreme syntheses of science-in-general and do not constitute particular laws conditioned by the universal laws. In positing a type of law at once particular and unconditioned, the *Critique of Judgment* established a new transcendental level, a level containing both poles, that of the transcendental validity and that of particularity. The laws of judgment, despite their reflective validity are laws conditioning experience, for they constitute the philosophical expression of the hypothesis of the rationality of nature.[6]

The scepticism manifest in the *Critique of Judgment* concerns the transcendental domain proper and does not refer to any immanent achievement of science. What Kant is questioning is not

[5] *Erste Einleitung in die Kritik der Urteilskraft* (Leipzig, 1927), p. 11.
[6] August Stadler, *Kant's Teleologie und ihre erkenntnistheoretische Bedeutung* (1874), p. 33

the validity of any specific material law of science which, because it does not fulfill its function, must be replaced by other laws. Kant assumes the possibility that the datum will not conform to the universal laws of the sciences. Therefore, when coming to specify how the gulf engendered by a possible gap of this sort can be bridged, he cannot utilize the laws of a particular concrete science, as the question he raises is prior to all posing of particular laws by any particular science.

So long as we do not safeguard against the possibility of a gulf between the component factors of cognition (between the domain of the concept and the domain of the sensuous datum), there are neither grounds nor reason for constructing a science. For so long as such a possibility exists, we construct the laws and conclusions of science in a vacuum, without guaranteeing their applicability to given contents. The *transcendental connotation of Kant's scepticism implies a doubt as regards the very possibility of constructing a science as a unified and consistent system with the aid of the apparatus of categorical laws provided by the Analytics.*

Kant's question is raised in, and therefore its answer can come only from, the domain which is prior to any particular science. Were we to attempt to answer this question by pointing to the achievements of science, we would be committing the fallacy of *petitio principii*: we would be questioning the possibility of rationalizing the intuitional datum with the aid of the categorical apparatus, and solving our problem with the aid of laws which presuppose the possibility and actuality of such rationalization. If the problem's solution must suit its meaning, then the introduction of particular laws that afford the possibility of experience as a unified system, implies the introduction of a special transcendental level to serve precisely this purpose. However, Kant asserts the validity of this transcendental level to be merely *reflective*. Were one to question the validity of, e.g. the law of gravitation, one would not thereby undermine the very possibility of constructing physics, let alone threaten the scientific construct in general.

The manner in which Kant presents his problem bears witness to, and is a manifestation of, a sceptical motif which questions the possibility of the conformity of form and matter in the domain of cognition. Were Kant's question to imply that there is no way of bridging the gulf between form and matter, we could regard it as an expression of absolute scepticism which categorically denies the possibility of constructing knowledge. Kant himself did not arrive at so far-reaching a sceptical conclusion, but neither did he intend to remove the doubt altogether, for he regarded the instrument of bridging the gulf between the factors as a reflective bridge, as a bridge the validity of which is not absolute. Let us examine the meaning of Kant's scepticism a bit more closely.

(4) Three points describe the character of Kant's scepticism:

(a) Kant regards the level of categorical laws, i.e. that of the principles, as the necessary minimum of all lawfulness, at the same time admitting that this minimum in itself is not capable of fulfilling the function of law-in-general, the function of unifying and assigning one meaning to the manifold of data. The necessary and constitutive categorical laws do not comprise the entire domain of laws that constitutes the grounds of science. Put positively, this point of Kant's scepticism asserts the domain of laws to be wider than the domain of the constitutive laws. Put negatively it asserts that the constitutive categorical laws present a minimum of lawfulness from which we cannot derive the nature of the laws which come to complement it, that is, it does not directly imply the assumption of reflective laws. Reflective laws are not derived or derivable from categorical-constitutive laws. Were they derivable from categorical laws, reflective laws would lose their independent status and would be regarded as a by-product of the laws of principles. Were this the case, reflective laws would not require a separate deduction assigning them a special logical status. Yet reflective laws are independent, primary and underived; they are rooted in a separate faculty (the faculty of reflective judgment) which guarantees their relative independence. We therefore might formulate this point of Kant's scepticism thus: the categorical laws are but the minimum of laws. On the other hand, the other, reflective laws, cannot be derived from the former and there is, therefore, a breach of a sort between the two planes of laws.

(b) What follows from the minimal nature of the principles is a possibility of *hiatus* between this minimum of laws and the intuitional contents which it has to subsume. Were we to confine ourselves to the *quid juris* position and maintain that the universal laws of cognition are the conditions of experience, there would be no grounds for questioning their validity. The very function of these universal laws within the confines of *quid juris*, guarantees their validity. Yet, if despite their transcendentality we regard these laws as comprising only a limited sphere within a broader framework of laws, then, although we grant them their validity as the conditions of experience, we at the same time are not obliged to assume that their limited domain is capable of fulfilling the function of the total framework of laws. So long as we do not identify the constitutive domain with the transcendental domain as a whole, there is a possibility of a breach between the constitutive domain and the experiential data. The principle of transcendentality implies only the necessity of non-experiential conditions for experience. It does not however imply that a number of specific conditions fulfills the function of the totality of conditions. The perspective of a possible breach between form and data implies the limitation of the domain of form. Limitation of the domain of form through the distinction between constitutive and regulative laws, in turn establishes the possibility of a breach between the partial domain of form (the total domain of form containing reflective as well as constitutive laws) and the intuitional datum.

(c) The third point of Kant's scepticism specifies that the domain of law serving to help the constitutive domain overcome its difficulty, is itself not constitutive and that the system established by these laws is *contingent*. This last point features a good deal of scepticism: for while stating that we can bridge the gap between form and data, it at the same time implies that there is no way of guaranteeing that the bridging-over will succeed. It is only a "happy chance" that the bridge fulfills its function. Yet if the success of the bridging function is only contingent, then the perspective of the gap is not entirely removed, that is, the removal of the breach is not necessary. It is the *quality* of the validity of the bridging-law that determines the nature of the third point of Kant's sceptic attitude.

However, here Kant's scepticism ends. Kant does not doubt the *validity* of the categorical-constitutive laws. His scepticism applies only to the *monopoly* of these laws (at least in the realm of our finite understanding) and one must clearly distinguish between the two views. Even when asserting that the categorical laws comprise only the minimum of laws, Kant does not doubt the necessity of this minimum, nor is his assumption of the possibility that the intuitional datum will not conform to law due to the doubt as to the validity of the universal laws. What he questions is the possibility of constructing a framework of laws *only* with the aid of constitutive laws. Thus the special status of the categorical laws is maintained. They are necessary laws and constitute the necessary conditions of scientific experience, *even though they do not constitute its sufficient* conditions, i.e. even though they do not comprise the totality of conditions of cognition. What is undermined is only the sufficiency of the lawfulness of the principles and not its validity. "Now, looking at the grounds of the possibility of our experience, the first thing, of course, that meets us is something necessary — namely the universal laws, apart from which nature in general (as an object of sense) cannot be thought. These rest on the categories applied to the formal conditions of all intuition possible for us, so far as it is also given *a priori*.... But... the objects of empirical cognition are... determinable in diverse ways, so that specifically differentiated natures... are further capable of being causes in an infinite variety of ways... we must think in nature of a possibility of an endless multiplicity of empirical laws, which yet are contingent so far as our insight goes, i.e. cannot be cognized *a priori*."[7] The "happy chance" does not refer to the lawfulness of the principles, i.e. to the lawfulness grounded in the categories. This lawfulness is necessary and is not impaired even when we regard it as the minimum only of laws. The "happy

---

[7] *Kritik der Urteilskraft*, ed. Cassirer, pp. 251–252; James Creed Meredith's translation, pp. 221–223.

chance" applies only to particular, reflective laws, which, although they are conditions of experience, are not necessary. It it here that the distinctive nature of Kant's scepticism becomes evident. The lawfulness of the principles is necessary even though it is not the only lawfulness constructing knowledge. All other laws, even though necessary for us, are not therefore objectively necessary, and it is only by chance that the infinite, variegated intuitional multiplicity lends itself to organization in determined forms. To summarize — Kant assumes the possibility of a breach between form and data not because he doubts the validity of form but because he questions the *sufficiency* of the *constitutive form*. It is the point that determines the distinctive nature of the problem of the breach between the components of cognition in Kant, that also determines the difference between his scepticism and that of Solomon Maimon.

(5) An additional aspect of this fundamental point in Kant's theory can be discerned if we consider our problem in the context of the *Critique of Pure Reason*, and disregard its special formulation in the *Critique of Judgment*. The constitutive laws presented in the Analytics, comprise the necessary framework of lawful knowledge, and establish the unity and transparence of the intuitive domain, a domain which initially lacks unity and transparence. Constitutive laws, however, are in a certain respect static. They cannot serve the scientist as a direct guide. They constitute, but cannot fill the framework of science. The task of establishing material laws, the specification of laws, belongs to the theory of regulative principles. With the aid of these principles we endeavor to ground the unified cognitive framework not only on universal, necessary foundations, but also on certain material foundations which complete the work of unification accomplished by the lawfulness of the principles. When positing a domain of regulative laws, we posit a domain of validity for scientific work, even if we deny the validity of these laws for the infinite understanding whose grasp of the world is simultaneous. One may state the position of regulative laws in Kant's doctrine thus: that regulative laws are necessary is due to the fact that science is not confined only to its established aspect but is rather a time-linked, open and

progressing framework. So long as there is a *process* of knowledge, it is necessary to assume the existence of laws governing this process, even though these laws are not necessary for the final conclusions of science, when these are detached from time. Regulative laws emerge as the buttress of finite-successive thought. Within the boundaries of finite understanding categorical laws do not suffice.

The function of the transcendental laws is to transform the chaotic aggregate of the intuitional contents into a lawful system, into a perspicuous whole. With the sole aid of the categorical laws, the finite understanding is not capable of fulfilling this function. It is therefore necessary to posit auxiliary laws which will enable the realization of this purpose. These auxiliary laws are *regulative* laws when we consider the dynamic-progressive aspect of science, and *reflective* laws when we take into account the variegated multiplicity of experiential contents which science must order. For our finite understanding, reflective laws fulfill the function assigned to the "Ideal" in the *Critique of Pure Reason*: the problem is how to grasp reality as a whole. Only with the full realization of this purpose will we have achieved the unity of experience, for only then will we be in a position to determine the place of each particular item within the totality of reality. Everything would be fully determined, were we to assign it something out of reality as a whole and eliminate the rest.[8] The establishment of the unity of experience, i.e. the substitution of a complete and necessary system for the experiential aggregate, would be possible were we to possess one perspicuous whole. Within the framework of this whole we would define the individual things so that each individual thing would fill a limited fragment within this whole and this filling would be identical with the essence of the particular thing. On the other hand, the particular thing would delimit itself from everything external to it so that its positive definition would be complemented by its negative delineation and the experiential framework would thus become an absolutely perspicuous system. Yet such a perspicuity is not possible for our understanding as the

---

[8] A. Stadler, *Kant's Teleologie*, etc., p. 37.

lawful determinations, with the aid of which we define the intuitional data, do not exhaust the entire content of the intuitional datum. They are but universal determinations that define the universal framework of the material statements, and nothing else. This framework is incapable of transforming the multiplicity of sensuous data into a perspicuous whole, for within the confines of our finite understanding we are not permitted to comply with the demands of the ideal, that is, we may not limit the whole and exclude the contents external to the delimited essence. We are obliged to make use of ancillary means which, while overcoming the absolute chaos, do not achieve absolute perspicuity. These ancillary means are the reflective laws. There being no other alternative, we turn to the reflective laws so as to enable the construction of science. The ideal postulated is a perspicuous system of experience having absolute validity. Within the confines of our limited understanding — the possible realization of this ideal is a subjective system. This solution bears witness to a sceptic trend in Kant's philosophy, a trend first manifest in his conception of the constitutive laws as the minimum of laws and culminating in his conception of the other transcendental laws, complementing this minimum, as reflective laws which serve to construct a system of experience, the validity of which is subjective alone.

The duality of understanding and intuition, a duality which in reality was not bridged, constitutes the element of moderate scepticism in Kant's doctrine. The duality was bridged because otherwise we would not be able to construct a cognition which is in need of both factors. Yet because we could not overcome the duality beyond the functional integration of the factors, the bridge was not of an absolute validity. Therefore the possibility of a breach between the mutually dependent factors remained; this possibility was not removed. The functional bridge, i.e. the introduction of reflective laws and the assertion that their validity is due to "happy chance," only permitted us to construct science despite the threat of a breach.

(6) It is the duality posited by Kant, i.e. the assumption of two heterogeneous domains, (of the concept and of the sensuous datum),

that underlies the scepticism of Solomon Maimon as well. Maimon's scepticism likewise grows out of the problem of the real validity of the forms of cognition applying to data external to them, a problem connected with the fact that cognition does not constitute an homogeneous system permitting a continuous transition from the *a priori* laws, (i.e. from form) to the data which they subsume. Were the cognitive system homogeneous, it would be absolutely perspicuous and would afford no grounds for doubt. But if the system is not an homogeneous one, and is essentially involved in the duality of its component factors, a duality which is not abolished within the confines of the experiential cognition of our finite understanding — then we are faced with the problem of the mutual concord of the two factors, i.e. the problem of the possibility of their integration and interrelation. Awareness of this problem leads us to doubt the real significance of the *a priori* form that refers to *a posteriori* data. Were our understanding capable of creating objects according to rules or conditions dictated by itself, without there being a need for a given datum from without, there would be no room for the entire question. Since such is not the case and since the objects subject to the rules and conditions must necessarily be given from without, the difficulty raises itself. The question arises: how can nevertheless Understanding subject to its rule, the given objects over which it has no power? Or else intuitions, even if they are *a priori*, are heterogeneous, as distinguished from the concepts of the Understanding.[9] Thus for Maimon the problem consists in the very positing of two heterogeneous factors as the stocks of cognition. The problem of the mutual concord of the two factors, despite their heterogeneity, had already arisen in Kant's philosophy and had engendered the need to posit an additional level of transcendental laws which would bridge, even if not completely, the gap between the heterogeneous factors. Maimon considers the problem of the mutual concord of the two factors, to be connected with the very assumption of their duality, and arrives at the conclusion that as long as we maintain the duality

---

[9] S. Maimon, *Versuch über die Transcendentalphilosophie* (Berlin, 1790), p. 64.

of the factors, there is no way out of the difficulty. Maimon's solution is of no interest to us in this context. What is of importance for us is the manner in which the question was presented by Kant and by Maimon.

Maimon's contribution consists in the specific meaning which he gave the breach between the factors, in his examination of its basis, and in his introduction of an epistemological criterion in the light of which its basic essence emerges. Kant was content to posit the possibility of a breach and considered this possibility to be due mainly to the gap between a limited number of forms, and an unlimited multiplicity of data which they serve to order. He did not, however, endeavor to show the reasons for the impossibility of bridging this gap, or under what conditions such a bridging over would be possible. Maimon, on the other hand, introduced an ideal type of true cognition. It is the impossibility of realizing this ideal type within the bounds of the empirial cognition delineated by the two poles — of concept and sensation — that is responsible for the gap between the factors. Because the cognitive ideal posited by Maimon demands an homogeneous framework for its realization, experiential cognition is denied the possibility of attaining this ideal, as the experiential framework is essentially heterogeneous. The sceptic conclusion implied by the breach between the factors composing cognition, and by the impossibility of overcoming it, asserts that within the realm of experience it is impossible to realize the type of true cognition, a type based on an internal relation between subject and predicate, as defined by the *law of determination*. The possibility of actually attributing a predicate to a subject is afforded only when it is shown that the predicate truly belongs to this subject, i.e., when the subject is the determinable and the predicate its possible determination.[10] To attribute a predicate in such a way is possible only in a totally perspicuous domain, i.e. in a domain wherein the full content of the subject is grasped, wherein the subject is seen to

---

[10] S. Maimon, *Versuch einer neuen Logik oder Theorie des Denkens* (Berlin, 1912), p. 151.

contain potentially the sum-total of contents which its analysis will reveal. The synthetical *a priori* wholes derive their power and validity from the fact that in the nature of the cognized there are analytical guides which they copy.[11] The ideal of the absolutely valid cognition is characterized by the reduction of all relations between cognitive contents (see e.g. Hume's discussion of these relations) to one pattern, to a one-one relation between a subject and its predicates. This ideal cannot be realized in the realm of experiential cognition as here the possibility of realizing the essential condition of this type of cognition, to wit, *the perspicuity of the cognized*, is not afforded. The given sensuous object is not transparent. For us, the sensuous object, which must be deciphered and rationally understood, does not contain the guide, the Ariadne thread, in virtue of which we only uncover what was contained in it from the first. From the point of view of potentiality, the predicate is not necessarily applicable to the sensuous subject and there is therefore room for doubting the validity of our assertion of the subject-predicate relation. The possibility of a breach recognized by Kant, is accounted for and proven. In contradistinction to the necessary, internal relation between the correlative terms, there prevails, in the realm of empirial cognition, only a psychological relationship of contents. The illusory employment of concepts is based on the law of association of ideas, which lacks absolute validity. Because that which is necessary is determined (in our sensation), the representation of the necessity and of the determination are connected with each other so that the representation of determination implies necessity.[12] In contradistinction to the logical relation based on a perspicuous whole, there exists a psychological relation, a relation of contingent linking of contents. It is the gulf between the valid logical relation and the psychological relation based on association, that leads Maimon to his scepticism. In addition to this systematic motif, one finds, in

---

[11] Friedrich Kuntze, *Die Philosophie Salomon Maimons* (Heidelberg, 1912), p. 57.

[12] S. Maimon, *Kritische Untersuchungen über den menschlichen Geist oder das höhere Erkenntnis–und Willensvermögen* (Berlin, 1797), p. 151.

Maimon's theory, a polemical motif which manifests not only his scepticism but also its referrent. Maimon questions not only the exclusiveness of the constitutive laws (this being the object and extent of Kant's scepticism) but the *very validity* of those laws as well. This polemical motif comes to cast doubt on the validity of the categorical domain as applying to data, by asserting the circularity of the proof of the applicability of form to data in Kant's deduction. Kant proves their objective validity by showing that without them, experience is not possible. Now experience is possible because, according to his assumption, it is real, and accordingly these concepts have objective reality. In another context, Maimon formulates this objection more pointedly, stating that the most the critical philosophy is able to do is to show that the *possibility* of experience-in-general, in the sense that it employs the concept of experience, presupposing universal synthetical principles (e.g. everything has its cause, etc.). Aside from this, for their reality (for their applicability to an object) the principles must presuppose experience as a fact. Thus critical philosophy must go around in a perpetual circle.[13]

Summing up: there is no possibility of establishing the validity of the supreme laws of cognition for empirical cognition because empirical cognition cannot become a cognition built on pure logical relations. On the other hand, the proof of the validity of the supreme universal laws rests on the assumption of their validity. The gulf between the foundations of cognition is fundamental and the bridging over of this gulf presupposes that the gulf is bridged, i.e., that there exists no gulf.

(7) "Hume or his representative"[14] directs his question at the validity of the supreme conditions of cognition; he asserts that form, as applied to data, is invalid; he casts doubt on the *validity of lawfulness in general* and is not content to assume the contingency of the particular-reflective laws. Maimon extends the scope of

---

[13] *Abhandlung über die Progresse der Philosophie*, p. 151, quoted in R. Kroner's *Von Kant bis Hegel* (Tübingen, 1924), I, 337–338.
[14] S. Maimon, *Versuch über die Transcendentalphilosophie*, p. 74.

doubt as his scepticism touches the very framework of the supreme transcendental laws. The problem of *quid facti* concerns all transcendental laws, and not only one level of them. The critical philosophy accepts the real thinking of objects in conformity to conditions based on the *a priori* cognitive faculty, as a fact of consciousness and only proves in what respect these are conditions, while scepticism doubts this fact.[15] What is questioned now is the validity of the supreme conditions of cognition, and not only the validity of *one level* in the framework of conditions. In other words, it is not only the sufficiency of the framework of principles that Maimon finds doubtful. We saw that Kant's scepticism referred to the sufficiency of the constitutive laws, not to their validity. The gulf between form and data is due to the fact that the constitutive laws do not comprise the totality of laws. However, this gulf is not due to the invalidity of those laws. Maimon's scepticism is directed at the very validity of the constitutive laws and asserts the gulf between form and data to be due to the invalidity of the form as applied to the given content. At any rate, form has no absolute validity and must content itself with "comparative universality." This is the first point that determines the nature of Maimon's scepticism and distinguishes it from the Kantian sceptic component of the *Critique of Judgment*.

(8) As a matter of fact, the laws that Kant considers constitutive, Maimon regards as reflective. Kant defined reflective laws as laws proceeding from the particular and searching for a suitable universal under which to subsume it.[16] The procedure of the reflective laws is from the bottom upwards, and is not based on a deduction that proceeds from the universal to which it subjects a particular. Reflective laws presuppose the totality of particular things as a given totality. Their function is confined to ordering this totality *ex post*, so as to enable it to enter the framework of scientific cognition. According to Kant, reflective laws, because they presuppose and do not themselves create, the given content, are not necessary.

---

[15] *Versuch einer neuen Logik*, p. 219.
[16] I. Kant: *Erste Einleitung zur Kritik der Urteilskraft*, p. 10.

All the particular laws that are placed in the framework of reflective laws (e.g. the law of classification, the laws of specification, etc.) — are laws that order given contents approaching them *ex post*; by ordering these contents these laws overcome their initial chaotic nature. The constitutive laws retain their constitutive status, i.e. their logical priority to all given data, they are employed in such a way as to subsume the contents, and do not constitute guides to revealing the laws potentially present in the contents. As stated, the domain regarded by Kant as constitutive was considered by Maimon to be essentially reflective. That is, Maimon did not attribute absolute validity to the laws applied to empirical data. The denial of their absolute validity follows from the opaqueness of the object to which they apply. The cognitive procedure within the realm of experience is therefore not accomplished from top to bottom, i.e. is not a procedure of deriving the predicate from the subject according to a guide contained in the latter. The procedure of determination by laws in the realm of empirical cognition is from the bottom upwards, deducing necessity from the context of things. Necessity is not given as an independent component. Determination by laws in the realm of empirial cognition remains subjective and of merely comparative universality. It must by no means be confused with the absolute law-determination.[17] Necessary law-determination is realized only in the *a priori* framework, or in the domain of the infinite understanding even when it cognizes those contents which for us belong to *a posteriori* reality. For us, any law-determination the referent of which is reality, remains an *ex post* determination, a determination proceeding step by step until it arrives at comparative universality. As a matter of fact, every law-determination in the domain of the datum, is a reflective determination and in no respect the spontaneous creation implied by constitutive laws. Reflectivity (to use a term not employed by Maimon to designate the subjective value of law-determinations in

---

[17] S. Maimon, *Kritische Untersuchungen*, pp. 57, 150. Obviously Kant's theory of Schematism is related to this context of ideas. Compare the present author's: "Kant's Schematism in its Context," *Dialectica* (Zürich, 1956).

the domain of empirial cognition), the universality of which is comparative only, is characteristic not only of the particular transcendental laws, but of the universal (constitutive, according to Kant) laws as well when these apply to real data.

True, Maimon also posits a special framework of particular laws, a framework differing from that of the universal principles, in that it refers directly to specific contents and does not constitute a framework determining the structure of objects-in-general. This framework of particular laws Maimon calls the *system of differentials*, the differentials, *qua* ideas of the understanding, i.e. the infinitesimal of every sensuous intuition and its forms provides the material for an account of the genesis of objects.[18] The differential is the rule for creating *specific* objects and contains all those necessary data that determine the multiplicity of particular objects within the framework of supreme law. The differential is a particular law because it refers to particular objects. It is here that we find the crucial difference between the doctrines of Kant and Maimon. Kant defines the particular transcendental laws as ordering laws, laws which because they apply to a given datum are of reflective value alone. Maimon the sceptic, regards even the universal (constitutive according to Kant) laws, as reflective laws. Yet Maimon the rationalist regards even the particular laws as constitutive laws constructing the object from *a priori* data. Maimon the sceptic demoted the constitutive laws, assigning them merely reflective value. Maimon the rationalist promoted the particular laws, assigning them constitutive value. For Kant, the datum always remains a datum, i.e. is always underivable; the most that can be done to overcome the chaotic, opaque nature of the datum is to order, organize it. Maimon in his rationalistic approach regarded the datum as a created factor. Cognition of the datum implies its creation, its transformation into a perspicuous *a priori* set-up.

Let us examine this central difference between the doctrines of Kant and Maimon from another angle. Kant assigned our finite

[18] S. Maimon, *Versuch*, p. 82.

understanding a constitutive function. According to him, it is the finite understanding that determines the principles comprising the constitutive framework of knowledge. Only one domain within the framework of conditions is not of constitutive value i.e. the reflective principles. Maimon, on the other hand, regarded all the methodological tools of the finite understanding as possessing purely reflective significance, constitutive significance being assigned to the infinite understanding for whom cognition of objects is their creation. The infinite understanding proceeds from the most universal, advancing (through determinations) with each step, towards the particular, accomplishing this only by means of an infinite progression. On the other hand, the infinite understanding proceeds from the particular and always advances (by means of abstraction) towards the universal, and this is accomplished in time.[19] To formulate this statement in Kant's terms: Maimon regards the finite understanding as an understanding that proceeds from a particular for which it endeavors to find a universal setting. Maimon's definition of finite understanding is accordingly equivalent to Kant's definition of the faculty of reflective judgment. As distinguished from the finite understanding, the infinite understanding according to Maimon proceeds from the universal, to which it subsumes the particular data. This corresponds to the function assigned the faculty of constitutive judgment, the faculty of the Schematism. The parallel functions of Maimon's finite and infinite understanding and Kant's reflective and constitutive judgments permit us to formulate the Kant-Maimon controversy thus: Kant assumes the existence of a certain domain of laws having unconditional validity vis-a-vis experience, to wit, the domain of the constitutive principles. This implies that our understanding can be of constitutive value even within the realm of empirical cognition. Maimon, on the other hand, thinks that within the realm of experience, the validity of law can be at the most the validity of merely comparative universality. This implies that within the realm of empirical cognition, our understanding is of reflective validity alone.

[19] *Versuch*, p. 443.

The significance of assigning reflective value to constitutive as well as particular laws, will become clearer when we examine the real meaning of laws the universality of which is merely comparative. Such universality is, according to Maimon, the universality of inductive conclusions. Philosophy has not as yet learned how to construct the bridge that will make possible the transcendental transition to the particular fact. So long as the philosopher remains within the boundaries of the transcendental, he can build a stronghold. But his position is good only for defensive and not for offensive action for he is not permitted to leave the transcendental realm and to use the *a priori* forms for determining specific and particular objects. Should he leave his high fortress, he will, it is true, be able, with the aid of light armies, such as induction, analogy, probability — to penetrate, here and there, the realm of truth. But his will not be sure conquests. In other words, because the universal assumptions of science have not been grounded, we must content ourselves when coming to answer the questions to which they give rise, with solutions which only come more or less *close* to the truth, without arriving at absolute truth.[20] The validity of the law-determinations in the realm of empirical cognition is equivalent to the validity of conclusions arrived at through induction, and accordingly is not absolutely necessary and universal. Some of Kant's interpreters understood the problem of the particular laws in the *Critique of Judgment*, as the problem of induction and its place in the methodological framework of the sciences. Because Kant himself describes induction as an advance from the particular to the universal (see his Logic), and because he offers the same description for the method of the faculty of reflective judgment, this interpretation of the problem of the *Critique of Judgment* is plausible. Induction — clearly means the use of the logical rules, the employment of which Kant calls reflection.[21]

The problem raised by Kant in the introduction to the *Critique*

---

[20] H. Bergmann, *Ha-Philosophia shel Shlomo Maimon* (Hebrew), (Jerusalem, 1932), p. 55.

[21] A. Stadler, *Kant's Teleologie* etc., p. 74. H. Cohen, *Kant's Theorie der Erfahrung* (Berlin, 1918), p. 701.

of Judgment is, accordingly, that of accounting for the possibility of induction. Induction is warranted when we introduce a certain extent of homogeneity into the totality of experience, or else when we transform the aggregate contained in it into a system, assuming a certain uniformity in experience. The validity of the law-determinations established on the basis of this contingent homogeneity cannot be absolute. This interpretation of Kant's theory brings into even greater relief both the affinity of his conception of reflective laws with Maimon's notion of laws of comparative universality and the differences between them.

We saw that according to Maimon, the finite understanding does not have constitutive significance within the realm of empirical cognition, where the only means to which it can resort are "the light armies of induction and analogy." Kant, on the other hand, regards the framework of principles, which is the sole methodological tool of our finite understanding, as necessary. According to Maimon, only the methodological tools of the infinite understanding have constitutive significance, and the constitutive value of our finite understanding depends on the extent to which it resembles the infinite understanding. Thus the infinite understanding is the condition of our finite understanding. Here we once again encounter the difference between the doctrines of Kant and Maimon. Kant also allows room for the infinite understanding and his description of its structure is the same as Maimon's. However, for Kant, the infinite understanding does not constitute the *precondition* of the validity of the methods of our finite understanding. Finite understanding is, to a certain extent, autonomous. Even if it does not create, but rather receives the datum, it nevertheless has constitutive validity *qua* cognizing the universal structure of this datum. Here lies the parting of Kant's and Maimon's ways; Maimon the empirical sceptic denies the validity of finite understanding, Kant the empirical rationalist asserts its validity even when maintaining that not all the methodological framework at its disposal is of constitutive value.

(9) Thus we find that while Kant is sceptical as regards only one level of the transcendental framework of laws, Maimon ques-

tions the validity of the entire framework as applied to the experiential datum. However, although their conclusions regarding the bridge over the gap between the factors composing cognition differ, their point of departure is the same, to wit — the problem of the duality of concepts and sensation. True, Maimon could not have been directly influenced by Kant's third *Critique*, for the simple (and a bit curious) reason that both the *Critique of Judgment* and the *Versuch über die Transcendentalphilosophie* appeared in the same year — 1790. All the same, one may ponder Maimon's thematic relation to Kant, for both developed the problem which is at once the starting point and outcome of the first *Critique*, the problem of the duality of the components of cognition, along parallel lines.

THE OCCASION OF THE INITIAL BREAK BETWEEN JUDAISM AND CHRISTIANITY

by MASSEY H. SHEPHERD, JR.

THE SEPARATION OF Judaism and Christianity in the generation following upon the death of Jesus was no doubt inevitable, however it is explained and justified by historians and theologians of the two religions respectively. The consequences of this break between two faithful peoples, who worship the same God and search out his revelation from the same Scriptures, have provided many tragic chapters to the historical records of their mutual relations. Yet there are brighter and less somber pages to this story; and none is more encouraging than the accomplishments of many modern Biblical and historical scholars, both Jewish and Christian, who have overcome by their researches so much misunderstanding and prejudice. In this endeavour, the name of none is more distinguished than Harry Austryn Wolfson. In particular, his studies in the common philosophy that underlies the work of Jewish and Christian theologians and apologists in the Hellenistic and Roman periods have set a standard which all can emulate but few can hope to equal.

The purpose of this small offering in tribute to Professor Wolfson, from a younger friend and admirer, is to pinpoint, if possible, the initial occasion when Christians became formally separated from Judaism and conscious of themselves as a distinct religious movement. It is our thesis that this event occurred in Antioch in the year A.D. 40–41, at the close of Caligula's and the beginning of Claudius' reign. It served as a precedent, a harbinger of other separations, in other cities and provinces of the Roman world, over the course of several decades. No doubt, these breaks in community between Jews and Christians took place more rapidly and decisively in the Diaspora, as we may surmise from the letters of Paul, where the Christian mission found a larger and readier response from Gentiles. Yet as late as the year 52, an intelligent Roman official, such as the Proconsul Gallio at Corinth, could not distinguish clearly Christians from Jews.[1] And, if the evidence of the Book of Acts is to be trusted, some five years later, when Paul reached Rome as a prisoner on appeal to Caesar, the Jewish leaders in Rome had no information regarding any apostasy of Paul from his ancestral faith.[2] However, when Nero attacked the Christians, in the summer of 64, the difference between Christianity and Judaism was well-known to the government.[3]

In Palestine, where the Christian churches remained predominantly Jewish rather than Gentile in membership, the stages of separation from the parent religion did not become critical until the decade of the 60's, when James the Just was martyred and, not long thereafter, the Jerusalem church over which he had presided took refuge in the Gentile city of Pella in order to disassociate itself from the Jewish rebellion against the Roman overlordship.[4] After the destruction of Jerusalem and the Temple in 70, relations between non-Christian and Christian Jews became increasingly strained — as one may judge from the traditions peculiar to the Gospel of Matthew.[5] The final seal of separation, however,

[1] Acts 18:15. For the date, see *The Beginnings of Christianity*, edited by F. J. Foakes Jackson and K. Lake, V (Macmillan, 1933), 460-64.

[2] Acts 28:21. Paul arrived in Rome ca. 58 (cf. *ibid.*, 464-67). When Paul wrote his letter to the Roman church, but a few years before his arrival, there were many Gentiles already members of that church; cf. Rom. 11:13.

[3] The account in Tacitus, *Ann.* xv, 44 provides no warrant for the position of Paul Styger, *Juden und Christen im alten Rom* (Berlin, 1934), that Jews were responsible for Nero's attack. More plausible is the theory that "strife and jealousy" within the Roman Christian community itself contributed to the tragedy; cf. O. Cullmann, *Peter: Disciple-Apostle-Martyr* (Westminster Press, 1953), pp. 107-09. See the judicious account of the Neronian persecution in E. G. Hardy, *Christianity and the Roman Government* (George Allen and Unwin, Ltd., 1925 [reprint of 1st ed. of 1894]), pp. 41 ff.

[4] Hegesippus in Eusebius *H.E.* II, 23, 4-18.

[5] See my remarks in *The Interpreter's Bible*, VII (Abingdon Cokesbury Press, 1951), 215-16.

came only with the virtual excommunication of the Christians from the synagogue, when in the latter years of the first century the *Birkat ha-Minim* was inserted in the synagogue liturgy.[6]

Whatever critical position one takes with respect to the intentions of Jesus, it would be difficult to maintain that he either desired, much less deliberately planned, the formation of a new religious institution distinct and separate from Israel. As Eduard Schweizer has recently pointed out, Jesus lived during his work on earth "entirely within the national and religious associations of Israel" and gave no sign to distinguish those who followed him from other Israelites, whether by special rite, creed, name, or office.[7] Even if one accepts the Last Supper as a ritual institution by Jesus for his disciples, it is clear from his words on that occasion that he intended it for a sign of their shared life with him in the coming Kingdom rather than as a sacramental rite of a new religion in history.[8] That Jesus was the "founder" of Christianity is a truism. But every effort to make his founding of the Christian religion a matter of organized planning or regulatory principles is shattered against the obvious fact of crisis produced in the primitive Church as soon as the preaching of its gospel was extended beyond the bounds of Judaism.

Similarly, Schweizer is also correct in his estimate, based upon the early chapters of Acts, that

...the primitive Church continued in its Jewish national and religious associations — this means that it regarded as valid the priesthood, the sacrificial system, the synagogue services, and

---

[6] This is dated as early as A.D. 80 by R. Travers Herford, *Christianity in Talmud and Midrash* (Williams and Norgate, 1903), pp. 125–37.

[7] *Church Order in the New Testament*, Studies in Biblical Theology, No. 32 (Alec R. Allenson, Inc., 1961), p. 20.

[8] Schweizer's remark that the institution of the Supper "does not imply an exclusive church that separates itself from the rest of Israel" (*ibid.*, p. 22) is justified. That non-believers were present at, if not participants in, the Lord's Supper in the Pauline churches is implied, I believe, by 1 Cor. 14:16. The "fencing of the table "is first noted explicitly in *Didache* 9:5; but the church-order material of this early document is certainly later than the definitive break of Christianity with Judaism.

the law. The kingdom of God remained in the future, and it was not for them to bring it in by reforms. All Israel, not just one severed group, was called to God's kingdom. Thus continuity between Israel and the open circle of Jesus' disciples was preserved; they were still a band of messengers.[9]

The first persecutions of the apostles by the Sanhedrin were directed against unlawful behavior, that is to say, an illegitimate exorcism in the Name of Jesus.[10] The teaching of the apostles about Jesus' resurrection was undoubtedly equally distasteful to the Sadducees, but it was not a sufficient ground for punishment. Even so, there was no threat of excommunication of the apostles from Israel. The persecution led by Paul before his conversion was confined to the Hellenist "deviationists" — whatever might have been the exact character of their unorthodoxy. But Acts distinctly says that the apostles were not scattered by this attack.[11] Their turn came some years later, in the time of Herod Agrippa. But this, as we shall now attempt to show, was consequent to significant developments at Antioch.

The oldest traditions concerning the beginning of Christianity in Antioch are gathered in Acts 11:19–30 and 13:1–3. The author has inserted into them a piece taken from another tradition,

---

[9] *Op. cit.*, pp. 34–35.

[10] Acts 4:7. The statement of the author of Acts in 4:2 that the arrest of the apostles was due to annoyance at their preaching the resurrection is certainly editorial. The real charge is given at the trial. See Foakes Jackson and Lake, *op. cit.*, IV, 40, 42.

[11] Acts 8:1. The exact character of the Hellenists continues to be debated — whether they were simply Greek-speaking Jews, or Jews who had adopted Grecizing ways of thought and life, or were possibly Gentiles, or proselytes. For recent discussion, see M. Simon, *St. Stephen and the Hellenists in the Primitive Church* (Longsman, 1958); O. Cullmann, "Samaria and the Origins of the Christian Mission," *The Early Church* (Westminster Press, 1956), pp. 185–92; Bo Reicke, *Glaube und Leben der Urgemeinde, Bemerkungen zu Apg. 1–7* (Zürich, 1957), pp. 116–17; C.F.D. Moule, "Once More, Who Were the Hellenists?" *The Expository Times*, LXX (1959), 100–02. Also note Johannes Munck, *Paul and the Salvation of Mankind* (SCM Press, Ltd., 1959), pp. 218–28 — but I cannot accept his view that the persecution affected the whole Jerusalem church, and not just the Hellenists.

[5] INITIAL BREAK BETWEEN JUDAISM AND CHRISTIANITY 707

possibly of the church in Jerusalem, about the persecution of the apostles by Herod Agrippa. The Antiochene traditions are lacking in precise dates, and are probably not even a continuous narrative, but a collection of distinct units of tradition arranged and edited by the author.[12] One of these units, introduced almost as it were parenthetically, may, however, provide a real clue in the problem of the separation of Christianity from Judaism. In 11:26 it is noted that "in Antioch the disciples were for the first time called Christians." This distinctive name, unlike other terms for the disciples in Acts (with the possible exception of Nazarenes in 24:5), suggests at least an identifiable party or sect, if not a different religious group.[13]

The interpretation of Acts 11:26 has been occasion of much dispute, not so much over the etymological meaning of the word "Christian," as over the source of the appellation. Who first called the disciples "Christians?" Was it unbelieving Jews, contemptuous Gentiles, government authorities, or Christian disciples themselves? Moreover, does this name reveal a distinctive emphasis in the belief and preaching of the early disciples in Antioch, centered in the confession that Jesus is the Christ, the Messiah? If so, does it mean that the differentiation of the disciples from other Jews took place within Antiochene Jewry itself, where the term "Messiah" could only bear any significant meaning, or did it occur amongst the Gentile believers for whom the word "Christ" had become, as already in the usage of Paul, virtually a proper name rather than a title? Behind this term there may lie either a peculiar Messianic enthusiasm of Jewish Christians or a cultic hero-divinity "Christ" of Gentile Christians.

All exegetes seem agreed that the word *Christianus* is formed from a Latin suffix to describe partisans or clients of a person, such as the words Caesariani, Augustiani, or Herodiani.[14] This

[12] For a form critical analysis of the text, see the commentary of Ernst Haenchen, *Die Apostelgeschichte* (Göttingen, 1956), *loc. cit.*

[13] See the note of H. J. Cadbury, "Names for Christians and Christianity in Acts," in Foakes Jackson and Lake, *op. cit.*, v, 375–92.

[14] The pertinent literature is listed by H. Karpp at the end of his article

fact lends weight to the interpretation of Erik Peterson and others that *Christianus* was an official appellation given by the Roman authorities, for whom the title Messiah-Christos would inevitably bear political connotations.[15] If this be true, then we must posit an incident, unrecorded in Acts, when Christians were hailed before the magistrates in Antioch, whether by the initiative of Jews or of pagans, as disturbers of the peace. An analogous case would be the accusation against Paul by the Jews in Corinth before the tribunal of Gallio, to which reference has already been made. If there is an analogy here, it is clear that Gallio had not as yet become familiar with an official, legal precedent for dealing with *Christiani* as distinguishable from Jews, unless (as is possible) the author of Acts has deliberately played down the opposition of the Roman magistracy to Christianity in the interest of his apologetic purposes. It is strange, to say the least, that Gallio in the year 52 would not be familiar with a legal precedent established in Antioch before the reign of Claudius. But this is what the chronology of Acts implies.[16]

Consequently, the older view of Bishop Lightfoot that *Christianus* arose in the first instance as a popular nickname rather than as an official governmental designation continues to have supporters. Lightfoot believed that the nickname was created by the heathen populace.[17] But it could have been formed by Hellenistic Jews who were politically sympathetic to Roman rule, or at least were discreet enough to appear sympathetic. For that matter, there were apostate Jews in the Diaspora, and we know of one such

---

"Christennamen," *Reallexikon für Antike und Christentum*, II, 1138. To this should be added C. Cecchelli, "Il nome e la 'setta' dei Cristiani," *Rivista di archeologia cristiana*, XXXI (1955), 55–73, and H. B. Mattingly, "The Origin of the Name *Christiani*," *The Journal of Theological Studies*, N.S., IX (1958), 26–37; C. Spicq, O. P., "Ce que signifie le titre de chrétien," *Studia Theologica*, XV (1961), 68–78.

[15] Erik Peterson, "Christianus," *Miscellanea Giovanni Mercati*, Studi e testi, 121, I (Citta del Vaticano, 1946), 355–72.

[16] Cf. Acts 11:28.

[17] J. B. Lightfoot, *The Apostolic Fathers*, Part II, Vol. I (2nd ed.; Macmillan, 1889), pp. 415–18.

unpleasant character at Antioch, a son of the chief magistrate of the Jews of the city. He was perhaps a super-patriot since his name was Antiochus. At the time of the Jewish war in Palestine against Rome, in 66–67, he inflamed the Gentile populace against his own people and received some kind of authority to persecute them on the basis of a specious charge that the Jews were plotting to burn the city.[18]

One should not overlook, however, the thesis of Elias J. Bickerman, that the verb in Acts 11:26 is active, not passive, and that it implies that the disciples themselves adopted the name Christian to designate themselves as the "agents, representatives of the Messiah... officers of the Anointed King in his kingdom."[19] This interpretation carries with it the supposition that the name was taken by Jewish Christians in Antioch, but at least by Jewish Christians who were sufficiently Hellenized in speech to have found it natural to employ a fashion of Latin loan-word formations. The strength of Bickerman's position lies in the fact that the early Church Fathers so understood the passage. Yet the evidence adduced by Bickerman is late — from the fourth century and after; and his documentation of Ante-Nicene usage of the verb χρηματίζω in an active sense is by no means conclusive.

The basic weakness of Bickerman's hypothesis is not so much philological as it is historical. For one must ask why, if the disciples themselves adopted the name "Christian" to express their primary conviction about Jesus as the Messiah — and that, too, in a church which became the focal center of extensive mission to the eastern Mediterranean world — the term is so sparingly used by Christians in the first two centuries. The author of Acts employs it in only one other place in his narrative, where it occurs somewhat contemptuously or flippantly on the lips of Herod Agrippa II (26:28). The word is never used by Paul, either in his letters or in the speeches

---

[18] Josephus *Bell.* vii, 46–53. See also G. Downey, *A History of Antioch in Syria from Seleucus to the Arab Conquest* (Princeton, 1961), pp. 199–200, 204–05.

[19] "The Name of Christians," *The Harvard Theological Review*, XLII (1949), 123–24; cf. Spicq, *op. cit.*

attributed to him in Acts. Elsewhere in the New Testament it occurs only in 1 Peter 4:16, a passage that suggests at least a non-Christian designation, in a context of persecution: "If one suffers as a Christian, let him not be ashamed, but under that name let him glorify God." The date of 1 Peter is uncertain, but it is hardly earlier than the reign of Nero. More probably it dates later in the first century. Even if we assume that it reflects the Neronian persecution, one may well ask why the author should encourage his fellow-believers not to be ashamed of the designation "Christian."

It is the more likely, therefore, that the term *Christianus* was first applied to the disciples of Jesus by outsiders, and most probable that it was coined by government officials. Since Paul never uses the term, the first datable example of its use is by Herod Agrippa II at Paul's hearing, when the king and his wife Bernice came to Caesarea to welcome the new Roman governor Festus, most probably in the late summer of 55 or 56.[20] As noted, Agrippa used the word with a certain air of contempt; nor does it appear from the context that the term was unfamiliar or needful of explanation. Is it possible that the term goes back, at least, to the time of his father, Herod Agrippa I?

We have noted that the initial persecution of the apostles by the Jewish authorities of Palestine did not entail their excommunication from Judaism. Nor did the Pharisaic action against the Hellenists, led by Paul, affect apparently the apostles in Jerusalem. However unpopular the belief of the disciples in Jesus' resurrection may have been with the authorities, serious trouble for the Christian believers was not likely until they attacked the Law and openly disobeyed it. Hence the first formal schism of Christianity and Judaism must be dated sometime between the persecution of the Hellenists — whether or not they were non-conformists with regard to the Law — and the decision of the apostolic conference in Jerusalem concerning the admission of Gentiles to full fellowship with Jewish-Christian believers without the necessity of the Gentiles having to observe the Law.

---

[20] Cf. Foakes Jackson and Lake, *op. cit.*, v, 464–67.

INITIAL BREAK BETWEEN JUDAISM AND CHRISTIANITY

The decision of the Jerusalem conference was not a sudden and unprecedented act of policy, but a ratification of a situation that had already arisen and had been causing tension within the Christian fellowship itself. Precedents had been established outside Judaea in the missionary activity of Paul and Barnabas in Syria and Cilicia, if not in wider areas such as Asia Minor and Greece. The conference of Paul and Barnabas with the "pillar" apostles in Jerusalem probably took place in 46 or 47, for this date fits the most likely time of the famine mentioned in Acts 11:28.[21] It also accords most naturally with the period of seventeen years related by Paul in Galatians 1:18 and 2:1 as having passed between the time of his conversion and his visit to Jerusalem for the conference. It is possible, however, to reduce the seventeen-year interval to one of fourteen years, by a different reading of the evidence in Galatians. In that case, the conference would have been held before the death of Herod Agrippa I in the spring of 44, or shortly thereafter.

Herod Agrippa I, King of Judaea from 41 to 44, had (according to Acts) already taken measures of persecution against the apostles — specifically James son of Zebedee and Peter — before the conference took place. He was an ardent Jew in his religious practice, and the only one of the Herods who enjoyed friendly relations with the Pharisees. His attack on the church leaders was probably supported by the Pharisees, in which case one may assume that the apostles had already shown indications of deviation from strict adherence to the Law. This, too, is suggested by Acts, since the author places the consorting of Peter with Gentiles before the persecution of Herod. It is possible that the combination of Pharisees and Herodians against Jesus, recorded in Mark 3:6, 8:15, and 12:13, actually reflects, as B.W. Bacon surmised,[22] the alliance of the Pharisees with partisans of Herod Agrippa I against

---

[21] For the date, see K. S. Gapp, "The Universal Famine under Claudius," *The Harvard Theological Review*, XXVIII (1935), 258–65. It is dated to 48–49 by J. Dupont, "Notes sur les Actes des Apôtres," *Revue Biblique*, LXII (1955), 52–55.

[22] *The Gospel of Mark, Its Composition and Date* (Yale University Press, 1925), pp. 74–76.

Christianity in the years 41–44. For it is difficult to accept any friendship of the Pharisees with the Herodians who had been partisans of Herod the Great or of Herod Antipas. One may note, also in passing, that there appears to have been one "Herodian" convert to the church among the early leaders in Antioch — the disciple Manaen, described in Acts 13:1 as "companion" or "fellow courtier" of Herod the tetrarch (i.e. Herod Antipas).

The disaffection between Jews and Christians exhibited in Herod Agrippa's persecution may well be rooted in the admission of Gentiles to the Church's fellowship. When, however, did this deviation from adherence to the Law begin? Can it be precisely or even approximately dated? According to Acts 11:20, the mission to the Gentiles began in Antioch through the preaching of the Hellenists scattered by the persecution following Stephen's death. It is true that Acts provides a precedent even for this, in the preaching of Peter to the household of Cornelius the centurion at Caesarea; and this took place, also according to the sequence of Acts' narratives, before Herod Agrippa's arrest of Peter. But we cannot give a definite date for this adventure of Peter in Caesarea, since we cannot determine how early Cornelius' Italic cohort was stationed in Caesarea.

We would probably have a better picture of the actual state of early Christian expansion if we would set the various narratives of Acts 8–11 in four parallel columns that would show a concurrent development of missionary activity. In one column we would place the story of Paul's conversion, his preaching in Damascus, his visit to Arabia, his return to Damacus, the first visit to Jerusalem, and the hurried departure secretly to his home in Tarsus. In a second column, concurrent with these events, would come the preaching of Philip in Samaria, his conversion of the Ethiopian eunuch, and his later preaching in the coastal cities until his settlement at Caesarea. The third and fourth columns would begin a little later than the first two. In the third would come Peter and John's visit to Samaria, followed by Peter's visits to the Christians in Lydda and Joppa, and ending in his extraordinary visit to Cornelius at Caesarea. The fourth column would show the activities of the Hellenists after their flight from Jerusalem — in Phoenicia, Cyprus, and Syria, with the beginnings of work in Antioch, the preaching to the Gentiles, the coming of Barnabas, and finally the arrival of Paul from Tarsus to help in the work at Antioch. All of this activity could be easily comprehended within a single decade or less following upon the death of Jesus in the year 30.[23]

If we place Paul's conversion within the year after Jesus' death,[24] then add at least three and possibly four years for his activities in Damascus and Arabia, then allow some time for a stay in Tarsus and Cilicia before he joined in the work at Antioch, we arrive at the year 36–37 as the most likely time of his arrival in Antioch. But by this time, Gentiles are already in the Christian movement. Acts tells us that Paul and Barnabas worked a whole year together in the Syrian capital. Were they then sent out on the so-called "First missionary journey" to Cyprus, Pamphylia and southern Galatia? Most probably they were; and what is more, the so-called "Second missionary journey" of Paul — to Galatia and Greece — may well have taken place sometime between the years 40 and 46–47, when Paul went up to Jerusalem for the conference. This is suggested by his arrival in Corinth shortly after Aquila and Priscilla had landed there from Italy, due to Claudius' expulsion of the Jews from Rome in 41.[25]

We are thus brought to the reign of Caligula, 37–41, as a fateful

[23] For the date, see the references in my article, "Are Both the Synoptics and John Correct About the Date of Jesus' Death?" *Journal of Biblical Literature*, LXXX (1961), 123–32.

[24] The only reason for placing Paul's conversion at a later time is the common assumption that Stephen must have been executed in the year of Pilate's recall, i.e. 36; but this is quite unnecessary if, as seems most probable, Stephen was lynched, not formally tried and sentenced by the Sanhedrin. See the following note.

[25] This chronology of Paul's career is not the "orthodox" one most generally current among New Testament scholars, for they are inclined to accept Orosius' dating the expulsion of the Jews from Rome, namely 49, and thus place at that date the arrival of Priscilla and Aquila in Corinth (cf. Acts 18:2). But the most likely date of Claudius' edict is 41; see H. Janne, "Impulsore Chresto," *Mélanges Bidez*, Annuaire de l'Institut de philologie et d'histoire orientales, Université libre de Bruxelles, II (1934), 531–53. For a trenchant

time in the relations of Judaism with the Christian movement. It was, in any event, a very fateful time in the fortunes of Judaism generally. Caligula's accession had held some promise for the easing of the fortunes of the Jews under Roman rule. For Tiberius' chief minister Sejanus had been hostile to them, and this had in turn probably been a major factor in the continuous affronts of Pilate to Jewish sentiment.[26] But Pilate had been recalled just before Tiberius' death, through the good offices of Vitellius, governor of Syria. Vitellius had also conciliated Jewish feelings, during his visit to Jerusalem in 37, by giving back to the Jews the custody of the high priest's vestments (which Pilate had kept locked in the castle of the Antonia, to be dispensed at his own pleasure to the high priest's use).[27] Moreover, Caligula was known to be a boon companion of Herod Agrippa I, and immediately after his accession he had not only released Agrippa from debtor's prison, but had given him the tetrarchy of his uncle Philip with the title of king.[28] Not long after Herod Agrippa arrived in Palestine he was favored in addition by having turned over to him the territories of his other uncle, Herod Antipas, who had fallen into disgrace, thanks in part to Agrippa's intrigues.[29] In any case, there was no question about the high popularity of Herod Agrippa with the new emperor. And, as already noted, he was the only one of the Herods whom the Jews liked.

But troubles had begun even before Agrippa arrived in Palestine to take over his client kingdoms. Stopping in Alexandria in August 38, on his way to Palestine, he had been publicly insulted by the pagan populace of that turbulent city under encouragement from

---

critique of the traditional Pauline chronology, see J. Knox, "The Pauline Chronology," *Journal of Biblical Literature*, LVIII (1939), with which I am more inclined to agree, contrary to views expressed by me earlier in my article in *Munera Studiosa* (Cambridge, Mass., 1946), pp. 95–96.

[26] E. M. Smallwood, "Some Notes on the Jews under Tiberius," *Latomus*, XV (1956), 314–29.

[27] Josephus *Ant.* XVIII, 4, 2–3.

[28] *Ibid.*, XVIII, 6, 10.

[29] *Ibid.*, XVIII, 7.

the governor Flaccus. A riot developed in which many Jews were killed, their possessions plundered, and — as a climax to the disturbance — a statue of the emperor had been erected in one of the synagogues. Embassies of both Jews and pagans were sent to Caligula, and the verdict of the emperor went against the Jews.[30]

Whether these disturbances in Alexandria (according to Josephus) or similar troubles in Jamnia in Palestine (according to Philo), led Caligula — by now definitely unhinged mentally — to proceed to his project of having his statue erected in the Temple at Jerusalem, need not be argued here. The story is well known. Not only did Petronius, the new governor of Syria, show courageous restraint in trying to delay this stupendous insult to the Jewish religion, but Herod Agrippa, visiting in Rome, risked his own life no less than his friendship with Caligula in an effort to ward off the catastrophe. The issue was only settled — fortunately for the Jews — by the emperor's assassination in January 41.

The trouble for the Jews was not confined to Alexandria and Palestine. The Antiochene historian Malalas relates that in the third year of Caligula (i.e., 40) factional strife between the Blues and the Greens in the circus at Antioch led to rioting that in short order involved the Jews, so that many of them were killed and their synagogues burned.[31] We do not know how the Jews became implicated, but considering the tensions and strains of all parties and the constant, underlying hatred of Jews and Gentiles for each other, it is reasonable to connect the Antiochene disturbances with either the disorders in Alexandria or the project of Caligula.

The story does not end here. Herod Agrippa, in Rome at the time of Caligula's assassination, was, in his customary way of opportunism, helpful in the establishment of Claudius on the imperial throne. The Jews apparently took this good fortune as a signal to take vengeance on their pagan oppressors. Renewed

---

[30] In addition to Josephus *Ant.* XVIII, 8, we have the excellent source material for these events in Philo's *In Flacc.* and his *Leg.*

[31] Cf. Downey, *op. cit.*, pp. 193–95.

disturbances broke out in Alexandria, in which, Josephus admits, the Jews were the aggressors.[32] A letter of Claudius to the Alexandrians, adjudicating the affair, has been preserved. The Alexandrians were confirmed in their privileges and the Jews in their rights. But a stern warning was given the Jews to be peaceable lest a heavy hand of punishment fall on them. In the same letter, Claudius admonished the Alexandrian Jews "not to introduce or invite Jews who sail down to Alexandria from Syria or Egypt, thus compelling me to conceive the greater suspicion; otherwise I will by all means take vengeance on them as fomenting a general plague for the whole world."[33] Thus it is clear that Jews in Syria were also involved with those in Alexandria in the disorders at the beginning of Claudius' reign.

Whether the preaching of Christians was a further exasperation to the troubles of the Jews at this time is a matter of conjecture. One is prompted to connect these disorders in the eastern Mediterranean with the tumults among the Jews at Rome at the very same time[34] — tumults which Suetonius says were instigated by "Chrestus" and which led to Claudius' edict of expulsion of the Jews from Rome.[35] "Chrestus" is certainly a vulgar form of "Christus," and may refer to the preaching about Jesus specifically, or to more general Messianic disturbances, or perhaps to both. Suetonius' reference is the only certain indication in our sources that Christians were involved in the explosive Jewish-Gentile tensions of these years. But the hypothesis of many New Testament scholars that links the apocalyptic materials of Mark 13 and of 1 and 2 Thessalonians to this crisis is attractive.

The project of Caligula must have seemed to both Jews and

---

[32] *Ant.* XIX, 5, 2.

[33] H. I. Bell, *Jews and Christians in Egypt* (British Museum, 1924), p. 29. This papyrus has provoked an extensive literature, but Bell's commentary remains fundamental; see also the review of H. Grégoire in *Byzantion*, I (1924), 644–46, and the pertinent literature listed by W. den Boer, "Claudius," *Reallexikon für Antike und Christentum*, III, 180–81.

[34] Suetonius, *Claud.* 25, 4.

[35] For the date of 41, see above, note 25.

Christians an impending fulfillment of the prophecy of Daniel about the "abomination." Christians may well have seen here the beginning of tribulations of the last times, immediately prior to the Parousia of the Lord. Such expectation would carry with it a more strenuous effort to preach the gospel to as many as would listen, to the Gentile no less than to the Jew.

The evidence of crisis in Judaism at the end of Caligula's and the beginning of Claudius' reigns is unmistakable, even though precise data regarding the involvement of Christians is slender. But if Christians were still a "party" within Judaism, it is hardly possible for them not to have been caught up into the excitement and tension of the times, especially in view of their own eschatological expectations. We would thus posit the hypothesis that this crisis of 40-41 marked a major turning point in the "origins" of Christianity, by producing the first significant break of Christianity away from its Jewish parent. It gave the Roman authorities their first indication that Christianity was a new religion, and not merely a party within Judaism — hence their adoption of the name "Christian" to distinguish the adherents of the new religious movement. It led also to the severer persecution of the primary apostolic leaders of the Christians initiated by Herod Agrippa I. Thus we would interpret the most probable time and occasion when "in Antioch the disciples were for the first time called Christians."

GUILLAUME DE CONCHES AND NEMESIUS OF EMESSA: ON THE SOURCES OF THE "NEW SCIENCE" OF THE TWELFTH CENTURY

by THEODORE SILVERSTEIN

GUILLAUME DE CONCHES the Chartrian cosmogonist has long held the interest of the chronicler of medieval thought, not only by the intrinsic merit of his treatises, but also by his importance among a distinguished group of teacher-philosophers whose influence was capital on the renaissance of letters in their time. As long ago as 1861 Von Prantl called attention to what he conceived to be the originality in Latin tradition of Guillaume's formal argument for the existence of God,[1] and the most recent general essay on his philosophy, both summarizing and advancing a century of studies, continues to testify to the range and variety of his speculations.[2] But the intellectual historian finds Guillaume's work of interest for other reasons also: for the clues which it offers, among further

[1] First proposed by Von Prantl in *Sitzungsberichte der königi. Bayerischen Akad. der Wissenschaften*, Philos.-phil. Cl., 5 January, 1861, and developed in *Geschichte der Logik im Abendlande*, II, 83 ff.; attributing the argument, mistakenly, from an early edition of the text in question, to William of Hirschau (amended in the 2nd ed. of *Geschichte der Logik*, pp. 127 ff.); cf. n. 4 below. He calls attention to Guillaume's priority over Anselm and the Arabs' supposed priority over both, suggesting that the Arabic line might have reached Guillaume through Constantinus Africanus. R.L. Poole, *Illustrations of the History of Mediaeval Thought and Learning* (new ed., London, 1920), pp. 293 ff., finds two objections to such a view: (1) that Guillaume's and Anselm's arguments are essentially different, (2) that the topic does not occur in Constantinus. For another history of the question, by implication refuting Von Prantl, see Tullio Gregory, *Anima mundi: La filosofia di Guglielmo di Conches e la scuola di Chartres* (Firenze, 1955), chap. II.

[2] Tullio Gregory, *Anima mundi*. See also J.M. Parent, *La doctrine de la création dans l'école de Chartres* Publications de l'Institut d'Études Médiévales d'Ottawa, no. VII, 1938, *passim*.

matters, as to the scientific books that were newly known in the earlier part of the twelfth century. After, roughly, the middle of the century, when the labors of the North Italian and Sicilian translators and the Arabic schools of Spain had begun to exercise their effect, such clues are found in various writers and with mounting frequency.[3] But in the earlier time they are rather scanty, with respect both to the Greek works that were the material sources of intellectual renewal in that age, and to the Arabic traditions based upon them, whether either was available directly or in Latin form.

The present article will call attention to a significant point in Guillaume's *Philosophia mundi* which raises afresh the question of such clues. Since that treatise, together with its revision the *Dragmaticon*, was for some centuries influential on Western cosmogony, the bearing of the problem is not confined to Guillaume de Conches alone. Nor has the topic under consideration eluded the scrutiny of scholarship; on the contrary, it has suffered recurring discussion. Yet it contains materials, intriguing in their nature, whose character, if not whose very presence, has escaped the searching eye.

The point in question occurs in a passage "De elementis,"[4] in which Guillaume attempts to form a definition by specifying other parts and combinations in nature and then eliminating them. An

[3] See especially C.H. Haskins, *Studies in the History of Mediaeval Science* (2nd ed., Cambridge, Mass., 1927), chaps IX, X, and XII *et passim*.

[4] Migne, *PL*, CLXXII, 48 D–51 A; XC, 1132 C–1134 B. The treatise is ascribed in these two editions to Honorius of Autun and Bede, respectively. A third edition, under the name of William of Hirschau, appeared in Basel, 1531. See M. Grabmann, *Handschriftliche Forschungen und Mitteilungen zum Schrifttum des Wilhelm von Conches*, Sitzungsb. d. Bayerischen Akad., phil.-hist., 1935, p. 5; and A. Vernet, in *Scriptorium*, I (1946–47), 243–59. For the attribution to Guillaume see Grabmann (pp. 5–6) and the references there to Rose and Jourdain; as well as Vernet, Gregory (pp. 4 ff.), and H. Flatten, *Die Philosophie des Wilhelm von Conches* (Bonn Diss., 1929), pp. 9 ff. Both Migne texts are imperfectly edited but that in *PL* CLXXII is in some respects superior, the one in *PL* XC printing *elementa* where *elementata* is required and suppressing the names of Guillaume's current medical authorities: cf. for example CLXXII, 48 D, 50 BC, 50 AB with XC, 1132 C, 1133 CD, 1133 C.

element, he argues, is the simple and minimal part of any body, simple as to quality and minimal as to quantity, *cujus expositio talis est*: *Elementum est pars simpla cujus non sunt contrariae qualitates*. By this definition such bodily substances as humors, bone and flesh, hands and feet are ruled out of consideration; for they are not, strictly, minimal parts. Similarly, earth, water, air, and fire, as we normally perceive them, are not elements in the proper sense, since each may have an admixture of a variety of qualities under a variety of actual circumstances; hence they are not simple, as required. In order to distinguish what the elements truly are, we are obliged to employ the method of division, and that is based, not on sense-perception, but on intellect.[5] The human body may be divided in fact into organs (hands and feet) and similar, or homogeneous, parts (bone and flesh); their further division, however, into humors and of humors into elements, can be accomplished by an intellectual act only. The intellect recognizes that what makes earth, water, air, and fire what they are, is the combination of *qualitates* peculiar to each, i.e. cold and dry, cold and moist, warm and moist, warm and dry, respectively; and that the minute particles of each of these peculiar mixtures, since they are simple and minimal parts ,are *elementa* in the absolute sense. The bodies which we ordinarily perceive in nature, though each may be dominated by the qualities of a single element, are not themselves *elementa*, but *elementata*. The further question is now raised whether the individual *qualitates* themselves are not simpler and more minimal than the particles in which they combine. Against those who, bringing the Chalcidian *Timaeus*, Johannitius, and Macrobius to their support, answer that the qualities are indeed simpler and hence to be considered elements, Guillaume argues that *elementa... non esse qualitates, sed qualitates esse in elementis*.[6] With respect to the "Pythagorean" position of those philosophers who assert that the elements are what we perceive by our various senses,

---

[5] Guillaume here refers to Boethius: *Vis est intellectus animi, conjuncta disjungere, et disjuncta conjungere*: *PL*, CLXXII, 49 CD; XC, 1133 AB. Cf. Boethius, *Comment. in Porphyrium*, Lib. i (*PL*, LXIV, 84 D).

[6] *PL*, CLXXII, 50 AB; XC, 1133 BC.

Guillaume maintains that there is nothing in his principles which contradicts that view.

This definition, which was destined to an extraordinary afterlife of both controversy and acceptance, sounds a new note in the Western Latin philosophy of the high Middle Ages. Not only does it invent the noun *elementatum* to express its essential distinctions, but in dealing with the distinctions and their consequences it displays a considerable philosophic talent. The noun itself became a pawn in subsequent maneuvering among cosmogonists, philosophers from the schools of Spain, Salernitans, anti-Salernitans, and encyclopedists, and finally found lodgment in the compilations of the lexicographers.[7] As to the argument, it has been used to describe Guillaume as Democritean, which is naive, and other accounts have sought to set the record straight.[7a]

What is new in Guillaume de Conches springs at once from a speculative temper, developed in the special atmosphere of his times, operating on a body of traditional topics, and from a further knowledge of new sources, chiefly in the theoretical realms of medicine. It produces in subsequent years a discussion relevant to "realism" and "nominalism," that has hitherto been neglected by those in modern times who describe the supposed medieval quarrel about "universals". With respect to the medical sources, Guillaume also knew and considered them from normal tradition, as witness his astronomical account of the seasons and their connection with human age, diseases and their cures, recording, though more fully, a common view found in Bede, Marcellus, and their predecessors.[8] But the entire section on

---

[7] Silverstein, "Elementatum: Its Appearance among the Twelfth-Century Cosmogonists," *Mediaeval Studies*, XVI (1954), 156–62; to which may be added the following further items among the Salernitans: Urso, *De Commixtionibus*, Bodleian MS. Digby 161, esp. fols 37v ff.; Urso, *Comment. in Aphorism.*, MS. Bodley 680, fols 32v, 46v, 75v, 79v, 90v; and an Introduction to the *Ysagoge*, as in Oxford MS. New College 171, fols 1v–3, but esp. 2, col. 2.

[7a] Among them the most recent and philosophically enlightening is that by R.P. McKeon, "Medicine and Philosophy in the Eleventh and Twelfth Centuries: The Problem of the Elements," *The Thomist*, XXIV (1961), 211–56.

[8] *PL*, CLXXII, 67 B–70 B; XC, 1150 B–52 C. Cf. Karl Werner, *Die Kosmologie*

the elements, both the passage above paraphrased and beyond, is testimony to his reading in fresh texts. In particular, it leans heavily for its support on Constantinus Africanus, whose name he mentions several times and whose eleventh-century translations or adaptations from the Arabic initiate a Casinensian-Salernitan influence, philosophic in bent, on Western medicine and natural science generally.[9] Guillaume also cites Johannitius and Theophilus *De urinis*, but it is to Constantinus' *Pantegni* that he goes directly for his definition of an element, deepening the implications, to be sure, yet paraphrasing if not exactly quoting its words; and his recourse to the method of division, while amplified from a knowledge of Boethius, is also suggested by Constantinus' text:

Philosophi diffiniunt simplam & minimam compositi corporis particulam esse elementum. Simplam autem rem dicimus quae cum eadem sit in essentia, similis est in partibus, ut ignis, aer, aqua, terra esse uidetur. Sunt tamen quaedam uisu simpla, intellectu composita, ut lapides, metalla & similia. Philosophi ergo uidentes elementa intellectu simpla, & omnia corpora constructioni & destructioni subiecta ex eis esse composita, uocauerunt ea prima elementa.[10]

His division of the body into four constituent parts — elements, humors, similars, and organs — is Galenic and likewise said by him to be based on Constantinus. It is to the same authority also that he expressly refers when maintaining the compatibility between his and the Pythagorean-Empedoclean views.[11] But there is a great deal more in the section which cannot be explained by Guillaume's use of the *Pantegni* (or indeed of Johannitius, as that

---

und Naturlehre des scholastischen Mittelalters mit specieller Beziehung auf Wilhelm von Conches (Wiener Sitzungsberichte, phil.-hist. Cl., LXXV. 3 [1873]), 344–46. See below n. 34. Marcellus means, in fact, his text of the Letter of Hippocrates to Antiochus (*De medicamentis*, ed. Helmreich, Leipzig, 1889, pp. 8–9), also known elsewhere in the Middle Ages.

[9] See Sudhoff, in *Archiv für Geschichte der Medizin*, IX (1916), 348–56; and Haskins, *Med. Sci.*, esp. pp. 39, 92, 374.

[10] *Pantegni*, i, 3 (*Opera*, Basel: Henricus Petrus, 1539, p. 4).

[11] *PL*, CLXXII, 50 C; XC substitutes *sententiae philosophorum* and *philosophus* for *Constantinus*. Cf. Silverstein, "Elementatum," pp. 157–58, n. 9.

abbreviated work deals with the subject[12]); moreover, even those passages which are closest to Constantinus contain language which cannot have been derived from that writer.

Thus, Constantinus' terms for the four bodily divisions, drawn as they are from Galen by way of the Arabic, are these: (1) *elementa*, (2) *humores*, (3) *similia* (or *consimilia*) *membra*, and (4) *officialia membra*.[13] And that is true also of Johannitius.[14] In Guillaume the list appears as (1) *elementa*, (2) *humores*, (3) *homiomeria, id est consimiles*, and (4) *organica, id est officiales*;[15] in which *homiomeria* and *organica* disclose a Greek source. What was that source?

We have no reason to suppose that Guillaume de Conches knew any Greek. And in the older traditions still preserved to us which were accessible to a humanist such as he, the four-fold classification is rather hard to find in full, and where it does appear the terms are not in Greek. Thus Apuleius *De Platone*, a book which as a Chartrian Guillaume surely read, provided an important account of the three *substantiae corporis* commenting on a part of the *Timaeus* which is missing from the Chalcidian version, hence was unavailable to the West in that form; but Apuleius' words are uniformly Latin:

> cum totius corporis ⟨tres⟩ dicat esse substantias, primam vult videri ex igni et aqua et ceteris elementis, aliam ex consimilibus partibus viscerum, ossiculorum, cruoris et ceterorum, tertiam de discrepantibus diversisque membris, id est capite, utero et articulis disparibus. unde et substantia, quae de simplicibus constat elementis, si id, quod necessitate victus extrinsecus adrogatur, quomodo congruit et generi singulorum, qualitatem corporis temperiemque custodit, et illis, quae de consimilibus, robur auget et iis, quae inter se disparia supra diximus, pulchritudinem nutrit....[16]

---

[12] See *Isagoge Joannitii*, in *Articella*, Venice: Baptista de Tortis, 1487, esp. f. 2, cols. 1 and 2.

[13] *Pantegni*, i, 2; ii, 1; iii, 1; in *Opera*, ed. 1539, pp. 2, 24, 48.

[14] *Isagoge*, in *Articella*, *loc. cit.*, and f. 5, cols. 1–2.

[15] *PL*, CLXXII, 49 A–C; XC, 1132 D–33 C.

[16] Ed. Thomas, in *Apulei opera quae supersunt*, III (Leipzig, 1908), 101.

As for *homiomeria*, the Latin text of Oribasius, which had a considerable survival in medieval medicine, offers in *Synopsis* v, 53, a reference both brief and unenlightening: *omiomerin quam nos firmissimam corporis substantiam dicere pateremus.*[17] Servius' commentary on *Aeneid* IV, 625, for the *lemma* "ex ossibus ultor," gives us a little more, but that hardly more informative, citing, as it does so, Lucretius:

secundum Anaxagoram qui homoeomeriam dicit, id est omnium membrorum similitudinem, esse in rebus creandis [id est] ex ossibus, ex sanguine, ex medullis: nam omnia pro parte sui transeunt in procreationem. Lucretius ⟨I,830⟩ *nunc ad Anaxagorae veniamus homoeomeriam.*[18]

It is the Lucretian passage itself, however, fully seen and at first hand, which provides the most striking account of the term, an account whose further details would have seemed to mesh conveniently with those of Apuleius:

Nunc et Anaxagoras scrutemur homoeomeriam,
....
Principium rerum quam dicit homoeomeriam:
Ossa videlicet e pauxillis atque minutis
Visceribus viscus gigni; sanguenque creari,
Sanguinis inter se multis coeuntibu' guttis:
Ex aurique putat micis consistere posse
Aurum: et de terris terram concrescere parvis:
Ignibus ex ignem; humorem ex humoribus esse;
Caetera consimili fingit ratione, putatque.
....
    Praeterea, quoniam cibus auget corpus, et ossa,
Et nervos alienigenis ex partibus esse:
Sive cibos omneis commisto corpora parva,
Ossaque, et omnino venas, parteisque cruoris;
Fiet, uti cibus omnis et aridus, et liquor ipse,
Ex alienigenis rebus constare putetur,
Ossibus, et nervis, venisque, et sanguine misto.   (I. 830–67)

[17] Ed. Molinier, in Bussemaker-Daremberg, *Oeuvres d'Oribase*, VI (1876), 90.
[18] Ed. Thilo and Hagen, I (Leipzig, 1881), 573.

Unfortunately, the knowledge in the Middle Ages of Lucretius, except for such bits as appeared in quotation or in the *florilegia*, is a matter of such doubt that we are almost obliged to rule it out of Guillaume's ken. Oribasius and Servius alone would have furnished him hardly anything beyond a word. If he had known them both or either of them, that word would perhaps have risen up in his memory and resounded against his new-laid Constantinian foundations; but missing from that echo would have been not only context of definition and classification, but also the further term *organica*. That term, ὄργανον, ὀργανικός, as Guillaume here understands it, goes back in particular to Aristotle, to such works as the *De historia animalium* and the *De partibus animalium*, where it specifies the several composite and instrumental parts of the body, in contradistinction to those that are simple and primary. But the relevant instances of its use in the Middle Ages, as the lexicographers have found them, all seem to be later than the *Philosophia mundi*.[19]

[19] See, e.g., Aristotle, *Hist. an.*, I, 6, 491a, 25–26, *Part. an.*, II, 2, 647b, 22–25; and cf. *Part. an.*, I, 5, 645b, 14, and *Genes. an.*, I, 2, 716 a, 24. The citations, therefore, in Stephanus, Forcellini, Du Cange, Bartal, Sella (*Glossario Latino Italiano*, Vatican City, 1944), and Souter (*A Glossary of Later Latin*, Oxford, 1949) are irrelevant, as also in Giovanni Balbi's *Catholicon*, ed. Petrus Egidius (Lugd.: Antonius du Ry, 1520), representing the tradition from Hugutio of Pisa. Mattheus Martin, *Lexicon philologicum* (Frankfurt, 1655), which, unlike Stephanus, retains many medieval "barbarisms," gives us: *Corpus organicum, habens certa organa, quibus anima ad distinctas actiones edendas utitur*. Baxter and Johnson, *Medieval Latin Word List* (London, 1934), records *organum* as for tongue or power of speech c. 1070 (for which cf. Prudentius, *Peristaphanon*, X, 2) and otherwise its useful instances are too late (c. 1167 and after). Scattered uses in the earlier period, chiefly of the noun rather than of the adjective, are not inimical to the general meaning that we want (as is also the case with numerous ancient employments in the Greek) but they are in themselves specialized largely to voice, breathing, singing, to figurative uses, or to the eye; and none, moreover, appears in a context distinguishing as an ordered group or kind members with dissimilar, from those with similar, parts. Thus, the medieval Latin Paulus of Aegina (ed. Heiberg, Leipzig, 1912, p. 44): *organicis uero paralisin thoraci afferre adiutoria, spiritus retentione et exclamatione uti* (cf. also Maigne d'Arnis, *Lexicon*, s.v. *organalis*); *organum pectoris* and *organi membra* [*de oculo*] in Claudianus Mamertus, iii, 9, and i,21

Among the new things available in Guillaume's time, however, there was a treatise whose definitions, classifications, and terms were remarkably apt to his hand. This was the work of Nemesius of Emessa περὶ φύσεως ἀνθρώπου.[20] Of that little treatise two Latin versions were known in the Middle Ages: one made by Burgundio of Pisa about the year 1155,[21] and the other by the eleventh-century archbishop of Salerno, Alfanus, under the odd but fitting title *Premnon phisicon*, that is, *The Trunk and Fount of Natural Things*.[22] The *Philosophia mundi*, written, as Guillaume tells us, in his youth, must have been produced some time late in the eleven-twenties, or not long thereafter.[23] Hence, it is in the Alfanus text, rather than in the later rendering by Burgundio, that we may expect to find the reward of special scrutiny.

In the first place, the *Premnon phisicon*, though not precisely

(ed. Englebrecht, *Corp. script. eccles. lat.*, xi [1885], 169 and 75); and all the instances in Arnaldi and Turriani, *Lexicon imperfectum*, pars iia (Bruxelles, 1951). The *Ars parva* as it appears in the *Articella* (ed. 1487, fols 153v–54) uses *organicae partes* though not *homiomeria*; but both translator and date of the text in that form remain to be established, despite Steinschneider, *Die europäischen Ubersetzungen*, i (1904), item 32a.7; cf. Thorndike and Kibre, *A Catalogue of Incipits* (1937), esp. col. 728, and Index s. nn. Constantinus Africanus and Galen. A proper Late and medieval Latin history of the word is evidently a desideratum and would affect any final view of the historical significance of its appearance in the *Philosophia mundi*.

[20] So called regularly in the editions. But for the question of the title see Benedict Einarson, *Studies in Nemesius* (Chicago University Diss., 1932), pp. 7–8 and nn. 22–27. Cf. below, n. 22.

[21] Ed. C. Burkhard, *Gregorii Nysseni (Nemesii Emeseni)* περὶ φύσεως ἀνθρώπου *liber a Burgundion in Latinum translatus*, in *Jahresbericht des k.k. Staats-Gymnasiums in XX. Bezirke von Wien*, nos. 8, 9, 13, 18, 19 (Vienna, 1891 – 1902). For the date see Haskins, *Med. Sci.*, p. 207.

[22] Ed. C. Burkhard (Leipzig: Teubner, 1917); p. 3: "Eritque ei titulus *Premnon physicon* hoc est *Stipes naturalium*, quia sicut ex uno stipite multi ramusculi pullulant, sic ex huius fonte doctrinae plurimi scientiae naturalium rivuli exuberabunt." *Premnon physicon* is Burkhard's emendation; the mss read *Pre'non phisicon*, *prepnon fisicon*, and *prennon fisicon*. Cf. below, n. 42 and its context. As for Burgundio's version, none of the surviving mss gives a Greek title; it is called, with a confusion of authorship, simply *Liber Sancti Gregorii Nyssae episcopi*, or variants thereof.

[23] For current opinions on the date see *Mediaeval Studies*, xvi, 157, n. 7.

Galenic in outlook, is yet founded at certain points in Galen's system and its analogues;[24] and this would have been attractive to Guillaume, whose interest in the physical structure of the universe and of man within it was indebted to the Galenic physiology as Constantinus Africanus and Johannitius provided it. Moreover, the particular subject of Nemesius' tractate — the nature of man, his soul and body, and the corporeal functioning of soul in body — is also, in considerable part, Guillaume's subject.

Now the *Premnon phisicon* has an extended passage on the elements, reflecting the same Galenic tradition but containing statements and language found in Guillaume and not in the other two writers which he names as sources. *Elementum mundanum*, Nemesius-Alfanus tells us,

> est pars minima confectionis corporum. Sunt autem elementa quattuor: terra, aqua, aer, ignis.... Ipsaque sunt prima et simplicia corpora quantum ad alia. Etenim omne elementum unius generis est his, quorum est elementum. Principium quidem non est unius generis his, quorum est principium, elementum vero omnino unius generis est. Quod autem terra et aqua, aer et ignis sint elementa, manifestum. Etenim in his extremae qualitates potestate et actu manifestae sunt. Sed nullum horum sensibilium elementorum simplex et non infectum est alio elemento.... Tamen in mixtura manifesta est natura eorum. Unumquodque vero elementorum qualitates habet specificantes illud. Est etenim terra sicca et frigida, aqua vero frigida et humida, aer autem humidus et calidus secundum suam naturam, ignis quidem calidus et siccus. Sed neque qualitates per se possunt esse elementa.[25]

This is Guillaume's argument in essence: the concern with

---

[24] See Einarson, esp. chap. 1, nn. 35, 36, 38, 39, 47; chaps. 2, 5–7, 9, 16–21, *passim*. Cf. B. Domański, *Die Psychologie des Nemesius*, Beiträge zur Geschichte der Philosophie des Mittelalters, III. 1, Münster, 1900, esp. pp. xviii; 1, n. 1; 9 ff.; 52; 96–130, *passim*.

[25] Ed. Burkhard (Teubner, 1917), p. 62. For the Greek see Nemesius, ed. Matthaei (Halle, 1802), pp. 150 ff. Cf. Burgundio, ed. Burkhard, in *Jahresbericht* no. 9 (1892), p. 29.

minima, the distinction between *elementum* and *elementatum* (though the new-coined noun does not appear), the denial that *qualitates* can *per se* be elements; and though it does not proceed explicitly by division, the method is implied in the reasoning and was in any case suggested to Guillaume by Constantinus' argument and supported by a reference to Boethius on Porphyry.[26]

More striking still is the *Premnon phisicon*'s account of the four divisions of the body, in which all the terms, Latin and Greek, are exactly those of the *Philosophia mundi* and established in a context which discloses their meanings as Guillaume understands them. The passage in Alfanus immediately precedes that on the elements and is directly connected with it:

Omne corpus ex quattuor *elementis* est compositum et ex his factum est. Singulariter autem sanguineorum animalium corpora ex quattuor *humoribus* constant.... Singulariter vero dicitur, quando principaliter ex eisdem aliquid fit, ut sit ipsa quattuor elementorum commixtio quattuor humores, humorum vera sint *homiomera* id est similes partes habentia, quae sunt membra corporis.... Omne vero non homiomerum ex homiomeris constat, ut caput ex nervis et carnibus et ossibus et similibus, vocantur autem et haec *organica* id est officialia.[27]

The relationship in kind between Guillaume and Alfanus is thus perfectly clear. Had Guillaume actually read the *Premnon phisicon*? Bliemetzrieder has argued plausibly that Nemesius' treatise was known to Adelard of Bath, who was of Guillaume's generation;[28] Alfanus was a friend of Constantinus Africanus, whose *Liber*

---

[26] See n. 5 above.

[27] Ed. Burkhard (Teubner, 1917), pp. 59–60; italics are the present writer's. For the Greek see ed. Matthaei, pp. 145 ff. Cf. Galen, *Comm. in Hippocratem de natura hominis,* Prooemium (ed. Kühn, xv [1828], esp. 7–8). Burgundio, who is in any case too late, uses the term *homiomeria* (and *consimiles*) but not *organica,* for which he gives a word (*Jahresbericht* no. 9, pp. 27–28) that does not appear in Guillaume: *anomiomerea* (=Alfanus *non homiomera*). Cf. Apuleius *discrepantes et diversa membra,* n. 16 above and its context.

[28] *Adelhard von Bath: Blätter aus dem Leben eines englischen Naturphilosophen des 12. Jahrhunderts und Bahnbrechers einer Wiedererweckung der griechischen Antike* (Munich, 1935), pp. 386–95.

aureus de stomachi affectionibus was written for the learned archbishop's benefit;[29] and Guillaume's interest in Casinensian and Salernitan medical theory suggests that he would have had access to so relevant a treatise produced in that milieu. But he never mentions the archbishop or his book, and that would seem to be a barrier to the view that either was known to a writer whose wont is to cite directly certain of the "new" things on which he drew. Yet it is not an absolute barrier; as far as the connection with Alfanus is concerned, all but one of the extant manuscripts of the treatise are anonymous and if they reflect a condition of Guillaume's time he might well have read it without knowing author or translator.[29a] However that may be, it would seem that the case for a connection between Guillaume and Alfanus must be argued chiefly from the obviousness of their similarities. Elsewhere in Guillaume's book are topics that Alfanus' Nemesius also discusses in considerable detail, especially human psychology with its physiological account of the so-called Internal Senses and the question of how soul and body can be said to unite.[30] Both these problems, however, have a complex history in

---

[29] Ed. Basel: Henricus Petrus, 1536, p. 215: *Alfano reuerendissimo Salernitanę ecclesię archipręsuli, Constantinus Africanus Cassinensis debitae subiectionis obsequium.... Idcirco huius culpę temeritatem magno animi aduersionis respectu considerans, hunc libellum de multis & eleganioribus antiquorum dictis tuę causa sanitatis conscripsi...* Alfanus himself was a physician of note, as well as archbishop, poet, and man of learning: see Haskins, *Med. Sci.*, p. 142, n. 5; and F.J.E. Raby, *A History of Christian-Latin Poetry* (2nd ed., Oxford, 1953), pp. 242—49, and its references. Cf. Raby, *A History of Secular Latin Poetry* (Oxford, 1934), I, 377–83. That Alfanus' work as *medicus* was not quickly forgotten is witnessed, for example, by the catalogue of Christ Church, Canterbury, in Prior Eastry's time (1284–1331), which lists a *Tractatus Alfani Salernitanensis, de quibusdam questionibus medicinalibus*: M.R. James, *The Ancient Libraries of Canterbury and Dover* (Cambridge, 1903), p. 59.

[29a] See ed. Burkhard (Teubner, 1917), p. 5, n. 1. Cf. below, n. 44.

[30] *PL*, CLXXII, 95, 98; XC, 1174 C–75 A. Cf. Alfanus, ed. Burkhard (Teubner, 1917), pp. 72 ff., esp. 87 and 89 (internal senses and their localization); 52–58 (union of soul and body). For an account of the development of the former of these subjects in medieval philosophy, see H.A. Wolfson, "The Internal Senses in Latin, Arabic, and Hebrew Philosophical Texts," *Harvard Theolo-*

the West: Guillaume would have been acquainted with the particulars of the first, as he and his contemporaries conceived it, from Boethius, Apuleius, Solinus, and other traditional sources, as well as from Constantinus Africanus and his "school"; and of the second from Boethius *Contra Eutychen et Nestorium*,[31] from the Chalcidian *Timaeus*,[32] and possibly also from Priscianus Lydus *Solutionum ad Chosroem liber* in the Carolingian Latin version which was known in the thirteenth century and was perhaps beginning to be studied during his age.[33] And nothing in Guillaume's language is so distinctive as to establish beyond doubt a relationship with Alfanus on these subjects, whether alone or primarily.

In another area, however, the likelihood of such a relationship appears to be more definite. That area comprises the particular subject *de homine et eius partibus*, on which Guillaume gives us several chapters, among them an elaborated account of the digestive system, whose sources Werner and Flatten have conceived to be, quite simply, Macrobius' *Saturnalia* and Constantinus.[34] Once more, nevertheless, Guillaume sets down details that do not coincide with anything in these authorities; nor, indeed, with anything in Theophilus *De urinis*, whom he also quotes,[35] though no modern study of his work has paused to remark the point. One such highly significant detail is a description of the tongue: *ad modum manus molendinarii illum* [i.e. *cibum*] *vertat, et sub dentes reducat, quae*

---

gical Review XXVIII (1935), 69–133; "Maimonides on the Internal Senses," *Jewish Quarterly Review*, N.S., XXV (1935), 441–67; and "Isaac Israeli on the Internal Senses," *Jewish Studies in Memory of George A. Kohut* (New York, 1935), pp. 583–98.

[31] Chaps IV, VI–VII (ed. and transl. H.F. Stewart and E.K. Rand, Loeb Library, 1918, pp. 90 ff., and 106–21).

[32] §§221 and 227 (ed. Wrobel, Leipzig, 1876, pp. 257 and 264–65).

[33] Ed. I. Bywater, *Prisciani Lydi quae extant*, Supplementum Aristotelicum, I. 2, Berlin, 1886, esp. pp. 50–52, and (for indications of influence, though incomplete), XII–XIII.

[34] *PL*, CLXXII, 91–93; XC, 1172–73 B. Cf. Werner, in *Wiener Sitzungsberichte*, phil.-hist. Cl., LXXV.3, 384; and Flatten, p. 166, following him.

[35] *PL*, CLXXII, 93 A; XC, 1173 AB, mistakenly changes the reference to Galen.

ad hoc spongiosa est, ut cibi succum recipiens, saporem discernat[36]; expanding a figure found in Galen *De usu partium*, XI, 4 (III, 855):

τὸ δ' ὥσπερ ὑπὸ μυλῶν τῶν γομφίων λειοῦσθαι τὴν τροφὴν τῶν μασητήρων ἔργον μυῶν. οὗτοι δ' αὐτοὶ καὶ μεταβάλλουσι τὰ σιτία καὶ τὰ τῶν ὀδόντων ἀποπίπτοντα πάλιν αὐτοῖς ἐπιβάλλουσι τεινόμενοι τε καὶ προσστελλόμενοι τῶν κροταφιτῶν μυῶν μηδὲν εἰς τοῦτ' ἔτι συμβαλλομένων. ἀλλ' ἡ γλῶττα μὲν οὐ σμικρὰ διαπράττεται περὶ τὴν ἐνέργειαν ταύτην οἷα χεὶρ ἀεὶ μεταβάλλουσα καὶ στρεφόυσα τὴν ἐν τῷ στόματι τροφὴν ὑπὲρ τοῦ πᾶν ὁμοίως αὐτῆς καταθραύεσθαι μέρος· ἔξωθεν δ' εἷς ἑκατέρωθεν ὁ μασητὴρ οὗτος μῦς οἷον ἑτέρα τις χεὶρ ἐπίκουρος τῇ γλώττῃ παρασκεύασται. μεγίστην δ' εἰς τοῦτο βοήθειαν αὐτῇ παρέχει τὰ κάτω πέρατα τῶν γνάθων τὰ δερματώδη τὰ πρὸς τοῖς χείλεσιν, εἰς ἃ καθήκουσιν οἱ λεπτοὶ καὶ πλατεῖς μύες εἷς καθ' ἑκάτερον μέρος ἅπαντι τῷ τραχήλῳ περιβεβλημένοι.[37]

The *De usu partium* itself would have been difficult of access to Guillaume, for the earliest Latin versions which we know, the *De iuvamentis membrorum* and the one by Nicholas of Reggio, were made after his time.[38] And in any case, the Galenic passage, basic as it is, could have furnished our author only the primary hint — teeth as mill and tongue as hand —, without his further simile of the miller. Again it is Nemesius, working the figure out

---

[36] *PL*, CLXXII, 91 D; XC, 1172 B. There is nothing relevant in Macrobius, *Saturnalia*, Bk. VII; and contrast also Constantinus, ed. Henricus Petrus, 1539, p. 62.

[37] Ed. Helmreich, II (Leipzig, 1909), 122, 11. 2–13. This figure is also used by Cicero, *De natura deorum*, ii, 54, §§ 134–35 (ed. Plasberg–Ax, Leipzig, 1933, p. 104; and p. 198, nn.), whence perhaps it passed to, among others, the early Christian apologist Lactantius (*De opificio dei*, x, 16). For the influence of the Ciceronian passage generally on the Church Fathers, see Eduard Norden, in *Jahrbücher für classische Philologie*, 19er Supplementband (1893), p. 434, n. 2.

[38] See Lo Parco, *Niccolò da Reggio* (1913), p. 298; and Thorndike and Kibre, *A Catalogue of Incipits* (1937), cols. 121, 211, 325. The version of *De iuvamentis membrorum* usually ascribed to Burgundio of Pisa does not seem to contain anything like the figure in question, at least as it occurs in mss which I have seen: Harley 3748, ff. 168–90, and Peterhouse 33, ff. 222 v ff.

[15]   GUILLAUME DE CONCHES AND MEMESIUS OF EMESSA   733

fully, which enlightens us; and, with the Alfanus version, in language very close to Guillaume's, including, for the Greek original's ἀλετρίς (that is *molitrix*, or mill woman), the masculine form *molendinarius*: *Maximam enim utilitatem lingua praestat masticationi coadunans escam dentibusque supponens, quemadmodum molendinarii manu frumentum molis subiciunt; sic quodammodo et lingua manus est masticationis.*[39]

Such evidence as this, the elaborate passage on the elements supported by the Nemesian description of the tongue, striking though together they may seem, cannot of course be taken as conclusive of a connection between our Chartrian and the churchman from Salerno. But if not from Nemesius, whence else did Guillaume get these patently uncommon items? At the very least they suggest that, whether he knew the treatise directly or not, he was acquainted with Casinensian-Salernitan sources that were influenced by materials which it embodies; by a Greek, in short, as well as an Arabic tradition.[40]

We need not leave the matter at that, however. There remains one further piece of external evidence which strengthens the appeal of our particular case. It is to be found in the *Metalogicon* of John of Salisbury, who had been to Chartres as a young man, studied there under Guillaume de Conches, and learned to know well his world and work.[41] At the end of a discussion of the power

---

[39] Ed. Burkhard (Teubner, 1917), p. 144. Cf. the Greek original, ed. Matthaei (Halle, 1802), p. 238. Burgundio's text omits the entire section in which the passage occurs. For the connection with Galen, see Einarson, p. 123, and p. 125, n. 6. Guillaume's further adjective for the tongue, *spongiosa*, present in neither version of Nemesius, is related to Constantinus in a description otherwise totally different; *Pantegni, iii*, 16 (ed. 1539, p. 62): *Lingua est instrumentum gustus et locutionis. Quae de carne molli componitur & spongię assimilatur.* *Pantegni, iii*, 23 (*De cibis*: ed. 1539, pp. 67–68) adds nothing useful to the account. None of this, however, explains the further detail in Guillaume that the tongue is porous *ut cibi succum recipiens, saporem discernat.*

[40] It should be added here that the entire subject of Western access to Graeco–Latin medical sources in the earlier twelfth century remains for serious investigation.

[41] For John's student days at Chartres see, *inter alia*, the well known

of the senses, the purpose of which is to establish, following Aristotle, that the arts and sciences derive from sensory perception, *Metalogicon* IV, 20 gives a list of further reading on the soul, including Plato, Aristotle, Cicero, the Fathers and Doctors of the Church, and Claudianus Mamertus; and then continues: *quos si quis non potest euoluere, uel Prenonphisicon legat, librum de anima copiosissime disputantem.*[42] To this John's modern editor C.C.J. Webb sets down the following note:

Phrenonphysicon: quasi περὶ φρενῶν φύσεως. Forsan ad librum quendam respicit qui *Physica Animae* inscribitur, et inter opera Willelmi abbatis S. Theodorici apud Remos, postea monachi Signiacensis, extat (Migne *P.L.* CLXXX. 707 seqq.). Obiit Willelmus post a. 1148 (*Hist. litt. de la France* XII. 331).[43]

Though it comes some eighteen years after his time with the Chartrian master, John's reference is precious and Webb quite mistaken in his guess. What the distinguished pupil of Guillaume de Conches is citing precisely, we now should recognize, is Nemesius' book, and that in the Latin version by Alfanus, as the use by John of the archbishop's title quaintly proves.[44]

---

accounts of Poole, *Illustrations*, esp. pp. 180–81; and C.C.J. Webb, *John of Salisbury* (London: SPCK, 1932), pp. 5–10 *et passim*.

[42] Ed. Webb, *Ioannis Saresberiensis episcopi Carnotensis metalogicon* (Oxford, 1929), pp. 187, 11. 1–7. Cf. n. 22 above.

[43] *Ibid.*, p. 187, n. 6.

[44] The fact that in the passage in question John cites authors for all but the *Premnon phisicon* suggests that, like Guillaume, he may not have known its author or translator. Cf. above, n. 29a and its context.

THE ACCOUNT OF SIMON MAGUS IN ACTS 8

by Morton Smith

Professor Wolfson's lucid analysis of the intellectual make-up of gnosticism has cleared the way for a restudy of the historical traditions concerning the individual gnostics, of whom Simon Magus was often said to have been the earliest.[1] The first major element in the Christian tradition about Simon is the story in Acts 8:4ff., probably written about 80 A.D. In the Revised Standard Version it reads as follows:

Now those who were scattered (from Jerusalem by the persecution which arose after the death of Stephen) went about preaching the word. Philip went down to a city of Samaria and proclaimed to them the Christ. And the multitudes with one accord gave heed to what was said by Philip, when they heard him and saw the signs which he did. For unclean spirits came out of many who were possessed, crying with a loud voice; and many who were paralyzed or lame were healed. So there was much joy in that city. But there was a man named Simon who had previously practiced magic in the city and amazed the nation of Samaria, saying that he himself was somebody great. They all gave heed to him, from the least to the greatest, saying, 'This man is that power of God which is called Great.' And they gave heed to him, because for a long time he had amazed them with his magic. But when they believed Philip as he preached good news about the kingdom of God and the name of Jesus Christ, they were baptized, both men and women. Even

---

[1] H.A. Wolfson, *The Philosophy of the Church Fathers* (Cambridge, 1956), I, 495 ff., esp. 512 ff. Simon appears as the first of heretics in Justin, *I Ap.* 26; Irenaeus I, 16 &c. and many subsequent writers.

Simon himself believed, and after being baptized he continued with Philip. And seeing signs and great miracles performed, he was amazed. Now when the apostles at Jerusalem heard that Samaria had received the word of God, they sent to them Peter and John, who came down and prayed for them that they might receive the Holy Spirit; for it had not yet fallen on any of them, but they had only been baptized in the name of the Lord Jesus. Then they laid their hands on them and they received the Holy Spirit. Now when Simon saw that the Spirit was given through the laying on of the apostles' hands, he offered them money, saying, 'Give me also this power, that any one on whom I lay my hands may receive the Holy Spirit.' But Peter said to him, 'Your silver perish with you, because you thought you could obtain the gift of God with money! You have neither part nor lot in this matter, for your heart is not right before God. Repent therefore of this wickedness of yours, and pray to the Lord that, if possible, the intent of your heart may be forgiven you. For I see that you are in the all of bitterness and in the bond of iniquity.' And Simon answered, 'Pray for me to the Lord, that nothing of what you have said may come upon me.'

This is a piece of Christian propaganda against the followers of Simon. Its primary object is to show that the cult of Simon is inferior to that of Jesus because Simon himself was converted to Christianity and baptized by a Christian. Moreover, it intends to show that Simon was inferior to the apostles, as well as to Jesus, because he never received the power to communicate the holy spirit to his followers, though he tried to buy it, and was publicly rebuked by the apostles and accepted their rebuke and asked them to pray for him. Just for good measure it adds that Simon had a shady past: He had previously been a magician and it was his magical prowess which had made his followers believe that he was the Great Power of God.

Of criticisms of the story to date, the most challenging has been one which takes as its point of departure the break in the middle.[2]

---

[2] Most effectively presented by A. Loisy, *Les Actes des Apôtres* (Paris, 1920), *ad loc.*

After Simon's baptism the narrative jumps to Jerusalem whence Peter and John are sent down to Samaria and by their prayers and laying on of hands bring down the holy spirit on those whom Philip had already baptized. Since there is a similar incident in Acts 19:1 ff. where Paul by rebaptism and laying on of hands gives the spirit to a group of disciples in Ephesus (who had hitherto been baptized only into the baptism of John) critics have supposed the notion that only apostles could give the spirit was a special concern of the author of Acts, who remodeled the story of Simon to introduce it. Originally the story represented Simon as trying to buy from Philip the power to do miracles, and getting his rebuke for that.

But Acts sometimes[3] represents the spirit as given without laying on of apostolic hands, so this theory of its motivation is dubious, and the internal evidence for remodeling is not conclusive. In particular, it is not likely that Simon the magician should be represented as bidding for the power to do miracles. Let us therefore turn from the question of the laying on of hands to the story of the baptism.

We have another example of a first-century Palestinian figure who was baptized into one Jewish sect and then proceeded to set up his own in competition. This was Jesus. The story of Simon's baptism looks very much like a Christian's telling against the Simonians the sort of story which the followers of John the Baptist were telling against the Christians to prove Jesus' inferiority to John. That such a story was told by the followers of John can be inferred with confidence from the Christian attempts to answer it, for instance, the way Mt. 3:13–15 develops the Marcan account of the baptism (Mk. 1:9–11) by making John protest his inferiority and Jesus demand to be baptized anyhow, "for thus it becometh us to fulfill all righteousness."[4] If Simon really was baptized by a Christian, the Simonians must have had their account of the matter,

---

[3] Acts 10:44 and 11:15.

[4] John's avoidance of the story of Jesus' baptism is no less informative in this respect than Matthew's apology for it.

explaining that it, too, was necessary "to fulfill all righteousness" (or something equally vague).

Thus considerations of polemic interest require us to question the report of the baptism and it is obvious that similar questions are raised by the report of the attempt to buy the power to confer the spirit. At most it *may* be evidence that the Simonians did not claim to confer the spirit by the laying on of hands and that Pauline Christians alleged this as proof of the inferiority of the Simonian sect and invented this story to rub in their allegation.[5] Similar questions, too, are raised by the charge that Simon practiced magic. That charge is common ancient abuse, applied alike to all sorts of people: Jesus, Apollonius of Tyana, the philosopher Apuleius and the emperor Tiberius. Used of religious leaders like Simon and Jesus it probably means that their fame as miracle workers was so well established that their opponents could not deny it. This is not to say that they may not also have practiced magic. Common abuse is often true, that's why it is common. But just because it is common we cannot (without further evidence) be certain of its truth in any particular instance.

Here let us cast a preliminary glance. What now seems to emerge from the story in Acts? It would seem to indicate that about 80 A.D. the author of Luke-Acts knew a tradition — either written or oral, we need not try to decide — to the effect that one Philip, of the Jerusalem community, had gone to Samaria to preach the gospel, and had made many converts there. Luke dated this after the death of Stephen, probably in the late thirties. He also knew and was anxious to embarrass the followers of a certain Simon, whom he believed to have been active in Samaria about that time. Simon had a great reputation as a miracle worker, which Luke could not deny, but explained by calling him a magician. To provide his fellow Christians with further ammunition against the Simonians he reported or elaborated or invented two stories, one, that Simon had been baptized by Philip, the other,

---

[5] For the basic importance of the gift of the spirit in Pauline circles, see Gal. 3:2 ff., a good commentary on Acts 19:1 ff.

that he had tried to buy from Peter and John the power to confer the spirit and had been refused and humiliated.

Of these two stories we have seen that the account of the baptism had a striking parallel in the account of Jesus' baptism being circulated by the followers of John the Baptist. This alone might have given Luke the idea of transferring it to Simon, but the idea would have been more easily come by if Simon had actually been baptized.

That Simon was baptized by a Christian, however, is quite unlikely, because Christian tradition contains a number of hostile accounts of him which depend on sources other than Acts. Had he really been baptized by a follower of Jesus, they would not have failed to emphasize the fact as a demonstration of his inferiority, just as Acts does. Since they say nothing about it, the probability is that it never occurred.

But this does not exclude the possibility of Simon's having been baptized by some other group, whose rite would not have had the same value for Christian propaganda (particularly if it has also been administered to Jesus), but would have sufficed to suggest to Luke (or his source) the slander which now stands in his text. And as a matter of fact it is reported that Simon was originally a member of the sect of John the Baptist.[6] Therefore it is not unlikely to suppose that he was at one time baptized by John or one of John's followers.

This supposition is confirmed by the details of the story in Acts, especially the facts that the baptism is in Samaria and that it is not accompanied, but followed, by the gift of the spirit. As remarked above, the other instance in Acts where a baptism is followed by a separate gift of the spirit is a case where the first baptism was Johannite. And in the fourth Gospel we have two contradictory traditions about the conversion of Samaria. On the one hand, this Gospel claims it was begun by Jesus;[7] on the other, it reports a saying of Jesus', addressed to his disciples, that in Samaria "others labored and you have entered into their labors," others

[6] *Clementine Homilies* 2,23.
[7] Jn. 4:41.

sowed and you reaped, "that the sower and the reaper may rejoice together."[8] This is very like another saying which the fourth Gospel puts in the mouth of the Baptist, making him declare himself the friend of the bridegroom who rejoices together with the bridegroom.[9] If the sower in Samaria who rejoices with the reaper is John who rejoices with Jesus, then the conversion of Samaria and the baptism of the converts must have been begun by John or his followers. A likely explanation of the above facts would be that Simon was baptized by them and later started a sect of his own, claiming to be the Great Power of God, come down to earth. Yet later Philip came from Jerusalem and won over many of the Samaritans, including a good many of Simon's followers, to Christianity. This may have been facilitated by the fact that Philip belonged to a group of Jerusalem Christians, the so-called "hellenists" which had many similarities with the Qumran sect, and the Qumran sect, in turn, had important points of contact with the Johannites and with Samaria.[10] If so, the story of the coming of Peter and John to Samaria and their introduction of the rite of giving the spirit by the laying on of hands, may reflect the yet later advent to the city of a Pauline type of Christianity, different in this and perhaps other respects from that of the "hellenists." But such speculations, though not inherently improbable, cannot be confirmed. The most we can say is that the story of Simon's baptism, in Acts, the report about Simon in the Clemen-

---

[8] Jn. 4:36–8.

[9] Jn. 3:29.

[10] For the similarities of the hellenists to the Qumran sect see M. Simon, *St. Stephen and the Hellenists* (London, 1958 [Haskell Lectures, 1956]), pp. 90–91, and the earlier studies by Cullmann and Johnson, referred to there. For Qumran's connection with Samaria, J. Bowman, "Centhct between Samaritan Sects and Qumran?," *Vetus Testamentum* 7 (1957), 184 ff.; with John, W. Brownlee, "John the Baptist," in *The Scrolls and the NT*, ed. K. Stendahl (N.Y., 1957), p. 33 ff.; S. McCasland, "The Way," *Jnl. Biblical Lit.*, 77 (1958), 222 ff., Cullmann's reconstruction, which refers the "others" of John 4:38 to the hellenists, is unconvincing because it supposes a greater separation between the hellenists and the twelve than that suggested by the account in Acts. Of course, the account in Acts is apologetic; nevertheless, as the evidence stands, it is better explained by taking the "others" to be the Johannites.

tina, and the contradictory traditions in the fourth Gospel about the conversion of Samaria, all fit together if we suppose Simon to have been a disciple of John the Baptist.

Acts says Simon has been astonishing the Samaritans by his magic "for a long time" before Philip arrived, so his career would seem to have begun about the same time as that of Jesus. But, like Jesus, he did not remain a Johannite; he started a sect of his own. In Luke's time his enemies reported that he claimed to be "somebody great" and his followers said that he was "that Power of God which is called Great."

The claim to be "somebody great" was also attributed by Rabban Gamaliel, if the western text of Acts reports him correctly,[11] to an earlier troublemaker called Theudas. Josephus[12] tells us that Theudas was a magician (i.e. worked miracles) and said he was a prophet and persuaded the people to follow him to the Jordan, saying he would divide the river by his command and enable them to cross. His followers were cut to pieces by a troop of Roman horsemen and he was beheaded. This was one of those Palestinian risings of which Eisler long ago demonstrated the messianic character.[13] We may take it, therefore, that the claim to be "somebody great" was a messianic claim and that by attributing it to Simon, Luke meant to stigmatize him as a messianic pretender like Theudas and — we may add, though Luke would have distinguished — like Jesus.

This is perfectly in accord with what is known about Samaritan history at this time. The Samaritans were no less agitated by messianic pretenders than were the Jewish sects. About 35 A.D., for instance, some unlucky leader persuaded many of them to assemble at their holy mountain, Gerizim, where he promized to reveal to them the holy vessels which were supposed to have been hidden there, and of which, it was believed, the revelation would mark the end of foreign rule and the beginning of the kingdom of God.

[11] Acts 5:36.
[12] *Antiquities* 20,97 f.
[13] R. Eisler, *The Messiah Jesus and John the Baptist*, tr. A. Krappe (London, 1931), p. 253 ff.

Pilate used troops to break up this gathering and a number of the participants were killed.[14] So it is no less likely that Simon claimed to be the Messiah than that Jesus did so.

But Simon's followers, like those of Jesus, conceived their Messiah as a supernatural being. Simon's are said to have identified him as "that Power of God which is called Great." So Acts reports, and the report is perfectly credible. The concept of "powers" as properties of objects is one of the most widespread and influential in Hellenistic thought, and the personification of "powers" as supernatural beings was common.[15] Such personification is not found in the Hebrew text of the Old Testament, but it appears in the Greek translations, beginning with the LXX. Here the Hebrew expression "the Lord of Hosts" is regularly translated "the Lord of the Powers," and the Powers of the Lord are urged to praise him.[16] This usage was taken over and developed by the Apocrypha and Pseudepigrapha,[17] Philo,[18] and the New Testament,[19] and is continued in the later Samaritan liturgy.[20] Moreover, it was certainly believed well before Simon's time that these powers occasionally came down and appeared on earth. Appearances of angels on earth were frequently reported by the Old Testament and (as Prof. Wolfson has shown)[21] angels were identified by Philo as those divine powers which God sent into the world for the care of mankind. From the Old Testament reports it was of course common belief that when the angelic powers

---

[14] Josephus, *Ant.* 18,85–87. On the revelation of the sacred vessels as one of the functions of the Messiah, A. Merx, *Der Messias oder Ta'eb der Samaritaner* (Giessen, 1909), ZAW Beiheft 17, pp. 28 and 39 ff.

[15] M. Nilsson, *Greek Piety*, (Oxford, 1948), pp. 103–10.

[16] II Sam. 6:2, 18 &c.; Pss. 102:21; 148:2; Dan. 3:61.

[17] II Macc. 3:28; IV Macc. 5:13; Enoch 61:10; T. Levi 3:33; T. Judah 25:2; T. Abr. 14; III Bar. 1:8; II Enoch 29:4; Ascen. Is. 1:3; 2:4; 4:2; 5:9 &c.; T. Sol. 2:4; 6.8(P) &c.

[18] *De fuga* 101; *de mut. nom.* 29; *de conf. ling.* 30 &c.

[19] Mt. 24:29; Acts 10:38(?); Rom. 8:38; I Cor. 1:24; 15:24; Eph. 1:21; I Pet. 3:22.

[20] A. Cowley, *The Samaritan Liturgy*, (Oxford, 1909), II, LVI, s.v. *ḥyl*.

[21] H.A. Wolfson, *Philo*, (Cambridge, 1947), I, 372 ff.

appeared in this world they did so in human forms and spoke and acted like men.

The notion that a particular historical human being was actually the appearance or incarnation of a particular supernatural power seems also to have been common in Palestine during the first century A.D. No less than five Palestinian teachers of this century — Dositheus, John, Jesus, Simon and Menander — were believed by their followers to have been such supernatural beings.[22] In the second century the pagan philosopher, Celsus, said that the wandering prophets of the Palestinian coast regularly made such claims, and his Christian opponent, Origen, did not deny this.[23]

Celsus' statement is confirmed by the frequency with which first-century Christian and Jewish literature either advances or attacks such claims to supernatural character. The claims made for Jesus are, of course, familiar; we need remark only that for Paul, our earliest witness, Jesus the Messiah was "the Power of God,"[24] as Simon the Messiah was for the Simonians. Moreover, Paul himself claimed to be an incarnation of the Messiah. "I live," he wrote, "no longer I, but the Messiah lives in me."[25] Some similar concept may have accounted for the claim of Menander, Simon's disciple, to supernatural status.[26]

The case of Menander, for lack of evidence, we cannot decide, and that of Paul, for variety of evidence, is so complex that we cannot discuss it here.[27] As far as our present purpose goes, it is enough to point out that Paul's conception of the indwelling of the Spirit of the Messiah in himself and in all believers is concrete

---

[22] Dositheus, Origen, *Against Celsus*, VI,11; John, *Clementine Recognitions* I,54; Vigilius of Thapsis, *Contra Arium* 20; Ephraem Syrus, *Commentaire de l'Evangile concordante, version armenienne*, tr. L. Leloir (Louvain, 1954), CSCO Armeniaci 2, 249; Menander, Justin Martyr, I *Apol.* 26; Epiphanius *Panarion*, XXII.

[23] Origen, *Against Celsus*, VII,9.

[24] I Cor. 1:24.

[25] Gal. 2:20.

[26] See above, note 22.

[27] See H. Windisch, *Paulus und Christus*, (Leipzig, 1934) and the discussion which it occasioned.

in the extreme. For instance, when believers do not know what to say in prayer, the Spirit dwelling in them, using their voices, makes supplication on their behalf with inarticulate groanings.[28] This is the same belief which we meet in the Gospels, where Jesus questions the demons dwelling in a man and they answer him, using the man's voice.[29]

A neglected corollary of this notion of the indwelling of the Messiah in the Christian is the notion of the indwelling of Belial in the unbeliever. Thus Paul argues that, since the Messiah and Belial cannot dwell together, there can be no marriage between a believer, who is a temple in which God dwells, and an unbeliever, who is an idol inhabited by a demon.[30] As by eating the Christian Eucharist the believer shares in the body and blood of the Messiah, so by eating things sacrificed to demons the unbeliever shares in the life of the demons.[31] As the ministry of Paul, the man of God,[32] reveals the incarnation of the Messiah "according to his working which works in me in power,"[33] so there is an anti-Paul, a man of Belial, who also claims to be an incarnation of God, but whose ministry is a revelation "according to the working of Satan in all power and signs and false miracles."[34]

Paul's further description of his opponent's claims echoes Daniel 11:36, which reflects the claim of Antiochus Epiphanes to be a manifest god.[35] Since Antiochus' time that claim had been made by many. Therefore it is not surprising that the synoptic Gospels make Jesus prophesy the coming of "false Messiahs and false prophets who will give signs and do wonders so as to lead

[28] Rom. 8:26.
[29] Mk. 5:9.
[30] II Cor. 6:14 ff.; Ep. Rom. 7:17.
[31] I Cor. 10:16 ff.
[32] I Tim. 6:11; II Tim. 4:17.
[33] Col. 1:29; cp. Rom. 15:18.
[34] II Thess. 2:3–9. The Greek "man of lawlessness" almost certainly renders the Hebrew "man of Belial"; see the evidence diligently connected and misunderstood by B. Rigaux, *Les Epitres aux Thessaloniciens* (Paris, 1956), pp. 656–7.
[35] J. Montgomery, *A Critical... Commentary on... Daniel* (N.Y., 1927), p. 461.

astray, if possible, the elect"[36] — a prophecy which early Christian commentators understood as referring to Simon Magus.[37] The letters of John were written, probably between 90 and 100, to Christians who believed such prophecies; the author assures them that anyone who denies that Jesus is the Messiah, or that he came in the flesh, is an antichrist, since in him dwells the spirit of the antichrist.[38] (The denial that Jesus came in the flesh appears later as one of the standard charges against the followers of Simon.)[39] Probably from about the same time, the *Didache* declares that "In the latter days (by which it means the time when it was written) false prophets will be multiplied... and then the deceiver of the world will be revealed as son of God and will do signs and wonders and the earth will be given over into his hands and he will do unlawful things which had never been done before."[40] (The Simonians were charged with all manner of unlawful practices.)[41] Similarly, the author of the Apocalypse saw "a beast from the sea" who had been given power by the devil to blaspheme God (in terms again recalling Daniel 11:36), make war against and defeat the saints, and be worshiped by all the rest of mankind; moreover, he had a false prophet, "a beast... from the land," who looked like a lamb but spoke like the devil, and who acted with the demonic power of the first beast and made all the inhabitants of the earth worship him and did great miracles, calling fire down from heaven and vivifying the image of the first beast so as to make it breathe and speak.[42]

---

[36] Mk. 13:22, cf. 13:6; Mt. 24:5 & 24; cf. Lk. 21:8.

[37] Origen, *On Mt.* 33 and 41; *On Jer.* 5:3; *On Jn.* 1:33(38); Hilary of Poitiers, *on Mt.* 24:5; Apollonaris of Laodicea, *on Mt.* 24:5; Jerome, *On Mt.* 4:24; Macarius Magnes, *Apocrit.* 4.15; *Opus imperfectum in Mt.*, on 24:5.

[38] I Jn. 2:18, 22; 4:3; II Jn. 7.

[39] So the *Epistula apostolorum*, Irenaeus, Pseudo-Tertullian, &c.

[40] Didache 16,3, for the date see J.–P. Audet, *La Didachè*, (Paris, 1958), and my review in *Anglican Theol. Rev.*, 1961.

[41] Celsus in Origen, *A.C.* VI,6; Irenaeus I,16 ff.; Clement of Alex. *Stromateis* 7,17,107; etc.

[42] Apoc. 13; *exousia* is *miraculous power*, not merely *authority*, cp. 19.20 and see the remarks in W. Bauer, *Wörterbuch zum NT* (Berlin, 1952), *s.v.*

It is generally conceded that such passages reflect ancient apocalyptic motifs, but the fact that they do so does not exclude the possibility that they refer also to contemporary persons and events.[43] Indeed, apocalytic literature generally — the Pseudepigrapha of the Old Testament and the works of the Qumran sect, no less than Christian works — is precisely the product of that vision which sees in contemporary events and persons the fulfilment of ancient prophecies and the manifestations of primaeval supernatural powers. The imaginative fusion and confusion of ancient motifs with modern figures is not merely the characteristic, but the essential content of these works. To produce it, both the ancient and the modern elements are deliberately distorted, in the effort to prove that the one prophesied the other. We cannot look to such literature for accurate pictures of contemporary individuals or events, but we can expect it to reflect in caricature the major concerns of the men who wrote it.

Therefore in estimating the significance of the above passages we must keep in mind the great success of Simon's church during the late first and the early second century. In the mid-second-century Justin Martyr declares plainly that Simon had had a great success in Rome and that "almost all Samaritans, and a few, even, among other peoples, confessing him to be the first God, do him worship."[44] Even at the end of the second century Irenaeus still considers Simon as the founder and father of all heresy.

That in the first century Simon was identified as the Antichrist is the most likely interpretation of Sibylline Oracles III,63ff. "From the men of Sebaste (Samaria) Beliar shall come hereafter, and will shake the height of the mountains, shall make the sea stand still, shall stop the great, fiery sun and the shining moon, and shall raise the dead and do many signs for men. But he shall have no power to fulfill (the prophecies, for which his signs gain credit). But, indeed, he deceives men. He shall deceive many believing

---

[43] See the wise remarks of W. Bousset, *The Antichrist Legend*, tr. A. Keane (London, 1896), pp. 11–12 (neglected by E. Lohmeyer, *Die Offenbarung des Johannes*, 2 ed., Tübingen, 1953, *hnt* 16, p. 113 f.).

[44] Justin, *I Apol.* 26.

and elect Hebrews and other, lawless, men who have not yet heard the word of God. But as soon as the threats of the great God draw near, then a fiery Power will come through the swelling sea to the land and will burn up Beliar and all overweening men such as put their trust in him." (And then the world shall be ruled by a woman, men shall throw their gold and silver into the sea, and God shall roll up the heavens like a book and all shall revert to fire). That this was written while Simon was alive is suggested by the fact that it expects him to be destroyed by a spectacular miracle which did not happen, and his destruction to be followed almost immediately by the end of the world. (That the world should be ruled by a woman is not a reference to Cleopatra, it is a thing as unlikely as that men should throw their gold and silver into the sea.)[45] Other passages in the Sibylline Oracles, notably II,166 f., may also refer to Simon, but are so vague that the reference is uncertain; his figure was evidently fused in apocalyptic imagination with that of Nero *redivivus*, whose coming was also expected to herald the end of the world, and in later passages we find Nero credited with miracles — raising the dead, flying through the air — which are undoubtedly parts of the Simon legend.[46]

A similar association of Nero and Simon (the Samaritan false prophet) appears in the *Ascension of Isaiah*, where both, again, are manifestations of Beliar.[47] Their association is the work of an early second century editor, who took older material, in which the individual figures had different references, and put it together as an expression of the concerns of his own time.[48] To investigate

---

[45] The interpretation proposed here is that of Geffcken, accepted most recently by A. Kurfess, *Sybillinische Weissagungen* (Tusculum, 1951), *ad loc.* W. Bousset's supposition (*The Antichrist Legend*, p. 96, followed by R. Charles and others) that *Sebastenon* means *of the imperial race*, is to the best of my knowledge, not supported by ancient usage of the term in that sense, cf. B. Rigaux, *L'Antéchrist* (Gembloux, 1932), p. 200.

[46] Sibylline Oracles 5,217 and 370; see the note by H. Lanchester to 5,216 in R. Charles, *Apocrypha and Pseudepigrapha* (Oxford, 1913), p. 401.

[47] Ascension of Isaiah 4:2; 5:9.

[48] R. Charles, *The Ascension of Isaiah* (London, 1900), pp. XI ff.; E. Tisserant, *Ascension d'Isäie* (Paris, 1909), pp. 56 ff.

the details of his reinterpretation — particularly his application to Jesus of the probably Simonian myth of the Messiah's descent through the heavens in disguise — would take us too far from our present concern, which is merely to demonstrate the frequency, in the first century, of the notion that a particular historical individual is a supernatural being, whether "appearing" or "embodied" of "indwelling," at all events, in one way or another, effectively present. (We cannot expect of first century thought an accurate awareness of the problems of fifth-century Christology.) We have seen this belief adopted by the followers of a number of first-century Palestinians (Dositheus, John, Jesus, Simon, Menander) and peculiarly developed by Paul. We have seen also that it accounts for the widespread expectation of a supernatural Antichrist. We may now, in conclusion, mention a number of miscellanaeous instances.

The Prayer of Joseph, a work probably of the first century, represents the patriarch Jacob as an incarnation of an archangel called Israel.[49] Incidentally, the *Prayer of Joseph* was also part of that apocalyptic literary tradition — *Jubilees, Enoch*, etc.– which Christianity had in common with the Qumran sect. We know of it chiefly because Origen quoted it to defend his own opinion that John the Baptist may have been a supernatural Power appearing on earth as a man.[50] This opinion, we have seen, was held by John's followers and also (according to the Gospels) by Herod Antipas[51] and by many others in Palestine who thought Jesus was a reappearance of John,[52] as Simon was later thought (and may have claimed) to be a reappearance of Jesus, i.e. of the Power which had appeared as Jesus.[53] The existence of some similar belief about Jacob is evidenced also by the occurrence of his name in lists of names of supernatural beings in the magical papyri (for

---

[49] M. James, *The Lost Apocrypha of the OT.*, (London, 1920), pp. 21 ff. The work was known by the editor of the *Ascension of Isaiah*, 4:22.

[50] On Jn. 2:31.

[51] Mark 6:14.

[52] Mark 8:28.

[53] Irenaeus I,16 and many subsequent authors.

instance, in the *Sword of Dardanus*, in the Paris Magical Papyrus, he is linked with Eros, Adonai and Iao.)[54] The same beliefs were held about Jesus in his own lifetime by persons who were not his followers, but who used his name, as the name of a supernatural being, to cast out demons.[55] And the same beliefs were held about Paul, too (if we can believe Acts), by the sons of a Jewish "high priest" who used his name, along with the name of Jesus, for the same purpose. Their opinion was confirmed by the demon's acknowledgment.[56]

In sum, then, the belief that a particular individual might be a supernatural Power come down to earth and appearing as a man, was reasonably common in first century Palestine. There is no cause whatever to doubt Acts' statement that the followers of Simon, in his own lifetime, believed him to be such a supernatural being. Whether or not Simon made the claim for himself, Acts does not say. He may well have done so.

---

[54] *Papyri Graecae Magicae*, ed. K. Preisendanz, I (Berlin, 1928), 126 (Pap. IV, lines 1730 ff.)
[55] Mk. 9:28.
[56] Acts 19:15.

HOW TO EDIT THE SEPTUAGINT

by ALEXANDER SPERBER

I. Lagarde's *Urseptuaginta* Theory

§ 1. ALMOST THIRTY YEARS AGO I published a paper in the Kahle-Festschrift (*Studien zur Geschichte und Kultur des Nahen und Fernen Ostens*, Leiden, 1935) under the title "Probleme einer Edition der Septuaginta." As a starting-point I used the well-known theory of Lagarde, in order to demonstrate the difficulties, which confront the editor of the Septuagint. This theory rests on the following three main theses:

a) The Septuagint has been handed down to us in a *"trifaria varietas,"* to use Jerome's expression. Lagarde explained this "threefold variety" to mean *three recensions*, in accordance with his interpretation of the pertinent passage in Jerome's *praefatio* to Chronicles, where this expression originates, and to which he himself had first called attention.

b) Our first step towards preparing an edition of the Septuagint must therefore be: to restore these *recensions* as individual and separate texts. Lagarde himself attempted to accomplish this task for at least one of them, the *recension* of Lucian; cf. § 20, below.

c) Only then, with the respective editions of the three *recensions* serving as bases, could we proceed to the final stage of our work: to combine them into one single text, which in turn would represent what Lagarde termed the *Urseptuaginta*.

Consequently, there could have been, according to Lagarde's way of thinking, only one genuine Greek translation of the Hebrew Bible, this *Urseptuaginta*. The text of this originally uniform *Urseptuaginta* had been, so argued Lagarde, variously modified in the course of time and as a result to such an extent changed that only by following the rather complicated procedure as just outlined could we hope for ever regaining it. But these changes, which were inflicted upon the *Urseptuaginta*, represent the "Ueberlieferungs-Geschichte" of the Greek Bible. They were achieved without the aid of or having recourse to its Hebrew *Vorlage*. This inner Greek development of the text had ultimately resulted, according to Jerome's statement as interpreted by Lagarde, in three different Greek *recensions* of the one original translation.

However, the result I arrived at in that paper was very discouraging. I expressed my disillusionment at our inability to separate the *recensions* (cf. point b in Lagarde's arguments) in the following concluding remark: "Ueberall nur Mischtexte und nirgendwo hat sich eine Rezension rein erhalten" (*ib.*, p. 46).

II. Facts *versus* Theory

§ 2. It is interesting to note that this inadequacy of the Septuagint theory as propounded by Lagarde was frankly admitted by his disciple Alfred Rahlfs, the head of the "Septuaginta-Unternehmen" of the "Goettinger Gesellschaft der Wissenschaften". This "Unternehmen" had been established with the explicit purpose to put into practice Lagarde's theories and "Richtlinien," by preparing critical editions of the various Biblical books according to the Septuagint. Rahlfs began with publishing the book of Ruth; the Genesis followed as the second specimen edition "Schon beim Buche Ruth zeigte sich die Unmoeglichkeit, die Richtlinien einzuhalten, die Lagarde einer Edition der Septuaginta vorgezeichnet hat. Rahlfs unterscheidet vier Gruppen-statt drei, wie es Lagarde verlangte. Dabei scheiden noch die beiden aeltesten und wichtigsten Handschriften, der Codex B (Vaticanus) und der Codex A (Alexandrinus) aus dieser Gruppeneinteilung aus und muessen separat behandelt werden. *Ueber die Ausgabe der Genesis urteilt Rahlfs selber, dass das, was er hier biete, noch viel weniger als das im Buche Ruth Gebotene dem Lagardeschen Ideal eines Aufbaues nach den beruehmten Rezensionen des Origenes, Lukian und Hesych entspreche.* Denn er unterscheide bloss zwei grosse, dafuer aber eine grosse Zahl kleinerer Gruppen. "*Aber*," schliesst Rahlfs, "*wenn wir vorwaerts kommen wollen, muessen wir uns nicht von vorgefassten Theorien, sondern lediglich von dem gegebenen Material leiten lassen.*" (cf. my *Septuaginta-Probleme*, Stuttgart, 1929, p. 2). Thus, instead of identifying *three* Septuagint *recensions* (cf. point a in Lagarde's arguments § 1), Rahlfs divided the manuscripts at his disposal into *several groups*. It is quite obvious that by no stretch of our imagination could we harmonize Lagarde's "Richtlinien" with these actual facts. For these "groups" represent only "Handschriften-Familien," such as any one has encountered, who has ever attempted to edit a text on the basis of a larger number of witnesses. The *family-characteristics*, which such a group has in common, usually consist in a considerable number of textual deviations from the basic text of the edition; they are not to be confused with *recensional characteristics*, as shown here in § 20. As a rule they are characteristic for the respective school of copyists only. However, instead of repeatedly listing several *sigla* to indicate variants shared by the identical manuscripts, the editor prefers to simplify his work and at the same time make it more "*uebersichtlich*", by introducing one *siglum* for them and terming them a "group." Hence, the unit called a "group" is the result of practical considerations only and does not represent the cristallization of theoretic reasoning.

I myself followed this practice in editing the Targum; cf. the "Prefatory Remarks," § 4 B (on p. vi) of my *Bible in Aramaic*, Volume I (Leiden, 1959). And what is even more relevant here, is that Rahlfs himself has admitted this very plainly (cf. the end of the lengthy quotation above). But, curiously enough, Lagarde has found, especially in this country, a number of followers, who like to consider themselves his "Schule," and who, unlike Rahlfs, do overlook the facts and persistently stick to Lagarde's theories (cf. H. M. Orlinsky in *JAOS*, 1941, pp. 81 ff.).

III. Recensions or Translations?

§ 3. In the intervening years since that paper of mine (cf. § 1) was written, I have continued to focus my attention on this so important problem of Biblical scholarship. The conclusions I reached now disprove my once so gloomy outlook. The turn began, when I examined the commentaries written by two Church Fathers, one from Egypt and the other from Asia Minor, on the identical Biblical books: the Minor Prophets. In these commentaries, each Church Father first quotes the Biblical verse and then proceeds to comment on it. Both the basic quotation and the explanatory remarks are in Greek. Now, if there ever existed such recensions of the Septuagint as are credited — according to Lagarde — to Lucian and Hesychius, these Church Fathers, who lived and labored in Asia Minor and Egypt, respectively, must have used them. Each of them must have considered that particular recension, which, again according to Lagarde's interpretation of Jerome's statement, had gained undisputed authority in his respective country, as his Bible, to the complete exclusion of the remaining other two recensions. Thus, Theodoret of Kyros must have considered Lucian's recension as authoritative and Cyril of Alexandria the work of Hesychius. I, therefore, collated the Bible quotations underlying these two commentaries in the hope of finding variants of such a nature which would point the way to a better appreciation of the work of Lucian and Hesychius than was heretofore possible.

§ 4. My collation resulted in approximately 1200 variant readings. As was to be expected, the great majority of these variants proved to be quite insignificant for the evaluation of the problem under consideration. But I consider myself very fortunate, indeed, that there also were 17 instances of real importance. They prove that the basic Greek Bible texts, which these two Church Fathers used for their commentaries do not represent two corresponding recensions of one and the same Greek Bible (cf. our definition of a "recension" in § 1), but go back to two independent translations of the Hebrew Bible into Greek. The results of this investigation were laid down in a paper "The Problems of the Septuagint Recensions" (*JBL*, 1935). Here I indicated the great importance of these 17 instances as compared with the relative insignificance of the bulk of the approximately 1200 variant readings, by the very way I chose in arranging the material. "I start with noting those variants which originate in a misunderstanding of the Hebrew text, either with regard to consonants or vowels, thus giving rise to translations which have no sense at all in their context. *Such misconceptions are the best linguistic proof that the texts... go back each to an independent translation*" (*ibid.*, p. 80). I stressed this point once more in my "New Testament and Septuagint" (*JBL*, 1940): "I published the results of an examination of the Greek Bible texts, which served these Fathers as bases for their commentaries. The variant readings are grouped and classified; they prove that these two Fathers used two different Bible texts in Greek, which in turn go back to two independent translations.... This is demonstrated by referring to variant readings which cannot be explained otherwise but as reflecting *a different approach to the* (scil. *identical*) *basic Hebrew text*. Differences of such a type may be seen in a translation which is based upon a mispronunciation of the Hebrew word or a mistake on account of the similarity in the script of certain Hebrew letters. They may be used as evidence for the fact that the translator was rather poorly equipped for his task, and thus account for so many other errors. *But they are, from the view-point of the philologian, the most trustworthy evidence for an assertion that their text with all its mistakes is really an independent translation, based upon a Hebrew original, and not a mere stylistic revision of an already existing Greek translation* (scil. *a recension*)" (*ibid.*, p. 268).

§ 5. Even a cursory glance at these 17 cases (cf. *JBL*, 1935, p. 82–3, paragraphs I to IV inclusive; 10 of them, which occur also in corresponding quotations from Origen's *Hexapla*, are also discussed in "New Testament and Septuagint," p. 269 f.) will suffice to make clear the correctness of my method and the soundness of the conclusion to any one who has exprience in dealing with problems of a related nature. I had previously applied the very same method and procedure in grouping and arranging the variants derived from a collation of certain Old Testament passages as they appear quoted in the New Testament with the way they are worded at their proper places in the Old Testament, both Old and New Testaments according to the identical Greek manuscript, Codex B (cf. my paper "האוונגליון ותרגום השבעים לתנ״ך" in the Hebrew quarterly תרביץ, Jerusalem, 1934, and briefly referred to in *NTS*, p. 200 f.). Thus, with the main thesis of my paper in *JBL* proven by these 17 instances, the remaining bulk of the variants between the texts of the two commentaries had to be disposed of in a methodical way, too. I grouped and classified them in accordance with certain linguistic characteristics, which they exhibit. They may still prove to be of value to the student of Greek grammar, syntax and style. But for the solution of the Biblical problems, which concern us here, they are of practically no importance.

It is worthwhile noting here that a spokesman for what I termed before (cf. § 2) the "Lagardesche Schule" apparently did not even grasp the vital importance of this way in which I arranged and listed the materials. For, in order to refute my conclusions, he merely referred to examples which I myself had listed as belonging to the "bulk" of the variants, as defined by my remarks just preceding here (cf. *JAOS*, 1941, pp. 87 f.). And it is even more characteristic of the manner, in which Biblical scholarship is conducted, to mention that this "refutation" of my theories has been taken at face value by scholars, who subsequently dealt with this topic (e.g. F. Pérez Castro in *Sefarad*, 1948, pp. 172 f.). No attempt has been made to consult my own publications in order to ascertain, whether I really based my conclusions on such a flimsy foundation as my critic would like his readers to believe.

§ 6. These researches of mine into the "Entstehung" of the Septuagint were continued. The results were embodied in my monograph "New Testament and Septuagint" (*JBL*, 1940). The conclusions at which I arrived there with regard to the problems, which concern us here, can be summed up briefly as follows: The Bible in Greek, which is known to us under the name of Septuagint, consisted originally of two independent translations from a Hebrew original; each of these Greek Bibles was subsequently even translated into Latin (*ibid.*, p. 278). This disposes of Lagarde's theory as far as the "recensions" of *Lucian and Hesychius* are concerned: they *were translations and not mere recensions*, which latter term implies: revisions of one and the same original (cf. § 1). But Origen's work in the fifth column of his *Hexapla*, which Lagarde termed: the Hexaplaric recension, was of a different nature. Here Origen offered a combination of these two translations into one text, indicating by the use of the so-called Hexaplaric symbols (an asterisk and obelus) the respective source and the extent of those readings which are particular to only one of these translations (*ibid.*, p. 279).

IV. The Complutensian Polyglot Bible

§ 7. With these results in mind we now approach anew the problem of How to Edit the Septuagint. But before formulating any suggestions of our own, it will be well to learn first which basic principles the previous editors of the Septuagint have adopted in their respective works. It is regrettable that the early editions of the Septuagint merely offer a text, but no explanation as to the method adopted in establishing it. The editor (or editors) even kept the very source, wherefrom their publication emanated, a secret, the disclosure of which became the subject of later research. Cf. Paul de Lagarde's remarks: "Versionis igitur graecae veteris [testamenti] constabat esse editiones quatuor. complutensem, aldinam, romanam, oxoniensem Ernesti Grabe. quae quum mirum in modum discordarent *primum eorum qui versione veteris testamenti graeca uti vellent negotium esse debebat, ut de editionum illarum et fontibus et pretio quaererent*" (*Librorum Veteris Testamenti Canonicorum... graece*, Gothingae, 1883, p. III). The relevant information is presented by Henry Barclay Swete in the *Preface* to his edition of *The Old Testament in Greek according to the Septuagint*, Vol. I (Cambridge, 1901). So we read concerning the Complutensian Polyglot Bible that "Documentary evidence has been produced... that the Vatican MSS. 330, 346 were lent to Ximenes, and a comparison of the Complutensian text with these MSS. shows an extensive and in places almost absolute agreement which suggests that they were largely used. Both MSS. are comparatively "late" (p. VI). But the question of the origin of the source (or sources) is only one of the problems that confront us. Granted that these two MSS. were actually used by the editors of the Septuagint in the Complutensian Polyglot Bible, it leaves the more important question unanswered: just *how* were they used? The "extensive and in places almost absolute agreement" could with equal justification be formulated as "but in other places complete disregard for their readings." This, at least, is the meaning which Swete's statement conveys by the limitations which he imposed on the agreements: "extensive", "in places" and "almost absolute". And it is exactly the *problem of the disagreements*, which interests us most. The same manuscripts could have been used by various scholars; but each of them would have left the imprint of his personality on the way *how* he used them. These two manuscripts may have been chosen by Vatican authorities or by the scholars on Cardinal Ximenes' staff; Swete does not indicate it. What reasons motivated them to deviate from their *Vorlage*? The disclosure of the nature and extent of such deviations would be by far more instructive than is the mere statement that the *Vorlage* has largely been followed.

§ 8. A few explanatory remarks will be best suited to bring out the importance of this problem. As is well known, there exists a difference in the way the Biblical material is arranged in the Hebrew Bibleand in the Septuagint; cf. the chapter "Differences of Sequence" in H. B. Swete's *Introduction to the Old Testament in Greek* (Cambridge, 1900), pp. 231 ff. The Complutensian Polyglot Bible with its columnar order is based on the principle that parallel columns contain the identical material in different languages. The difficulty of different arrangement, whenever it presented itself, was solved in the following manner: the Complutensis adopted the order of the Hebrew Bible and adjusted the Septuagint accordingly. No reference to the original order of the chapters and verses involved according to the Septuagint was given. However, the problem became more complicated in cases, where the actual amount of Biblical material as offered in the Septuagint differs from that of the Hebrew Bible. These differences represent either omissions or additions in the Septuagint. a) Cases of omissions in the Septuagint, according to Codex B, are e.g. Ex. 25:6, 28:23, 26–28; 35:8, 18; 36:10–34; 37:11–12, 25–28; 39:39; 40:7, 11, 28; Josh. 20:4–6; Jer. 25:14; 27:1, 7, 13, 21; 29:16–20; 30:10–11, 15, 22; 34:14–26; 39:4–13; 46:1; 48:45–47; 49:6; 51:45–48; 52:2–3, 15, 28–30; Ezek. 1:14; 10:14; 11:11–12; 27:31; 32:19; 33:25–26; 40:30. The Complutensis was faced with a "drucktechnisches" problem: how to preserve the uniform appearance of the printed pages and cover up the *lacunae* in the corresponding Septuagint material. This result was achieved by adequately spacing the material at disposal. b) The additional material found in the Septuagint is mainly of a doublet-nature. In a paper entitled: "The Codex Vaticanus (B)," which was published in *Miscellanea Giovanni Mercati* (Vol. I, pp. 1–16; Vatican City, 1946) I have shown that the Septuagint sometimes offers "Lengthy Passages in Two Translations" (*ibid.*, p. 7 ff.). They are found either in close proximity to one another, or set far apart. But in the Complutensis with its columnar arrangement there is room for one translation only; thus one translation had to be omitted. The problem now is: which translation was included and which one was rejected? And what were the criteria for the inclusion or rejection? The location (whether identical with that of the corresponding verses in the Hebrew Bible or not) could not have been considered so all-important; for the different arrangement of the Septuagint has been adjusted to that of the Hebrew Bible even elsewhere. Perhaps: faithfulness to the Hebrew text? Or: polished Greek style? Only a very detailed examination of all the passages involved could give us the answer to these questions.

§ 9. A different treatment must be accorded to those passages in the Septuagint, which are additions only when compared with *MT*, but which may be translations of a Hebrew Bible differing from our *MT*; cf. § 12, where I warned against identifying the Hebrew *Vorlage* of the Septuagint with our *MT*. In *NTS*, p. 242 ff.

I pointed out the "direct interdependence between the obelus-type (of the Septuagint) and the corresponding readings of the Hebrew Pentateuch of the Samaritans" (*ibid.*, p. 243), which "does not represent the Bible of the heretic sect of the Samaritans, but was originally another recension of the Hebrew Pentateuch" (*ibid.*, p. 242). Later on (*ibid.*, p. 266) I concluded there that Codex "B shows close affinity to the obelus type." As a characteristic of the Samaritan Pentateuch I noted (*ibid.*, p. 243 ff.) cases of harmonization, a phenomenon, which is also evident in the obelus type of the Septuagint. Codex B shares this characteristic with the obelus type, as will be seen from these two examples: 2 Sam. 8:7. Here, the translation of the verse ends with: καὶ ἤνεγκεν αὐτὰ εἰς Ἰερουσαλημ. The following: καὶ ἔλαβεν αὐτὰ Σουσακειμ βασιλεὺς Αἰγύπτου ἐν τῷ ἀναβῆναι αὐτὸν εἰς Ἰερουσαλημ ἐν ἡμέραις Ἰεροβοαμ υἱοῦ Σολομῶντος is such a harmonizing addition; cf. 1 Ki. 14:25 ff. Similarly in the next verse, 8 the translation ends with: χαλκὸν πολὺν σφόδρα. Then follows: ἐν αὐτῷ ἐποίησεν Σαλωμων τὴν θάλασσαν τὴν χαλκῆν καὶ τοὺς στύλους καὶ τοὺς λουτῆρας καὶ πάντα τὰ σκεύη; cf. 1 Ki 7:23 ff. Such passages were omitted in the Complutensis, probably because there was no corresponding Hebrew text for the parallel column. But we should not hastily term them as additions; for the equivalent Hebrew text may actually have been contained in the *Vorlage* of Codex B. This assumption finds a very strong support in the following observation: The events narrated in 2 Sam. 8 are retold in the parallel chapter 1 Chron 18; cf. my *BE* § 49. Verse 8 in both these chapters ends in Codex B with the identical words, as quoted above. However, the harmonizing addition of 2 Sam. 8:8 appears in 1 Chron. 18:8 in a somewhat different wording: ἐξ αὐτοῦ ἐποίησεν Σαλωμων τὴν θάλασσαν τὴν χαλκῆν καὶ τοὺς στύλους καὶ τὰ σκεύη τὰ χαλκᾶ. But here in 1 Chron. this is no addition at all; for *MT* has the Hebrew equivalent for it: בָּהּ עָשָׂה שְׁלֹמֹה אֶת יָם הַנְּחֹשֶׁת וְאֶת הָעַמּוּדִים וְאֵת כְּלֵי הַנְּחֹשֶׁת. Thus, I hope to have demonstrated that the important problem before us is not to identify the manuscripts, which the editors of the Complutensis had used, but to realize the way *how they had used them*. The conclusion from the preceding observations is: *the Complutensis does not represent an edition of the Septuagint at all* but offers the Hebrew Bible with the corresponding portions of the Greek translation according to the Septuagint, wherever available.

V. Codex Vaticanus (B)

§ 10. For his own edition Swete used the Codex Vaticanus (B) as basic text. "The text of the Vatican MS. was selected" (namely: by the Syndics of the Cambridge University Press) as that "which on the whole presents the version of the Septuagint in its relatively oldest form" (*ibid.*, p. XI f.). Though this statement is carefully worded ("on the whole", "relatively"), I have my grave doubts as to its tenability: On what basis does this "*Werturteil*" rest? Wherein lies the superior value of Codex B as compared with the "comparatively late" manuscripts of the Complutensis? The *age of a manuscript* is determined by external criteria (like palaeography, ink, writing material) and is of interest to the antiquarian. But the scholar concerns himself with the *comparative age of its text*, and this can be determined on internal evidence alone. I am under the impression that in selecting Codex B, the greater age of the manuscript was erroneously taken as an indicator of the equally superior relative age of its text. In my paper in *JBL*, 1935, to which I have already referred (above § 4), I pointed out several obviously corrupt readings (because they are utterly nonsensical) in the text of Codex B on the Minor Prophets, the correct *Vorlagen* for which are still traceable in the commentary of Cyril of Alexandria (*JBL*, pp. 81 and 83). I list them here again, and in order to make my point clear, I have added here a few explanatory remarks to each of these items:

Hos. 7:4:B: ἀπὸ φυράσεως στέατος: "from the mixing of the *fat* (until it be leavened)." But "fat" never gets "leavened"! The correct reading is found in Cyril's commentary: σταιτός: *dough* = *MT*: בָּצֵק

Hos. 9:10:B: καὶ ὡς σκοπὸν ἐν συκῇ... εἶδον πατέρας αὐτῶν: "and like a *goal* in a fig-tree... saw I their fathers." Has a fig-tree a "goal" or "aim"? And if so, what might it be?! Cyril has correctly: σῦκον, *a fig* = *MT*: כְּבִכּוּרָה (cf. also *NTS*, p. 270).

Amos 1:11:B: καὶ ἐλυμήνατο μητέρα ἐπὶ γῆς: "and he utterly destroyed (literally: to the earth) *the mother*." But this cannot be a translation of our verse, which reads: רַחֲמָיו Hence cf. Cyril: μήτραν: *the womb*, thus interpreting the *MT* רַחֲמָיו as a derivate from רֶחֶם.

Micah 4:14:B: ἐν ῥάβδῳ πατάξουσιν ἐπὶ σιαγόνα τὰς πύλας τοῦ Ἰσραηλ: "with a rod do they smite upon the cheek the *gates* of Israel." But "gates" have no "cheeks." And smiting a wall with a mere rod will bring no results, either. Hence cf. Cyril: φυλάς: *the tribes*; the שֵׁפֶט of the Hebrew text was mistaken for שֵׁבֶט; cf. *HPT* § 13. (cf. also *NTS*, p. 285, on 1 Chron. 17:6).

Jonah 2:5:B: καὶ ἐγὼ εἶπα· Ἀπῶσμαι ἐξ ὀφθαλμῶν σου· ἆρα προσθήσω τοῦ ἐπιβλέψαι πρὸς τὸν λαὸν τὸν ἅγιόν σου: "And I said: I am cast out from before Thine eyes; yet I will look again toward Thy holy *people*." There is no logical connection between the two clauses in this verse: Jonah first complains that he is removed from the presence of the Lord and is in fear not to see the Lord any more. ἆρα προσθήσω brings a ray of hope into the picture: "yet...." But what follows, is not what we expected to learn; for even though Jonah is hopeful that he will see again λαόν *the people*, this could not relay his fear expressed before of not seeing *the Lord*! Now, Cyril reads: ναόν: *temple* = *MT*: הֵיכָל. The temple is the place, where the Lord's presence dwells; cf. *NBT* § 25 on Amos 4:2.

Micah 5:1:B: ὀλιγοστὸς εἶ τοῦ εἶναι ἐν χιλιάσιν Ἰουδα· ἐξ οὗ μοι ἐξελεύσεται τοῦ εἶναι εἰς ἄρχοντα τοῦ Ἰσραηλ: "Thou art too little to be among the thousands of Judah, *out of which* shall come forth unto Me (one) to be as a ruler of Israel." But this is against the meaning of the Hebrew text which clearly indicates that, little though בֵּית לֶחֶם may be, it still will bring forth the ruler of Judah. Thus, Codex B seems to have reduced to naught the very idea, which Micah wished to stress. However, Cyril reads: ἐκ σοῦ = MT מִמְּךָ: *out of thee*! (cf. also *NTS*, p. 196 f.).

Hab. 1:13:B: καθαρὸς ὀφθαλμὸς τοῦ μὴ ὁρᾶν πονηρά· καὶ

ἐπιβλέπειν ἐπὶ πόνους ὀδύνης: "Pure of eyes (art Thou) lest Thou behold evil, and look on the toils of *grief.*" But "grief" is in no way a proper parallel to the thought expressed by "evil." Cyril has instead: οὐ δυνήσῃ = MT: לֹא תוּכָל: *Thou canst not.*

§ 11. But as most conclusive (from the point of view of defying common sense) I consider the example from Hos. 13:3. Here Codex B reads: καὶ ὡς ἀτμὶς ἀπὸ δακρύων: "and like smoke from tears." This is sheer nonsense! Sometimes, perhaps, smoke may bring tears in our eyes; but never will tears in our eyes result in smoke! The Hebrew text points the way how this obvious error originated, מֵאֲרֻבָּה (chimney or smoke stack) was erroneously read as מֵאַרְבֶּה (locust), and consequently rendered by Theodoret (or his *Vorlage*): ἀπὸ ἀκρίδων. This in turn led to the confusion with δακρύων, probably because of the greater familiarity of the copyist with that word.

I wonder whether Swete's characterization of Codex B as representing the Septuagint "in its relatively oldest form" can still stand in the light of these corruptions taken from parts of the Minor Prophets alone! Does not the Church Father, who in his works exhibits the respective correct readings, deserve more consideration from an editor of the Septuagint, even though his works are contained in manuscripts of comparatively younger date than Codex B? (cf. also *NTS*, pp. 264 and 269).

§ 12. The Septuagint is a Greek Bible, which goes back to a Hebrew Bible as its *Vorlage*. This implies that it must fulfill two requirements: a) it must be identifiable as a translation from the Hebrew; and b) it must be understandable to the Greek speaking readers. Of course, I do not imply that the Hebrew *Vorlage* of the Septuagint was our *MT*. But the textual deviations between this *Vorlage* and our *MT* were of a relatively minor importance; they mostly come under the heading of such scribal errors, as are even generally assumed as criteria by the textual criticism of the Bible. The main thesis in my paper "The Codex Vaticanus (B)," (cf. § 8) was the assertion "that the Hebrew Bible is indispensable for the understanding of the Septuagint" (p. 1). The Septuagint must in all its readings be retrovertible into Hebrew. The *Vorlage* which we thus reconstruct by retroversion may sometimes even be illogical, yielding no sense (cf. my paper in *OLZ*, 1929, p. 538 and 540). Such, indeed, was the case with Hos. 13:3: מֵאֲרֻבָּה: which Theodoret renders with: ἀπὸ ἀκρίδων, and which I discussed in the preceding paragraph. Smoke does not come from a locust! And, still, this is a genuine translation; for the translator mistook the Hebrew word, which means "chimney," and confused it with "locust", which is spelled with the identical consonants in Hebrew. Thus, ἀπὸ ἀκρίδων is retrovertible into Hebrew. But Codex B confused this Greek word ἀκρίδων with another Greek word: δακρύων, and thus offers a reading, which cannot be translated back into Hebrew as defined above, even making due allowance for errors of the translator. For the error lies not in the incompetence of the translator, but of the later copyist. The same is the case with all the instances listed in § 10. The readings in Codex B are not genuine translations or even mistranslations, but Greek corruptions of original translations or mistranslations. Now, one might argue that Swete did not intend to present us with a real edition of the Septuagint, but considered it as his task merely to publish Codex B of the Septuagint. The difference between editing a text and printing a manuscript is too striking to require any further elucidation. But it is one of the most basic duties of any scholar, who even only publishes a manuscript, to see to it that such obvious corruptions do not mar the usefulness of his work. Overlooking them constitutes a grave case of neglect of duty.

§ 13. But the Septuagint must also present itself in such a form, which makes sense for those, whose native tongue was Greek. For the Septuagint owes its very origin to the desire to make the Bible accessible to Greek speaking people. No knowledge of Hebrew should therefore be presupposed, nor reference to a *Vorlage* in Hebrew necessary in order to understand at least the simple sentences of the narrative and legal portions. Of course, nobody would expect to find here a model of Greek style; because, being a translation, the Septuagint followed the syntax of the *Vorlage*, as was common practice in such cases in ancient times;

cf. my paper "Zur Sprache des Prophetentargums," *ZAW*, 1927, pp. 272 ff.

We must bear in mind that in ancient times translators were more intent literally to follow their *Vorlage* and to translate each individual word adequately, than to present a polished language. Thus, in matters of Greck style, a Biblical book, which was originally written in Hebrew and only subsequently translated into Greek, cannot be measured by the same standards as an original Greek text. In the case of a translation, the syntax is identical with that of the *Vorlage*. This is true not only of Greek translations, but of any translation, done in ancient times. I have demonstrated this fact in my still unpublished Introduction to my edition of the Targum, both for these Aramaic translations as well as for Abū Saʿīd's Arabic translation. It is obvious that with Aramaic and Arabic being Semitic languages themselves, these adaptations to the Hebrew *Vorlage* are more evident in the vocabulary (the respective Hebrew word with a makeshift Aramaic ending instead of the genuinely Aramaic equivalent) or morphology (the praedicate in the plural, though the two subjects would make the use of the dual imperative in Arabic), than in the syntax. But I see no reason why the Greek of the Septuagint should be singled out as foreign sounding by terming it "barbaric" (E. Bickerman in the *Alexander Marx Jubilee Volume*, New York, 1950, English Section, p. 150). The *Vetus Latina* is just another example for such a foreign or "barbaric" style; and an even cursory study of the *Vetus Latina* might induce a classical philologist to revise such a harsh pronouncement on the language of the Septuagint. The only difference in this case is that while the *Vetus Latina* found in Jerome a well-qualified revisor of its style (resulting in the *Vulgate*) and subsequently was withdrawn from circulation in its original variety of forms, the Greek of the Septuagint was not interfered with, luckily for Biblical research.

Consequently, a grammar of Septuagint Greek deals with morphology only, and there is no need for a chapter on the syntax. But imitation of Hebrew "Wortstellung" does not imply the formation of sentences like these, which are found in Codex B, and which could be neither translated into English, nor even interpreted at all:

2 Sam. 18:18:B: καὶ Ἀβεσσαλωμ ἔτι ζῶν καὶ ἔστησεν ἑαυτῷ τὴν στήλην ἐν ᾗ ἐλήμφθη καὶ ἐστήλωσεν αὐτὴν λαβεῖν....

2 Sam. 21:1:B: καὶ ἐζήτησεν Δαυειδ τὸ πρόσωπον τοῦ κυρίου· καὶ εἶπεν κύριος Ἐπὶ Σαουλ καὶ ἐπὶ τὸν οἶκον αὐτοῦ ἀδικία διὰ τὸ αὐτὸν θανάτῳ αἱμάτων περὶ οὗ ἐθανάτωσεν τοὺς Γαβαωνείτας.

2 Sam. 1:9:B: καὶ εἶπεν πρὸς μέ Στῆθι δὴ ἐπάνω μου καὶ θανάτωσόν με. ὅτι κατέσχεν με σκότος δεινόν, ὅτι πᾶσα ἡ ψυχή μου ἐν ἐμού.

1 Ki. 2:7:B: καὶ τοῖς υἱοῖς Βερζελλει τοῦ Γαλααδείτου ποιήσεις ἔλεος, καὶ ἔσονται ἐν τοῖς ἐσθίουσιν τὴν τράπεζάν σου....

1 Ki. 8:59:B: ....τοῦ ποιεῖν τὸ δικαίωμα τοῦ δούλου σου Ἰσραηλ ῥῆμα ἡμέρας ἐν ἡμέρᾳ ἐνιαυτοῦ.

2 Sam. 8:7:B: καὶ ἔλαβεν Δαυειδ τοὺς χλίδωνας τοὺς χρυσοῦς οὓς ἐποίησεν ἐπὶ τῶν παίδων τῶν Ἀδρααζαρ βασιλέως Σουβα, καὶ ἤνεγκεν αὐτὰ εἰς Ἰερουσαλημ.

2 Sam. 8:10:B: καὶ ἀπέστειλεν Θοου Ἰεδδουραν τὸν υἱὸν αὐτοῦ πρὸς βασιλέα Δαυειδ ἐρωτῆσαι αὐτὸν τὰ εἰς εἰρήνην καὶ εὐλογῆσαι αὐτὸν ὑπὲρ οὗ ἐπάταξεν τὸν Ἀδρααζαρ· καὶ ἐπάταξεν αὐτὸν, ὅτι κείμενος ἦν τῷ Ἀδρααζαρ....

It is obvious that such sentences could not have been part of the original translation, but are only the result of later scribal confusions. They thus reflect on the place, which we have to assign to Codex B in the history of inner Greek corruption of the Septuagint.

§ 14. Let us now consider the two postulates as formulated in § 12 together, and examine in their light the problem of doublets. Our demand that the Septuagint be *a* translation also implies that it be *one* translation. The Hebrew *Vorlage*, no matter whether correctly or incorrectly interpreted, should be presented in one translation only. The fact in itself that doublets occur in the running text of a manuscript (cf. *NTS*, p. 248–257 and *Miscellanea Giovanni Mercati* pp. 4–7), is evidence of the long development its text must have gone through before it reached the present stage with two translations combined into one text. From the point of view of the uncritical reader, for whom the Septuagint after all was intended, there could be no objection to such cases, as long as the combination of the two renderings resulted in a smoothly running Greek text; cf. the cases listed in *NTS* on p. 254 under b, c, and d. But in all the many other instances, which I have listed there on p. 250 ff., the resulting Greek text must have sounded repugnant to any one who spoke Greek as his native language. The characteristics of Codex B as disclosed there by the occurrence of such doublets tend to prove that far from presenting an old form of the Septuagint, this manuscript stands, at the end of a long historical development with progressing deterioration of the Septuagint text.

§ 15. Codex B was chosen for the Cambridge Septuagint edition not only because it supposedly exhibits the oldest form of the Septuagint (a claim which I hope was definitely refuted in the preceding paragraphs), but also because of its being free from what Swete terms "hexaplaric influence" or "hexaplaric revision." Now, what are we to understand under these terms? They cannot refer to an interference with the shaping of the *text* of such manuscripts, as were exposed to "hexaplaric influence." Because every Septuagint manuscript either goes back to one of the two original independent translations (cf. *NTS*, p. 278), or represents — as is generally the case — an already mixed type. The hexaplaric influence or revision can therefore only refer to the affixing of the hexaplaric symbols, in order to separate the readings, which are characteristic for the respective translation, from the bulk of the text by enclosing them accordingly with an asterisk or obelus. Those manuscripts which, like Codex B, are supposedly free from hexaplaric influence, do not exhibit these symbols; but they do exhibit the characteristic reading of their respective translation, nevertheless, be it the asterisk — or the obelus-type; only the identifying marking is missing. Consequently, the hexaplaric influence can be written off entirely as a criterion for the relative age of its text.

§ 16. The shortcomings of Codex B, which I have pointed out in the preceding paragraphs, can be traced *mutatis mutandis* in

Codex A also, which is generally considered to be next to Codex B in importance. In *NTS*, p. 248 ff. I have subjected both these codices to a critical scrutiny, which led me to the following conclusion: "... taking ... B and A as entities, the divergencies displayed therein largely reflect similar variant readings of the two types of the hexaplaric Septuagint; thus, B shows close affinity to the obelus-type, and A to the asterisk-type. Neither of them can be regarded as representing their respective basic textual type in all its details" (*ibid.*, p. 266). The same holds true of any other individual Septuagint manuscript we may examine. There is no consistency to the type, but only the mixed type prevails. We thus realize that *no matter which individual Septuagint manuscript we adopt as basic text for an edition, the result will remain the same: a conflated text*. On the other hand, we cannot even think of applying the eclectic method in selecting or rejecting individual readings, because we have no reliable criterion to serve us as guide in these decisions. The result would only be a new textual combination of our own making, the genuineness of which could never be proved. On Lagarde's attempt to edit Lucian's text, cf. § 20.

VI. The Church Father's Greek Bible

§ 17. How, then, shall we edit the Septuagint? I wish to suggest an entirely new procedure, representing a complete break with the past: *NO* Septuagint manuscript at all to serve as basic text! But to adopt a procedure similar to that which is the only way open to us in publishing the daughter-translation of the Septuagint, the *Vetus Latina*. Here we print, under the common denominator of *Vetus Latina*, various texts which externally are not related to one another. One book may be preserved here, the other there; sometimes large parts of a Biblical book, but more often small portions only, and very rarely a complete book. We do not expect these texts to go back to one translator, or even to one school of translators; and as a matter of fact, they do not even claim such uniformity. All they have in common is that they represent attempts to render into Latin their Greek *Vorlage* of the Bible. An analysis of these texts attests to the great differences that existed in the skill and qualification of the various translators as well as in the textual type of their respective Greek *Vorlagen* (cf. *NTS*, pp. 272–8). And now I ask: are not these the very characteristics, which are typical for what we term as "Septuagint"? (cf. Henry St. John Thackeray: *A Grammar of the Old Testament in Greek*, Cambridge, 1909, pp. 1–16). Every one of the better known Septuagint manuscripts exhibits the selfsame characteristics, which I have just outlined with reference to the *Vetus Latina*. Codex B is far from representing a uniform text, not only when we take the codex as an entity, but even when we review only portions of it. Thackeray has already demonstrated that the Biblical books of adequate bulk were subdivided into two or more parts and translated by different men in a different manner. And even in its external form Codex B is the work of at least three and possible even four different copyists (cf. Swete's *Introduction*, p. 128). Thus, it was only the book binder, who created the illusion of a uniform volume. It is high time that we free ourselves from this illusion and face realities. "Septuagint" as currently known, is nothing but a common denominator, which combines the works of different translators and pretends that they present a unity.

§ 18. This fact that different hands were at work in the creating of what now pretends to be a unity called Septuagint, is also revealed by the different ways, how the identical Biblical names appear in transliteration at their various occurrences in the Bible. I have discussed this aspect of the problem in my "Hebrew based upon Greek and Latin Transliterations" (*HUCA*, 1938) in paragraphs IV and XXIII. My observations there are summed up in the statement "that Codex A, not only when considered as an entity covering the entire Bible, but even on the individual Biblical books goes back to different sources. The same is true of Codex B also" (*ibid.*, p. 148). Cf. also e.g. אָחָז in Isa. 1:1: Ἀχας, but *ibid.* 7:1: Ἀχαζ; in 2 Ki. 16:1: Ἀχαζ, but in the following verse 2 referred to as: Ἀχας. Similarly, the identical name sometimes is merely transliterated, but some other times this transliteration is even "hellenized"; e.g. אֲחַזְיָהוּ in 2 Ki. 8:25 and 26 is "hellenized" as: Ὀχοειας but *ibid.*, v. 29 simply transliterated, Ὀχοζει. In the following chapter 9, too, we find both forms in close proximity, v. 16: Ὀχοζειας, but v. 21: Ὀχοζει .

§ 19. Thus, the editor of the Septuagint has to face the same problems as the editor of the *Vetus Latina*. Consequently, I suggest that he adopt a procedure parallel to that employed for the publication of the *Vetus Latina*. In other words: we shall aim at the publication of the Greek *Vorlage* or *Vorlagen* (plural!) of the *Vetus Latina*. I would like to coin a new term for it: *the Church Fathers' Greek Bible*. To this end we shall start with excerpting the Old Testament quotations in the commentaries, Homilies and other theological writings of the Greek Church Fathers. In this fashion, we may not get together translations of complete Biblical books; but our material will probably represent a purer form of the respective original translation. The relationship of *the Church Fathers' Greek Bible* to the text (or texts) now commonly known as Septuagint will perhaps be comparable to that of the *Vetus Latina* to Jerome's Vulgate. This does not imply that *the Church Fathers' Greek Bible* will necessarily prove to have been the Greek *Vorlage* of the *Vetus Latina*. But I do hope that these texts will show a much closer affinity than that which a comparison of a Septuagint text with the corresponding portion of the *Vetus Latina* reveals. I wish to substantiate the reasonableness of this expectation of mine by pointing to a few examples, which I picked at random while reading in E. Ranke's *Par Palimpsestorum Wirceburgensium* (Vienna, 1871). In listing the two parallel Old Latin translations, I follow the arrangement of the two corresponding Greek Bibles, which supposedly served them as *Vorlagen*; they can be traced in the commentaries of Cyril of Alexandria (listed here on the left) and Theodoret of Kyros (noted on the right), both according to the edition of Migne:

Hos 1:1: Ἀχαζ, Ἐζεχίου — καὶ Ἀχαζ καὶ Ἐζεκίου
        Achaz, Ezechiae— et achas et ezechiae

Hos. 1:2: ἐν Ὡσηε — πρὸς Ὡσηε (cf. *NTS*, pp. 264 and 277)
        in osee — ad osee

Hos. 1:4: πρὸς αὐτόν — vacat
ad eum — vacat

Just as the Biblical texts in their present form, as they appear in Migne's edition, cannot be regarded as genuinely pure, but merely as indicative in a general way of their underlying original Greek Bible Versions, so have we also to view the two Old Latin texts of Ranke's edition. But even in the form as they appear now can these Old Latin texts be useful in our endeavor to restore original readings of their Greek *Vorlagen* (cf. my paper in *MGWJ*, 1937); cf. Ranke p. 244 on Hos. 2:3: dilecta — misericordia consecuta; (corresponds to: ἀγαπημένη — ἐλεημένη); *ibid.*, on Hos. 2:2: haec non est — haec non and ego non sum — ego non (cf. *NTS*, p. 217 on Jer. 33:9: אשר אנכי עשה and *ibid.*, p. 221 under § 5 d: ἐγώ εἰμὶ ποιήσω and ἐγὼ ποιήσω).

§ 20. But the question could be asked: isn't this postulate of ours part of Lagarde's own theory, forming the basis for the editing of the three "recensions" as individual and separate texts (cf. point b in § 1?) For, according to Lagarde, "Septuagint manuscripts were to be assigned to one of the three recensions according to the agreement of their readings with the Bible quotations of a given Church Father. If, for instance, a Church Father, who had lived in Syria, quoted in his works a Biblical passage in the same form as we find it in a certain manuscript, this fact would lead to the conclusion that the manuscript in question belongs to Lucian's recension" (*JBL*, 1935, p. 75 f.). With this theoretic reasoning in mind, Lagarde himself has published what he considered to be Lucian's recension of the Bible: *Librorum Veteris Testamenti Canonicorum pars prior Graece* (Goettingen, 1883): "Luciani recognitio, cuius editionem dedi post aliquot annorum studium molestissimum in gravioribus omnibus satis fidam, et conlatis codicibus versionibusque eam praebentibus *et patribus ea utentibus* excussis efficiendum erit *ut etiam in minutioribus adcurate edita dici merito possit*" (p. XV). Now, is his claim to exactness right? In my *Septuaginta-Probleme* (Stuttgart, 1929, p. 93 on Ps. 104:18), and, more in detail, in my paper in the *Kahle-Festschrift* (cf. § 1) on pp. 43–45, I have pointed out the significance of the variant translations for Hebrew שָׁפָן or אַרְנֶבֶת: The Greek equivalent for these words, λαγωός, had to be circumvented by all means in Egypt, out of consideration for the ruling house. But in Syria, where the Seleucids ruled, there could have been no objections to the use of the term λαγωός in these cases. Consequently, we have here a very important indicator for the "Heimat" of a manuscript: any avoidance of the use of λαγωός proves Egypt to be the "Heimmat"; the respective manuscript thus belongs to Hesychius. We now turn to Lagarde's edition of Lucian. Here we read in Lev. 11:5: καὶ τὸν χοιρογρύλλιον (for Hebrew וְאֶת הַשָּׁפָן) and *ibid.*, v. 6: καὶ τὸν δασύποδα (for Hebrew וְאֶת הָאַרְנֶבֶת). This might be considered only circumstantial evidence that the text which Lagarde published as Lucianic, in reality represents Hesychius. But we have also explicit proof that in Syria (Lucian) λαγωός was actually read in these verses: cf. Theodoret of Kyros (Migne, Vol. 80, p. 315 A): ὡς κάμηλος καὶ λαγωός. And Chrysostomus (IX, p. 727, cf. Holmes and Parsons on Ps. 104:18) has the doublet: τοῖς χοιρογρυλλίοις καὶ τιοῖς λαγωοῖς. Cf. also the doublets in two manuscripts on Lev. 11:5, according to the Brooke–McLean edition of the Septuagint: ms. g reads: τον δασυποδα // λαγωον, while ms. n has: τον αλογον // δασυποδα. This is additional proof of the importance of the minuscule Mss. of the Septuagint; cf. my *Septuaginta-Probleme*, p. 55 f. Of course, this proves only that the Leviticus-passage under consideration in Lagarde's edition reflects Hesychius, and does not implicitly reflect on the edition as a whole, which may or may not represent Lucian. However, the fact that this edition abounds in doublets must be taken as sufficient proof that it is based upon a "Mischtext"; cf. e.g. Gen. 15:11: ἐπὶ τὰ σώματα // τὰ διχοτομήματα (cf. *NTS*, p. 251); Ex. 26:13: τοῦ ὑπερέχοντος τῶν δέρρεων // ἐκ τοῦ μήκους τῶν δέρρεων (cf. *NTS*, p. 251); cf. also all the doublets in the Greek Pentateuch, which I discussed in *NTS* pp. 250–256, and which almost without any exception are to be found in this so-called Lucianic recension. Lagarde thus failed to realize that the text, which he offered, was the result of a combination of two original translations, as can be seen from the fact that doublets occur there (and in so great a number!);

and even such characteristic Egyptian renderings as those noted above on Lev. 11:5 and 6 did not attract his attention. Cf. also Robert H. Pfeiffer: *Introduction to the Old Testament* (New York, 1941), p. 112 for references to "sharp criticism" of this edition.

ON THE PLAN OF *THE GUIDE OF THE PERPLEXED*

by Leo Strauss

I BELIEVE THAT it will not be amiss if I simply present the plan of the *Guide* as it has become clear to me in the course of about twenty-five years of frequently interrupted but never abandoned study. In the following scheme Roman (and Arabic) numerals at the beginning of a line indicate the sections (and subsections) of the *Guide* while the numbers given in parentheses indicate the Parts and the chapters of the book.

A. Views (I 1–III 24)

A1. Views regarding God and the angels (I 1–III 7)

1. *Biblical terms applied to God* (I 1–70)

(a) Terms suggesting the corporeality of God (and the angels) (I 1–49)

   (1) The two most important passages of the Torah which seem to suggest that God is corporeal (I 1–7)

   (2) Terms designating place, change of place, the organs of human locomotion etc. (I 8–28)

   (3) Terms designating wrath and consuming (or taking food) which if applied to divine things refer to idolatry on the one hand and to human knowledge on the other (I 29–36)

   (4) Terms designating parts and actions of animals (I 37–49)

(b) Terms suggesting multiplicity in God (I 50–70)

   (5) Given that God is absolutely one and incomparable, what is the meaning of the terms applied to God in non-figurative speech? (I 50–60)

(6) The names of God and the utterances of God (I 61–67)
(7) The apparent multiplicity in God consequent upon His knowledge, His causality, and His governance (I 68–70)

II. *Demonstrations of the existence, unity and incorporeality of God* (I 71–II 31)
   (1) Introductory (I 71–73)
   (2) Refutation of the Kalām demonstrations (I 74–76)
   (3) The philosophic demonstrations (II 1)
   (4) Maimonides' demonstration (II 2)
   (5) The angels (II 3–12)
   (6) Creation of the world, i.e. defense of the belief in creation out of nothing against the philosophers (II 13–24)
   (7) Creation and the Law (II 25–31)

III. *Prophecy* (II 32–48)
   (1) Natural endowment and training the prerequisites of prophecy (II 32–34)
   (2) The difference between the prophecy of Moses and that of the other prophets (II 35)
   (3) The essence of prophecy (II 36–38)
   (4) The legislative prophecy (of Moses) and the Law (II 39–40)
   (5) Legal study of the prophecy of the prophets other than Moses (II 41–44)
   (6) The degrees of prophecy (II 45)
   (7) How to understand the divine and the divinely commanded actions and works as presented by the prophets (II 46–48)

IV. *The Work of the Chariot* (III 1–7)

A[2]. VIEWS REGARDING BODILY BEINGS WHICH COME INTO BEING AND PERISH AND IN PARTICULAR REGARDING MAN (III 8–54)

V. *Providence* (III 8–24)
   (1) Statement of the problem: matter is the ground of all evils and yet matter is created by the absolutely good God (III 8–14)

(2) The nature of the impossible or the meaning of omnipotence (III 15)
(3) The philosophic arguments against omniscience (III 16)
(4) The views regarding providence (III 17–18)
(5) Jewish views on omniscience and Maimonides' discourse on this subject (III 19–21)
(6) The book of Job as the authoritative treatment of providence (III 22–23)
(7) The teaching of the Torah on omniscience (III 24)

B. ACTIONS (III 25–54)

VI. *The actions commanded by God and done by God* (III 25–50)
   (1) The rationality of God's actions in general and of His legislation in particular (III 25–26)
   (2) The manifestly rational part of the commandments of the Torah (III 27–28)
   (3) The rationale of the apparently irrational part of the commandments of the Torah (III 29–33)
   (4) The inevitable limit to the rationality of the commandments of the Torah (III 34)
   (5) Division of the commandments into classes and explanation of the usefulness of each class (III 35)
   (6) Explanation of all or almost all commandments (III 36–49)
   (7) The narratives in the Torah (III 50)

VII. *Man's perfection and God's providence* (III 51–54)
   (1) True knowledge of God Himself is the prerequisite of providence (III 51–52)
   (2) True knowledge of what constitutes the human individual himself is the prerequisite of knowledge of the workings of providence (III 53–54)

The *Guide* consists then of 7 sections or of 38 subsections. Wherever feasible, each section is divided into 7 subsections; the only section which does not permit of being divided into subsections, is divided into 7 chapters.

The simple statement of the plan of the *Guide* suffices to show that the book is sealed with many seals. At the end of its Introduction Maimonides describes the preceding passage as follows: "It is a key permitting one to enter places the gates to which were locked. When those gates are opened and those places are entered, the souls will find rest therein, the eyes will be delighted, and the bodies will be eased of their toil and of their labor." The *Guide* as a whole is not merely a key to a forest but itself a forest, an enchanted forest, and hence also an enchanting forest: it is a delight for the eyes. For the tree of life is a delight for the eyes.

The enchanting character of the *Guide* does not appear immediately. At first glance the book merely appears to be strange and, in particular, to lack order and consistency. But the progress in its understanding is a progress in becoming enchanted by it. Enchanting understanding is perhaps the highest form of edification. One begins to understand the *Guide* once one sees that it is not a philosophic book — a book written by a philosopher for philosophers — but a Jewish book: a book written by a Jew for Jews. Its first premise is the old Jewish premise that being a Jew and being a philosopher are two incompatible things. Philosophers are men who try to give an account of the whole by starting from what is always accessible to man as man; Maimonides starts from the acceptance of the Torah. A Jew may make use of philosophy and Maimonides makes the most ample use of it; but as a Jew he gives his assent where as a philosopher he would suspend his assent (cf. II 16).

In accordance with this, the *Guide* is devoted to the Torah or more precisely to the true science of the Torah, of the Law. Its first purpose is to explain Biblical terms and its second purpose is to explain Biblical similes. The *Guide* is then devoted above all to Biblical exegesis, although to Biblical exegesis of a particular kind. That kind of exegesis is required because many Biblical terms and all Biblical similes have an apparent or outer and a hidden or inner meaning: the gravest errors as well as the most tormenting perplexities arise from men's understanding the Bible always according to its apparent or literal meaning. The *Guide* is then devoted to "the difficulties of the Law" or to "the secrets of the Law." The most important of those secrets are the Work of the Beginning (the beginning of the Bible) and the Work of the Chariot (Ezekiel 1 and 10). The *Guide* is then devoted primarily and chiefly to the explanation of the Work of the Beginning and the Work of the Chariot.

Yet the Law whose secrets Maimonides intends to explain, forbids that they be explained in public, or to the public; they may only be explained in private and only to such individuals as possess both theoretical and political wisdom as well as the capacity of both understanding and using allusive speech; for only "the chapter headings" of the secret teaching may be transmitted even to those who belong to the natural elite. Since every explanation given in writing, at any rate in a book, is a public explanation, Maimonides seems to be compelled by his intention to transgress the Law. There were other cases in which he was under such a compulsion. The Law also forbids one to study the books of idolaters on idolatry, for the first intention of the Law as a whole is to destroy every vestige of idolatry; and yet Maimonides, as he openly admits and even emphasizes, has studied all the available idolatrous books of this kind with the utmost thoroughness. Nor is this all. He goes so far as to encourage the reader of the *Guide* to study those books by himself (III 29–30, 32 and 37; *M.T.*, H. 'Abodah zara II 2 and III 2). The Law also forbids one to speculate about the date of the coming of the Messiah, and yet Maimonides presents such a speculation or at least its equivalent in order to comfort his contemporaries (*Epistle to Yemen*, 62, 16 ff. and 80, 17 ff., Halkin; cf. Halkin's Introduction pp. XII–XIII; *M.T.*, H. Melakim XII 2). Above all, the Law forbids one to seek for the grounds of the commandments, and yet Maimonides devotes almost twenty-six chapters of the *Guide* to such seeking (III 26; cf. II 25). All these irregularities have one and the same justification: Maimonides transgresses the Law "for the sake of heaven," i.e. in order to uphold or to fulfill the Law (I Introd. and III Introd.). Still, in the most important case he does not strictly speaking transgress the Law, for his written explanation of the secrets of the Law is not a public but a secret explanation. The secrecy is achieved in three ways. Firstly, every word of the *Guide* is chosen with exceeding care; since very few men are able or willing to read with exceeding care, most men will fail to perceive the secret teaching. Secondly, Maimonides deliberately contradicts himself, and if a man declares both that *a* is *b* and that *a* is not *b*, he cannot be said to declare anything. Lastly, the "chapter headings" of the secret teaching are not presented in an orderly fashion but are scattered throughout the book. This permits us to understand why the plan of the *Guide* is so obscure. Maimonides succeeds in obscuring the plan immediately by failing to divide the book explicitly in sections and subsections or by dividing it explicitly only into three Parts and each Part into chapters without supplying the Parts and the chapters with headings indicating the subject matter of the Parts or of the chapters.

The plan of the *Guide* is not entirely obscure. No one can reasonably doubt for instance that II 32–48, III 1–7 and III 25–50 form sections. The plan is most obscure at the beginning and it becomes clearer as one proceeds; generally speaking it is clearer in the second half (II 13–end) than in the first half. The *Guide* is then not entirely devoted to secretly transmitting chapter headings of the secret teaching. This does not mean that the book is not in its entirety devoted to the true science of the Law. It means that the true science of the Law is partly public. This is not surprising, for the teaching of the Law itself is of necessity partly public. According to one statement, the core of the public teaching consists of the assertions that God is one, that He alone is to be worshipped, that He is incorporeal, that He is incomparable to any of His creatures and that He suffers from no defect and no passion (I 35). From other statements it would appear that the acceptance of the Law on every level of comprehension presupposes belief in God, in angels and in prophecy (III 45) or that the basic beliefs are those in God's unity and in Creation (II 13). In brief, one may say that the public teaching of the Law insofar as it refers to beliefs or to "views," can be reduced to the 13 "roots" (or dogmas) which Maimonides had put together in his *Commentary on the*

Mishna. That part of the true science of the Law which is devoted to the public teaching of the Law or which is itself public, has the task of demonstrating the roots to the extent to which this is possible or of establishing the roots by means of speculation (III 51 and 54). Being speculative, that part of the true science of the Law is not exegetic; it is not necessarily in need of support by Biblical or Talmudic texts (cf. II 45 beginning). Accordingly, about 20 per cent of the chapters of the *Guide* contain no Biblical quotations and about 9 per cent of them contain no Hebrew or Aramaic expressions whatever. It is not very difficult to see (especially on the basis of III 7 end, 23 and 28) that the *Guide* as devoted to speculation on the roots of the Law or to the public teaching consists of sections II–III and V–VI as indicated in our scheme and that the sequence of these sections is rational; but one cannot understand in this manner why the book is divided into 3 Parts nor what sections I, IV and VII and most, not to say all, subsections mean. The teaching of the *Guide* is then neither entirely public or speculative nor is it entirely secret or exegetic. For this reason the plan of the *Guide* is neither entirely obscure nor entirely clear.

Yet the *Guide* is a single whole. What then is the bond uniting its exegetic and its speculative element? One might imagine that, while speculation demonstrates the roots of the Law, exegesis proves that those roots as demonstrated by speculation are in fact taught by the Law. But in that case the *Guide* would open with chapters devoted to speculation and the opposite is manifestly true. In addition, if the exegesis dealt with the same subject matter as that speculation which demonstrates the public teaching par excellence, namely, the roots of the Law, there would be no reason why the exegesis should be secret. Maimonides does say that the Work of the Beginning is the same as natural science and the Work of the Chariot is the same as divine science (i.e. the science of the incorporeal beings or of God and the angels). This might lead one to think that the public teaching is identical with what the philosophers teach while the secret teaching makes one understand the identity of the teaching of the philosophers with the secret teaching of the Law. One can safely say that this thought proves to be untenable on almost every level of one's comprehending the *Guide*: the non-identity of the teaching of the philosophers as a whole and the 13 roots of the Law as a whole is the first word and the last word of Maimonides. What he means by identifying the core of philosophy (natural science and divine science) with the highest secrets of the Law (the Work of the Beginning and the Work of the Chariot) and therewith by somehow identifying the subject matter of speculation with the subject matter of exegesis may be said to be the secret par excellence of the *Guide*.

Let us then retrace our steps. The *Guide* contains a public teaching and a secret teaching. The public teaching is addressed to every Jew including the vulgar; the secret teaching is addressed to the elite. The secret teaching is of no use to the vulgar and the elite does not need the *Guide* for being appraised of the public teaching. To the extent to which the *Guide* is a whole, or one work, it is not addressed to the vulgar nor to the elite. To whom then is it addressed? How legitimate and important this question is appears from Maimonides' remark that the chief purpose of the *Guide* is to explain as far as possible the Work of the Beginning and the Work of the Chariot "with a view to him for whom (the book) has been composed" (III beginning). Maimonides answers our question both explicitly and implicitly. He answers it explicitly in two ways: he says on the one hand that the *Guide* is addressed to believing Jews who are perfect in their religion and in their character, have studied the sciences of the philosophers and are perplexed by the literal meaning of the Law; he says on the other hand that the book is addressed to such perfect human beings as are Law-students and perplexed. He answers our question more simply by dedicating the book to his disciple Joseph and by stating that it has been composed for Joseph and his like. Joseph had come to him "from the ends of the earth" and had studied under him for a while; the interruption of the oral instruction through Joseph's departure which "God had decreed," induced Maimonides to write the *Guide* for Joseph and his like. In the Epistle dedicatory addressed to Joseph, Maimonides extolls Joseph's virtues and indicates his limitation. Joseph had a passionate desire for things speculative and especially for mathematics. When he studied astronomy, mathematics and logic under Maimonides, the teacher saw that Joseph had an excellent mind and a quick grasp; he thought him therefore fit to have revealed to him allusively the secrets of the books of the prophets and he began to make such revelations. This stimulated Joseph's interest in things divine as well as in an appraisal of the Kalām; his desire for knowledge about these subjects became so great that Maimonides was compelled to warn him unceasingly to proceed in an orderly manner. It appears that Joseph was inclined to proceed impatiently or unmethodically in his study and that this defect had not been cured when he left Maimonides. The most important consequence of Joseph's defect is the fact, brought out by Maimonides' silence, that Joseph turned to divine science without having studied natural science under Maimonides or before, although natural science necessarily precedes divine science in the order of study.

The impression derived from the Epistle dedicatory is confirmed by the book itself. Maimonides frequently addresses the reader by using expressions like "know" or "you know already;" expressions of the latter kind indicate what the typical addressee knows and expressions of the former kind indicate what he does not know. One thus learns that Joseph has some knowledge of both the content and the charater of divine science. He knows for example that divine science in contradistinction to mathematics and medicine requires an extreme of rectitude and moral perfection, and in particular of humility, but he apparently does not yet know how ascetic Judaism is in matters of sex (I 34, III 52). He had learned from Maimonides' "speech" that the orthodox "views" do not last in a man if he does not confirm them by the corresponding "actions" (II 31). It goes without saying that while his knowledge of the Jewish sources is extensive it is not comparable in extent and thoroughness to Maimonides' (II 26, 33). At the beginning of the book he does not know that both according to the Jewish view and according to demonstration angels have no bodies (I 43, 49) and he certainly does not know strictly speaking that God has no body (I 9). In this respect as well as in other respects his understanding necessarily progresses while he advances in his study of the *Guide* (cf. I 65 beginning). As for natural science, he has studied astronomy but is not aware of the conflict between the astronomical principles and the principles of natural science (II 24), because he has not studied natural science. He knows a number of things which are made clear in natural science but this does not mean that he knows them through having studied natural science (cf. I 17, 28; III 10). From the 91st chapter (II 15) it appears that while he knows Aristotle's *Topics* and Farabi's commentary on that work, he does not know the *Physics* and *On the Heaven* (cf. II 8). Nor will he acquire the science of nature as he acquires the science of God and the angels while he advances in the study of the *Guide*. For the *Guide* which is addressed to a reader not conversant with natural science, does not itself transmit natural science (II 2). The following remark occurring in the 26th chapter is particularly revealing: "It has been demonstrated that everything moved undoubtedly possesses a magnitude and is divisible; and it will be demonstrated that God possesses no magnitude and hence possesses no motion." What "has been demonstrated" has been demonstrated in the *Physics* and is simply presupposed in the *Guide*; what "will be demonstrated" belongs to divine science and not to natural science; but that which "will be demonstrated" is built on what "has been demonstrated." The student of the *Guide* acquires knowledge of divine science but not of natural science. The author of the *Guide* in contradistinction to its addressee is thoroughly versed in natural science. Still, the addressee needs some awareness of the whole in order to be able to ascend from the whole to God, for there is no way to knowledge of God except through such ascent (I 71 toward the end); he acquires that awareness through a report of some kind (I 70) which Maimonides has inserted into the *Guide*. That report is characterized by the fact that it does not contain a single mention of philosophy in general and of natural science in particular. The serious student cannot rest satisfied with that report; he must turn from that report to natural science itself which supplies the demonstration of what the report merely asserts. Maimonides cannot but leave it to his reader whether he will turn to genuine speculation or whether he will be satisfied with accepting the report on the authority of Maimonides and with building on that report theological conclusions. The addressee of the *Guide* is a man regarding whom it is still undecided whether he will become a genuine man of speculation or whether he will remain a follower of authority, if of Maimonides' authority (cf. I 72 end). He stands on the point of the road where speculation branches off from acceptance of authority.

Why did Maimonides choose an addressee of this description? What is the virtue of not being trained in natural science? We learn from the 17th chapter that natural science was treated as a secret doctrine already by the pagan philosophers "upon whom the charge of corruption would not be laid if they exposed natural science clearly:" all the more is the community of the Law-adherents obliged to treat natural science as a secret science. The reason why natural science is dangerous and is kept secret "with all kinds of artifices" is not that it undermines the Law — only the ignorant believe that (I 33) and Maimonides' whole life as well as the life of his successors refutes this suspicion. Yet it is also true that natural science has this corrupting effect on all men who are not perfect (cf. I 62). For natural science surely affects the understanding of the meaning of the Law, of the grounds on which it is to be obeyed and of the weight which is to be attached to its different parts. In a word, natural science upsets habits. By addressing a reader who is not conversant with natural science, Maimonides is compelled to proceed in a manner which does not upset habits or does so to the smallest possible degree. He acts as a moderate or conservative man.

But we must not forget that the *Guide* is written also for atypical addressees. In the first place, certain chapters of the *Guide* are explicitly said to be useful also for those who are beginners simply. Since the whole book is somehow accessible to the vulgar, it must have been written in such a way as not to be harmful to the vulgar (I Introd.; III 29). Besides, the book is also meant to be useful to such men of great intelligence as have been trained fully in all philosophic sciences and as are not in the habit of bowing to any authority — in other words, to men not inferior to Maimonides in their critical faculty. This kind of reader will be unable to bow to Maimonides' authority; he will examine all his assertions, speculative or exegetic, with all reasonable severity; and he will derive great pleasure from all chapters of the *Guide* (I Introd.; I 55, 68 end, 73, tenth premise).

How much Maimonides' choice of his typical addressee affects the plan of his book, the judicious reader will see by glancing at our scheme. It suffices to mention the fact that no section or subsection of the *Guide* is devoted to the bodies which do not come into being and perish (cf. III 8 beginning and I 11), i.e., to the heavenly bodies which according to Maimonides possess life and knowledge, or to "the holy bodies" to use the bold expression used by him in his *Code* (*M.T.*, H. Yesode ha-torah IV 12). In other words, no section or subsection of the *Guide* is devoted to the Work of the Beginning in the manner in which a section is devoted to the Work of the Chariot. It is more important to see that Maimonides' choice of his typical addressee is the key to the whole plan of the *Guide*, to the apparent lack of order or to the obscurity of the plan. The plan of the *Guide* appears to be obscure only as long as one does not consider for what kind of reader the book is written or as long as one seeks for an order agreeing with the essential order of subject matter. We recall the order of the sciences: logic precedes mathematics, mathematics precedes natural science, and natural science precedes divine science; and we recall that while Joseph was sufficiently trained in logic and mathematics, he is supposed to be introduced into divine science without having been trained properly in natural science. Maimonides must therefore seek for a substitute for natural science. He finds that substitute in the traditional Jewish beliefs and ultimately in the Biblical texts correctly interpreted: the immediate preparation for divine science in the *Guide* is exegetic rather than speculative. Furthermore, Maimonides wishes to proceed in a manner which changes habits to the smallest possible degree. He himself tells us which habit is in particular need of being changed. After having reported the opinion of a pagan philosopher on the obstacles to speculation, he adds the remark that there exists now an obstacle which the ancient philosopher had not mentioned because it did not exist in his society: the habit of relying on revered "texts," i.e. on their literal meaning (I 31). It is for this reason that he opens his book with the explanation of Biblical terms, i.e. with showing that their true meaning is not always their literal meaning. He cures the vicious habit in question by having recourse to another habit of his addressee. The addressee was accustomed not only to accept the literally understood Biblical text as true but also in many cases to understand Biblical texts according to traditional interpretations which differed considerably from the literal meaning. Being accustomed to listen to authoritative interpretations of Biblical texts, he is prepared to listen to Maimonides' interpretations as authoritative interpretations. The explanation of Biblical terms which is given by Maimonides authoritatively, is in the circumstances the natural substitute for natural science.

But which Biblical terms deserve primary consideration? In other words, what is the initial theme of the *Guide*? The choice of the initial theme is dictated by the right answer to the question as to which theme is the most urgent for the typical addressee and at the same time the least upsetting to him. The first theme of the *Guide* is God's incorporeality. God's incorporeality is the third of the three most fundamental truths, the preceding ones being the existence of God and His unity. The existence of God and His unity were admitted as unquestionable by all Jews; all Jews as Jews know that God exists and that He is one, and they know this through the Biblical revelation or the Biblical miracles. One can say that because belief in the Biblical revelation precedes speculation, and the discovery of the true meaning of revelation is the task of exegesis, exegesis precedes speculation. But as regards God's incorporeality there existed a certain confusion. The Biblical texts suggest that God is corporeal and the interpretation of these texts is not a very easy task (II 25, 31, III 28). God's incorporeality is indeed a demonstrable truth but, to say nothing of others, the addressee of the *Guide* does not come into the possession of the demonstration until he has advanced into the Second Part (cf. I 1, 9, 18). The necessity to refute "corporealism" (the belief that God is corporeal) does not merely arise from the fact that corporealism is demonstrably untrue: corporealism is dangerous because it endangers the belief shared by all Jews in God's unity (I 35). On the other hand, by teaching that God is incorporeal, one does not do more than to give expression to what the Talmudic Sages believed (I 46). However, the Jewish authority who had given the most consistent and the most popularly effective expression to the belief in God's incorporeality, was Onkelos the Stranger, for the primary preoccupation of his translation of the Torah into Aramaic which Joseph knew as a matter of course, was precisely to dispose of the corporealistic suggestions of the original (I 21, 27, 28, 36 end). Maimonides' innovation is then limited to his deviation from Onkelos' procedure: he does explicitly what Onkelos did implicitly; whereas Onkelos tacitly substituted non-corporealistic terms for the corporealistic terms occurring in the original, Maimonides explicitly discusses each of the terms in question by itself in an order which has no correspondence to the accidental sequence of their occurrence in the Bible. As a consequence, the discussion of corporealism in the *Guide* consists chiefly of a discussion of the various Biblical terms suggesting corporealism, and vice versa the chief subject of what Maimonides declares to be the primary purpose of the *Guide*, namely, the explanation of Biblical terms, is the explanation of Biblical terms suggesting corporealism. This is not surprising. There are no Biblical terms which suggest that God is not one whereas there are many Biblical terms which suggest that God is corporeal: the apparent difficulty created by the plural *Elohim* can be disposed of by a single sentence or by a single reference to Onkelos (I 2).

The chief reason however why it is so urgent to establish the belief in God's incorporeality is supplied by the fact that that belief is destructive of idolatry. It was of course universally known that idolatry is a very grave sin, nay, that the Law has so to speak no other purpose than to destroy idolatry (I 35, III 29 end). But this evil can be completely eradicated only if everyone is brought to know that God has no visible shape whatever or that He is incorporeal. Only if God is incorporeal is it absurd to make images of God and to worship such images. Only under this condition can it become manifest to everyone that the only image of God is man, living and thinking man, and that man acts as the image of God only through worshipping the invisible or hidden God alone. Not idolatry but the belief in God's corporeality is a fundamental sin. Hence, the sin of idolatry is less grave than that of believing in God's being corporeal (I 36). This being the case, it becomes indispensable that God's incorporeality be believed in by everyone regardless of whether he knows by demonstration that God is incorporeal or not; as regards the majority of men it is sufficient and necessary that they believe in this truth on the basis of authority or tradition, i.e. on a basis which the first subsections of the *Guide* are meant to supply. The teaching of God's incorporeality by means of authoritative exegesis, i.e. the most public teaching of God's incorporeality, is indispensable for destroying the last relics of paganism: the immediate source of paganism is less the ignorance of God's unity than the ignorance of His radical incorporeality (cf. I 36 with *M.T.*, H. ʿAboda zara I 1).

It is necessary that we should understand the character of the reasoning which Maimonides uses in determining the initial theme of the *Guide*. We limit ourselves to a consideration of the second point. While the belief in Unity leads immediately to the rejection of the worship of "other gods" but not to the rejection of the worship of images of the one God, the belief in Incorporeality leads immediately only to the rejection of the worship of images or of other bodies but not to the rejection of the worship of other gods: all gods may be incorporeal. Only if the belief in God's incorporeality is based on the belief in His unity as Maimonides' argument indeed assumes, does the belief in God's incorporeality appear to be the necessary and sufficient ground for rejecting "forbidden worship" in every form, i.e. the worship of other gods as well as the worship of both natural things and artificial things. This would mean that the prohibition against idolatry in the widest sense is as much a dictate of reason as the belief in God's unity and incorporeality. Yet Maimonides indicates that only the theoretical truths pronounced in the Decalogue (God's existence and His unity), in contradistinction to the rest of the Decalogue, are rational. This is in agreement with his denying the existence of rational commandments or prohibitions as such (II 33; cf. I 54, II 31 beginning, III 28; *Eight Chapters* VI). Given the fact that Aristotle believed in God's unity and incorporeality and yet was an idolator (I 71, III 29), Maimonides' admiration for him would be incomprehensible if the rejection of idolatry were the simple consequence of that belief. According to Maimonides, the Law agrees with Aristotle in holding that the heavenly bodies are endowed with life and intelligence and that they are superior to man in dignity; one could say that he agrees with Aristotle in implying that those holy bodies deserve more than man to be called images of God. But unlike the philosophers he does not go so far as to call those bodies "divine bodies" (II 4–6; cf. Letter to Ibn Tibbon). The true ground of the rejection of "forbidden worship" is the belief in creation out of nothing which implies that creation is an absolutely free act of God or that God alone is the complete good which is in no way increased by creation. But creation is, according to Maimonides, not demonstrable, whereas God's unity and incorporeality are demonstrable. The reasoning underlying the determination of the initial theme of the *Guide* can then be described as follows: it conceals the difference of cognitive status between the belief in God's unity and incorporeality on the one hand and the belief in creation on the other; it is in accordance with the opinion of the Kalām. In accordance with this, Maimonides brings his disagreement with the Kalām into the open only after he has concluded his thematic discussion of God's incorporeality; in that discussion he does not even mention the Kalām.

It is necessary that we should understand as clearly as possible the situation in which Maimonides and his addressee find themselves at the beginning of the book, if not throughout the book. Maimonides knows that God is incorporeal; he knows this by a demonstration which is at least partly based on natural science. The addressee does not know that God is incorporeal; nor does he learn it yet from Maimonides: he accepts the fact that God's incorporeality is demonstrated on Maimonides' authority. Both Maimonides and the addressee know that the Law is a source of knowledge of God: only the Law can establish God's incorporeality for the addressee in a manner which does not depend on Maimonides' authority. But both know that the literal meaning of the Law is not always its true meaning and that the literal meaning is certainly not the true meaning when it contradicts reason, for otherwise the Law could not be "your wisdom and your understanding in the sight of the nations" (Deuteronomy 4:6). Both know in other words that exegesis does not simply precede speculation. Yet only Maimonides knows that the corporealistic expressions of the Law are against reason and must therefore be taken as figurative. The addressee does not know and cannot know that Maimonides' figurative interpretations of those expressions are true: Maimonides does not adduce arguments based on grammar. The addressee accepts Maimonides' interpretations just as he is in the habit of accepting the Aramaic translations as correct translations or interpretations. Maimonides enters the ranks of the traditional Jewish authorities: he simply tells the addressee what to believe as regards the meaning of the Biblical terms. Maimonides introduces Reason in the guise of Authority. He takes on the garb of authority. He tells the addressee to believe in God's incorporeality because, as he tells him, contrary to appearance, the Law does not teach corporeality, because, as he tells him, corporeality is a demonstrably wrong belief.

POST-BIBLICAL HEBRAISMS IN THE PRIMA CLEMENTIS

by ERIC WERNER

THE CONTROVERSIES, which the recent studies on Judaeo-Christianity by H. J. Schoeps,[1] J. Danielou,[2] H. Thyen[3] and others have kindled, and which the detailed studies and analyses of the Dead Sea Scrolls (= DSS) enlivened, seem more and more to center about the Apostolic Fathers. Unlike chemical compounds that yield to analysis the exact percentages and proportions of their constituent elements: and equally unlike certain cases well-known in the annals of philology, where texts were falsely attributed to famous authors, or where interpolations could be proved and eliminated by a quasi anatomical dissection of the text, the literature of the Apostolic Fathers does not lend itself to quantitative analysis. Even the most minute and incisive examination of texts and ideas will somewhere approach a limit, beyond which we must resort to more or less plausible inferences. For so organic is the interpenetration of the basic components, viz. biblical, rabbinic, and sectarian Judaism, Hellenism, and Gentile Christianity, that in many cases the attempt to separate them from each other is idle and will yield nothing but verbal or theological hairsplitting. And yet, so farreaching were the consequences and influences of these texts for the further development of Christianity and Judaism, that the research into this unpromising field is hardly going to lose momentum; the less so, the more Hellenistic and Judaistic sources, hitherto unknown, are brought to light. This factor will eventually

[1] H. J. Schoeps, *Theologie und Geschichte des Judenchristentums* (Tuebingen 1949).
[2] J. Danielou, *Théologie du Judéo-Christianisme* (Tournai, 1958).
[3] H. Thyen, *Der Stil der juedisch-hellenistischen Homilie* (Goettingen, 1955).

outweigh the misgivings of scholarly prudence. This essay, then, is undertaken in the full knowledge that the final verdict might be a plain "*non liquet.*"

I

Our examination of First Clement will be confined to the study of post-biblical elements of Jewish origin in its text, structure, and ideas. In particular some of the hitherto unidentified quotations and allusions of the epistle will be traced; its basic unity will be re-examined in the light of midrashic elements previously overlooked, and a hypothesis about the genesis of this important document will be tentatively formulated.

According to the penetrating monographs by J. B. Lightfoot,[4] W. Wrede,[5] A. v. Harnack,[6] E. Peterson,[7] A. W. Ziegler,[8] K. Lake,[9] a. o. the following passages, singled out by Clement as scriptural quotations, have thus far resisted any definite identification: ch. 8:3; 17:6; 23:3–5; 29:3; 34:8; 35:6; 46:2, to which must be added some other *obiter dicta*, esp. 28:3, which resemble certain scriptural verses but deviate considerably from the MT or LXX text.

Ad 8:3. The text of this quotation is usually viewed as a "loose" allusion to Ezek. 33:11+18:30; the continuation ἐὰν ὦσιν αἱ ἁμαρτίαι ὑμῶν ἀπὸ τῆς γῆς ἕως τοῦ οὐρανοῦ, καὶ ἐὰν ὦσιν πυρρότεραι κόκκου καὶ μελανώτεραι σάκκου, καί ἐπιστραφῆτε πρός με ἐξ ὅλης τῆς καρδίας καὶ εἴπητε, Πάτερ, ἐπακούσομαι ὑμῶν ὡς λαοῦ ἁγίου κτλ. however, contains also references to Is. 1:18; Ps. 103:11; and Jer. 3:19, 22, (all according to the LXX, not the Hebrew text). Some scholars conjecture from this and some similarly compound quotations either a non-canonical text of

[4] J. B. Lightfoot, *The Apostolic Fathers*, Rev. ed. (London, 1890).
[5] W. Wrede, *Untersuchungen zum Ersten Klemensbrief* (Goettingen, 1891).
[6] A. v. Harnack, *Das Schreiben der Roemischen Kirche an die Korinthische*, I. Clemensbrief, (Leipzig, 1929).
[7] E. Peterson, *Fruehkirche, Judentum und Gnosis* (Rom-Wien, 1959).
[8] A. W. Ziegler, *Neue Studien zum Klemensbrief* (Muenchen, 1958).
[9] K. Lake, *The Apostolic Fathers*, I (London-New York, 1919).

Ezek., or they assume the existence of so-called "books of testimonies," where suitable compilations of scriptural passages were topically arranged.[10] M. R. James devotes an entire chapter of his book *The Lost Apocrypha of the OT* (London, 1920) to the apocryphal Ezekiel.[11] J. Danielou accepts this hypothesis without any reservation; indeed, he goes on to assert that "le terme Πατήρ, appliqué à Dieu, s'il se trouve dans l'Ancien Testament (Jer. 3:19) a une resonance chrétienne." And the entire reference in Clement is an "agglomérat paraît bien de main chrétienne." While he does not give a shadow of a proof, we shall try to trace this particular combination of scriptural verses in rabbinic literature. Indeed, the verses Jer. 3:22, Hos. 14:2, and Ezek. 33:19 are juxtaposed in Yoma 86, and culminate in the profound idea of Resh Lakish that the virtue of repentance is so great, that (in the case of a repentant sinner) premeditated sins are accounted as though they were merits, as indicated in our verse Ezek. 33:19.[12]

Ad 17:6. Professor S. Lieberman has kindly pointed out to me: "The usual translation of ἀτμὶς ἀπο κύθρας — smoke from a (boiling) pot is erroneous. It should read: 'as vapour from a (boiling) pot'. Thus the Syriac version (ed. Bentley, Cambridge 1899, p. 16) conveys the correct meaning להגא מן קדרא. In like fashion the rabbis interpret בהבליהם in Deut. 32:21 as 'vapour which ascends from the pot' להבל זה שעולה מן הקדירה. (Cf. *Sifre* Deut. sect. 320, ed. Friedmann 137a, ed. Finkelstein p. 367.) From here it is just one short step to the parable of Moses' humility. According to b *Hullin* 89a Moses and Aaron, humbler even than Abraham, said 'What are we' (Ex. 16:7) ואנחנו מה, which was coupled by Nachmanides and other sages with Ps. 144:3 מה אדם ותדעהו continuing

---

[10] Cf. B. F. Westcott, *General Survey of the History of the Canon of the NT* (Cambridge, 1881), pp. 560–62; also R. Harris, *Book of Testimonies*, I, (Manchester, 1917) p. 8–9; and E. Hatch, *Essays in Biblical Greek* (Oxford, 1889), p. 202 f.

[11] Numerous ancient sources testify to apocryphal chapters in Ez. Among them we find Josephus, (*Ant*. X, 5, 1), Clement of Alexandria, (*Paed*., I, 10, 91), and Tertullian (*De carn. Chr.* 23.).

[12] Cf. J. Danielou, *op. cit.*, p. 119.

with אדם להבל דמה man is like vapour. The definite link and association with Clement's text occurs in *Kohelet R.* I, 1, where the above Psalm-verse is attributed to David, whereas Solomon, his son, specified the vapour: הבל הבלים —vapour of vapours. 'like a man who sets (on burning coals) seven pots one upon another, and the vapour of the seventh pot has no substance' (at all). It seems that Clement preserved the entire Midrash: משה אמר: ואנחנו מה; היך מה דכתיב מה אדם ותדעהו וגו', אדם להבל דמה להבל זה שעולה מן הקדירה".

Ad 23:3 — 4. The operative word in this admonition is δίψυχοι, the double-minded. Prof. Lieberman suggests: "It corresponds to the midrashic, חלוק לב which occurs in *Mek.* בשלח ed. Lauterbach, I, p. 192.[13] Comp. Hos. 10:12. In *Sifre* Deut. sect. 32, ed. Finkelstein, p. 55 we read: שלא יהא לבך חלוק על המקום do not doubt concerning the Lord".[14] Clement's metaphor is closely related to the allegorical almond-tree in Philo's *Life of Moses*, and seems to belong to the "stock-in-trade" parables of the Hellenistic Synagogue.[15] The antecedent verse "we have heard these things even in the days of our fathers and behold we have grown old, and none of these things has happened to us," is cited as a scriptural text by Clement, although the verse does not occur in this form in the Bible.[16] Of recent authors especially J. Danielou has paid considerable attention to the passage. Taking his departure from Resch's conjecture that the verse represents a Christian *agraphon*, he continues — without any serious proof: ". . . il semble plutôt faire partie de la collection des *Logia*. De toute façon son caractère chrétien est certain. Le terme δίψυχος surtout est caractéristique de la spiritualité chrétienne archaïque."[17] Let us examine this remark. The word

---

[13] שהיה לבו חלוק אם לרדוף.

[14] Dr. Lieberman suggests the Greek equivalent μὴ θιψυχήσῃς περὶ τοῦ θεοῦ. Comp. *Deb. Rabba* ed. Lieberman (1964), p. 70, n. 3, and Supplement ibid.

[15] Cf. *Vita Moysis*, ed. Colson, II, ch. 34, (186). See also R. Bultmann, who links the parable with Mk. 4:26–29, in his *Theologie des NT.* (1953), p. 7.

[16] The same verse is quoted in the Ps.-Clement Homily (#11) introduced by the words λέγει γὰρ καὶ ὁ προφητικὸς λόγος.

[17] Cf. J. Danielou, *op. cit.*, p. 120. An extended version of his conclusion

δίψυχος does not occur in LXX; it does occur in Jam. 1:8, 4:8, also in Hermas and the *Didache* 4 (οὐ διψυχήσεις πότερον ἔσται ἢ οὔ), where it has the connotation of a sceptic or fickle-minded character. All three sources are Judeo-Christian by nature, and we may safely assume their familiarity with the Hebrew key-phrase (Deut, 32:20) כי דור תהפכת המה. The midrashic counterpart of δίψυχος, הפכפך of לבב[17a] is introduced in the *Sifre* to the passage from Deut. Hence it is by no means evident that this is "characteristic of ancient Christian spirituality," as Danielou claims. Moreover we find a related phrase in the "Hymns of Thanksgiving":

"They have scoffed at Thy teaching,
Nor given ear to Thy word,
But have spoken of the vision of Thy knowledge
'It is not certain'. . . ."[18]

Clement's subsequent warning, (23:5) reads: "Truly His will shall be and suddenly accomplished, according to Scripture's testimony:
'He shall come quickly and shall not tarry;
and the Lord shall suddenly come to His Temple,
and the Holy One, for whom ye look.' "

This is similar to what follows Deut. 32:20, is parallel to the admonition of the δίψυχοι and the parable of the vine, and could appropriately follow the verse quoted from *Hodayot*. This eschatological vision consists of Is. 13:22 with Mal. 3:1, but nowhere alludes to the second coming of Christ.[19] We are thus unable to see in this composite passage a typically Christian conception. If anything, we should heed and accept Clement's assertion of OT Scriptural foundation for his statement and take note of the absence of any anti-Jewish interpretation of the Scriptural source.[20]

also on p. 420. Against this interpretation the sole E. Peterson has, in his profound book *Fruehkirche, Judentum und Gnosis* (Rome-Vienna, 1959), p. 293, stressed the Jewish character and importance of the conception of δίψυχος.

[17a] See Jastrow, Dictionary, *ad. verb*, הפכפכן.
[18] Cf. DSS, *Hodayot*, IV:18.
[19] Cf. A. W. Ziegler, *Neue Studien zum Ersten Klemensbrief* (Muenchen, 1958), p. 56.   [20] Harnack, *op. cit.*, p. 111, says simply: "As this is quoted as γραφή, it was Jewish, not Christian."

Ad. 26:2a. This consists of a mixture of two Psalm-verses, which seems to indicate either that Clement was quoting from memory, or else had at his service a collection of Pss.-*centos* of the sort which we encounter in early Jewish and Christian liturgies.[21] Ps. 3:6 is quoted almost verbatim after the LXX, and the foregoing καὶ ἐξαναστήσεις με καὶ ἐξομολογήσομαί σοι is a mere paraphrase of the Septuagint version of Ps. 27:7 (Gr).

Ad 28:3 Clement uses here the term γραφεῖον to indicate the כתובים of the Jewish tradition of the canon, spread to the Hellenistic world by Sirach, Prologue. (τοῦ νόμου, καὶ τῶν προφητῶν, καὶ τῶν ἄλλων πατρίων βιβλίων, κτλ.)[22] Clement's verse amounts to a paraphrase of Ps. 139:7–10, which resembles the targumic interpretation.

Ad 29:2. Clement claims OT authority for the sentence: "When the Most High (ὕψιστος) divided the nations, when He scattered the sons of Adam, He established the bounds of the nations according to the number of the angels of God. His people Jacob became the portion of the Lord, Israel was the lot of His inheritance." Lightfoot's emendation of Deut. 32:8, 9 (LXX κατὰ ἀριθμὸν ἀγγέλων θεοῦ למספר בני אלהים) makes very good sense when coupled with its midrashic elaborations, which support his conjecture. Indeed, the *Tanchuma* (ויצא, ב) as well as Jubil. 15:31, the Palestinian Targum to Deut. 32:8, and Pirke de R. Eliezer, c. 24 all base their interpretation upon the LXX version, whereby various angels are assigned to specific nations. Pirke de R. Eliezer reads: "God assigned an angel to each specific people, but Israel fell to His own portion and possession. . . ."[23] This preference of the LXX text is supported by early Midrashic and Hellenistic

---

[21] Cf. my *Sacred Bridge* (London-New York, 1959), ch. IV.

[22] Cf. W. Wrede, *Untersuchungen zum Ersten Klemensbrief* (Goettingen, 1891), p. 68 stresses in this connection the predominance of quotations from the book of Psalms, Job, and Proverbs — the so-called "poetic books" of the OT Canon.

[23] Cf. G. F. Moore, *Judaism*, III, 62; also Test. Naphtali, and E. Peterson's fine study "Das Problem des Nationalismus im alten Christentum," in *op. cit.*, p. 51 ff.

sources. Philo knows this version in *De Plantat.* 14. This demonstrates clearly the dependence of Clement upon the tradition of the Hellenistic Synagogue.

Ad 34:8. Text in K. Lake's translation:
> "for he (or Scripture) says: 'Eye hath not seen, and ear hath not heard, and it hath not entered into the heart of man, what things the Lord hath prepared for them that wait for Him.'"

This is perhaps the most interesting and ambiguous quotation of the epistle. At first glance it appears to be a mere repetition of I Cor. 2:9.[24] Yet already Paul uses this esoteric-poetic *theologoumenon* as a Scriptural quotation.[25] It is not so much the unknown origin of the passage which puzzles us. The difficulty arises from its insertion as a climax after the emphatic and solemn Thrice-Holy in the same chapter. While the passage has a certain eschatological ring, its intent is anti-apocalyptic. Still, it deviates somewhat from Clement's usually moralistic and didactic inclination.

Both Paul and Clement associate this verse with angelology and with an esoteric σοφία. E. Peterson has shown convincingly that Paul polemicizes through this verse and its context against Jewish mystics of his time.[26] The paraphrase of Is. 64:3, tinged with a gnostic-apocalyptic hue stems, according to Origen and Jerome, from a lost Elijah-Apocalypse.[27] In what connection and for what

[24] Paul has here ὅσα ἡτοίμασεν ὁ θεὸς τοῖς ἀγαπῶσιν αὐτόν, while Clement reads ὁ κύριος τοῖς ὑπομένουσιν αὐτόν.

[25] It is not clear why R. Knopf, (*Der erste Clemensbrief*, in T & U, NF, vol. V, Leipzig, 1899) p. 181, assumes that the *logion* is ascribed by Clement to the pre-existent Christ. A list of the quotations of our verse is offered in Ph. Bachman, *Der Erste Brief des Paulus an die Corinther* (Leipzig, 1910), p. 127, n. 2.

[26] Cf. E. Peterson, *op. cit.*, p. 48 f. The author conjectures that the liturgical occasion of Paul's homily I. Cor. 1:16 ff. was a Jewish fast-day, and surmises the transposition of the liturgical occasion to a Christian day of penitence, possibly Holy Saturday. I have reached similar conclusions concerning the transposition of *Yom Kippur* to Holy Saturday in my *Sacred Bridge* (London-New York), pp. 81, 86 ff. As for rabbinic parallels to our verse, cf. J. Prigent in *Theol. Zeitschrift*, XIV (1958), fasc. 6.

[27] Cf. Lightfoot II, p. 106 ff., where the entire bibliography of the older sources is listed; also M. R. James, *The Lost Apocrypha of the OT* (London, 1936), p. 53 f. See also A. Resch, *Agrapha*, p. 154 ff. The two extant versions of

purpose does Clement use the quotation? In ch. 34 he admonishes the addressees "to be prompt in well-doing (ἀγαθοποιίαν)." For God will pay (ἀποδοῦναι) each a reward according to his work, (and the obedience to His will). Without much transition Clement then draws his reader's attention to "the multitude of His angels, how they stand ready and minister to His will." There follows a combination of Dan. 7:10 and Is. 6:3 — whereupon he again warns the faithful to gather in concord "in their conscience," closing his argument with the verse under discussion. Apparently he stresses the promise of a divine reward; but equally emphatically he denies that mortal eye and ear have perceived what the nature of this reward might be. Why does Clement conclude his vision of the heavenly *Qedusha* with this apocryphal *theologoumenon*?

I do not believe that Clement simply quoted Paul; aside from the textual deviation the verse is here inserted in a quite different framework. Supposing then that both authors made use of an (apocryphal) source, whether it was the Apocalypse of Elijah or simply a book of OT testimonies, is it possible to find the underlying reason for this denial of human knowledge concerning the Hereafter? Had anyone made claims to the contrary? Indeed, the books of Enoch, Jubilees, IV Esra all contain descriptions of eschatological rewards; so do — though much more cautiously — the Dead Sea Scrolls.[28] Is it thinkable that Clement polemicizes here against those apocalyptic writers of his own time, or at least against an apocalyptic interpretation of canonic texts? It does not seem impossible; for the author of our epistle appears as a responsible,

---

the apocryphon are in Hebrew (ed. Buttenwieser, 1897), and in Coptic (ed. Steindorff, 1899).

[28] In *Manual of Discipl.* IV:7; *Hodayot* VIII:10–14; *War-Scroll* XII:3 et passim. The talmudic literature also offers various interpretations of Is. 64:3–4; three of them by R. Chiya bar Aba, (in the name of R. Yochanan): a messianic one, an eschatological one, and one referring to the Hereafter, (b *Ber.* 34b): אבל לעלם הבא. עין לא ראתה אלהים זולתך etc. and the parallel passages *Sanh.* 99 a, *Shabb.* 63 a. A variant of it in *Ab. Zara* 65 a concludes the interpretation with an aggadic story about Raba and a heathen called Bar-Sheshak. The trend of the story is anti-apocalyptic and moralistic. On the other hand, see the remark of Rab in *Ber.* 17 a.

[9] HEBRAISMS IN PRIMA CLEMENTIS 801

sober-minded and prudent statesman, who does not prod the faithful ones into light-hearted, apocalyptic martyrdom, but emphasizes instead the need of steadfast faithfulness.

A similar correspondence with a Paulinic epistle, this time with Rom. 1:32, appears in Clem. 35:6; and again the similarity of text and the difference of intent let us surmise a common source available to both authors.[29]

As to the hotly debated *Qedusha* quotation itself, which is of great importance for the history of Christian liturgy, only a few words must suffice here.

In a recent study W. C. van Unnik has demonstrated the non-liturgical character of the passage in Clement. Although some of his premises are shaky, to say the least, he affords, we believe, a cogent and generally convincing argument. He senses clearly the logical gap between verses 6 and 7 of ch. 34, and, not too familiar with the structure of Jewish prayers, concludes that the verse following Dan. 7:10 and Is. 6:3 is an *ad hoc* exhortation suitable for a prayer-meeting, but holds no significance for the history of "fixed" liturgies. This verse (7) reads in van Unnik's new translation:

"Therefore, [noticing thus unity in multitude], we too in concord brought together (συναχθέντες) to one place by compliance to the Lord's will [and not by fear for the judgment], let us as from one mouth cry (βοήσωμεν πρὸς αὐτὸν ἐκτενῶς) [for help in our dangerous situation] unto Him with fervor in order that we may become [after the judgment] sharers in His great and glorious promises."[30]

---

[29] Cf. E. Peterson, *op. cit.*, p. 96, n. 4, where the author draws attention to the passage in *Test. Asher* VI:2, which also shows similarity with Clement's text.

[30] Cf. W. C. van Unnik, "I Clement 34 and the Sanctus," in *Vigiliae Christianae*, V (Amsterdam, 1951) p. 214 ff. The brackets indicate the author's added exegetical remarks. In his argumentation Unnik simplifies or misunderstands Elbogen's observations concerning the age of the liturgical usage of Is. 6:3. As *Tos. Sanh.* 37 b, and b *Ber.* 21 b (the speaker is R. Huna, a contemporary of R. Jehuda) clearly show, the *Qedusha* was a well-established institution early in the second century. Elbogen quotes all pertinent sources in the notes of his third edition. Prof. A. Stuiber (Bonn) was kind enough to stress in a personal communication to me the absence of the Thrice-Holy in the first

This interpretation of βοήσωμεν πρὸς αὐτόν κτλ., after translating συνείδησις with "compliance with the will of God" comes now very close to the meaning and the attitude of the *Qedusha d'Yotzer*, where the compliance with the will of God is symbolized by the "yoke of the kingdom of heaven" עול מלכות שמים willingly borne by the angels; this text did not exist in our present form at the time of Clement, but its ideas antedate him.

Whatever the significance of the *Qedusha* in Rev. 4:8, (which again in intent resembles the *Qedusha d'Yotzer*), it is not as clear in this case or even in Clement as van Unnik seems to believe.

According to rabbinic law the praise and sanctification of God must precede any prayer of supplication or thanksgiving, and one may conjecture that Clement followed this custom — a custom with which Paul was most familiar. (Cf. Ph. 4:5; I Thess. 5:16.) If this be the case, we might consider the *Sanctus* passage in Clement as a part of a *program* of prayer, rather than a prayer itself. Such strong leanings towards Jewish practices would again strengthen the assumption of Clement's Jewish origin.

Ad 39:2. The text reads: τί γὰρ δύναται θνητός; ἢ τίς ἰσχὺς γηγενοῦς; Both the general phraseology and the term γηγενής hark back to LXX; they also occur in classical Greek authors. In LXX the word simply corresponds with אדם;[31] but beneath this plain interpretation we fathom an older and more mythical significance of the word γηγενής = earth-born. The daily morning prayer contains a sentence מה צדקנו, מה ישועתנו, מה כוחנו, מה גבורתנו, מה נאמר לפניך ה' אלהינו... הלא כל הגברים כאין לפניך ואנשי השם כלא היו...[32] which E. Peterson links with Baruch 3:26,

---

Eucharistic service (in Hippolytos). This fact might support our conjecture that Clement gives in ch. 34 not a prayer, but a program of praying.

[31] Ps. 49:3 גם בני אדם גם בני איש is rendered οἵ τε γηγενεῖς καὶ οἱ υἱοὶ τῶν ἀνθρώπων. Cf. Lightfoot I, p. 118, n. 4.

[32] Cf. Elbogen, *Der Juedische Gottesdienst*, 3rd ed., 1931, p. 91, where these sentences are traced to R. Yochanan and Mar Samuel in b *Yoma* 87 b. E. Peterson, elaborating upon Lightfoot's interpretation, connects אנשי השם with the רפאים (LXX Prov. 3:26; 9:18), while Theodotion and Σ render it γίγαντες or θεομάχοι, In Peterson's opinion Baruch 3:26 οἱ γίγαντες οἱ

where the אנשי השם are the γίγαντες οἱ ὀνομαστοί. Indeed, shortly after this verse we encounter (3:29) an anti-apocalyptic passage of the same type which Clement had utilized before in 34:8 τίς ἀνέβη εἰς τὸν οὐρανὸν καὶ ἔλαβεν αὐτήν. We are inclined to believe that all these rhetoric questions are subtle attacks upon, or defenses against, some apocalyptic speakers of the time; perhaps also against an incipient *gnosis*.

Ad 46:2. The biblical דבק is generally expressed by the LXX and the *Koine* by κολλάω or κολλάομαι. The sentence for which Clement claims scriptural authority κολλᾶσθε τοῖς ἁγίοις, ὅτι οἱ κολλώμενοι αὐτοῖς ἁγιασθήσονται has more than one parallel in Talmudic and Midrashic literature, e.g. מי שהוא דבוק באחר : אוי להם לרשעים ודבקיהם, ואשריהם לצדיקים ולדבקיהם.[33] The negative formulation of the saying follows in the next verse, being a close paraphrase of the LXX rendition of Ps. 18:26 (Gr. 17:26). Again we are reminded of the morning prayer, where we read: והרחיקנו מאדם רע ומחבר רע. ודבקנו ביצר הטוב ובמעשים טובים, which can be traced back to a Tannaitic stratum of b *Ber.* 16 b. Even more closely akin to Clement's admonition are the passages of the Dead Sea Scrolls: לרחוק מכול רע ולדבוק בכול מעשי טוב: וכן משפט כל באי בריתו אשר לא יחזיקו באלה... לפוקדם לכלה ביד בליעל. (Manual I, 5, ed. Habermann p. 60, add Damascus Scroll, 8:1–2.)[34] Dr. S. Lieberman has kindly pointed out to me the rabbinic adage: -הדבק לשחין ויישת חן לך (*Sifre* II, sect. 6, ed. Finkelstein, p. 15, and parallels) which Clement might have paraphrased הדבק לקדושים ותתקדש. For other parallels, see S. Lieberman, *Hellenism in Jewish Palestine*, p. 216, with reference to Tertullian's *De orat.* 26.

Whether or not Clement was familiar with the literature of the

---

ὀνομαστοὶ οἱ ἀπ' ἀρχῆς, I. Cor. 1:18, the Hebrew morning prayer, and Clement all go back to the same source. See also Dead Sea Scrolls, Dam. II, 18, 19.

[33] Cf. *Tanchuma*, בראשית 21, where both the positive and negative consequences of adherence ("cleaving to") are assessed.

[34] Cf. D. Flusser, "The Dead Sea Scrolls and Pre-Paulinic Christianity," in *Scripta Hierosolymitana*, IV (Jerusalem 1958), p. 215 ff.; esp. p. 219; also Y. Yadin, the Dead Sea Scrolls and the Epistle to the Hebrews, *ibid.*, p. 36 ff.

Qumran sect, some of its ideas, common to the ethical thinking of contemporary Judaism, did certainly reach and impress him. The parallel ἁγίοις ἁγιασθήσονται is not to be found in the corresponding Hebrew sources; hence we may assume that most of Clement's knowledge of Scripture as well as of contemporary Jewish thought came from the Hellenized orbit of the Diaspora and its often syncretistic and sectarian synthesis of Rabbinic, Essenian, exoteric as well as esoteric, but generally non-apocalyptic ethics. Thus it is not surprising that the idea of 46:2 appears also in a series of early Christian canons, which Hilgenfeld named "The Two Ways" or "Judgment of Peter."[35]

II

When we examine the compact midrashic allusions in Clement, they appear in a quite different light than the supposedly biblical quotations. Two of these are quite conspicuous: the story of Rahab in ch. 12 and the reference to the sacrifice of Isaac in ch. 10:7 and 31:3.

Clement opens the case of Rahab with the words: "For her faith and hospitality Rahab the harlot was saved." He then proceeds to tell her story in accordance with the biblical account given in Jos. 2. Remarkable, however, are certain deviations: (1) he errs in his narration, when he says that Rahab lead the *pursuers* in the wrong direction, whereas in MT and LXX she directs the spies in the opposite direction;[36] (2) he lapses into Hebraisms, such as Γινώσκουσα γινώσκω ἐγώ, κ.τ.λ. The LXX has here simply ἐπίσταμαι; (3) he adds an allegorization of the scarlet thread: "And they proceeded (προσέθεντο) to give her a sign, that she should hang out from her house a scarlet thread, thereby showing beforehand that through the blood of the Lord there shall be redemption unto all them that believe and hope in God. Ye see, dearly beloved, not only faith, but prophecy is found in the woman."[37] Lighfoot conjectures here that Clement had the

[35] Cf. M. R. James, *op. cit.*, p. 88.
[36] Cf. Lightfoot II, p. 48, also W. Wrede, *op. cit.*, p. 67.
[37] Clement's logic is apparently confused here. If the allegorical significance

story from Heb. 11:31 and Jam. 2:25. None of these authors, however, praise her as a prophetess! On the other hand, we find to our surprise that Rahab is mentioned in the genealogy of Jesus (Matt. 1:4). Did Clement know this tradition? It is not probable, to say the least, since the evidence indicates that Clement was familiar with only a few *logia*, which were widely known long before the gospel of St. Matthew and its genealogy of Jesus. The only *logia* which are remembered, are contained in ch. 13:2 and in 46:8 f. The latter quotation combines Matt. 26:24, Luke 17:2, Matt. 18:6, Mk. 9:42, and Mk. 14:21.[38] Harnack explains the paucity of the *logia* by stressing the conservatism of the "*Lehrtradition*," which only reluctantly permitted words of Jesus to be coupled with passages from the OT.[39]

Undoubtedly the authors of Hebrews as well as of James, and certainly the editor of the Matth.-genealogy thought highly of Rahab. In the genealogy she is the only woman of the four mentioned in all, who did not *have to be included*: Tamar, (mother of Perez); the "wife of Uriah" (mother of Solomon); Ruth (great-grandmother of David), were indispensable, if the Davidic descent of Jesus was to be established. All of them happen to have been outstanding personalities as well. Rahab was neither. Thus we must ask now, whence James, Hebrews, and the genealogy had the tradition of Rahab the heroine, and Clement and his followers the conception of the harlot as seeress and great mother?[40]

of the scarlet thread constitutes the evidence of Rahab's prophetic gift, it must be observed that in both the MT and in Clement's own account it was the *spies* who suggested the use of the scarlet thread. The midrash is, as we shall see later, well aware of this circumstance.

[38] Cf. Harnack, *op. cit.*, p. 110: "The deviation from Matt. and Luke are considerable."

[39] Cf. Harnack, *op. cit.*, p. 74. The new interpretation of the Rahab-passage in A. W. Ziegler, *op. cit.*, pp. 77–84, whereby the mantic gifts of Rahab are juxtaposed with those of the Delphian Pythia, is interesting enough, but hardly convincing.

[40] Both the prophetic character of Rahab and the christological interpretation of the scarlet thread occur in Justin, *Dial.* # 111, and afterwards in Irenaeus, Barnabas, Origen, and later patristic authors. Cf. Lightfoot, II, p. 49–50, n. 19. The puritan Harnack observes: (*op. cit.*, p. 109, n. 12): "*Das*

This image of Rahab is familiar indeed to the Aggadic tradition. She is there a seeress, a mother of prophets and of kings. In the following we quote the most important references.

I. Rahab was the mother of seven kings, hence the ancestress of David and the Messiah, Son of David: אבל רחב הזונה נתקבלה בתשובה. ר׳ אליעזר ב׳ יעקב א׳ למה נקרא שמה רחב. etc. ויצאו ממנה שבעה מלכים ושמונה נביאים.[41]

II. She became the wife of Joshua and the ancestress of eight prophets and of the prophetess Hulda.[42]

III. The covenant with Yonadab, the son of Rahab, was greater than the covenant God made with David.[43]

IV. She was the founder of the house of Ashbea, (I Ch. 4:21), and the ancestress of the prophets Jeremiah, Helkiah, Zeraiah, Machzariah, Baruch, Neraiah, Hanamel, and Shallum, also of Hulda the prophetess.[44]

V. Among her descendants were also Ezekiel and Buzi.[45]

VI. Her daughter married into priesthood, and it is said of her: לכך נאמר שלום על ישראל כלם שמצינו ברחב הזונה וכו׳.[46]

VII. Tamar's second son was called Zerah; ... the two, Perez and Zerah, were sent out as spies by Joshua. The scarlet thread which Rahab bound in her window ... was received from Zerah. It was the scarlet thread that the midwife had bound, at his birth, upon his hand, to distinguish him from his twin brother.[47]

In addition to the main lines of this "sacred gossip," as it might be termed, there are even more phantastic legends about Rahab

Gewerbe und die Luege des Weibes genieren Clemens so wenig wie Jacobus, den Verfasser des Hebraeerbriefs und Justin..."

[41] Cf. *Ps.-Pirqe R. Eliezer* (in *Seder Elijahu Zuta*), ed. Friedmann (Vienna, 1904), p. 37, *perek* 3; cf. with it b *Meg.* 14 b, according to which Joshua "stooped down" when he married Rahab.

[42] Cf. *Sifre* Numbers, 78, ed. Friedmann (Vienna, 1864).

[43] Cf. *Mekilta*, ed. Lauterbach, Amalek, p. 187 (ch. 4).

[44] Cf. *Sifre*, # 78, (p. 52), ed. Friedmann (Vienna, 1864).

[45] Cf. *Sifre Zuta*, 75, ed. Horovitz (Breslau, 1910).

[46] Cf. *Bamidbar R.*, ed. Vilna 1887, *perek* 8 (end).

[47] Cf. Cf. *Midrash haggadol*, I, ed. Schechter, 579 (Cambridge, 1902).

extant in the various Midrashim; one of them connects her with the Rechabites because of the similarity of the respective names.

Of the Sages named as conveyors of the tradition concerning Rahab we name here R. Eliezer b. Jacob, R. Elazar b. Shammua, R. Juda b. Ilai, R. Nathan, R. Shimon, R. Alexander; they all belong to Tannaitic and early Amoraic generations. Inasmuch as most of them transmitted older material, recognizable by the plethora of parallel passages, (to which we could add at least five or six more), and also by its incorporation in the Epistles to the Hebrews, to James, and in the Matt.-genealogy, we are clearly dealing here with an old, certainly pre-Christian stratum of Midrashic tradition.

Aside from the glorification of the prostitute — a cause not easily championed by puritanical rabbis — we find a particularly interesting tradition in *Ruth Rabba* II, 1, where Rahab's descendants are identified with the clan of Shela, the son of Juda, who founded the families of fine linen workers and embroiderers (I Chr. 4:21). These families worked for the Temple. It is in this connection that we are reminded of the apocryphal gospels, esp. of the *Protevangelium Jacobi*, the oldest of them. This apocryphon tells that young Mary worked as an embroiderer, both before and after her betrothal to Joseph, in the precincts of the Temple.[48] Where does the legend of the weaving vestals in the Temple originate? The Talmudic testimony on this point is most enlightening. According to b *Hull.* 90 b, b *Ketub.* 106 a, b *Yoma* 71 b, a number of highly trained ladies occupied themselves regularly with the weaving and embroidering of the *parachot* of the Temple.[49] These ladies worked within the precincts of the Temple and had a special

[48] Cf. C. de Tischendorf, *Evangelia apocrypha*, sec. ed. (Leipzig, 1876) p. 20 ff.; also introduction p. XII f. See also W. Michaelis, *Die Apokryphen zum NT* (Bremen, 1956) p. 80 ff., and M. R. James, *The Apocryphal NT* (Oxford, 1955) p. 43; and K. L. Schmidt, *Kanonische und Apokryphe Evangelien* (Basel 1944) ch. 1, pp. 9, 10.

[49] Cf. S. Krauss, *Talmudische Archaeologie*, vol. I, p. 570, n. 321 (Leipzig, 1910) where all talmudic and later rabbinic sources are given. Very dramatically describes the *Pesikta Rabbati* the self-sacrifice of the weaving virgins of the Temple in *Pis.* 26.

overseer to direct them. Thus, the often disputed passages of the *Protevangelium Jacobi* seem to be vindicated.[50] Both the stories of Rahab's descendents and of Mary's youth in the Temple are founded upon a tradition once well known, which the editor of the Matth.-genealogy and other Christian authors freely utilized. Clement, who was familiar with the epistles to the Hebrews and of James, seems to have known the Aggadic concept of Rahab as seeress and mother of kings, of which the other two sources say nothing. Here we encounter the first unquestionable dependence of Clement upon post-Biblical, and especially upon Midrashic sources.

Another Midrashic element of considerable interest is Clement's allusion to the sacrifice of Isaac. We quote his text in English and, where necessary, in Greek:

I Clement, 10:7.

"Because of his faith and hospitality a son was given him in his old age, and in his obedience he offered him (προσήνεγκεν) as a sacrifice to God (θυσίαν τῷ θεῷ) on the mountain which He showed him."

I Clement, 31:3.

"Isaac in confident knowledge of the future was gladly brought himself as a sacrifice." (γινώσκων τὸ μέλλον ἡδέως προσήγετο θυσία.)

We also find a definite assertion that the sacrifice of Isaac was completed in Heb. 11:17, a strange passage indeed: "By faith Abraham, when he was tested, offered up, (προσενήνοχεν) Isaac, and he, who had received the promise, offered (προσέφερεν) his only son...." As Clement quotes Hebrews more than once, this epistle may have been his source of doctrine concerning Isaac's consummated sacrifice; but this does not fully explain Clement's stress of Isaac's foreknowledge.[51]

A great deal of the Midrashic tradition which underlies the

[50] Cf. M. R. James, *The Apocryphpal New Testament* (Oxford, 1955), p. 43, and S. Lieberman, *op. cit.*, p. 167 ff.

[51] This idea of Isaac's prophetic gift can be traced to midrashic tradition, as will be demonstrated *infra*.

consummation of Isaac's sacrifice is collected and interpreted in S. Spiegel's penetrating study מאגדות העקדה.[52] The crucial passage contained therein occurs in the *Midrash Haggadol*, 360, to the opening of Gen. 22:19:

וישב אברהם... ויצחק היכן הוא, אלא אמר ר׳ אלעזר ב׳ פדת: "אף על פי שלא מת יצחק מעלה עליו הכתוב כאלו מת ואפרו מוטל על גבי המזבח, לכך נאמר "וישב אברהם...".[53]

To this interpretation the remark in b *Seb*. 62a should be added: ור׳ יצחק נפחא אמר: אפרו של יצחק ראו שמונה באותו מקום. In later tradition, Isaac was "transported" by God and spent three years in the Garden of Eden, (a euphemism for death) and then he returned alive.[54] In spite of the fact that this "uncanonical," yet often repeated story of the sacrificed Isaac is quoted in Strack-Billerbeck, Commentary to the NT, and also in D. Lerch's study *Isaaks Opferung*, the passages Hebr. 11:17 as well as the corresponding ones in I Clement have been overlooked, as far as I can see, by many NT scholars.

Yet even the assumption of Clement's familiarity with the Rabbinic tradition through Hebr. cannot fully explain his suggestion that Isaac had foreknowledge of a "happy ending;" nor does it adequately account for the prophetic qualities and venerability attributed by Clement to Rahab. Nor is this all. In addition to Clement's post-Biblical Hebraisms and his familiarity with certain Midrashim which are not extant in Hellenistic Judaism, we must also try to interpret the undeniable resemblance of some of Clement's closing prayer to certain portions of the *Amida*.

III

Since Lightfoot had drawn attention to the kinship of the paraenetic prayer (ch. 59–61) with the *Tefilla*, most later scholars — not all! — were wont to consider this part of the epistle a previously

---

[52] In the Alexander Marx-*Festschrift* (New York, 1950) p. 471 ff.; Comp. S. Lieberman *op. cit.*, p. 162, nn. 73–75 *ibid*.

[53] R. Eleazar b. Pedat, d. 279, was an *Amora* of the second generation, a disciple of Rab.

[54] Also *Pirqe de R. Eliezer* 31, (16b) in the name of R. Judah. Cf. Also Strack-Billerbeck, III, p. 746, and D. Lerch, *op. cit.*, p. 43f, and p. 8–9.

fixed segment of a Jewish homily or even a direct legacy of the Hellenistic Synagogue. Harnack goes so far as to trace certain phrases, such as the expression ἀρχεγόνος (59:3) to gnostic influence. He relates additional unspecified allusions to ideas derived from mystery-cults.[55] However, he is fully aware of the Jewish basis of the prayer. Much more detailed are E. Petersons's remarks, which view the prayer plainly as an intercessary oration of Hebrew (not Hellenistic) origin.[56]

We are more concerned with the deviations from the Hebrew *Vorlage* than with correspondences with it; for these deviations should indicate the trend of thought which Clement pursued, and hence the degree of his dependence upon or independence from these sources.

The prayer opens with an invocation of "the Name," the "original source of all creation," uses the familiar Hebrew metaphor "eyes of our heart" and confirms "that Thou alone art the highest in the highest and remainest holy among the holy." The preceding verse (59:2) contains as a preamble the "supplication that the Creator of the Universe" (ὁ δημιουργὸς τῶν ἁπάντων) may guard unhurt the number of His elect that has been numbered in all the world through His beloved servant Jesus Christ, through whom He called us from darkness to light, from ignorance (ἀπὸ ἀγνωσίας) to the "full knowledge of His Name" (εἰς ἐπίγνωσιν δόξης ὀνόματος αὐτοῦ).

The three invocations of "the Name" are, it goes without saying, a direct legacy of the Synagogue. Conspicuous in the invocation is also the reference to the "elect" (ἐκλεκτῶν), which has here a peculiarly sectarian ring. Aside from Rev. 7:4 ff, where a similar idea of the "elect remnant" kindles a wide eschatological phantasmagoria, it is mainly the *Qumran* documents, where the term בחירים plays such an eminent role.[57]

Does Clement use this term (as also in 2:4) simply as "the"

---

[55] Cf. Harnack, *op. cit.*, p. 119–20.

[56] Cf. E. Peterson, *op. cit.*, p. 111, n. 14; p. 115, n. 30; p. 179.

[57] The biblical בחיר is consistently translated in the LXX by ἐκλεκτός e. g. Ps. 106:23; 89:4; Is. 43:20; Ps. 105:6, 43. (all MT) As for the DSS, see Habermann's *Concordance* (Jerusalem, 1959) *ad verbum* בחירי, ובחירי, לבחירי etc.

LXX-designation of God's elect, or does he pit here one set of elect (the Christian) against another (the *Qumran* Jews)? The context seems to favor the first assumption; yet the sectarian overtone remains discernible, whatever the interpretation. The general tenor of the invocation is plainly of Jewish vintage. Lightfoot's comparison of these passages with the *Amida* have retained their validity to the present.[58] The most characteristic and revealing deviations seem to be:

59:3 (end)"... Thou dost raise up the humble and abase the lofty, thou makest rich and makest poor, Thou dost slay and makest alive, Thou alone art the finder of spirits and art God of all flesh ... Thou dost multiply nations upon earth and hast chosen out from them all those that love thee through Jesus Christ, Thy beloved servant...," closing δι' οὗ ἡμᾶς ἐπαίδευσας, ἡγίασας, ἐτίμησας. The intercession through Christ appears here not only superfluous, but artificially added, as in ch. 20, where a similar passage is called "glued on" by Harnack.[59]

59:4 "We beseech thee, Master, to be our '*help and succour.*' Save those of us, who are in affliction, have mercy on the lowly, raise the fallen, ...Succour (ἀντιλήπτορα ἡμῶν), this is the equivalent of מגני in Ps. 119:114. The Pseudo-Clementine liturgy knows this term, too, (VIII, 12, obviously quoted from the epistle), but uses for מגן אברהם πρωτόμαχε [or πρόμαχε] 'Ἀβραάμ. At the end of the verse the name of Christ is again "glued on," interrupting a chain of Scriptural quotations, esp. II Kings 19:19 + Ps. 100:3.[60] On the other hand, Clement follows the practice of the Synagogue by starting his prayer with praise, continuing with supplication, (60:2–3), and by closing it with thanksgiving and a formal doxology (61:3). Verse 60:1 (ὁ ἀγαθὸς ἐν τοῖς ὁρωμένοις) is, according to Lightfoot II, p. 176, inspired by *Sap. Salomonis* 13:1 καὶ ἐκ τῶν ὁρωμένων ἀγαθῶν. The continuation of the verse, however, contains neither a parallelism nor an antithesis. Hence I suggest the emendation ὡρισμένοις —πεποιθόσιν ἐπὶ σέ "Thou art good to those who are bound [by Thy law], faithful to those who trust

[58] *Op. cit.*, I, p. 393 ff.   [59] *Op. cit.*, p. 111.   [60] *Op. cit.*, p. 111.

in thee," which shows kinship to the 13th *berakha* of the *Tefilla* (על הצדיקים).[61]

60:4. Even the English translation shows the surprising *non sequitur* transition to 61:

"Give concord and peace to us and to all that dwell on the earth, as Thou didst give to our fathers who called on Thee in holiness with faith and truth, and grant that we may be obedient to Thy almighty and glorious Name, and *to our rulers and governors upon the earth*."

This obviously added and padded ending leads to the extensive prayer for the Roman government, which was apparently composed *ad hoc*, whereas the preceding material is derived from familiar synagogue tradition.

And yet, this dignified recognition of a government profoundly hostile to Christianity, is hardly of the same spirit as Paul's principle (Rom. 13:1–3):

"Let every person be subject to the governing authorities. For there is no authority except from God, and those that exist have been instituted by God. Therefore he who resists the authorities resists what God has appointed, and those who resist will incur judgment. For rulers are not a terror to good conduct, but to bad... ."[62]

Clement's attitude towards the government is closer to the thought of the Rabbis, as we encounter it in b *Ber*. 58 a. Even the traditional *berakha* at the sight of a monarch is more akin to Clement's ideas than Paul's basically pessimistic attitude. We might, to quote but one instance, consider R. Shela a man closer to the spirit of the Roman author — as is easily seen by comparing R. Shela's exposition of the God-given rank of a sovereign with Clement's prayer in ch. 61. The similarity is more one of thought than of expression.[63]

---

[61] Clement's ἀγαθὸς ἐν τοῖς ὁρωμένοις has a certain similarity to the saying of R. Eliezer b. Hyrcanos : עשה רצונך בשמים ממעל ותן נחת רוח ליראיך בארץ והטוב בעיניך עשה in *Tos. Ber*. 3, 7.

[62] The tragic consequences of a too narrow interpretation of this doctrine have become notorious in the history of Western civilization, especially noteworthy in recent German history.   [63] Cf. b *Ber*. 58 a.

Clement 61.	Ber. 58a.
Thou, Master, hast given the power of sovereignty to them through thy excellent and inexpressible might, that we may know the glory and honor (δόξαν καὶ τιμὴν הגדולה והגבורה) given to them by Thee .... For Thou, heavenly Master, King of eternity, (βασιλεῦ τῶν αἰώνων = מלך העולם) hast given to the sons of men glory and honor and power over the things which are on the earth....	"לך, ה' הגדולה" זו מעשה בראשית...(Job 9:10=) והגבורה זו יציאת מצרים... (Ex. 14:31) והתפארת... והנצח... וההוד... (Num. 21:14)כי כל בשמים ובארץ ... לך ה' הממלכה (Jud. 5:20) והמתנשא לכל ... (Ex. 17:16) לראש...(Ez. 38:3; 39:1).

Even the practical and authoritative advice to the malcontents in Clement Ch. 55 and 63, to go into exile voluntarily, has its parallel in *Ber.* 56a, where we read: אמר, איקום ואגלי; דאמר מר: גלות מכפרת עון (cf. *Sanh.* 37, b). Of course, the punishment of being exiled was at that time generally practiced, especially among the Romans. Interesting is here only the (non existing) Scriptural reference that (voluntary) exile atones for sin.[64]

After a genuinely Christian doxology, built in magnificent rhetorical language (ch. 64), Clement closes the epistle with the identification of the messengers and a brief doxological benediction.

We ought to be able by now to reach certain conclusions concerning (a) the genuine unity of the document, (b) possible sources of the author, and finally (c) the personality and nationality of the author.

---

[64] Clement bases his suggestion of voluntary exile upon gentile authors; the מר in the talmudic reference alludes to R. Juda b. Chiya.

IV

It will be more practical to decide questions (a) and (c) after having investigated the possible sources or *Vorlagen* of the epistle. Aside from the LXX we noted evidently Rabbinic elements in the Midrashic portions, and, not quite as certainly, apocryphal, yet anti-apocalyptic, elements; finally we noted the Hebraisms of a few passages and the closing prayer with its synagogal phraseology. Yet all of these elements — except linguistic Hebraisms — have been smoothly incorporated in the Greek language and style. There remains the question if the Midrashim were accessible to Clement in a Hellenized form, a question which this writer is unable to answer.[65]

What are the Christian sources of Clement? Here we are in full agreement with the ideas of Drs. Yadin and Flusser.[66] The latter gives an entire list of theological terms occurring with equal significance in the Epistle to the Hebrews, in Paulinic, apostolic, and subapostolic literature. He states, "The terms ... were evidently coined in the Hebrew language (such as "spirit of grace," "holy ghost," "the elect ones," etc.) and passed in a Hebrew medium into Christianity. They passed as true meaningful theological terms, not as empty or vague locutions." And: "It is highly improbable that each of the NT authors... was directly and independently influenced by the Qumran sectarians.... Therefore we must suppose that there existed a stratum of Christian thought which was especially influenced by Sectarian ideas, and that John the Evangelist, Paul, and the authors of most other NT epistles based themselves on the theological achievements of this stratum."[67]

To this theory we might add that Clement found these *theolo-*

---

[65] cf. Th. Schermann, *Griech. Zauberpapyri, und das Gemeindegebet in I. Klemens-Brief*, (in T. & U., 3 Reihe, 4. BD.) Leipzig 1909, p. 50. *"Zur Beleuchtung der Religionsgeschichtlichen Stellung der altchristlichen Dankgebete sei noch auf Philo hingewiesen, in dessen Eroerterungen... sich die meisten Gedanken Klements schon finden."*

[66] See *supra* n. 34.   [67] D. Flusser, *op. cit.*, p. 216.

goumena already in smooth Hellenistic Greek, which only seldom betrays its Hebraic origin. However, we consider it improbable that the Paulinic literature, as we know it, was fully available to Clement, and that he identified himself with Paul's philosophy and theology. If nothing else, the high respect in which he speaks of the Jewish nation and its institutions, would strongly testify against Paulinic thinking.[68] E. Peterson has shown the Jewish attitude to the problem of Israel and the Nations and demonstrated its transformation in early Christianity.

After these deliberations it will be easier to consider the basic unity of our document. We believe that the epistle presupposes a Jewish-Hellenistic stratum of *theologoumena*, some Midrashic knowledge, and a Christological, not necessarily Paulinic, foundation, which seems to be closely linked to the ideas of the epistle to the Hebrews. Enclosed in this Christological basis are not only ideas of the Qumran sectarians, but *also theological and mental reservations and defenses against them*. These three strata were connected by the hand of a statesman and very able homilist.

That the author was familiar with *Testimony-books*, was already indicated; but it is quite instructive to investigate the mentioning of Jesus Christ in the various chapters of the epistle. Sometimes his name appears to be "glued on" at the end of an older passage or prayer; sometimes he is invoked at the very beginning of an otherwise non-Christian argument; and frequently his name and person are organically and closely involved in the text and ideas of a chapter. In the following we give a tabulation of the occurrence of the name Jesus, as it appears in the epistle.

The tabulation shows the existence of three "blocks" in the text, which have no Christological significance at all: ch. 8–12; 25–32; and the prayer 59:2–61:2 with an added and inorganic reference to Christ at the very end. Of these blocks the first one contains a simple OT exegesis of didactic character, the second a universalistic and allegorical defense of the doctrine of immortality and resurrection, cauched in liturgical language, the third a paraphrase of a synagogal prayer.

[68] Cf. esp. W. Wrede, *op. cit.* p. 95 ff.; and recently E. Peterson, *op. cit.*, p. 51 ff.

	A		B	C	
	BEGINNING OF CHAPTER		BULK OF CHAPTER	END OF CHAPTER	
	(a) Necessary for the argument	(b) Not necessary		(a) Necessary	(b) Not necessary
	Praescript				
			1		
	2				
			3		
			5		
			7		
			12		
			13		
	16		16	16	
	17				
				20	
			21		
			32	32	
	36		36		
					38
	42		42		
	44		44		
	47		47		(47)
			48		
		49	49	49	
			50		50
			54		
		57			
			58	58	
	59		59		59
				61	
	64				
				65	

Yet even in those chapters, where Jesus is mentioned, he does not appear as God, or as One with God. Wrede has sensed this fact and comments upon it: "All these arguments cannot destroy the impression that Christ was not a living, organic part of the author's faith. There is for Clement no religious attitude (*Verhalten*) which would directly refer to Christ, and that would be deprived of its character, if one does not associate it with Christ. It is an absolutely correct observation... by Ritschl that Clement expresses faith solely with reference to God, not to Christ."[69]

We believe to be justified in assuming that Clement used at least some Jewish sources first hand; *they were more or less fixed and needed only Christological interpretation or an appended Christian doxology to make them acceptable to the early Church.* This situation elicits the question of the author's nationality. *For* his Judeo-Christian origin speak: familiarity with Midrashim; the term "the elect," a few Hebraisms of the text; the respect of the author for Jewish institutions such as Kingdom or Temple; the reluctance of identifying Jesus with God himself; and the absence of all anti-Jewish polemics. *Against* his Judeo-Christian origin speak: the total silence about the problem of Jewish law and observance; the absence of remarks concerning the Paulinic thesis of the nullification of the Law; Clement's trinitarian allusions, (although the concept is nowhere fully developed); and the author's identification with the Apostles (but also with "our fathers," such as Abraham and Isaac). Of the positive reasons two were *argumenta e silentio*; also two of the negative reasons. If we disregard them equally — which seems not unfair — the remaining arguments speak strongly for a Judeo-Christian author, who maintained some tenuous relations with Jews, (perhaps sectarians), and was well versed in Judeo-Christian literature, especially the epistle to the Hebrews.

It might also be added that the author of an epistle which undoubtedly had a concrete and actual motivation felt no reason for taking a stand to the question concerning the Law or the Paulinic Doctrine. For in Corinth the definite split between Synagogue and Church had already taken place in Paul's time, if we consider the Acts of Apostles a historically reliable document; in 18:5-17 — we find the report of the schism.[70] As we know of the existence of an orthodox Jewish community in Corinth centuries

---

[69] W. Wrede, *op. cit.*, p. 103.

[70] For the correct interpretation of the passage and its revision in the *Codex Bezae*, cf. W. M. Ramsay, *The Church in the Roman Empire* (London, 1893), p. 158.

later, the Christian congregation of Corinth was obviously not Judeo-Christian in character or doctrine; hence Clement would hardly have been understood by the gentile Christians of Corinth, had he discoursed at length on the problem of the Law in Christianity. Instead, he assumed only a certain knowledge of the OT as he might justly expect from the presbyters of his church. If we find elements and ideas in Clement's epistle, which are remote or apocryphal, we must not fail to observe that all these more obscure sources are only of secondary importance for his argument; in fact, he might have done just as well without them. As they "lay in the air" of his time and were probably the subjects of discussion in his circle, they found their way into his epistle.[71]

---

[71] For numerous suggestions and hints I am indebted to my friends and colleagues Dr. E. Kiev and the late Dr. A. Kahana of the Hebrew Union College — Jewish Institute of Religion, and to my dear and patient friend, Rabbi Dudley Weinberg of Milwaukee.

MORAL JUDGMENT AND VOLUNTARY ACTION

by MORTON WHITE

ALTHOUGH AN ENORMOUS amount has been said in the history of philosophy about the nature of moral judgment and the nature of voluntary action, and although it has often been asserted that a moral judgment about a human action implies that the action is voluntary, the meaning of the word 'implies' in this context is rarely explained with as much care as it deserves. The subject is not only interesting in its own right but takes on extra significance because some philosophers have suggested that we can infer from some moral judgments that the will is in some sense free. According to such a view, a moral judgment of an action implies a statement that the judged action is voluntary, so that, from an acceptable moral judgment as a premise one should be able to deduce, and in this way prove, the statement that we perform voluntary actions at least on some occasions. I think this argument is fallacious for reasons which deserve serious attention. I shall try to present these reasons in this paper and then go on to propose an alternative view of the relationship between moral judgments and statements in which an action is said to be voluntary. Having briefly treated the matter elsewhere,[1] I now wish to probe more deeply into the relationship between the moral judgment and the statement of the voluntariness of the action in an effort to see what is meant when it is said that moral judgments about actions imply that the actions are voluntary. My basic conviction is that this implication is not logical implication and that that is

---

[1] In my *Religion, Politics and the Higher Learning* (Cambridge, Mass., 1959), pp. 79–81.

why we cannot validly offer a "proof" of the freedom of the will like that previously mentioned. For this reason I think that G. E. Moore once spoke misleadingly when he said that the proposition that an action is morally wrong *entails* that the agent could have made a choice different from the one he did make.[2] It is just such a use of 'entails' that may lead some philosophers into wrongly supposing that they can prove the freedom of the will in the manner previously described. In the pages to follow I shall first try to show why this relationship is not that of logical implication or entailment, and then try to say more positively what the relationship is.

In advance of presenting my argument I should point out that I shall limit myself to one kind of moral judgment and to one notion of voluntariness as applied to actions. I shall be concerned with those moral judgments in which it is either asserted that a given action is right or that it is wrong. Strictly speaking, therefore, I shall not be concerned with the telegraphically formulated philosophical doctrine that 'Ought' implies 'Can,' but rather with its sister-doctrines that 'Right' and 'Wrong' imply 'Can.' I should also add that I do not think we can automatically transfer the conclusions reached in this paper to the dictum that 'Ought' implies 'Can.' But that is another story, too long to be told here.

1. In order to discuss the main issues concretely I shall use two statements as examples. My first illustrative statement, which I shall call (*a*), is, 'Booth acted wrongly in shooting Lincoln.' And I shall construe it as equivalent in meaning to, 'Booth acted wrongly when he shot Lincoln,' 'Booth's action in shooting Lincoln was wrong,' and 'It was wrong for Booth to have shot Lincoln.' My second statement, which I shall call (*b*), is 'If just before shooting Lincoln, Booth had chosen not to shoot Lincoln, he would not have shot him.'

As we have seen, there is a temptation to construe the relationship between (*a*) and (*b*) as logical implication or entailment. But this, I think, is a temptation to be avoided. It does not seem to

---

[2] See *The Philosophy of G. E. Moore*, ed. P. A. Schilpp, (Evanston, Illinois, 1942), p. 624.

me that the statement, 'Booth acted wrongly when he shot Lincoln,' or any of its equivalents, entails the statement, 'If just before shooting Lincoln, Booth had chosen not to shoot Lincoln, he would not have shot Lincoln.' And I might add that *a fortiori*, statement (*a*) does not entail the conjunction of this last statement, (*b*), and the statement that Booth could have chosen not to shoot Lincoln.

Although I have serious philosophical doubts about the analysis of entailment and related notions, I shall assume for purposes of this discussion that those doubts might be removed. And so, granting that we can say truly — if not analyze clearly what we mean when we say — that the statement 'Jones is a bachelor' entails the statement 'Jones is unmarried,' or that the premises of a syllogism entail the conclusion, or that the statement 'this is scarlet' entails the statement 'this is red,' I do not believe we can say that the relationship between (*a*) and (*b*) is the same as that which holds in these other cases. None of the usual tests that some philosophers apply with confidence in these standard cases give the usual results in the case of (*a*) and (*b*). Conjoin (*a*) and the denial of (*b*) and you do not seem to "involve yourself in contradiction." Nor is it easy to see that (*b*) expresses "part of the meaning" of (*a*). Moreover, I am not aware of any other test for the presence of a relation of entailment which will do the trick. Note also that it is possible to say truly of a man who has done something wrong: 'It was wrong of him to do it, but he couldn't help doing it.' And when we say this we are not normally accused of contradicting ourselves even though we are conjoining statement (*a*) and a denial of its voluntariness in the sense of statement (*b*).

2. Next, I wish to offer an argument which is most easily expressed in logical terminology. If (*a*) were to entail (*b*), the denial of (*b*) would entail the denial of (*a*). But some moral philosophers hold that the moral judgment which is a denial of (*a*), namely, 'Booth was *not* wrong in shooting Lincoln,' also implies (*b*). If they construe both of these entailments as logical implications, they are committed to the view that the denial of (*b*) logically implies both the denial of (*a*) and the denial of the denial of (*a*).

This in itself indicates that there is something queer about the view that 'Not Wrong' and 'Wrong' entail 'Voluntary.'

3. Lastly, I mention an argument which I find less convincing than some philosophers might find it, but it is worth mentioning in a general airing of this subject. If a moral statement like (*a*) entails a statement of voluntariness like (*b*), and if you construe a statement of voluntariness like (*b*) as an 'is'-statement about an action, then you must conclude that the denial of an 'is'-statement entails the denial of a 'wrong'-statement. It is plausible to suppose that those philosophers who think that moral statements are not deducible from 'is'-statements would also say they are not deducible from 'is not'-statements. In that case, as I have said, this argument should carry weight with them. My own hesitation about using this argument (as opposed to mentioning it) stems from doubts about its basic assumption — about the non-deducibility of moral statements from 'is'-statements. But it is certainly an argument that should move the minds of those who speak glibly of something called the naturalistic fallacy.

Before proceeding, I wish to say that of all the arguments I have offered or mentioned, the most compelling in my opinion is the first: I simply do not see how we can say that statement (*a*) contains as part of its meaning what is asserted in (*b*). I simply do not see how we can say that a man who asserts (*a*) and denies (*b*) involves himself in a contradiction. Nor do I see that something that has been called "pragmatic implication" is involved here. Saying 'Booth acted wrongly but he couldn't help it' is not like saying 'It is raining but I don't believe that it is.'

4. It might be argued, therefore, that the voluntariness of an action in the sense of statement (*b*) as construed earlier is a *presupposition* of statement (*a*). I mean 'presupposition' in the sense of P. F. Strawson's *Introduction to Logical Theory*. Strawson says that it is the relation which holds between a statement like 'All of Queen Elizabeth's children are asleep' and the statement that Queen Elizabeth has children.[3] The former does not entail the

---

[3] P. F. Strawson, *Introduction to Logical Theory* (New York, 1952), pp. 175–179.

latter; therefore, the denial of the latter does not entail the denial of the former. This encourages an analogous view of the relationship between our statements (*a*) and (*b*). On such a view of the relationship between them, the voluntariness of the action would be entailed, not by a moral statement, but rather by the assertion that the moral statement is true-or-false, the point being that if the action in question were not voluntary, the question of the truth or falsity of the moral statement about the action would not arise.

I believe that this is a step in the right direction. However, it does not of itself bring out a cardinal difference between presupposing that the children of Queen Elizabeth exist when you state that all of them are asleep, and presupposing that an action is voluntary when you state that it is wrong. And this difference must be seen if we are properly to understand the relationship between our statements (*a*) and (*b*). Before trying to describe this difference, I want to say that from the point of view of my argument one of the chief virtues of construing the relationship between (*a*) and (*b*) as presupposition is that it shows why we cannot *prove* that there are some voluntary actions merely by asserting a true moral statement about an action and then deducing that the action about which we make the statement is voluntary. Even if Queen Elizabeth's having children is a necessary condition for making true-or-false statements by the use of the sentence, 'All of Queen Elizabeth's children are asleep,' we cannot *prove* that she has children by deducing their existence either from this statement or from the statement that we have made a true-or-false statement by uttering those words on a given occasion. To show that she has children we must engage in biological investigation, and no amount of metalinguistic assertion can take its place. In the same way, to show that Booth's action has the characteristic of voluntariness expressed in our statement (*b*) we must engage in a kind of investigation which cannot be replaced by a deductive argument of the kind previously considered.

5. Having said that the relationship between our statements (*a*) and (*b*) is that of presupposition rather than entailment, I now wish to describe what I have called a cardinal difference between

the two examples of presupposition considered so far — the one in which we presuppose the voluntariness of an action and the other in which we presuppose the existence of Queen Elizabeth's children. To see this difference it is well to consider the difference between saying that our statement (*a*) presupposes the *voluntariness* of Booth's shooting of Lincoln, and saying that the same statement presupposes his *shooting* of Lincoln. I am assuming, of course, that there is a difference between performing (or failing to perform) an action, and performing (or failing to perform) it voluntarily. On this assumption it would be proper to say that Booth shot Lincoln even if he had been hypnotized into shooting him, in which case we would say that he did not shoot Lincoln voluntarily. Therefore we may think of Booth's shooting of Lincoln as something which is presupposed by the statement that his shooting of Lincoln was a wrong action.

What I want to bring out here is that a truism underlies the statement that 'Booth acted wrongly in shooting Lincoln' presupposes Booth's having shot Lincoln, whereas no such truism underlies the statement that 'Booth acted wrongly in shooting Lincoln' presupposes Booth's having shot Lincoln voluntarily. The truism which underlies the presupposition of the existence of the action, as in the case of the existence of Queen Elizabeth's children, is that you can not make a statement that is true-or-false if there is nothing for it to be true of or false of. But I do not think it truistic to say that you can not make a moral statement like (*a*), which is true-or-false of Booth's action, if his action is not voluntary in the sense expressed in statement (*b*) above. When Strawson is considering the illustration of a man who uses a sentence like 'All of Queen Elizabeth's children are asleep,' Strawson says it would be "incorrect (or deceitful) for him to use this sentence" unless (1) he thinks he is referring to some children whom he thinks to be asleep; (2) he thinks that Queen Elizabeth has children; and (3) he thinks that the children he is referring to are Queen Elizabeth's.[4] But there is no reason to suppose that it would

---

[4] P. F. Strawson, *Introduction to Logical Theory*, p. 175.

be *deceitful* for a man to use our sentence (*a*) if he did not think our statement (*b*) was true. Would it be "incorrect?" Here, I am inclined to say that it *would* be incorrect, but only according to certain moral codes. In other words, it seems to me that underlying the presupposition of our statement (*b*) by our statement (*a*) is a *moral* conviction on the part of those who speak in a certain way; while underlying the presupposition of 'Queen Elizabeth's children exist' by 'All of Queen Elizabeth's children are asleep' is something that might more properly be called a truism.

When an action has been performed, the question can arise whether it is true-or-false to say that it is right, whether it is true-or-false to say that it is wrong. And this may be conceived as the question whether that action is susceptible to moral judgment. But I think that the question whether an action is *subject* to moral judgment or *susceptible* to moral judgment is the question whether we are morally right in passing moral judgment on the action. Corresponding questions in more theoretical cases are different. If you think, for example, that you cannot predicate colors of numbers, you might express this too by saying that a number is not *subject* to color-predication or that it is not *susceptible* of colour-predication. But you would not say that it is not morally right for a number to be called violet, blue, green, yellow, orange, or red. And this is crucial for the understanding of my point. In our case the question is the moral question whether the judged man should be judged morally. And that is one reason why I think there is a crucial difference between the dictum that you can not make a true-or-false statement like 'All of Queen Elizabeth's children are asleep' unless certain things exist, and the dictum that you can not make a true-or-false statement of rightness or wrongness about non-voluntary actions.

One consequence of this way of looking at the matter may be expressed by contrasting what a man must conclude when he is informed that the presupposed children do not exist in the case where he thinks he is making a statement like 'All of Queen Elizabeth's children are asleep,' with what a man must conclude when he is informed that an action that he has judged right or wrong is not voluntary in the sense in question. In the former case I think that he must conclude that he did not make a statement that is true-or-false, although he had previously thought he had. In the latter case, I do not think that he must say that he did not make a statement that is true-or-false though he had previously thought he had. In the second case the man could respond by continuing to say that the person criticized did something wrong, only adding that this person might be excused.

One further consideration. In an illuminating philosophical exchange, G. E. Moore was persuaded by A. C. Garnett that Moore in his book *Ethics* failed to realize that it is not sufficient in the case of an action to be judged morally that the action merely be one which the agent would have not done if he had chosen.[5] Garnett argues that a person with a certain disease which prevents choice might fail to do something (and a failure is here construed as a kind of action), in which case it would be true to say that he would not have failed to do it if he had chosen otherwise. The trouble was that he could not *choose* otherwise. Now when Moore is prevailed upon to acknowledge the fact that his original characterization of actions subject to moral criticism was deficient and that he must add that the person must be able to choose, I submit that he is being moved to see that it would be morally wrong to criticize this diseased person negatively.

6. My main conclusions are: that a moral judgment like (*a*) does not entail a statement of freedom like (*b*), and that although it is illuminating to say that (*a*) presupposes (*b*), we should not be misled by the latter formulation into neglecting the fact that the basis of our presupposition is a moral conviction. I think that we can imagine a society in which people do not accept the principle 'Wrong' presupposes 'Voluntary,' so to speak. Moreover, I think that there are people in our own society who do not really accept it, who make moral judgments on others for performing what they (the judges) think are non-voluntary actions. Such people

---

[5] See Garnett's contribution to *The Philosophy of G. E. Moore* and Moore's reply to Garnett in the same volume.

punish wrong-doers who act non-voluntarily, and they often go through the same procedures as we do for testing their judgments of right and wrong, even though they do not think that they can judge only agents who have acted voluntarily. Therefore it seems parochial to *define* moral judgment as that which must entail belief in the voluntariness of the action judged. One may try to advocate to such people a more enlightened way of engaging in the process of moral judgment, of deciding who should be visited with pain and who should be treated to pleasures; but one should realize that such advocacy is large-scale moral advice rather than logical or metaphysical instruction.

7. It is not my intention to assert that a moral code is simply a glorified legal code, and therefore the argument I am about to offer should be construed as no more than analogical. It will probably be granted that from a legal point of view the rules which fix responsibility are not logical in character. If a code says that a man is legally responsible only if he is a sane adult not acting under duress, it does not base this on some logical assertion to the effect that being legally responsible *logically entails* satisfying this condition, or that we would contradict ourselves if we said that a man was legally responsible but did not satisfy the condition. Of course, we might say this *after* we had promulgated a rule of this kind, but we would not justify its promulgation by citing a pre-established logical implication or connection between the statement that the man is legally responsible and the statement that he is a sane adult who is not acting under duress. Moreover, we may debate the moral wisdom of such a convention just as we debate the moral wisdom of setting the voting age at 21. Why, then, should the situation change so radically when we come to an analogous issue involving *moral* responsibility? Why should we think that the connection between our statements (*a*) and (*b*) is fundamentally different from that between the statements (*a'*), 'Booth acted illegally when he shot Lincoln' and (*b'*), 'Booth was a sane man who was not acting under duress when he shot Lincoln?' Behind the notion that there is a fundamental difference there may lie a parochialism about the nature of moral judgment

which we have managed to outgrow in our thinking about the law.

8. Some philosophers might wish to argue that within logical theory itself one can find issues that are very much like those that surround the acceptability of the dictum that 'Right' and 'Wrong' presuppose 'Voluntary.' According to logicians who operate with the conventions of modern mathematical logic, a statement of the form 'All S is P' is *true* if there are no things to which the predicate 'S' applies. In other words, they do not adopt the dictum regarding presupposition which is used by Strawson. The decision of the mathematical logician to treat 'All S is P' as true where 'S' does not apply to anything, is intimately connected with his construal of 'All S is P' as meaning the same as 'For every x, if x is S, then x is P,' where the connective 'if — then' is in turn construed in such a way that a conditional statement is true if its antecedent is false. And part of the motivation for this decision concerning the use of 'if — then' is to avoid what have been called "truth-value gaps." It is desirable from a mathematical logician's point of view that he should be able to attribute truth or falsity to every well-formed formula of his language, and therefore he calls a conditional statement with a false antecedent true, even though in ordinary language we might refuse to call it true or false. It follows that he must call a universal statement like 'All S is P' true when nothing is S.

Now it might be said that these considerations which are adduced by the mathematical logician in defense of his departure from ordinary linguistic practice are similar in kind to those which might be adduced by a society which wished to justify its abandonment of the dictum that our statement (*a*) presupposes our statement (*b*). And, of course, representatives of such a society might argue that the whole language of moral judgment becomes less complicated when one says that a statement of rightness or wrongness is true-or-false irrespective of whether the action judged is voluntary. They too might appeal to the linguistic advantages of eliminating all truth-value gaps where statements of right and wrong were concerned. But my point is that they might, and probably would, defend their divergence from *our* practice — assuming that we *do* treat (*a*) as presupposing (*b*) — by giving arguments of a kind that might be better construed as moral. That is to say, they might defend the *moral* worth of regarding it as true-or-false that an action is right, quite apart from whether this action is voluntary in the sense of (*b*). Their mode of attributing rightness and wrongness, they might say, leads to certain desirable social consequences or to conformity with the moral attitudes of their own people, and not merely to smooth-running logical accountancy. They might argue, for example, that their "language game" diminishes the amount of frustration which is characteristic of ours, because we must check our natural impulse to condemn in moral language those who have ostensibly done wrong and our natural impulse to speak praisingly of those who have ostensibly done right, in order to be sure that they have acted voluntarily.

9. I cannot see why any philosopher would wish to deny that an alternative linguistic situation of the kind I describe might exist. I realize, of course, that he might be tempted to say that people who make moral judgments in my imaginary society do not use the words 'right' and 'wrong' as we do, or that they do not conceive the activity of moral judgment as we do. But everything will now depend on how we understand the crucial word 'use' in this context, and also on what we understand by the phrase 'conceive the activity of moral judgment.' The imagined situation is as I have imagined it, and if a philosopher chooses to say that I am picturing a group of people who do not use the words 'right' and 'wrong,' as we use them, he may do so. But he should realize that in the situation I imagine, the words 'right' and 'wrong' could mean the same thing — — in one sense of that difficult phrase — — for my imaginary people as they mean for us. The difference between them and us would emerge, as it were, not in the interpretation of the *predicates* of the statement forms '*x* is right' and '*x* is wrong,' but rather in the range of the variable. *We* would limit that range to voluntary actions, saying that the resulting sentences cannot be used to make true-or-false statements

when we substitute the names of non-voluntary actions; whereas the people of the other society would not be so restrictive. If it be said that an anthropologist who studied my imagined people would certainly not translate their moral predicates as 'right' and 'wrong' precisely because these people do *not* adopt our dicta of presupposition, I cannot agree. The anthropologist might describe it as a situation in which, meaning by the words 'right' and 'wrong' what we do, the people in question apply them in cases where we do not. And he could add that they, for moral reasons, do not adopt the same dicta of presupposition as we do concerning statements of right and wrong.

10. I can see that another philosopher might describe the situation under discussion by saying that those who do make moral judgments on actions where the actions are not voluntary have a different *conception* of moral judgment from those who do. He might say that one group means one thing by 'moral judgment' while those who think and operate differently in this area mean another thing by it. But my quarrel with such a way of looking at the situation is that it tends to obscure the fact that one culture can influence another to adopt the other's presuppositions concerning moral judgment without thinking that it has persuaded the other culture to change the meaning of moral words, or to take up moral judgment at last. I find it difficult to imagine a conversation in which a representative of a culture which adopts the principle "'Wrong' presupposes 'Voluntary'" says to a representative of a culture which might not: "Why don't you start meaning by 'moral judgment' what we mean by it?" I should rather construe the dialogue as beginning: "Why don't you adopt the moral practice of judging morally only those actions which are voluntary?"

Those who cannot bring themselves to broaden their use of the term 'moral judgment' may be asked what they shall call an activity which is in every other respect just like what they call moral judgment except for the fact that those who make the judgments do not feel obliged to limit such judgments to voluntary actions. Surely we cannot deny that such an activity is conceivable. Many of us take ourselves to make moral judgments about action whose voluntariness we do not in fact investigate. What are we doing? Surely something. Well, then, there might be societies in which it is morally permissible to do this thing. Such people would punish, that is, inflict pain for wrong-doing. And if it be replied that they could not be said to punish when they do not think that the action punished is voluntary because in that case their punishment would have no point, I say that it all depends on what you mean by 'point.' Call them savages if you will, but not logical blunderers. We must not allow ourselves to be enticed into the view that people punish only with the alteration of the conduct of the punished person in mind. Some people punish in a spirit of vengeance. Shall we say that the judgment they make prior to punishing, *viz.* 'This man acted wrongly' is therefore not a "moral" judgment? Shall we say that their infliction of pain for wrong-doing is not punishment? I think this would be absurd. It would be more plausible to say that they judge as wrong and punish actions that they should not so judge and punish.

Among the advantages of this view of the relation between moral judgment and voluntary action is the fact that it makes it easier to view the principle that 'Right' and 'Wrong' presuppose 'Voluntary' as one that need not be held by people who are capable of ratiocination. For I think it *is* logically surrenderable, not self-evident, probably not accepted by all cultures, or even by all members of our own. For that reason it is a very fragile link in supposedly knock-down arguments for freedom of the will. For the same reason, persuading people to accept it requires more than training them in logic.

CAMILLUS RENATUS CALLED ALSO LYSIAS PHILAENUS AND PAULO RICCI (c. 1500 — c. 1575): FORERUNNER OF SOCINIANISM ON INDIVIDUAL IMMORTALITY

by GEORGE HUNTSTON WILLIAMS

INTRODUCTION

PROFESSOR WOLFSON has distinguished in the history of philosophy three views of immortality. In so doing with typical clarity, he has helpfully simplified the long and complicated history of the problem.[1] The first view he calls "individual immortality by the grace of God;" the second, associated with Averroes (d. 1198), "universal [impersonal] immortality by nature;" and the third, associated with Avicenna (d. 1037), "individual immortality by nature." In the opening of the Reformation Era the common Christian view of individual immortality by grace (the first view above) had here and there, under the influence of Renaissance Platonism, given way to a belief in a natural immortality of man (the third view above). It was, in any event, on the premise of either individual immortality by grace or by nature that the papal Church militant exercised sway over the vast realm of the suffering Church of purgatory. The V Lateran Council ending in 1517 had confirmed this position; and Protestantism, for the most part, perpetuated the traditional Catholic view of immortality, although it eliminated purgatory and otherwise modified the doctrine of the afterlife in the perspective of its strong emphasis upon election, reprobation, and saving faith.

---

[1] "Spinoza and the Religion of the Past," *Religious Philosophy: A Group of Essays* (Cambridge, 1961), pp. 263 f. See also the whole essay "Immortality and Resurrection in the Philosophy of the Church Fathers," *ibid.*, pp. 69–103.

Over against the main Christian positions in the Reformation Era regarding the soul was that of the psychopannychists, soul sleepers, or mortalists. These psychopannychists, working within the presuppositions either of Averroist or Alexandrist Aristotelianism, repudiated "individual immortality by nature;" and, while ultimately classifiable as exponents of "individual immortality by grace," they differed from the majority under this heading in interposing a period of psychic death or quiescence before the attainment of immortality in the re-creative miracle of the Holy Spirit at the second advent of Christ. During the sixteenth century there were three groups among the exponents of the Radical Reformation who, abandoning the traditional Catholic view of the general and immediately realized immortality of the individual sentient soul, espoused various forms of psychopannychism.[2] Psychopannychism has come to be the generic term for a complex of sectarian views about the death or sleep of the soul after the death of the body, pending the resurrection of all the dead *or* of the elect alone. The three religious groups espousing psychopannychism in the Reformation Era were the Spiritual Libertines, the Anabaptists, and the Socinians.

All three groups seem to have been directly or indirectly influenced by the speculations emanating from two schools of interpreters of Aristotle in the northern Italian universities of Padua, Bologna, and Ferrara. Common to these two schools was the acceptance, in dependence upon Aristotle, of the natural *mortality* of the soul.

These two Italian schools of interpreters of Aristotle stood apart from the Thomists, who had, of course, sought to harmonize Aristotle with Christian dogma, and also from the Avicennists, who contrived their adherence to the aforementioned doctrine of

---

[2] I have traced the various expresions of psychopannychism, including thnetopsychism and quoted the pertinent decree of the V Lateran Council in *Radical Reformation* (Philadelphia, 1962), pp. 20–24, 104–106, 580–592, and *passim*. LeRoy Edwin Froom, ranking Seventh Day Adventist Church historian, projects a comprehensive history of the doctrine of the provisional sleep of the soul, "Conditional Immortality."

"individual immortality by nature." The first school was that of the Italian followers of Averroes (d. 1198) who, with the aid of Neoplatonist elements, had propounded a monopsychism whereby it was possible to salvage at least an impersonal or universal immortality through absorption at death back into the eternal universal intellect (*anima intellectiva*). The other school was that of the Italian followers of Alexander of Aphrodisias (d. c. 200 A.D.) who, more boldly, had denied that the "multiple" souls of men could ever, even in a sublimated form, survive the death of the body.

From the purely philosophical and often medically trained Averroists and from the often humanistically trained Alexandrists the sectarian psychopannychists differed, of course, markedly. For while the psychopannychists accepted from these two kinds of interpreters of Aristotle as practically and philosophically evident the fact that the personal soul (*anima rationalis*) is extinguished with the death of the body, they would not resort to the purely nominal affirmation of immortality as a datum of faith based on revelation and authoritative ecclesiastical tradition, nor would they accept as binding the Scriptural arguments advanced rather perfunctorily in the condemnation of the Averroist and the Alexandrist positions by the V Lateran Council which drew to a close in 1517. Instead, the radical reformers of psychopannychist persuasion, yielding to the philosophical-medical argumentation in the northern Italian universities, had recourse to a neglected, minor theme running through the New Testament and the Church Fathers which placed the eschatological hope entirely in the general resurrection as a final re-creative action of God. It is possible that they related this impending mighty act of God to the ongoing operation of His Holy Spirit as *Creator Spiritus* in the resuscitation of the spirits and the bodies of the elect. In any event, they rejoiced in such Scriptural assurances as I Thessalonians 4:13–18 that the saintly dead would awake to the sound of the trumpet of God; and in the meantime they vigorously attacked all medieval institutions which rested upon the claim of the Church to control allegedly *sentient* souls in purgatory and to manipulate the supererogatory merits of the saints in paradise.

Liberated from Catholic ecclesiasticism in the general Protestant upheaval of the century, the sectarian psychopannychists, indigenous to Italy, freely avowing the death of the soul with the body, proclaimed the saving gospel that, by a miracle no less prodigious than creation *ex nihilo*, God would at the end re-create the bodies of the dead or form new bodies and, re-animating them, bring them before him for bliss or punishment according to their merit. Psychopannychism, linked with the doctrine of election, was the Italian counterpart of solafideism in Luther's Germany and of predestination in Calvin's Switzerland. As such it was a basic thrust in what proved to be an abortive reformation in the northern Italian city-states and principalities.

In the course of the seventeenth century the psychopannychist hope largely subsided among the Libertines who accommodated themselves completely to the world as a cultured, political faction in advanced circles in Italy, France, and Holland. The same stern and radical hope among the Anabaptists of a much humbler walk of life was gradually mitigated by sentiments flowing from their Catholic or Protestant environment which tended to revive the expectation of a natural immortality. Alone among the original groups of psychopannychists, the Socinians persisted throughout the seventeenth century and beyond in their radical faith in the eventual re-creation of the ensouled bodies of the saintly dead.

Among the influential figures in the rise of Socinianism was Camillo Renato. He was an associate of the young Sienese Laelius Socinus who became much concerned about the *quies* of the soul and the final resurrection.[3] Dying in 1562, Laelius left his library and his own writings to his nephew Faustus Socinus, the refounder of the Reformed-Anabaptist Minor Church of Poland and the fountainhead of the Socinian movement.

In recognition of the fact that Professor Wolfson has been throughout his career at Harvard associated with the Faculty of Divinity which has had in the past a Socinian strain; because also

---

[3] Besides his Confession and his correspondence with John Calvin on the subject, see also his "De resurrectione" as edited by Lech Szczucki, "Z Eschatologii Braci Polsckich," *Archiwum historii filozofii*, I (1957), 5–41.

he has himself in the Ingersoll Lecture[4] at the Divinity School dealt probingly with the problem of immortality and resurrection; and finally because he has been the animating force behind the series devoted to the Averroistic *corpus*,[5] I have chosen to recount in his honor the early career of the seminal but erratic psychopannychist, the proto-Socinian Camillo Renato, called also Lisia Phileno.

Camillo Renato was not "the gentle mystic" idealized in the Socinian tradition. He was, rather, a man of brilliance, daring, duplicity, passion, excess, turmoil, and inconstancy. He is to be classed with others on the margins of the Reformation: Michael Servetus, David Joris, and Bernardino Ochino, all four of whom were chameleon-like figures, readily changing their names. All four sought for a season to camouflage themselves, first in inquisitorial-Catholic society and then in established-Protestant lands. In an age of thousands of martyr pyres, they, like the mythical salamander, flourished close to the flames. A trait common to these four men was their espousal of toleration, never without at least a trace of histrionic self-indulgence.

These four men of the Left Wing of the Reformation are difficult to place, however refined our typology. In fact, the major interest attaching to Camillo Renato, who moved like a storm up the Italian peninsula from Palermo in Sicily to Chur in Switzerland, is that he was genetically and morphologically an important nodal point connecting three branches of the Radical Reformation: Spiritualism, Evangelical Rationalism, and Anabaptism. However, Camillo is of interest not only as a representative figure but also in his own right, especially now that we can with certainty annex to his biography several episodes in which he featured under the name of Lisia Phileno, heard twice by the inquisition.[6]

---

[4] Reprinted as "Immortality and Resurrection in the Philosophy of the Church Fathers," *Religious Philosophy*, pp. 69–103.

[5] "Plan for the Publication of a *Corpus Commentariorum Averrois in Aristotelem*," *Speculum*, VI (1931), 412–427. A revision of this prospectus in the light of the publication to date and the new items is in press, *ibid.*, XXXVIII (1963). See also his "Twice-Revealed Averroes," *ibid.*, XXXVI (1961), 372–392.

[6] The identification of Lisia Phileno and Camillo Renato was first suggested

The life and thought of Camillo Renato fall into two phases: Lisia Phileno: unfrocked Franciscan humanist of Venice, Bologna, Modena, and Ferrara (c. 1500–1542) and Camillo Renato: Radical Reformer in Rhaetia (the Grisons and Valtellina) (1542–c. 1572). We shall confine ourselves to his career under the names of Paolo Ricci and Lisia Phileno.[7]

Lisia Phileno: Radical Franciscan Humanist (c. 1500–1542)

The life of Camillo Renato before his capture near Modena in 1540 can be only a sketch with traits drawn from a half dozen personal references in the documentation of the year of his arrest and trial and inferences drawn from the full name as given in the final trial: Lysias Philaenus Paulus Riccius Siculus.[8]

Camillo Renato, henceforth to be called Phileno, was born

by F.C. Church, *The Italian Reformers, 1534–1564* (New York, 1932), p. 39, n. The identification was virtually proved by Alfredo Casadei, "Lisia Fileno e Camillo Renato," *Religio*, XV (1939), 356–440 (the fifth and last, undistributed fascicule); and it was accepted by Delio Cantimori, *Eretici italiani del Cinquecento* (Florence, 1939; German edition, Basel, 1949), with a few amplifications. The author has come into epistolary contact with Professor Antonio Rotondò of Modena who is engaged in a study of heresy in Modena from 1540 to 1570, in which Camillo Renato features as an important figure. Professor Rotondò has very kindly permitted me to remark that his researches, when published, will further harden the Casadei thesis in his forthcoming article in *Rinascimento*.

[7] I have dealt briefly with the whole career of Ricci-Phileno-Renato in *Radical Reformation*, pp. 546–559; 562–571. I shall deal with his later career (1542–1572) in *Italian Reformation Studies*, "Collana Pietro Rossi" of the University of Siena (Florence: Le Monnier, 1964). This volume, devoted to Laelius Socinus on the occasion of the four hundredth anniversary of his death in 1562, will be edited by Mr. John Tedeschi, to whom I am much indebted for help at several stages in the preparation of this study in Italy and at home.

[8] The "Apologia," prepared by Phileno while in prison in Ferrara and the Record of the trial at Ferrara constitute a major source of the present study: "Apologia Lisyae Philaeni Pauli Ricci Siculi Ferrariae nomine haereseos detenti, feliciter Hercule II imperante, Duce IV, 1540." This is MS No. B 1928 in the Biblioteca Comunale dell' Archiginnasio of Bologna. See Albano Sorbelli

presumably as Paolo Ricci between 1500 and 1510[9] in what had until 1503 been the Aragonese Kingdom of the Two Sicilies, hence the recurrent toponymic Siculus (Siciliano). It is less likely that he was born in the Spanish Kingdom of Sicily (commonly called the Kingdom of Naples) than on the island (called the Vice-royalty — *vicereame*). One could conjecture on the basis of the name of Lysias, which he later assumed, that he had some connection with Syracuse; for the Attic orator Lysias who died c. 380 B.C. was the son of an Athenian metic born in Syracuse.[10] But our only specific reference to origins in the documentation points to Palermo and the neighboring province of Trapani[11] as the region of his birth. A rather prominent Franciscan tertiary of high birth and of the same surname who died in Palermo in 1599[12] might have

et al., *Inventari dei Manoscritti delle Biblioteche Italiane*, LXXX (Florence, 1954). The "Apologia" records utterances of Phileno during his trial at Ferrara in December 1540. It will be critically edited by Antonio Rotondò in *Rinascimento* and interpreted by him in a comprehensive account of the sectarian history of Modena. Professor Rotondò will also publish the complete text of the *Trattato sul Battesimo e sulla Eucaristia*, recently printed in part and identified by Delio Cantimori as a later work of Phileno-Renato (cf. n. 6 above).

I am most grateful to Professor and Mrs. Rotondò, the latter an expert palaeographer, for the transliteration of folio 26: "Quod sanctorum nondum in Paradisum animae." For the rest I am depending upon a microfilm of the text and the immense help of Dr. David Pingree, Harvard Junior Fellow and prospective Research Associate of the Oriental Institute, University of Chicago.

[9] The date is inferred from Tommasino de' Bianchi detto de' Lancellotti, *Cronaca Modenese* VI (Parma, 1868) *Monumenti di Storia 'Patria delle Provincie Modenesi*, VII, 410; Casadei, "Fileno," p. 369. But the governor, *loc. cit. supra*, refers to him in 1540 as "giovane di età." As for the name Fileno, it might have been *originally* a toponymic. We know of a Dominican house in Calabria, elevated to the rank of priory "in locum Fileni" in 1558. See Andreas Frühwert, *Acta capitulorum generalium ordinis Praedicatorum*, V (Rome, 1901), 16; cf. p. 100 where it is spelled "Filenae."

[10] Lysias' father earned his living making shields.

[11] The reference to Palermo is found in the letter of the governor of Modena to the duke of Ferrara, 16 October 1540; Casadei, "Fileno", pp. 364 f.

[12] Geronimo Riccio (Riccius) of Trapani (1514–1599) who went to Rome in 1544 to be elected procurator general of the order of the Discalced Franciscan Tertiaries. See Giuseppe Mira, *Bibliografia Siciliana*, II (Palermo, 1881), 285 and especially Giuseppe M. di Ferro, *Biografia degli Uomini Illustri*

been a relation. Presumably our Paolo Ricci Phileno came of a family of means and culture, for he was later to move with ease in the habitations of patricians and nobles. He is described as "a big man and well formed."[13]

It may have been while he was quite young that Phileno joined the Franciscans. In the first third of the sixteenth century this could have meant theoretically one of five main branches of the Franciscan family, namely, the Observants, the Conventuals, the Third Order of St. Francis, the Hermits of St. Francis of Paola in Calabria (d. 1507), and the Capuchins. Phileno surely had none of the distinctive characteristics of a Capuchin. An eighteenth-century literary historian assumes that he was a Conventual, without adducing reasons.[14] This account is based, in turn, upon a contemporary description[15] which says somewhat curiously that Phileno was "della religion de S. Francesco de Napole." It is just

---

Trapanesi, IV (Trapani, 1850), 138–140. It is not certain whether this "gracious" and "celebrated orator" who wrote the statutes of his order in Italian belongs to the family of the somewhat later Geronimo Riccio, baron of S. Anna. This noble family is known to have had connections with Naples. There are several members of this family, renowned in both branches of law, in literature, and theology who originated in the town or the province of Trapani and ended their careers in Palermo. The Ricci (Riccio) family originating in the province of Trapani would have been keenly conscious, because of the local monuments and traditions, that their ancestors were once within the marine empire of Carthage and as such had valiantly fought the Romans. The later assumed name of our very literate Siciliano might have been intended to evoke the memory of both the Grecian (Syracuse) and the Carthaginian (Trapani) beginnings of civilization in Sicily: Lysias, to Syracuse and Philaenus, to Carthaginian Trapani and Palermo at the other extreme of the storied island. On the heroic Carthaginian brothers Philaeni, see below at n. 30.

[13] The description of Phileno as "homo grando, e ben formato" is that of Lancellotti, *Cronaca*, p. 410; Cf. that of Alessandro Tassoni, "Cronaca di Modena," *Monumenti di Storia Patria delle Provincie Modenesi: Serie Delle Cronache*, XV (Modena, 1888), p. 331; Casadei, "Fileno," p. 373.

[14] Girolamo Tiraboschi, *Biblioteca Modenese*, I (Modena, 1781), 12.

[15] Lancellotti, *Cronaca*, p. 410; Tassoni, "Cronaca," p. 331; Casadei, "Fileno," p. 373; letter of vicar to bishop of Modena, 26 October 1540; printed in C. Cantù, *Gli Eretici d' Italia* (Turin, 1866), II, 175, also Casadei, "Fileno," p. 371, n. 1.

possible that *Napole* is the transcribing editor's misreading of *Paola*; and that we have here a reference to the rapidly rising new order of Calabrian Minimi or Hermits of San Francesco of Paola. This order was particularly given to a strenuous life of Lent throughout the year and to the defense and alleviation of the poor and downtrodden. Some of Phileno's traits, like his concern for the poor, his later chronic ill health which could have been caused by excessive fasting in his youth, his eschatology, his reforming zeal, and the fact that he is never in the later hearings and trial identified with any of the older branches of the Franciscan family (who might conceivably have sought to protect him) could be explained by his having as a youth joined the Minimi who, though they spread rapidly from Calabria and Sicily to France,[16] were not at this time strong in Emilia. It is equally plausible that Phileno could have been a Discalced Tertiary of St. Francis who also wore a distinctive habit with scapular and cord.

At some point in his monastic career Phileno was ordained a priest.[17] A powerful preacher, he became a Master of Theology.[18]

[16] It is just possible that *Palermo* in another source is also a misreading of a manuscript *Paolo* and that Phileno-Ricci came from the same family in Calabria which produced at the beginning of the next century a bishop for the joined and diminutive Calabrian sees of Cerenzia and Cariati. One Mauritius Ricci became bishop of these two sees in 1619. Pius Bonifacius Gams, *Series Episcoporum* (Regensburg, 1873), p. 869. Girolamo Marafioti, *Croniche et Antichita di Calabria* (Padua, 1601), folios 112 v; 268 v. Cerenzia, a mere village on the Sila, is not distant from the casale San Fili between Cosenza and Paola. The Castello Melicucco is not far off. On the Sila near Cerenzia is located the mother house of Joachimism, San Giovanni in Fiore. In this same region, in a castle between San Fili and Paolo, St. Francis of Paola, devoted to the poor and to extreme austerity "of the life of Lent" throughout the year — founded the order of the Hermits of St. Francis of Assisi called the Minimi, with its mother house above Paolo and with thirty-two convents established by his death in 1507. For the castle, near San Fili, see Marafioti, *op. cit.*, folio 168 v. In this same region two thousand Waldensians were put to death on the Sila 10 June 1530. Gertrude Slaughter, *Calabria the First Italy* (Madison, Wisconsin, 1939), p. 270.

[17] That he was ordained is inferred from a later statement that he celebrated the Mass in Modena. Lancellotti, *Cronaca*, p. 410; Casadei, "Fileno," p. 369. [18] Lancellotti, *Cronaca*, p. 410; Casadei, "Fileno," p. 369.

Presumably it was at the University of Naples that he studied.[19] Here he may have established contact with other learned members of his clan, for several Riccis are attested among the *lectores* at the *Studium* of Naples in this period.[20] Perhaps it was at this point in his career as friar, preacher, and *scholaris*, that Phileno became intensely concerned with the reformation of Christendom and the renewal of the Church.

Phileno apparently left Naples for Padua,[21] and perhaps matriculated at the university. He then went on to Venice where, during the nunciature (1526–28) of Altobello Averoldi (bishop of Pola), Phileno was accused of heresy by several people of ill will, detained, and investigated but not condemned.[22]

As it happens another Paolo Ricci appears at about this time in the Venetian records. This was the converted Jew who served as physician and astrological advisor of Maximilian I and Ferdinand I. It was during the nunciature of Averoldi's successor, Girolamo Aleander, that a certain work of this Austro-Italian Ricci, perhaps his *Apologeticus* on the Cabbala, was sequestered and burned.[23] But we have no record apart from a reference in

[19] Lancellotti, *Cronaca*, p. 410.

[20] Giangiuseppe Origlia, *Istoria dello Studio di Napoli* (Naples, 1753), I, 246; II, 39.

[21] This is inferred from his answer to the inquisitorial question whether he had been held for a hearing in Padua. "Apologia," folio 6A: "Respondit (Phileno) numquam Patavii hoc nomine accusatum aut inquisitum fuisse *ante* detentionem Venetam."

[22] "Apologia," folio 6A: "Venetiis de hac questione non fui accusatus ullo pacto neque inquisitus ut in actis preberi potest." It is scarcely possible that the hearing would have taken place under Averoldi's earlier nunciature in Venice (1517–1523). For these dates, see F. Gaeta, "Origine e sviluppo della rappresentanza stabile pontificia in Venezia," *Annuario dell' Istituto Storico per l' età moderna e contemporanea*, IX–X (1957/58), 40.

[23] Aleander refers to his condemnation of one work by Ferdinand's Ricci in a letter to Pietro Carnesecchi, Franco Gaeta, ed., *Nunziature di Venezia*, I (Rome, 1958), item 58, 7 February 1534, p. 165. Pier Paolo Vergerio, later an associate of Phileno-Renato, delivered an oration on the death of Averoldi in 1531. Cf. Franco Gaeta, "Un inedito Vergeriano," *Rivista di Storia della Chiesa in Italia*, XIII (1959), 397. Gaeta here calls attention to a *miscellanea*

[11] CAMILLUS RENATUS AND INDIVIDUAL IMMORTALITY 843

the later trial in Ferrara, [24] of Ricci-Phileno's hearing in Venice.

For what was at least a decade, 1528–1538, we lose track of Phileno. It is possible that he stayed on in Venice and came to know Pietro Paolo Vergerio who delivered the funeral oration for Averoldi in 1531, who became papal nuncio himself in Germany in 1533, and who in 1531 began a career as reforming bishop successively of Modrus and Capodistria. Vergerio is mentioned at this point because after his exile, he was to become briefly associated in Rhaetia with Phileno (under the name Camillo Renato) and to propound a plan for a political unification of the reformation movement. It is plausible to assume that it was in relatively tolerant Venice, full of Greeks, Armenians, Jews, and the ambassadors and merchants from Lutheran cities and principalities to the north, that Phileno formulated his own grand design: "In pacificanda Germania cum Ecclesia Romana."[25] It is remotely possible that an oration printed as though delivered at the diet of Speyer in 1529 (and from internal evidence composed in 1528), commonly ascribed to Ferdinand's physician, was actually composed by our Paolo Ricci Phileno as his contribution to the uni-

---

manuscript in the Biblioteca Nazionale Marciana, which besides Vergerio's oration on the death of Nuncio Averoldi, contains a list of heretical writers of the north, from John Hus to Theobald Billicanus, and including Paolo Ricci. After his name Gaeta mentions the specific works condemned: "Apologetica plures charte e Apologetica intera." It is possible that we have here a reference to the Austrian Ricci's *Apologeticus... adversus obtrectatorem Cabbalae sermo*. The condemnation of one of the Austrian Ricci's works only adds interest to the fact that Ferdinand was so basically confident in the worth of his Jewish convert that he on two occasions proposed him to Clement VII as bishop for the see of Trent, first in 1531 and then in 1534. See *Enciclopedia Italiana*, XXIX (1936), 247. For the fact that this Ricci was a physician for Maximilian I as well as Ferdinand I and that he was perhaps responsible for the expulsion of Jews by the former from certain Austrian domains, see Emanuel Baumgarten *Die Juden in Steiermark* (Vienna, 1903), pp. 28 f. For the numerous writings of the Austrian Ricci, see the catalogues of the British Museum and of the Bibliothèque Nationale, and Christian Gottlieb Jöcher, *Gelehrten-Lexikon*, Ergänzungsband VI (Bremen, 1819), coll. 2095 f.

[24] See below, p. 860.
[25] "Apologia," folio 35.

fication of Christendom against the Turk.[26] But this is very unlikely, since the oration appeals primarily to Germanic and ancient Roman patriotism in calling for concerted war on Mohammedanism. Our Ricci-Phileno, from his known views, was not interested in the defense of Christendom by war but rather in the reunification of Christendom through the radical reformation and by direct appeal to the Pope.

It was Phileno's intention to go Rome (at some unidentified moment in his career) and to confer with "the most reverend and learned cardinals" there; for he was confident that by restoring the Mass "to its dignity and integrity" rather than by suspending it (as in Reformed lands) "the whole of Christendom (*rem Christianam*) and the mutual concord of the whole Church" might be served. He was certain that the more enlightened prelates in Rome including the Pope himself would like to see the way to clearing the Church of its superstitions, both those not hitherto recognized as such and those long tolerated. One of Phileno's basic convictions concerning the renewal of the Church was that the priest and his parishioner should alike be able to give a full and refined account of the articles of faith, including the *beneficium Christi*, the will of God, the Fatherhood of God, and the dignity and institution of the Christian life.[27] It is not certain at what date Phileno intended to present his work in Rome,[28] nor is there any evidence that he ever went there.

It is possible that it was in Venice that our Sicilian Franciscan changed his name from Paolo Ricci to Lisia Phileno and also

---

[26] The oration, *Ad principes, magistratus, populosque Germaniae in Spirensi conventu habito*, is printed by Marquard Freher, *Germanicarum rerum scriptores*, III (Hanover, 1611), 379–386. Here it is dated as of 1544. For earlier editions, all of which except the first are ascribed to Paolo Ricci, see the catalogues of the British Museum and the Bibliothèque Nationale. For a summary of the contents and for the fact that the address was not actually delivered at Speyer, although in German Ferdinand himself expressed some of the same ideas, see Johannes Kühn, *Deutsche Reichstagsakten*, jüngere Reihe, VII:1 (Stuttgart, 1935), long note on p. 552 f.

[27] "Apologia," folio 36 r.

[28] "Apologia," folio 37 v.

his habit from that of a Franciscan to that of a gentleman scholar. In the documentation from Bologna, where he appeared in 1538,[29] he was known under the name of Paolo Ricci and that of Lisia Phileno (Fileno). It is very unlikely that a Franciscan while still under orders would have so boldly changed his name in such a programmatically classical sense. We have already referred to the Attic orator whose name he assumed. As an eloquent preacher, proud to the point of vanity, our Siciliano probably thought of himself as Lysias (Lisia) reborn to proclaim the reform in classic cadences. His assumed name, Phileno, may have been originally a toponymic, spelled Fileno, more specific than Siciliano. On this view, once he assumed the name of Lysias he gave a classical turn to his toponymic as well, spelling it occasionally Philaenus in clear allusion to the two Carthaginian brothers of that name who allowed themselves to be buried alive to mark the extreme boundary of Punic Carthage over against Cyrenaica.[30] That Phileno thought of himself as an academician and a great orator is clear from our documentation. That he would have allowed himself and any brother in faith to be buried alive to mark and hold the eastern-most boundary of a reformed Christendom seems less in character.[31]

---

[29] The date of 1539 is inferred from Phileno's testimony in the "Apologia," folio 43 r, where he says in 1540 that he had studied in Bologna "biennio fere." Abbot Tiraboschi, working with MS materials in the Ducal Archive of Modena, says that Phileno had, on his arrival in Modena, "deposto l'abito religioso," *op. cit.*, p. 12.

[30] The story is told by Sallust, *Bellum Jugurthinum*, 79; repeated by Pomponius Mela, *Chorographia*, i, 31–38; Valerus Maximus, *Memorabilia*, vi, 4; and Pliny, *Naturalis Historia*, v, 4. For the possible significance of the choice of a Carthaginian name, see the reference above to the Tertiary Franciscan Geronimo Riccio (1514–1599) of "Carthaginian" Trapani and Palermo, n. 12. Alas, for any theory of a fraternal relationship between these two is the assertion that Geronimo was the first born of the illustrious Aloisio and Agnese. We have postulated for Paolo Ricci (Riccio) Phileno a birth c. 1500, at the latest 1510.

[31] The Paolo Ricci who composed an ideal oration for the diet of Speyer, urging a joint Catholic-Protestant war against the encroachments from the east, could more plausibly have called himself Lysias Philaenus, but the *Ad principes* (cf. n. 26) is connected with the name Riccius not Philaenus.

Lysias Philaenus or Paulus Riccius matriculated at the *Studium* of Bologna in 1538, at least a decade after his brush with the papal nuncio in Venice. Unlike a Franciscan under conventual discipline, Phileno appears to have spent a good deal of his time in the homes of Bolognese patricians and nobles, like the Lambertini, Danesi, Biancani, Manzoli, and Bocchi.[32] Count Cornelio Lambertini, for example, whom Phileno names as one of his hosts, later appears in the Bolognese chronicle as a senator. Another host, Achille Bocchi, would soon form the Academia Bocchiana. From the library of Giacomo Biancani of Bologna are preserved fifteen manuscript Latin poems (*carmina*) composed by Phileno mostly on domestic personalities and occasions.[33] Phileno devoted himself in Bologna to literary, philosophical, and theological studies. He apparently made many friends among fellow *scholares* and discussed with them and his patrons the issues of the hour. He reports somewhat immodestly that he was greatly admired for his ability, erudition, his zeal in humane letters, and his good habits.[34]

---

[32] "Apologia" folio 44r. For Count Cornelio Lambertini, either the same as the one referred to by Phileno or perhaps his son, see Salvatore Muzzi, *Annali della Città di Bologna* (Bologna, 1844), VI, pp. 589, 622.

[33] The fifteen *carmina* begin as follows: Ad Annam Parthinean Pontanorum Dominam, In Fantutii de Fantutiis obitum, Ad Cassandram Troianam, Ad Hilarium Taurum, De Flora, Ad Angelum Danesium, Ad Octavium, Ad Ludovicum, De quodam puero sordidulo, In D. N. Jesu Christi nata, Ad Memmium de sole, nubibus, tonitru, fulmine, pluvia. These are to be found in Codice latino 83 (52, Busta II, No. 1) of the Biblioteca Universitaria in Bologna, ff. 438–450. The titles are listed by Lodovico Frati, "Indice dei codici latini... di Bologna," *Studi Italiani di Filologia Classica*, XVI (1908), 137 f. They should be compared with the only other known *carmen* of the same humanist friar under the name of Camillo Renato, in defense of Michael Servetus, 1554. The text of this *Carmen* is printed in Calvin, *Opera Omnia*, XV (*Corpus Reformatorum*, XLVIII), No. 2017, coll. 239–245. As for Giacomo Biancani in whose library the fifteen *carmina* were preserved, he was not a contemporary of Phileno. We await an examination of the manuscript "Notizie storiche genealogiche della famiglia Biancani di Bologna," by Baldassare Biancani, MS B 2526 of the Archiginnasio, Sorbelli, *op. cit.*, LXXXII, 90.

[34] "Apologia," folio 43v.

He was clearly at home *in scholis* as well as in the piazzas and the churches. In view of his command of patristic and scholastic theology, as evidenced by his "Apologia" of 1540, it would appear that Phileno had come to Bologna prepared to specialize.

The *Studium* of Bologna had for some time been divided into the University of the Legists, for which the city had long been famous, and the *Universitas Artistarum*, which embraced all the other disciplines besides law, including medicine. Lectures in theology, however, were not given regularly under the auspices of the *Artisti*; and, when announced, they were most commonly given by a learned friar lecturing in his own convent.[35]

The Averroists Alessandro Achillini and Tiberio Bacilieri,[36] both doctors of medicine, had taught philosophy at the opening of the century; and the more radical Alexandrist, Pietro Pomponazzi, had come to Bologna from Padua in 1512, publishing his *De immortalitate animae* in 1516, teaching that the immortality of the *anima intellectiva*, though a datum of the faith, cannot be demonstrated by reason. In 1520 Pomponazzi came out with his *De fato, de libero arbitrio et praedestinatione*.

At the time of Phileno's sojourn in Bologna, there were three professors of philosophy and medicine who lectured *on the soul*. One of them was Antonio Francesco dalla Fava (Faba, Fabius), another Antonio dal Fiume (Flumeneus).[37] Both of them had begun their teaching careers within a year or two after the death of Pomponazzi in 1525. It is quite probable that Phileno heard

[35] Paul Oskar Kristeller, "The University of Bologna and the Renaissance," *Studi e Memorie per la storia dell' Università di Bologna*, n.s. I (Bologna, 1956), 320 f. For lectures in theology in a convent instead of the usual precincts of the *Artisti*, cf. Umberto Dallari, *I Rotuli dei Lettori Legisti e Artisti dello Studio Bolognese*, II (Bologna, 1889), 5.

[36] Carlo Calcaterra, *Alma Mater Studiorum: L'Università di Bologna nella Storia della Cultura e della Civiltà* (Bologna, 1948), pp. 162 f.; Bruno Nardi, *Saggi sull' Aristotelismo padovano dal secolo xiv al xvi* (Florence, 1960), ch. viii, ix.

[37] Dallari, *Rotuli*, II, p. 91; Serafino Mazzetti, *Repertorio di tutti i professori... di Bologna* (Bologna, 1847), items 1174 and 978; Calcaterra, *op. cit.*, p. 175.

these men lecturing on the mortality of the individual soul. It is almost certain that he knew the third, the last master of Bolognese Averroism, Ludovico Boccadiferro (Buccaferreus), who belonged to the circle of Phileno's protector, Achille Bocchi. Boccadiferro attempted to harmonize Plato, Arictotle, and Averroes in his *Lectiones super tres libros de anima* (Venice, 1556) and in "Quaestio de immortalite animae."

We know that Phileno himself was pressed, as he says, by certain among the students (*ex scholaribus*), on the immortality of the souls of the saints, and that he was amazed to find that there were indeed many passages in Scripture [38] and among the Fathers indicating that the souls of not even the saints had yet been admitted to paradise. He specified the books of Irenaeus, Lactantius, Ambrose, and Augustine.[39] He also became much interested in the Council of Basel-Ferrara-Florence and specifically referred to the Greek views about purgatory in the debates of June–July 1438.[40] Phileno was apparently to become quite impressed by the Orthodox arguments which interpreted the New Testament texts eschatologically as referring solely to a future rather than a provisional, present blessedness or purgation immediately after death. The Greeks were explicit that there was no present purgation by fire. Phileno reports that he at first tried to controvert the testimony of these passages by others of a more traditional content and that he consulted with "other students and friends" over a number of years (*superioribus annis*) and particularly with the otherwise unidentified preacher (*concionatorem*) of San Petronio in Bologna at the beginning of the year 1540. Phileno claims later, in his "Apologia," that his fellow students, "who were always eager to discuss all new and wayward doctrines," involved

---

[38] Cf. Oscar Cullmann, *Immortality of the Soul or Resurrection of the Dead in the New Testament* (New York, 1958). [39] "Apologia," folio 26 r.

[40] Mansi, *Sacrorum Conciliorum... Collectio*, XXXI, coll. 485 ff. Phileno says that the book of the Acts which he consulted in prison had been "recentissime impresso," "Apologia," folio 8. Phileno will have been particularly interested in the views of Metropolitan Mark Eugenicus of Ephesus. The most recent account of the discussion on purgatory is by Joseph Gill, *The Council of Florence* (Cambridge, 1959), pp. 117–125.

him so much in speculative discussion that he, as a mature scholar perhaps still in orders, was implicated as the very fountainhead of student ferment. But there can be little doubt that, despite his later protestations before a tribunal, he himself had come to espouse and even elaborate those views, accepting as probable that "the souls of the elect have not yet entered (paradise or) heaven" and that "they rest (*quiescere*) with Christ" "along with the Spirit" (*Spiritum vero secus*) "until resurrected at the day of judgment" and that there is no present hell or purgatory.[41] Phileno must have adopted other radical views also which were theologically and socially unsettling.

Yet everything seemed to be going well for Phileno until the Lent of 1540. There came to San Giacomo, the church and convent of the Austin Friars, a famous preacher of the order from Naples with, from Phileno's lofty point of view, an unwarranted reputation for Scriptural learning. Phileno scornfully describes his grave demeanor, his inept pronunciation, and his actual perversion of Scriptures. One is relieved, in the interest of safeguarding Phileno's own reputation, to ascertain that he could not have been referring to Girolamo Seripando of Naples, general of the Hermits of St. Augustine and later the papal legate at the Council of Trent.[42] Seripando had, to be sure, been resident in Bologna for six years, and in 1540 he would visit and preach in the city between April 11 and April 30.[43] But Phileno's difficulties with an unnamed Austin Friar from Naples began on Ash Wednesday, February 11, 1540[44] when the preacher spent two wearisome

[41] *Ibid.*, and folio 5v.

[42] Hubert Jedin, *Girolamo Seripando: Sein Leben und Denken im Geisteskampf des 16. Jahrhunderts*, 2 vols. (Würzburg, 1937).

[43] *Ibid.*, II, 412. See below.

[44] In "Apologia," folio 43r. Phileno specifies "primo die quatragesime." Easter in that year fell on March 28. Hence we have a specific date for the onset of Phileno's troubles. That Seripando could not have made an earlier visit to Bologna that year is inferred from his itinerary ascertained by reference to his sermons calendared by Jedin, *op. cit.*, II, 407–426. He was in Perugia on January 18 and then went to the Adriatic, moving up the coast from Fermo, February 14; Ancona, February 26; Pesaro, March 6 and 8; Rimini, March 9-April 2.

hours on the trivialia of fasting, "as if every father in Bologna were not fully acquainted with the law of the Church on the subject." Phileno, "with much civility as was becoming," made bold to apprise the preacher of his opinion that more edifying and needful topics could be dealt with in the ensuing Lenten sermons. At this the Neapolitan Augustinian was enraged, declared that Phileno was "a prophet of Martin Luther sent into Italy" and that he was an excommunicated apostate; and he proceeded to inform the local Dominicans of the renegade in their midst.

Bologna was the seat of the Dominican provincial chapter of Lower Lombardy. The Dominicans mobilized to apprehend Phileno "in the church, in the assembly, in the schools, in the square, and throughout the city." Given the original provocation, we must henceforth be prepared to find the evidence of Phileno's having eaten meat and dairy products during Lent and his almost hypochondriacal itemization of ailments that justified his use of forbidden proteins bulking very large in the extant documentation. We shall try to keep this kind of material to a minimum.

Phileno had powerful protectors among the highborn citizens. Moreover, he was confident that his ideas of reform were much closer to those of the reforming Roman Pontiff (Paul III) than the Austin Friar's. Phileno's strategy was therefore to appeal from the Dominican inquisitor and from the bishop of Bologna (Alessandro Campeggio) to the papal legate in Bologna, the newly appointed Bonifazio Ferrero, cardinal bishop of Ivrea,[45] or to his deputy. In the meantime, the whole of the town became aroused by the charges, the preachers of San Petronio and of the Dominican Church joining with the preacher of the Austin Friars in San Giacomo, in denouncing Phileno as a heretic, an apostate, an excommunicate, and a seditious person to be avoided for the religious and social turmoil he was causing men and women in houses and parishes. Before Phileno could manage to state his case before the legate, the latter fell ill.[46]

[45] "Apologia," folios 17 v. 45 r. For the appointment of the new legate, see Pompeo Vizani, *Diece libri delle historie della sua patria* (Bologna, 1608), supplementary book XI, pp. 16 f. [46] "Apologia," folio 45v.

Although before this unfortunate turn of events, Phileno had never considered fleeing, he now decided to depart from Bologna with a view to visiting his *patria*, then Rome itself, and finally to leave Italy altogether, not without visiting "the ancient cities of Modena, Mirandola, and Mantua."[47] Because of an abscess in his right armpit, from which he was suffering at the time, he thought he would perish. In the company of several friends he got away to Nonantola; and to prove his innocence he boldly asked admittance at the local Dominican convent, two of whose members he names.[48] He hoped through the intercession of these two learned and reasonable men to vindicate his honor and orthodoxy. With these friars, whom he presumably had known earlier, at least by reputation, he stayed for five or six days, talking with them at table about all the problems astir in Bologna. They agreed with all that he put forward, but the bishop of Nonantola, a member of the same order, remarked to his brother that Phileno was obviously "maximus Lutheranus."

As his abscess grew worse, Phileno went on to Modena, staying in bed for almost a month. Scarcely cured, he went back toward Nonantola, to the villa or palace of Thomaso Carandino at Staggia (at that time in the territory of Nonantola; today a *frazione* of the commune of San Prospero). Henceforth Staggia will bulk large in the account of Phileno in his own "Apologia" and in the Histories of the two Modenese chroniclers, the contemporary Lancellotti and the later Tassoni. It is here the place to note that the lady of the villa was the extraordinarily independent and unconventional Anna Carandina, natural daughter of Count Sigismondo Rangoni. The Rangoni family protected Phileno as long as possible and may have compassed his final escape from Italy after his impending trial and incarceration in Ferrara. But this is to anticipate.

The other hearth for the half fugitive Phileno was the Academy in Modena. Here he was received as Messer Lisia Phileno, Siciliano,

[47] "Apologia," folio 45v.
[48] Angelus Valentinus and Bartholomeus Giselinus Mirandulanus, lector of the Dominican convent in Modena. "Apologia," folio 45v.

accomplished in Latin literature and in Scriptural learning. It is possible that within the circle of the academicians he assumed still another name, that by which he was solely known after his flight to Rhaetia–Camillo.[49] The Academy of Modena was, at this time, under the direction of the physician Giovanni Grillenzoni, a former student of Pietro Pomponazzi. Other members were the Cretan Francesco Porto, teacher of Greek in Modena from 1536 to 1546 and later, reader at the University of Ferrara and teacher of the daughters of Duchess Renata; the equally learned Lodovico Castelvetro;[50] and Carlo Segonio, the famous historian of Roman and Bolognese antiquities. It is of interest that Castelvetro and Porto ended up as Calvinists in Switzerland. Count Ercole Rangoni had come in a very brief time apparently to consider Phileno as a friend, deeply impressed as he was by the unfrocked friar's "*virtù*, imposing doctrine, singular judgment, highest competence in all branches of literature, especially the Bible."[51] The Count noted also the accomplished friar's "incomparable magnanimity and love, the holiness of all his ways, exemplary to those close to him and far from any personal ambition and quest for glory."[52] Alas, this evaluation is at variance with what Phileno freely says proudly in his "Apologia" about his sense of mission, his achievements as a preacher, conversationalist, and writer, everywhere esteemed and praised.

It was during his very brief and interrupted visits in Modena that Phileno gave clearest expression to his views about poverty and the duties of the monks and friars to help the poor and to safeguard them from exploitation. His utterances were called forth by the famine[53] caused by extended drought which oppressed the

[49] There is a bit of evidence that in Modena he took a new name, Camillo Renato. The manuscript evidence for this will be presented by Rotondò in his forthcoming work. As *scholaris* in Bologna he used both Phileno and Ricci.

[50] Letter of Papino (n. 77); Casadei, "Fileno," p. 368. Information on Porto from Francesco Lemmi, *La Riforma in Italia* (Milan, 1939), p. 76.

[51] Tassoni, "Cronaca," p. 331; Casadei, "Fileno," p. 359.

[52] Letter of Count Ercole to Duke Ercole, 18 October 1540, Archivio di Stato di Modena: Particolari; Casadei, "Fileno," pp. 365–367.

[53] Lancellotti, *Cronaca*, pp. X, 402 *passim*.

region at this time. That some of Phileno's teaching bore on the Franciscan theme of apostolic poverty and in the socially radical context of a local famine is suggested also by the fact that the *letterati* of the Academy had, even before his arrival, made the demand that the religious in their convents should be expected to give even more for the poor and the needy than Christians living in the world.[54] There was so much commotion stirred up from the pulpits of the churches, including the cathedral, among the various orders, particularly between the Austin Friars and the Observant Franciscans, that the governor of Modena, Battistino Strozzi, had to report to Count Ercole in a long letter of 18 April 1540.[55]

Social and religious reform will surely have been in the air as a consequence of the meeting of the provincial chapter of the Austin Friars after the Lenten season. The principal preacher was a powerful orator, by many thought to be favorable to Lutheranism, perhaps Seripando himself, present in Bologna April 11 to April 30.[56] Despite Phileno's unfortunate encounter with another Austin Friar earlier in the year in Bologna, one cannot doubt but that he sought out Seripando or an even more congenial representative of the order and that he surely entered into the general discussion following in the wake of his visit. Phileno himself is reported to have preached, possibly from the pulpit of the Conventual Franciscan church and to have challenged the religious orders, the Franciscans included, demanding that they give up their corporate wealth for the benefit of the poor, the better to follow the evange-

[54] Lancellotti, *Cronaca*, p. 205; Casadei, "Fileno," p. 362. The date of this entry is 17 September 1539, a year before Camillo's arrival in Modena.

[55] The letter of Strozzi, said to be in the "Ducale Archivio segreto," is adduced by Tiraboschi, *Biblioteca Modenese*, I, 13. The chronicle of the conflict among the friars is given by Lancellotti, *Cronaca*, pp. 317–336.

[56] The chapter meeting of some two hundred friars began after Easter, March 28. *Ibid.*, pp. xii, 308. On April 18 a preacher of the Austin Friars, Fra Latantio, preached a "most beautiful sermon" in S. Agostino and made known from the vicar of the Dominican inquisitor that his listeners should denounce whoever had or whatever shop sold a little book entitled *El Summario della Sacra Scrittura. Ibid.*, p. 321.

lical counsels which they professed. He is reported to have celebrated the Mass perhaps in some parish church under the patronage of the Rangoni.[57] The latter phrase could, of course, mean also that Phileno conducted the Eucharistic service along the simplified lines permitted in the chapel of Duchess Renata in Ferrara, with communion in both kinds. In his sermons Phileno will have approached Luther's doctrine at several points, for example on the preeminence of faith and election.

Taking leave from the conventual churches and from the company of the Court and the Academy, Phileno also sought out, as occasion afforded, the religiously more radical groups which, in rather large numbers before his arrival in town, had already been meeting in conventicles and private chapels, as perhaps at Staggia. In these circles, some of which had friendly contacts with the Swiss and South German divines, Phileno began to read and comment on the epistles of Paul and guided the study of Scripture in general. The hostile chronicler Tassoni says that in 1540 the wise and the stupid, men and women, professed to decide the sense of Scripture: "Not only men of every condition, learned and ignorant and devoid of a knowledge of letters, but also women, whenever occasion was given — in public places, in squares, shops, and churches, — disputed about faith and the law of Christ, and all out of the Holy Scriptures, promiscuously quoting Paul, Matthew, John, the Apocalypse, and all the doctors whom they never saw."[58]

About the end of August Phileno went out from Modena some twenty kilometers to stay in the villa of the reform-minded Carandini in Staggia, then under the jurisdiction of Nonantola.[59] His hostess, Anna Carandina (1502–1552),[60] and his host, Thomaso

[57] Lancellotti, *Cronaca*, pp. 410; Casadei, "Fileno," p. 369.

[58] Tassoni, "Cronaca", as given by Cantù, *Eretici*, II, 158. The material is also presented in Girolamo Tiraboschi, *Storia della letteratura italiana*, VII:1 (Milan, 1824), 135 f. Cf. above, n. 56.

[59] A sojourn of a month and a half at the palace is based upon the testimony of a Modenese witness at the trial. "Apologia," folio 31v.

[60] She lived a rather unconventional life, remarried after the death of her husband, was called before the judicatory in Ferrara for mistreating a servant,

[23] CAMILLUS RENATUS AND INDIVIDUAL IMMORTALITY 855

Carandino, were possibly induced by Phileno to introduce, as patrons of the local church, a new liturgy (*officium novum*) perhaps modeled on that of Duchess Renata in Ferrara.[61] Phileno is said, however, to have gone only once to attend this service. It was noted by the local rustics, alas, that during Phileno's sojourn at the villa in Staggia for a month and a half his host and hostess did not go to Mass and that he himself was often seen walking with others around the grounds of the palace or nearby at the hour of Mass or shortly thereafter.[62] At his trial Phileno would later deny this hotly and recall that, despite the severe trouble which his thirty-eight year old hostess was having with her feet, she, her husband, their children, and the entire household and retinue walked regularly to Sunday Mass, and he would call down upon the false witness the condign punishment of the law.

At the same time it is clear from Phileno's testimony that he was disgusted by the ignorance and the disorderly lives of the two local priests.[63] One of them was by common rumor a counterfeiter (*monetarius*), the other so inept at Latin that he made no sense of the liturgy, stringing the words together, and subverting the sense. Moreover, both were utterly superstitious, preying on the credulities of parishioners still more simple than themselves. Shabby priests, they gave themselves over to gluttony, games of chance, and various frivolities, thereby incurring the frequent rebuke of Phileno and his noble companions.

It is clear that Phileno would have been loathe to attend Mass celebrated by such priests. He had also compelling physical reasons for abstaining. Besides his recently cured abscess, he was apparently suffering from numerous ailments of the head, liver, stomach, limbs, and notably of his eyes which were so afflicted with discharges that the left one seemed threatened with blindness.[64] All

and because of family altercation was twice interred. Lancellotti, *Cronaca Modenese*, Monumenti, XII, 289 f.

[61] The *officium novum* is mentioned by a witness at the trial. "Apologia," folio 31v.

[62] "Apologia," folios 31v and 38r.   [63] "Apologia," folio 38v.

[64] "Apologia," folio 38r. It is a further evidence of the identity of Phileno

his ailments required medical attention and the therapy of hot and cold baths and medical applications. On some days, he later records, he was scarcely able to rise from his bed in the morning. Then, to compound his difficulties, he seriously hurt his foot on a rock when he was returning from Mirandola and for almost a fortnight he had to keep to his abode.

The best that can be made of the conflicting evidence is that the spirited lord and lady of Staggia undoubtedly attended the local church from time to time in the company of their learned guest but that the center of their religious speculation at Staggia was the palace salon; and our radical Franciscan undoubtedly celebrated the Eucharist in the palace chapel in a quasi-Protestant manner, restored, as Phileno would have explained, to its original "dignity and integrity."

The rancor of the local priests, the enmity of other denizens of the region, and the persistence of the aggrieved Austin Friars and Dominicans of Bologna finally combined to bring about the capture of Phileno in plain day in the open road. It was "il messo della Croce," or a *missus* of the local sodality of cross-wearing informers, the *societas Crucesignatorum*, usually summoned by a bell,[65] who pointed out Phileno to the detachment of knights in search of him. Phileno says the capture took place on October 14 with many Modenese in the crowd.[66]

The Modenese chronicler, in contrast, says that the arrest took place suddenly on Sunday 17 October 1540 when Phileno and several of his followers were presumably gathered for worship in the villa of Madonna Anna Carandina.[67] The chronicler says further that the knights were retainers of Duke Ercole II, who had ordered the arrest from his seat in Ferrara. It is also reported that but for his foolhardiness (*leggerezza*), Phileno, duly warned, could easily have saved himself. Trusting "too much in himself,"

---

and Camillo Renato that Camillo is known to have died blind in one eye.
[65] Paul Hinschius, *System des katholischen Kirchenrechts*, V:1 (Berlin, 1893), 461.
[66] "Apologia," folio 43r.
[67] Lancellotti, *Cronaca*, p. 410.

he wished "to tempt God."[68] The foolhardiness consisted in Phileno's openly moving back and forth between Staggia and Modena, carried in a two-wheeled cart (*cisium*) because of his several ailments, even after he knew himself to be under suspicion.[69]

Count Ercole Rangoni of Modena almost at once wrote to his superior Duke Ercole in Ferrara, the spouse of reform-minded Duchess Renata (Renée), declaring his confidence in the probity of the "poor innocent" friar, in words quoted more fully above, charging the Dominicans with jealousy and machination in having the attractive Franciscan preacher and humanist arrested. He implored the duke to see to it that the trial, should it come to that, be conducted fairly and if possible by non-partisan judges.[70] Rangoni apparently took steps to arrange the amelioration of the place of Phileno's detention and was presumably seconded by the governor of Modena, Battistino Strozzi, who apprised the duke in Ferrara of the arrest and of the condition of "the highly cultured" occupant of the castle prison.[71]

The vicar of the bishop of Modena had an entirely different opinion of the prisoner from that of the incredulous count of Modena. In a letter of 16 October to his bishop, Giovanni Morone (soon to be named cardinal), at the time papal nuncio in Germany,[72]

---

[68] The order for the arrest was dated 10 October. Letter of the governor of Modena (n. 11). Lancellotti gives both the date, 17 October, and the name of Anna Carandina, *Cronaca*, pp. 403, 405, 410. It is of interest that at the trial of Pietro Antonio Cervia, beginning 1563 in Modena, a certain Claudio Carandino is cited as heretical. See John Tedeschi, *Miscellanea Sozzini*. The *frazione* of Staggia continued to harbor persons like Phileno. We have a letter of his fellow academician, Castelvetro, from his villa in Staggia, 8 October 1545. Giuseppe Cavazzuti, *Lodovico Castelvetro* (Modena, 1903), p. 72; cf. p. 197, n. 1. The fact that Phileno courted arrest is inferred from the letter of Cypriano Quadrio to Giulio Milanese, 13 February 1541. See below, at n. 85, Casadei, "Fileno," pp. 326, 377.

[69] "Apologia," folio 46v.

[70] Letter of Count Ercole to Duke Ercole, n. 52 above.

[71] Letter of governor of Modena, n. 11 above.

[72] Morone was named bishop of Modena in 1529, but had not been able to take possession of his see because of the interference of Cardinal Ippolito d'Este. Letter of vicar to bishop, n. 15 above.

the vicar described among "the sowers of heresy in the diocese" our radical Franciscan who "according to his manner, calls himself by various names."[73] The vicar called the friar a "ribaldo" who had, moreover, proceeded to excite social unrest among the peasants and artisans imprisoned with him. Surely the biased vicar was going on rumour only when he included homicide along with heresy among the charges now brought against the friar; for violence does not feature in any of the more circumstantial reports of the hearings and the final trial. At best, we can only conjecture that there is here a distorted echo of the armed attempt on the open roads to prevent the passage of the Dominican inquisitors intent on entering Modena on an errand possibly related to the apprehension or prosecution of suspects associated with Phileno.[74] Morone himself in a letter from Worms to Cardinal Farnese, 27 December 1540, was closer to the truth when he observed in simple dismay that there was more heresy in his Modena than in Bohemia and in Germany and proceeded to specify the teachings that were being openly proclaimed in his diocese, against purgatory, against the Mass, against ecclesiastical power, and against the invocation of the saints, all with the tacit support of the supposed defenders of the city.[75] From Morone's letter and from that of his vicar, as from other sources already cited, it is clear that Phileno did not lack for intercessors who repudiated the charges of sedition, immorality, and heresy, saying that he was being calumniated merely "for being exceedingly learned in Scriptures and in Platonic [sic] doctrine."[76] The Rangoni and other noble supporters felt so strongly about Phileno that through their direct or indirect armed intervention the Dominican inquisitor of Bologna was prevented from transferring the records of the first hearing in Bologna to reinforce the findings in Modena.[77]

[73] The vicar gives only the two names already introduced: Fileno and Paolo.
[74] Letter of Papino, n. 77 below.
[75] Ludwig Cardauns ed., *Nuntiaturberichte aus Deutschland* (1533–1559), VI (Berlin, 1910), No. 270.   [76] Letter of vicar to bishop, n. 15 above.
[77] The letter of the inquisitor Papino to the duke of Ferrara, 28 October 1540; Casadei, "Fileno," p. 368.

[27] CAMILLUS RENATUS AND INDIVIDUAL IMMORTALITY 859

Despite the efforts of Modenese supporters, including the count and the academicians,[78] the hearing of Phileno as a "Lutheran heretic" began in the prison of the castle in Modena 26 October under the direction of Dominican inquisitors from both Bologna and Ferrara.[79] By 28 October 1540 sufficiently incriminating evidence had been assembled to justify the transfer of the trial this time to the ducal capital, Ferrara.[80] The evidence brought forward in the Modenese hearings was not of such a character as to undermine the devotion of all the heretical friar's followers. The excited populace was perhaps divided in its passions. Phileno was taken, bound, out of town by armed guard at night; and the populace was diverted by an officially inspired rumor that he would be conducted through the gate leading to Bologna to be burned instead of to Ferrara for another hearing.[81]

In the meantime Cardinal Gasparo Contarini had become interested in Phileno, or rather, in the theological points at issue in the hearings. A letter of 16 November 1540 from Duke Ercole to his ambassador Bonifacio Ruggieri (former *podestà* of Modena)[82] indicates that the most powerful Italian ecclesiastic in favor of irenic efforts to conciliate German Protestants had already made discreet inquiries about the heretical Sicilian.[83] In view of his own very difficult position among his confrères in the Italian hierarchy, Cardinal Contarini will have been somewhat concerned lest the Augustinian (Lutheranizing) doctrine of election and justification be compromised in high circles by the vagaries of an irresponsible friar. Since the cardinal himself was at variance also with the popular Catholic conception of free will and merit,

[78] "The Academy wished to help him." Lancellotti, *Cronaca*, p. 405.

[79] The hearing in the castle prison began 26 October. Lancellotti, *Cronaca*, p. 405; Casadei, "Fileno," p. 367.

[80] Letter of Papino, n. 77 above.

[81] Lancellotti, *Cronaca*, pp. 410, 419 f.; Tassoni, "Cronaca," p. 331; Casadei, "Fileno," pp. 369, 372 f.

[82] The *cavaliere* Ruggieri was *podestà* in 1538. Luigi Napoleone Cittadella, *Notizie relative a Ferrara per la maggior parte inedite* (Ferrara, 1864), p. 369.

[83] Archivio di Stato di Modena: Dispaccio da Roma, filza 28; Casadei, "Fileno," p. 371.

he was doubtless anxious that the interrelated doctrines of salvation by faith and predestination not be imperiled by the taint of moral improbity on the part of the eloquent Modenese preacher of ecclesiastical reform, divine election, and psychopannychism. The cardinal's inquiries had apparently turned up not only the usual charge of Phileno's being "a very seditious person" but also the extraordinary rumor that Phileno's "ribaldry" was nothing less than bigamy or rather that the friar had "had four (women)."[84] Since no moral charges will be brought against Phileno in the records closest to the hearings and the final trial at Ferrara, we may assume that this rumor, like the other, even worse, contained in the correspondence with Cardinal Morone, can be ascribed to frenzied inferences and deliberate distortions on the part of the opponents of the popular humanist. It is not to be excluded, however, that in the fellowship of the popular conventicles meeting in the homes of the radicals of several social classes in and around Modena and earlier in Bologna the conduct of the friar was open to criticism.[85] It may be sufficient, however, to safeguard Phileno's honor to state that even after the trial, Duke Ercole continued to speak of Phileno as a man "of quality" and crossed out of his letter the charge against Phileno as "tristo et ribaldo," replacing it simply with the charge of his being a heretic.[86]

We turn now to the details of this trial of Lisia Phileno *alias* Paolo Ricci in Ferrara. There are four principal sources: the XLIII Articles[87] of Bologna and the "Apologia," the Abjuration and

---

[84] *Ibid.*, filza 27; Casadei, "Fileno," p. 376. In the text the word is *bigomio*. The letter containing it comes after the completion of the trial; but the rumor, reported to the duke by Ruggieri as something mentioned by Contarini, must have been picked up previously.

[85] It is of interest in this connection that one Giulio Milanese, later to become pastor in Vicosoprano and then Poschiavo in Rhaetia, was acquainted with the *leggerezza* of Renato-Phileno, when he was himself under judicial scrutiny in Venice in the spring of 1541.

[86] Letter of Duke Ercole to Bonifacio Ruggieri, 28 December 1540; B. Fontana, *Renata di Francia* (Rome, 1893), II, 137; Casadei, "Fileno," p. 375.

[87] The XLIII Articles in the Archiginnasio of Bologna with other new

Alessandro Tassoni's now published "Cronaca di Modena." The "Apologia" in forty-eight folios was prepared in several copies[88] by Phileno in the prison of the Dominican convent of the no longer extant Santa Maria degli Angeli,[89] where Girolamo Savonarola had once taken his vows. Attached to the "Apologia" are nine folios containing the trial and signed by the notary Boethius de Sylvestris.

The final trial in Ferrara took place in a chamber above the prison of Degli Angeli in four sessions beginning 12 December 1540. The trial proceeded in the presence of two judges: the one, the suffragan bishop[90] as the representative of Cardinal Giovanni Salviati, archbishop of Ferrara; the other, Fra Stefano Foscharara, Dominican inquisitor from Bologna.[91] The presence of the Cardinal's vicar, Bishop Ottaviano, would appear to represent Duke Ercole's accommodation to Count Ercole's request that "the poor innocent" be given as impartial a trial as possible. Six consultors heard the testimony of a score of witnesses including at least one woman of Modena. The most moderate of the consultors, appointed advocate for Phileno, was Lodovico de Silvestris, doctor (of canon law).

Before we listen to the verdict of the consultors and hear the sentence of the lord inquisitor and overhear the abjuration of the heretic, it is appropriate to bring together the main points espoused by Phileno in order to have before us a balanced delineation of the kind of radical reform he was preaching in various circles. They were, in fact, brought as IX Accusations at the trial in Ferrara.[92]

---

materials will be adduced in article of Antonio Rotondò, "Per la storia dell' eresia a Bologna nel secolo XVI," *Rinascimento*, XIII (1962).

[88] "Apologia," folio 1A.

[89] A picture of church and convent, built in 1440, may be seen in Dante Balboni, "Briciole Savonaroliane," *Studi Savonaroliani*, Atti e Memorie della Deputazione Provinciale Ferrarese di Storia Patria, n.s., III, Part III (Ferrara, 1932/33), opp. p. 66.

[90] Ottaviano da Castello Vescovo di S. Leone.

[91] Tassoni, "Cronaca," pp. 331 f.; Cantù, *Eretici*, pp. 157–159; Casadei, "Fileno," pp. 373–375.

[92] The following is based upon Phileno's avowals and abjurations. Tassoni,

These in turn can be grouped under three main headings, namely, 1) that salvation depends utterly upon the divine election with no meritorious use of one's free will; 2) that the souls of the righteous and the wicked expire at the death of the body and have no abiding place until the general resurrection and the last judgment (psychopannychism); and hence 3) that all the liturgical and penitential practices based on the alleged existence of a purgatory filled with sinners and of a paradise filled with saints constitute a religious deception that has given rise to intolerable social exploitation of simple believers by the professionally religious.

As for the first, his doctrine of election, Phileno stood with the Protestant Reformers to the north and could therefore be plausibly accused of being a Calvinist or a Lutheran. Nevertheless, as we have already noted, Cardinal Contarini (himself concerned to preserve or recover the fullness of the Augustinian doctrine which belonged to the common heritage) had found occasion to observe that on this first point Phileno was improperly accused of heresy. And, precisely on this point Phileno, citing several patristic and scholastic authorities, contended against his detractors and misinterpreters that he acknowledged the freedom of the will but he claimed also that because of original sin this will, without being "liberated by the power of the Holy Spirit,"[93] could never perform anything but evil. He adduced in his favor the whole tradition of the Fathers and the Schoolmen, specifying Cyprian, Augustine against Pelagius, Ambrose, the epistles of five bishops to Pope Innocent I, the Council of Mileve against Pelagius and Coelestius in 416, the II Council of Orange (under Caesarius of Arles) in 529 against the Semipelagians, Popes Gregory I and Leo I, and Thomas Aquinas. At the end he was forced to repudiate his view "that man does not have a free will except to do evil" and to avow instead "that man has a free will both to do good and to do evil, although, to be sure, he cannot perform works worthy of eternal life without the special grace of the Holy Spirit."

"Cronaca," pp. 331 f.; Casadei, "Fileno," pp. 373–375; and the MS "Apologia."
[93] "Apologia," folio 25 r, cf. folio 5A.

With what Phileno would have preferred to call simply the Pauline (rather than either the Lutheran or the Augustinian) view of predestination and of the bondage of the will and with his second main doctrine concerning the provisional death of the soul Phileno had forged a highly sharpened two-edged sword which he could wield with frightening skill in cutting away the vestiges of the ecclesiastical merit system surviving, as he would later say, in even the Reformed churches. We turn to examine this second edge of Phileno's trenchant theology.

The view that the soul at the death of the body falls into a dreamlike sleep and the starker conception of the complete extinction of the soul, in either case, with the hope of resuscitation with the body at the resurrection and for the final judgment are to be found, as noted by way of introduction, in the New Testament. It is not likely, however, that Phileno drew his eschatology directly from the Scriptures but rather from the theories of the *Studium* of Padua and Bologna where philosophical and medical speculation had worked with the Averroistic idea of the death of the sentient *anima* with the body and the absorption of the individuated *anima intellectiva* into the universal intellect (*intellectus universalis* or *agens*) and the even more drastic Alexandrist idea about the mortality of the soul expounded by Pomponazzi. That Phileno's espousal of the provisional death or sleep of the soul could be interpreted by the inquisitorial court of Ferrara as one with the most extreme heresies, exceeding in gravity even Calvinism, is suggested by the title of a work of the humanist crypto-Protestant Celio Secondo Curione writing in Lucca in the year after Phileno's trial, *De immortalitate animorum*, which was specifically directed against "Anabaptists," "Epicureans," and "Sadduces."[94]

To use as nearly as possible his own words, Phileno presumably

---

[94] On the background, also with special reference to Renato-Phileno, see Delio Cantimori, "Anabattismo e Neoplatonismo nel xvi secolo in Italia," *Rendiconti della R. Academia Nazionale dei Lincei*, cl. di. sc. mor., May/June, 1936, pp. 521–561.

held prior to his trial "that the souls of the saints and the others justified have not yet entered heaven and will not enter in fact until after the last judgment" and therefore that they do not yet "enjoy the delights of paradise" nor "the vision of the highest God."[95] By the same token, the souls of sinful believers are not suffering in purgatory. And this leads to the third major feature of Phileno's radical reformation.

The whole complex of ecclesiastical practices which presupposed the survival of the sentient soul in the interim before the general resurrection completely gives way in Phileno's theology under the pressure of his stress on eschatology and predestination. The saints are not yet in heaven to intercede on behalf of the living. Or at least — so he preferred to argue in the presence of the tribunal — the Old Testament and the New and even the early canons of the Church are aware of the great danger of idolatry and therefore do not require prayers to the saints as a matter of faith. Since like all souls, the soul of the Virgin Mary is at peace until the general resurrection, prayer even to her is of no avail, only the *Pater noster* as taught by Jesus being efficacious.[96] Since, then, all prayers and ecclesiastical practices based upon the assumption of a natural immortality of the sentient soul susceptible of pain or pleasure are without Scriptural warrant, not only are all Masses for the dead invalid but also all prayers of intercession, and the whole penitential system of confessions and fasts, especially during Lent. Moreover, the Mass should be celebrated in its primitive simplicity just as it was instituted by Jesus and recorded by the evangelists and Paul. Chapels, convents, and monasteries which exist partly by reason of the endowments for the saying of Masses for the dead should be disbanded and vows should be dissolved. As for this last point, which was existential for him as a friar who had once taken vows, and for the devout poor, Phileno declared expressly that "one should not make a vow to God or

---

[95] These phrases are from the abjuration, and they appear also in the "Apologia."

[96] "Apologia," folios 13r, 26v.

to the saints and that, even having done so, one should not fulfil it," once liberated by the true gospel.[97]

Given the radical character of Phileno's teachings, it is a wonder that the inquisitors in the proceedings begun at Bologna, continued at Modena, and terminated at Ferrara just before Christmas 1540, took so long to declare Phileno a heretic.[98] The fact is that the brilliant rhetorician and well-versed theologian had been so resourceful in parrying the charges of the witnesses by citing such ancient authorities as Cyprian and Chrysostom and such later writers as Scotus and Erasmus that the advocate among the six consultors, Lodovico de Silvestris, could contend that Phileno was not "formally heretical," that he had effectively advanced Scriptural, patristic, and scholastic reasons for his doubts, and that he had all told offered enough explanation of the spirit in which he was probing for answers "to alleviate his case" and to justify the tribunal in sparing him the ordinary penalties for stubborn heretics. Until persuaded by the majority, Lodovico proposed that the tribunal find some "extraordinary" remedy suitable to the case.

The five remaining consultors found Phileno indeed guilty of heresy; but at least one, Fra Girolamo dei Landi, O.P., lector on metaphysics at the University of Ferrara, urged that the normal punishment be mitigated lest Phileno "fall into despair." The three consultors who voted for the normal punishment of a clever but obdurate heretic were Fra Giovanni Verato, Carmelite professor of theology at the University of Ferrara, Dom Giacomo Emiliano of Ferrara, doctor of law, and Fra Andrea da Imola, O.P., lector and priest in the convent of Santa Maria degli Angeli in Ferrara. The most severe in his judgment among the consultors was Dom Lanfranco di Lugo, doctor and professor in Ferrara, who was certain that Phileno, because of his pertinacity in responses, his excuses, evasions, and frivolities, was at heart impenitent, and that he should therefore be given over to the secular arm for the ultimate punishment. It would appear that Lanfranco, though

[97] Abjuration and "Apologia," folio 8A.
[98] The opinions of the six consultors are found in "Apologia," folio 9A.

the most pitiless, was also the most discerning of the consultors!

The final sentence was that Phileno should make a public abjuration and that he should be verbally degraded from his ecclesiastical rank and consigned to perpetual imprisonment. That he was only *verbally* degraded confirms our impression that for some time, perhaps since his stay in Venice, Phileno had not been wearing the habit of a friar.

According to the sentence, Phileno publicly recanted all his heresies. The accounts all agree that after the recantation there was "a solemn procession," at the end of which Phileno's sentence as a convicted "Lutheran" was read and he was mitred.[99] After his confession of the Catholic faith,[100] Phileno went on to promise that he would not in future adhere to any of the aforementioned heresies; that he would not seek to win any others to them; that he would not harbor any heretical books; that, if in future he should know of any one infected with any of these heresies or to be in possession of such books, he would inform on them before the two ecclesiastics who had conducted his trial; that he would neither flee nor leave without the approval, permission, and consent of the local authorities; that he would not complain about the penance to be exacted of him; and, finally, that if he should ever contravene his solemn promises, he would willingly submit to all the penalties due the relapsed according to the canon law. The provisions here enumerated strangely suggest that there was in fact an effort (inspired perhaps by Duchess Renata) to rehabilitate the much-admired preacher in return for his formal recantation. These provisions point to a kind of house arrest or gentleman's detention on good behavior rather than life imprisonment for penance. Yet the very document which contains the abjuration and these conditions states elsewhere that he was sentenced to

---

[99] Letter of Duke Ercole to Ruggeri, n. 86, above; Lancellotti, *Cronaca*, pp. 419 f.; Casadei, "Fileno," p. 372.

[100] These special provisions coming at the end of the abjuration are to be found in Tassoni, "Cronaca," pp. 31 f.; Casadei, "Fileno," pp. 374 f.; Cf. "Apologia," folio 5A.

imprisonment[101] for life. A third source, Duke Ercole[102] in his letter to his ambassador in Rome with information for Contarini, in mentioning the sentence of life imprisonment, interprets it as in itself the act of clemency secured by him in recognition of the fact that the penitent heretic was a man "di tale qualitade".

It is possible that the duke himself chose to interpret the sentence of confinement more liberally than the inquisitors. Phileno was at some point after the trial taken from Ferrara to a prison in Bologna, as we learn from an entry in the Modenese chronicle under date of 11 May 1541.[103] The same source reports that Phileno "was said to have accused many persons of heresy," as indeed he had promised he would in the abjuration forced from him in Ferrara.

There is, however, no evidence that his alleged delations affected his followings in Modena, Bologna, and presumably Ferrara. At least his ideas remained a potent influence. One Modenese chronicler observed that "the evil seed sown by him had, in the meantime, taken deep root;" another, that the doctrine of the immortality of the soul was the subject of an important sermon in the cathedral.[104] Moreover, three letters from Martin Bucer in Strassburg, dated 17 August, 10 September, and 23 December 1541,[105] indicate that radical ideas about predestination and the

[101] Lancellotti, *Cronaca*, pp. 49 f.; Casadei, "Fileno," p. 373. This report is based on one Andrea Barco Cancelero of Modena who happened to be in Ferrara on the day of the solemn sentence, having gone there to present the duke with some fine pigs. Andrea is reported to have described the punishment as that of Phileno's being bound for life in the galley (*galéa*), but this is probably a misreading for prison (*galera*).

[102] Letter of Duke Ercole, to Ruggieri, n. 86 above.

[103] Lancellotti, *Cronaca*, VII, 53; Casadei, "Fileno," p. 375.

[104] Tassoni, "Cronaca," quoted by Cantù, *Eretici*, II, 137 f.; Lancellotti, *Cronaca*, p. 52, under date of 9 May 1541. The Phileno affair was to be remembered as a *cause célèbre* in Modena well into the seventeenth century. See Lodovico Vedriani, *Historia della antichissima città di Modona* (Modena, 1667), II 528.

[105] Bucer or pseudonymously as Aretius Felinus writes three letters: "to the Italians," "to the brethern in Bologna and Modena," "to the Italians," (perhaps in Lucca). Works of Bucer arranged topically by Konrad Hubert

Lord's Supper were agitating the evangelical conventicles of Bologna and Modena at this time. These evangelicals whom Bucer addressed as brothers were exercised by the question "whether God is the author of sin"[106] and whether Christ was in any sense present in the elements of the communion. Lacking, as we do, the letters by which or the informants through whom Bucer learned of the controversy in Bologna and Modena, we can only infer from certain locutions that the Strassburg divine was dealing with a doctrinal ferment more radical than he realized, and that the questions posed were precisely those raised by Phileno.

There is, for example, a faint trace in Bucer's coping with the eucharistic problem of sacrament, mystery, and symbol of the terminology known to have been employed by Phileno at least at a later date. There is a bare suggestion in the terms employed by Bucer for the proper conduct of the eucharistic service that the Italians, under Phileno's influence, had already introduced an *agape* before the communion and that in the observation thereof the distinction between the minister and the *plebs* had been programmatically obliterated.[107] Such egalitarianism suggests Phileno's known ecclesiological views, commonly pilloried as subversive.

Scripta Anglicana (Basel, 1577), pp. 687–689. It is of interest that the conciliatory work of Contarini at Regensburg (Ratisbon) in 1541 was preceded by that of Martin Bucer and Johann Gropper at Worms in the *Liber Ratisbonensis*) presented at the Colloquy of Regensburg.

[106] A certain Alexander is mentioned in the letter of 23 December. The fact that in this letter Bucer mentions the recent death of Capito (3 November 1541) suggests that one of the mediators of information from Bologna and Modena might have been Francesco Negri, at the time in Chiavenna (whither Phileno would presently flee); for Negri had studied with Bucer and Capito in Strassburg between 1529 and 1531 and would have given currency among the Italian Evangelicals to the name of the otherwise much less widely known Capito. It is, of course, also possible that Calvin had familiarized the Reform-minded circle with the name of Capito, during his stay at the court of Duchess Renata in 1536.

[107] See especially the letter of 10 September wherein Bucer insists that only the Scriptural words and not those of the minister should be employed and that the *ministri* were present "ad distribuendum et sumendum, plebs, ad sumendum" and the injunction: "edamus et bibamus, non circumferamus vel

Some time in 1542 Phileno escaped from the prison in Bologna, perhaps with the connivance of Duchess Renata, and appeared in Tirano in the Valtellina, a protectorate of the Rhaetian Republic, itself confederated with the Swiss. From Tirano he addressed a letter under date of 9 November 1542[108] to Heinrich Bullinger in Zurich; and, signing himself perhaps for the first time "Camillo Renato," he began therewith his extraordinary career within and against the Reformed Church of Rhaetia.

In 1548 Phileno-Renato and his followers would be anathematized by the chief spokesman of the Italian-speaking Reformed churches, the ex-Austin Friar, Agostino Mainardo, pastor in Chiavenna. The first of the XXII Anathemas will read: "We damn those who say [like Renato] that the rational soul (*anima rationalis*) is mortal, that it dies along with the body, but that on the Last Day it will be resurrected with the body, and that then the whole man will be made truly immortal."[109]

Phileno-Renato was to be condemned by the Reformed Church of Rhaetia not only for his psychopannychism but also for his Libertine formulation of the doctrine of election; also for his observance of the Eucharist as a nourishing *agape* or fellowship meal for commingled rich and poor, natives and refugees, in the mountainside parish of Caspano under the patronage of the locally powerful Paravicini family; for introducing adult or

---

includamus." These words could, to be sure, just as well be used by Bucer to mark off the evangelical from the elaborate Catholic observances; but in the context Bucer seems to be warning against extremes on the left rather than on the right. It should be remarked that not only in the evangelical conventicles but also even in the Cappella di Renata di Francia in Ferrara, "la messa di sette punti" was observed, modeled no doubt on the simplified service as observed at the court of Navarre, with communion in both kinds.

[108] Traugott Schiess, *Bullingers Korrespondenz mit den Graubündern*, three volumes, Quellen zur Schweizer Geschichte, XXIII (1904), XXIV (1905), XXV (1906), No. 37, pp. 48–51.

[109] The XXII Anathemas of Mainardo are printed by Petro Domenico Rosio da Porta, *Historia Reformationis ecclesiarum Raeticarum*, 2 volumes (Chur, 1771/74), I:2, 83–86. Cf. Mainardo's letter to Bullinger, 10 December 1548, Schiess, *op. cit.*, XXIII, 139 f.

believers' baptism; and for preaching religious toleration and defending Michael Servetus in another long *carmen*.

In the meantime he will have found occasion to share his convictions with a youthful visitor from Bologna, Laelius Socinus. The ideas and practices, the strengths and weaknesses, the vision and the vacillation of Ricci-Phileno-Renato were to be perpetuated in Socinianism.

PROSELYTES AND PROSELYTISM DURING THE SECOND COMMONWEALTH AND THE EARLY TANNAITIC PERIOD

by SOLOMON ZEITLIN

IN THE RABBINIC LITERATURE the term for a convert to Judaism, a proselyte is *ger*. It has another connotation in the Pentateuch, sojourner, one who came to live in the country for a while. The Pentateuch refers to the children of Israel as *gerim* who came from the land of Canaan to live in Egypt.[1] The Pentateuch as well as the early prophets did not recognize conversion. Yahweh was held to be an ethnic God, the God of the children of Abraham, Isaac and Jacob with whom He made a covenant. Yahweh was the God of the descendants of those whom He had brought out of Egypt, the land of slavery. Hence those who were not descendants of Abraham, Isaac and Jacob and whose ancestors were not slaves in Egypt could not worship Yahweh.

During the time of the Second Commonwealth the Judaean religion went through a revolutionary transformation due to the influence of the prophets and the teaching of the Pharisees. Yahweh was no longer believed to be an ethnic god, the God of the Judaeans alone; now He was held to be the God of the entire universe. The four letters, the Tetragrammaton, were now pronounced *Adonai*, the Lord of the universe. Anyone could accept Him. Hence conversion not only became possible but desirable.[2]

The author of the book of Ruth relates that Ruth, the Moabite, who after her husband's death returned to Judaea said to her mother-in-law, Naomi, "Thy people shall be my people, and thy

---

[1] Ex. 23: 8. כי גרים הייתם בארץ מצרים.
[2] Cf. S. Zeitlin, *The Rise and Fall of the Judaean State*, I. Idem. "The Pharisees," *JQR* (Oct. 1961), 29–33; 269–281.

God my God."³ These words could not have been uttered when conversion was unheard of. The author wanted to stress the desirability of conversion. According to the Pentateuch "an Ammonite or a Moabite shall not enter into the assembly of Yahweh; even to the tenth generation shall none of them enter into the assembly of Yahweh forever."⁴ The author of the book of Ruth made Ruth say, "Thy people shall be my people, and thy God my God" and she later married Boaz, a leading man of Judah. King David, the anointed of God, was a descendant of this union. It is true that later the Sages, in order to reconcile the contradictory and opposing view between the book of Ruth and the book of Deuteronomy, said that the Pentateuchal prohibition regarding the Moabites referred only to the male but not to the female.⁵ At a still later period the Sages advanced the view that the Pentateuchal prohibition regarding the Moabites did not refer to the period after the time of Sennacherib, the king of Assyria.⁶

The author of the book of Judith relates that one of the generals of Holofernes named Achior, an Ammonite, after the victory of the Israelites over the hosts of Holofernes, "joined unto the house of Israel."⁷ The book of Judith is not based on historical facts. It is fictitious. It may be that some current event prompted the author to write the book. It is primarily a religious book, emphasizing that righteousness will ultimately triumph, and that the Jews will be victorious over their enemies as long as they observe the laws of God. He also brought out the idea of proselytism, purposely making the general of the Holofernes army an Ammonite who spoke in favor of the Jews. He said to Holofernes

---

³ 1:16. עמך עמי ואלהיך אלהי.

⁴ 23:4. לא יבא עמוני ומואבי בקהל ה׳ גם דור עשירי לא יבא להם בקהל.

⁵ M. Yeb. 8, 3. עמוני ומואבי אסורים ואיסורן איסור עולם אבל נקבותיהם מותרות מיד.

⁶ Yad. 4. בו ביום בא יהודה גר עמוני לפניהם בבהמ״ד אמר להם מה אני לבא בקהל א״ל ר׳ גמליאל אסור אתה א״ל ר׳ יהושע מותר אתה... כבר עלה סנחריב מלך אשור ובלבל את כל האומות... והתירוהו לבא בקהל. Tosefta ibid., 2, 17.

⁷ 14:10.

that as long as the Jews will observe the laws of God none can vanquish them. Ultimately this Ammonite general became a convert to the Jewish religion. The author emphasizes that Ammonites, like any other foreigners, are welcome to become converts to Judaism and a member of the Judaeans.

In the books of Ruth and Judith conversion to Judaism is clearly stated. The former, a canonical book, states that Ruth, a Moabite, became converted to Judaism. The latter, an apocryphal book, states that an Ammonite was converted to Judaism. These two conversions are in direct contradiction to the laws given in Deuteronomy against the Moabites and the Ammonites. The book of Ruth was written in Judaea and the book of Judith was written in the Diaspora. Both books were written in the period when the Judaeans were influenced by the Pharisees who held that Yahweh is the God of the universe, the father and the ruler of all mankind.

In the book of Esther it is related that after Haman was hanged the Jews "had gladness and joy. And many from among the peoples of the land מתיהדים; for the fear of the Judaeans was fallen upon them."[8] The word מתיהדים is rendered by the JPS translation "became Jews." The same rendering is given in the authorized version. Rashi, in his commentary on the word, has מתגיירים "became converts." The translation of the word, מתיהדים to mean that the people of the land became Jews, is faulty. At the time of the composition of the book of Esther there could not have been conversions to Judaism. That Yahweh was the God of the Universe was not yet the prevailing belief of the Judaeans. The word מתיהדים is to be rendered "they pretended to be Judaeans," i.e., the fear of the Judaeans which fell upon the people of the land made them pretend to be Judaeans. A similar word is given in the story that when King Jeroboam sent his wife to the prophet Ahijah to inquire about the illness of his son she disguised herself in order that the prophet should not recognize her.[9] The expression

---

[8] ורבים מעמי הארץ מתיהדים כי נפל פחד היהודים עליהם.
[9] I Kings 14:5–6. והיא מתנכרה... למה זה את מתנכרה.

given is מתנכרה "she will feign herself to be another woman." Similarly in the book of Samuel it is related that when Ammon fell in love with Tamar, his sister, and wanted her to come to him, his friend Jonadab advised him to התחל "to pretend to be sick."[10] Thus it is clear that the words מתנכרה, מתיהדים have the connotation "to pretend to be what one is not."

When conversion to Judaism was made possible, the term for it was מומר changer, i.e., one who changed his god for the God of Israel.[11] Conversion became prevalent at the time when theocracy was abolished and nomocracy, i.e. the rule of the law was established. Thus a convert to Judaism was called a changer to the law. One who left the Judaeans and adopted another religion was termed a changer of the law, i.e. he changed his religion.[12] Josephus wrote that when Epiphanes, the son of King Antiochus, refused to marry Drusilla, the sister of King Agrippa, the reason was that he did not want to change to the Judaean law,[13] he did not want to be a changer. On the other hand one who left Judaism was also called a changer. The author of III Maccabees said that Dositheus was born a Jew but became a Hellene, using the phrase "he changed his laws."[14] Similarly the author of II Maccabees used the expression "change" in the case when a Jew changed his laws for the customs of the pagans.[15] In the Tannaitic literature a person who abandoned Judaism for another religion was termed מומר, a changer.

In the later Tannaitic literature a convert to Judaism was called a *ger*. The word *ger* occurs frequently in the Pentateuch where it has the connotation of a stranger, a newcomer to the land of Israel. The same term was applied to one who became a convert to Judaism, a newcomer to the Jewish people. In the Septuagint the word *ger* is translated *proselytos* with the same connotation, a newcomer to a foreign land. When the word *ger* was applied

---

[10] II Sam. 13:5–6. שכב על משכבך והתחל... וישכב אמנון ויתחל.
[11] Jer. 2:11. ההימיר גוי אלהים... ועמי המיר.
[12] *Pes.* 96. המרת הדת. *Suk.* 56. שהמירה דתה.
[13] *Ant.* 20.7.1 (139). ...'Ιουδαίων ἔθη μεταλαβεῖν [μεταβαλεῖν].
[14] 1:3. μεταβαλὼν τὰ νόμιμα.   [15] 6:24.

[5] PROSELYTES AND PROSELYTISM 875

to a convert to Judaism the same Greek word *proselytos* also came to mean a convert to Judaism. However one who left Judaism was still named מומר, changer.

Neither the term *ger*, in the sense of a convert to Judaism, nor the term *proselytos*, with the same connotation, occurs in the early literature of the Second Commonwealth. It is true that in a story related in the Talmud about a foreigner who came to Hillel to be converted to Judaism the word *ger* is used.[16] We have to bear in mind, however, that the story does not come from Hillel but was related at a later period. The word *proselytos*, in the sense of a convert to Judaism, does not occur in the apocryphal literature nor in the writings of Josephus. Philo employs *proselytos* three times in his writings. In two instances he copies the term from the Septuagint which renders the word *ger* by *proselytos*, a sojourner.[17] In the third instance he may have used *proselytos* in the meaning of convert to Judaism.[18]

Originally a *proselyte* did not have to undergo particular rites. That he had rejected idols and accepted the God of Israel as the God of the universe was sufficient. In the above mentioned story about the foreigner who came to Hillel to be converted, Hillel said to him, "What is hurtful to you do not do to your fellow man, the rest is commentary; go and study." Hillel implied that when the foreigner accepted the God of Israel as the God of the universe he had already embraced the main principle of Judaism. The next principle was the relationship between man and man, and this he should study. To use a later rabbinic expression, — one who denies idol worship recognizes the entire Torah.[19] In the story related in *Antiquities* about the conversion of Izates, the son of Queen Helena, a Jew named Ananias persuaded him to

---

[16] *Shab.* 31. מעשה בנכרי [גוי] שבא לפני שמאי אמר ליה גיירני ע״מ שתלמדני כל התורה כולה כשאני עומד על רגל אחת דחפו באמת הבנין שבידו בא לפני הלל גייריה אמר ליה דעלך סני לחברך לא תעביד זו היא כל התורה כולה ואידך פירושה היא זיל גמיר.

[17] *On Dreams*, 2.272; *Special Laws*, 1.308.   [18] *Ibid.* 51.

[19] *Sifre* (I, sect. 111, ed. Horovitz, p. 116, bot.) כל הכופר בע״ז מודה בכל התורה. Cf. *Meg*, 13 כל הכופר בע״ז נקרא יהודי.

embrace Judaism and did not exact any rites, even that of circumcision. He told Izates that "worship of God was of a superior nature to circumcision."[20] However, when another Jew, Eleazar whom Josephus portrayed as very learned in the law, entered the palace and found Izates reading the Laws of Moses, he reproached him for not being circumcised saying, "You do not consider, O king! that you unjustly break the principle of those laws, and are injurious to God Himself; for you ought not only to read them but chiefly to practice what they enjoin you. How long will you continue to be uncircumcised?"[21]

Circumcision actually became a *sine qua non* for any man who wanted to embrace Judaism. To again quote Josephus who stated that Agrippa gave his sister Drusilla in marriage to Azizus, King of Emesa, only upon the condition that he be circumcised. Circumcision became imperative for Jews as Tacitus said: the Jews adopted circumcision, "to distinguish themselves from other peoples by this difference."[22] It was indeed a mark of distinction. By remaining uncircumcised a person transgressed the Pentateuchal law all the time. Again, when Antiochus Epiphanes forced Hellenization upon the Judaeans he prohibited circumcision and ordered anyone discovered to be circumcised to be put to death. Thus the Jews throughout the ages emphasized the importance of circumcision. However, halakicly, legal, a Jew who was uncircumcised was considered a Jew but regarded as מומר לדבר אחד.[23] According to the Halakah, if it happened in a family that children died resulting from circumcision a new born child was exempted from circumcision.[24]

According to Rabbi Joshua if a pagan became a convert to Judaism and underwent ritual immersion but was not circumcised he was considered a proselyte, a Jew.[25] According to the school of Hillel circumcision *ex opere operato* is valid.[26] If a pagan was

---

[20] 20. 2. 4 (45–46).   [21] *Ibid.* (47–48).
[22] *Hist.* 5.5. *Circumcidere genitalia instituerunt ut diversitate noscantur.*
[23] Cf. *Hulin* 4.   [24] *Ibid.*
[25] *Yeb.* 46. טבל ולא מל ר' יהושע אומר הרי זה גר.
[26] *Tos. Shab* 15, 9. גר שנתגייר כשהוא מהול... אין צריך (להטיף ממנו דם).

circumcised before he was converted to Judaism he did not have to undergo another ritual. According to Rabbi Eliezer if a pagan who wanted to embrace Judaism was circumcised but had not undergone the ritual of immersion he was considered a proselyte, a Jew.[27] Immersion for proselytes was not instituted as a ritual *per se* for converts to Judaism. It became a requirement for proselytes for another reason. At the Conclave in the year 65 C.E. it was decreed that all gentiles are *ipso facto* unclean, in the category of a *zab*.[28] In consequence of this decree any gentile who wished to enter the Jewish community had to undergo the ritual of immersion. This was the underlying reason for the institution of baptism for proselytes and was introduced after the year 65 C.E. Rabbi Joshua laid stress on baptism while Rabbi Eliezer laid stress on circumcision.[29]

Prior to the year 65 C.E. pagans were not deemed susceptible to the laws of impurity and were never subject to the laws of impurity and purity. Many statements to this effect are found in the Tannaitic literature that pagans are not susceptible to the laws of impurity ...הגוי והבהמה,[30] and also that pagans affected by leprosy do not impart impurity.[31] Therefore a pagan, not being considered unclean, was not obliged to be baptised upon becoming a proselyte. Hence baptism with regard to proselytes is not mentioned in the aprocryphal literature nor in the writings of Josephus when reference is made to converts to Judaism. According to the Tannaitic literature a proselyte, besides undergoing the rituals of circumcision and baptism, had to offer a

---

[27] *Yeb.* 46. גר שמל ולא טבל רבי אליעזר אומר הרי זה גר תני גר שמל ולא טבל טבל ולא מל הכל הולך אחר המילה דברי רבי אליעזר רבי יהושע אומר (אף) הטבי־ לה מעכבת. *Yer. Kid.* 3, 12.

[28] *Tos. Zabim* 2, 1. כזבין לכל דבריהם. Cf. also, S. Zeitlin, "L'origine de L'institution du Baptême pour les Prosélytes," *REJ* (1934).

[29] Cf. S. Zeitlin, "The Halaka in the Gospels and its Relation to the Jewish Law at the Time of Jesus," *HUCA*, 1.

[30] *Tos. Neg.* 7. 10. Cf. also *Tos. Oh.* 1. 4. שמת [גוי] נכרי ...הגוי והבהמה; טהור מלטמא במשא שאין טומאתו אלא מדברי סופרים. *Ibid. Nida* 9, 14. Cf. also *Sifra* (ריש פ׳ זבים, ed. Weiss, 74d) ואין הגוים מיטמים בזיבה.

[31] *Tosefta, Neg.* 2, 13. בהרת בגוי....

sacrifice.[32] This sacrifice consisted of two doves. Such a sacrifice was brought by a *zab*.[33] Hence the sacrifice which had to be brought by a proselyte was not because he embraced Judaism but because he was no longer in the status of a *zab*. The rituals of baptism and sacrifice were introduced for proselytes because they were no longer considered *zabim* and had the right to enter the Jewish community. The rituals of baptism and sacrifice for proselytes were introduced after the year 65 C.E.

Jews were zealous to make proselytes and regarded them as superior to natives. Horace also refers to the eagerness of the Jews to proselytize.[34] The Gospel of Matthew relates that Jesus accused the Pharisees of proselytizing, "Woe unto you scribes and Pharisees, hypocrites, for you compass sea and land to make one proselyte."[35] Justin Martyr also accused the Jews of sending men to preach against Christianity, "You select and send out of Jerusalem chosen men throughout the land to tell that the godless heresy of the Christians had sprung up."[36] The historian Dio, in writing about the Jews, stated, "The country (Palestine) has been named Judaea, and the people themselves Judaeans. I do not know how this title came to be given them, but it applies also to all the rest of mankind, although of alien nationalities, who affect their laws. This class exists even among the Romans, and though often repressed has increased to a very great extent and has won its way to the right of freedom in its observances."[37] From this account it is clearly indicated that there were many proselytes even among the Romans.

Many in the pagan world followed the Jewish customs and practices. Was this due to the zeal of the Jews to spread their religion or to the decline of Hellenism and the yearning of the pagans for mysteries? The spread of the observance of Jewish customs, particularly of the Sabbath and the kindling of the lights, was probably the result of all of these causes. Josephus, in *Contra*

---

[32] *Ker.* 9. [33] Lev. 15:14; cf. also *ibid.* 12:6–8.
[34] *Sat.* 1.4.143. *ac veluti te Iudaei cogemus in hanc concedere turbam.*
[35] 23:15.
[36] *Dialogue With Tryhpo*, 108. [37] *Roman History*, 37.

Apionem, wrote "The masses have long since shown a zeal to adopt our religious observances, and there is not one city, Hellene or barbarian, nor a single nation to which our custom of abstaining from work on the seventh day has not spread, and where the fasts and the lighting of the lamps and many of our prohibitions in the matter of food are not observed."[38]

The Roman writers also showed their acquaintance with the Sabbath and other Jewish customs. Horace makes reference to the Sabbath, "Today is the thirtieth Sabbath," he said, "Would you affront the circumcised Jews?"[39] Ovid also refers to the Sabbath, "On that day," he writes, "less fit for business, whereon returns the seventh day feast that the Syrians of Palestine observe."[40] In another place he wrote, "Nor let Adonis bewailed of Venus escape you, nor the seventh day that the Syrian Jew holds sacred."[41] Juvenal in his satires makes reference to Sabbath observance and other Jewish customs, "Some who have had a father who reveres the Sabbath, worship nothing but the clouds, and the divinity of the heavens, and see no difference between eating swine's flesh from which their father abstained and that of man; and in time they take to circumcision. Having been wont to flout the laws of Rome, they learn and practice and revere the Jewish law, and all that Moses committed to his secret tome, forbidding to point out the way to any not worshipping the same rites and conducting none but the circumcised to the desired fountain. For all which the father was to blame, who gave up every seventh day to idleness, keeping it apart from all the concerns of life."[42] Some Roman writers misunderstood the significance

---

[38] 2. 282.

[39] *Sat.* 9. 69. *hodie tricesima sabbata; vin tu curtis Iudaeis oppedere?*

[40] *Artis Amatoriae*, 1.415. *Quaque die redeunt rebus minus apta gerendis, Culta Palestino septima festa Syro.*

[41] *Ibid.*, 75. *Nec te praetereat Veneri ploratus Adonis, Cultaque Iudaeo septima sacra Syro.*

[42] *Quidam sortiti metuentem sabbata patrem nil praeter nubes et caeli numen adorant, nec distare putant humana carne suillam, qua pater abstinuit mox et praeputia ponunt; Romanas autem soliti contemnere leges Iudaicum ediscunt*

of the Sabbath and attributed the ceasing of work on that day to laziness of the Jews.[43]

The observance of Jewish customs became widespread among the pagans. Many of them, although not converted to Judaism, were God fearing יראי ה׳, יראי שמים and worshipped the God of Israel, without becoming *gerim*. Poppea, the mistress wife of Nero Caesar, was attracted to Jewish customs. Josephus called her a religious woman.[44] From the writings of Josephus we learn that many in the pagan world were attracted to Judaism and revered the God of Israel. In his book, *Antiquities*, describing the wealth of the Temple, he stated, "For all the Judaeans throughout the habitable world, and those who revered God, even those from Asia and Europe, had been contributing to it for a very long time."[45] During the time of the revolt against the Romans in Syria the pagan population arose against the Judaeans who lived there and massacred them. Josephus wrote that although the Judaeans were annihilated, the Syrians were still in a state of fear, "For although believing that they had rid themselves of the Judaeans, still each city had its Judaizers who aroused suspicion; and, while they shrunk from killing off hand this equivocal element in their midst, they feared these neutrals as much as those who were of foreign religion."[46] In describing the massacre of the Judaeans in Damascus Josephus wrote that the pagans feared their own wives, "who with few exceptions adhered to the Judaean customs, and so their efforts were mainly directed to keeping the secret from them."[47] In describing the status of the Jews in Antioch and the wealth of the synagogue Josephus wrote, "They were constantly attracting to their religious ceremonies multitudes of the

et servant ac metuunt ius, tradidit arcano quodcumque volumine Moyses non monstrare vias eadem nisi sacra colenti, quaesitum ad fontem solos seducere verpos sed pater in causa, cui septima quaeque fuit lux ignava et partem vitae non attigit ullam. Sat. 14, 96–106.

[43] Cf. also Tacitus, *Hist.* 5.4. *dein blandiente inertia septimum quoque annum ignaviae datum.*

[44] θεοσεβής. *Ant.* 20. 8. 11 (195).

[45] σεβομένων τὸν θεόν. *Ibid.* 14. 7. 1 (110).

[46] *Wars* 2. 18. 2 (463). [47] *Ibid.* (559–560).

Hellenes, and these they had in some measure incorporated with themselves."[48] Not all of those who revered the God of Israel and accepted Jewish customs became proselytes. Josephus, in his book *Contra Apionem*, made the following statement, "Many of them have agreed to adopt our laws; of whom some have remained faithful, while others, lacking the necessary endurance, have again seceded."[49]

A *ger* was one who accepted Judaism without qualification. If a pagan wanted to become a proselyte but stipulated that he would not adhere to one of the precepts he was not accepted as a *ger*. There were *no* semi-proselytes. A *ger torshab* was a foreigner who lived in the land of Judaea. He had to observe the Noachite laws, i.e., *jus gentium*.[50] The fearers of *Adonai* were pagans who, although they worshipped their own gods, yet feared and revered the God of Israel. The psalmists already made reference to the fearers of *Adonai*.[51] From the book of Kings we learn that the Kutim, who were transported from their land by the Assyrians to the land of Israel, worshipped their gods yet feared *Adonai*.[52] The term "fearers of Heaven", which was originally applied to the pagans who feared and revered the God of Israel, was later applied to pious Jews.

A proselyte was considered on a par with a native Jew.[53] However those who adhered to the view, as did the Sadducees, that Yahweh is an ethnic God, the God of the descendants of Abraham, Isaac and Jacob with whom He had made a covenant and whom He brought out of the land of Egypt, regarded the proselyte as not the equal of a native Jew. Although this view was contrary to the philosophy of the Sages of the Second Commonwealth and the Tannaitic period and rejected by them it did influence later Judaism.

---

[48] *Ibid.* 7. 3. 3 (45).   [49] 2. 10 (123).
[50] Cf. *Ab. Zarah* 64. איזהו גר תושב כל שקיבל בפני ג׳ חברים שלא לעבוד עבודה זרה דברי רבי מאיר וחכמים אומרים כל שקיבל עליו שבע מצות שקבלו עליהם בני נח
[51] Ps. 115:13. Cf. also S. Zeitlin, "The Hallel," *JQR* (July, 1962), 24–25.
[52] II Kings 17:33.
[53] Cf. *Mekilta, Mishp.* 18. כמה חביבים הגרים... ונקראו הגרים אוהבים.